New Social Movements in Western Europe

Social Movements, Protest, and Contention

Series Editor: Bert Klandermans, Free University, Amsterdam

Associate Editors: Sidney G. Tarrow, Cornell University
                      Verta A. Taylor, Ohio State University

New Social Movements in Western Europe

A Comparative Analysis

Hanspeter Kriesi, Ruud Koopmans, Jan Willem Duyvendak, and Marco G. Giugni

Social Movements, Protest, and Contention
Volume 5

University of Minnesota Press
Minneapolis

Published by the University of Minnesota Press
111 Third Avenue South, Suite 290
Minneapolis, MN 55401-2520

Printed in the United States of America on acid-free paper

Library of Congress Cataloging-in-Publication Data

New social movements in Western Europe : a comparative analysis /
    Hanspeter Kriesi ... [et al.].
        p.   cm. — (Social movements, protest, and contention ; v. 5)
    Includes bibliographical references and index.
    ISBN 0-8166-2670-7 (hc). — ISBN 0-8166-2671-5 (pb)
    1. Social movements—Europe.   I. Kriesi, Hanspeter.   II. Series.
HN373.5.N495   1995
303.48'4'094—dc20   95-13671

The University of Minnesota is an equal-opportunity educator and employer.

FTW
AHT 1439

Contents

Preface

This study is the product of a collaborative effort that has lasted for more than seven years. The project on the comparative analysis of new social movements in Western Europe was launched by Hanspeter Kriesi when he was still at the Department for Collective Political Behavior of the University of Amsterdam in 1987. Jan Willem Duyvendak was the first assistant to be hired by the department for this project the same year. Ruud Koopmans joined the project a year later thanks to the Amsterdam School for Social Research, which provided him with an assistantship. After Hanspeter Kriesi moved to the University of Geneva, he obtained two research grants from the Swiss national science foundation, which allowed Marco Giugni to join the project in 1989. In the course of the following years, the project has also been supported by the Department of General Political Science and the faculty of political and social-cultural sciences at the University of Amsterdam, by the Dutch national science foundation (NWO), and by the Department of Political Science of the University of Geneva. Without the generous support we have received from these various institutions, we could never have gone as far as we have.

In the course of the project, four country-specific volumes have been completed — one for each of the four countries we have chosen to compare: first, Jan Willem Duyvendak, Hein-Anton van der Heijden, Ruud Koopmans, and Luuk Wijmans (1992) edited a book on the Netherlands, to which several additional authors have contributed. Then, three Ph.D. theses have been completed: Jan Willem Duyvendak (1992, 1994b) wrote about France, Marco Giugni (1992) about Switzerland, and Ruud Koopmans (1992a) about Germany. All these individual studies share the same general conceptual framework which we have developed and discussed in many joint workshops in

Amsterdam and Geneva during the years of our collaboration. The present study is an attempt to integrate the country-specific findings of the previous publications into a systematically comparative whole. All the chapters of the present volume share the same general perspective, and have been intensively discussed among ourselves on several occasions. However, they have been written by variable combinations of us four, and the final responsibility rests with the particular authors of each chapter. More specifically, Jan Willem Duyvendak wrote chapter 7 on the gay movement and contributed to chapters 1, 4, and 6, as well as to the Conclusion. Marco Giugni wrote the final two chapters on diffusion and outcomes (chapters 8 and 9), and coauthored chapter 4 and the Introduction. Ruud Koopmans is the author of chapter 5 on the dynamics of protest waves and of the technical appendix, and he contributed to chapters 2 and 6 as well as to the Conclusion. Hanspeter Kriesi wrote chapter 3 on alliance structures and coauthored the Introduction and chapters 1 and 2.

In addition to institutional support, we have also received support from a number of colleagues and friends. We would like to express our gratitude to the coders who helped us with the coding of the events in France, Germany, and the Netherlands. We are indebted to the three reviewers of the University of Minnesota Press—Bert Klandermans, Chris Rootes, and Sidney Tarrow—whose comments have been very helpful in improving our manuscript. In developing our ideas, we have also profited from stimulating discussions with a large number of colleagues at several workshops that have been held on social movements over the past few years. Finally, we would also like to thank our colleagues Hein-Anton van der Heijden and Luuk Wijmans from the University of Amsterdam, and Florence Passy of the University of Geneva, who, at various stages of our common project, discussed concepts and results with us and otherwise contributed to our well-being. Meeting with one or the other of them in Geneva or in Amsterdam, we not only worked hard, but we also enjoyed some beautiful hikes and pleasant meals together.

Hanspeter Kriesi
Ruud Koopmans
Jan Willem Duyvendak
Marco G. Giugni
Geneva, Berlin, Amsterdam, New York
May 1994

Introduction

October 22, 1983, will be remembered in the history of the Federal Republic of Germany, as *Le Monde* observed.[1] As early as four o'clock in the morning, the first special trains arrived in Bonn, bringing participants to what was to become the greatest peace demonstration the capital had seen since the beginning of the mobilization two years earlier against the stationing of cruise and Pershing II missiles in Germany. In the morning, the demonstrators formed chains linking the Theater Square in nearby Bad Godesberg with the embassies of the nuclear powers — China, France, Great Britain, India, South Africa, the Soviet Union, and the United States. At noon, under a magnificent sky, a huge train flowed back from Bad Godesberg to Bonn, where, at two in the afternoon, an enormous crowd was gathering in the Hofgarten. An estimated 250,000 to 500,000 people took part in this impressive demonstration of force by the German peace movement. The event was not clouded by the slightest incident, apart maybe from the fact that Willy Brandt, who was supposed to be the star speaker of the day, got a rather lukewarm reception from the crowd. After extended negotiations, the organizers had allowed the president of the Social Democratic Party to address the meeting, but many of those attending had not forgotten that it was a Social Democratic chancellor who had agreed to the NATO decision to station the Pershing II and cruise missiles on German territory.

The meeting in Bonn was not the only great event of the day. All over Germany, the peace movement demonstrated against nuclear weapons. Thus, in southern Germany, the movement organized a human chain of 220,000 demonstrators linking the headquarters of the U.S. forces in Germany at Stuttgart-Vaihingen to the Wiley barracks near Ulm, more than 100 kilometers away. Given the number of participants (which exceeded all expectations), the chain could have gone as far as Munich, to the seat of the Christian Social Union (CSU), the party that most assiduously defended the double-track decision of NATO. Moreover, the events of the weekend had been preceded by an action week that mobilized very large numbers of people. Innumerable professional groups had launched appeals to the general public—among them "artists for peace," "architects for peace," "judges and public prosecutors for peace." There was hardly a professional group that did not publish a statement. All over Germany, schools too had been participating in this peace week. Many special events had been held, such as a hunger strike in Frankfurt organized to manifest the people's "hunger for peace." All in all, between two and three million people took part in the events of this peace week. The news magazine *Spiegel* spoke about the greatest challenge the Federal Republic had ever had to face: never before had a protest movement put the establishment under such pressure.[2] The impact of the movement was particularly far-reaching for the Social Democratic Party (SPD), which, *Spiegel* maintained, had become entirely "lafontainized." In other words, the SPD was now following the lead of one of its figureheads, Oskar Lafontaine, who had already sided with the peace movement and who was to become the party's candidate for the chancellorship in the 1990 national elections.

If the German challenge was the most important one, Germany was not the only country to be rocked by the peace movement during that weekend in October 1983: 500,000 people protested against nuclear weapons in Rome (the Communist *Unità* claimed that they numbered one million); 250,000 marched from the River Thames to Hyde Park in the center of London, an unprecedented success of the British Campaign against Nuclear Disarmament (CND); between 120,000 (the police estimate) and 400,000 (according to the organizers) gathered in Brussels, which had not seen such a massive demonstration in two years; more than 100,000 Spaniards (according to the most credible estimates, as was stressed by *Le Monde*) demonstrated their solidarity with the international campaign in Madrid. One week later, the Dutch movement staged its largest demonstration ever in The Hague; with its 550,000 participants, this event was even bigger than the one the movement had organized two years earlier in Amsterdam. Even in Switzerland, the protest against the stationing of cruise missiles in Western Europe was impressive, although this neutral country was not directly affected by NATO's decision; in one of the largest demonstrations that had ever taken place in Switzerland, between 30,000 and 40,000 people supported by more than fifty organizations demonstrated their solidarity with the international campaign in the capital of Bern on December 5.

France turns out to be a deviant case. On its first page, *Le Monde* spoke about a "weak mobilization" in France. In Paris, two separate demonstrations were held during the weekend in question: one on Saturday, organized by the Communist-dominated Mouvement de la Paix, the Communist Party (PCF), and the largest trade union (the Communist CGT); and one on Sunday, organized by the Comité pour le désarmement nucléaire en Europe (CODENE), the second-largest trade union (CFDT), and the major party of the new left, the Unified Socialist Party (PSU). Both events only attracted comparatively small numbers of people: between 15,000 and 20,000 marched on Saturday; 7,000 to 8,000 formed a human chain between the United States embassy on the Avenue Gabriel and the Soviet embassy on the Boulevard Lannes on Sunday morning; and about 5,000 met at the Bastille on Sunday afternoon. The main speaker at this last gathering challenged the Socialist Party and the Socialist government, both hostile to any pacifist manifestation. In the rest of France, the mobilization was even weaker: about 2,000 were mobilized in Marseilles, Lyons, Grenoble, and Lille, about 1,000 in Nancy and Bourges, and 200 in Toulouse—the hometown of the French aircraft industry.

From the comparative perspective we take in this study, the surprise is not so much the enormous success of the movement's mobilization all over Europe, but its relative absence in France. Why did more people not turn out to demonstrate in France in October 1983? The reader might be tempted to invoke the historical or cultural specificity of the French to explain their exceptionalism. At its most general level, however, such an argument is not very persuasive: each of the countries mentioned earlier has its own historical and cultural peculiarities, but in spite of these many peculiarities, all of them, except for France, participated massively in the movement's protest. At a more specific level, the reference to historical or cultural roots could be more promising. Thus, one might refer to the tradition of the *grande nation* that has maintained a rather distanced relationship with NATO and had, therefore, not been directly concerned by NATO's double decision. But, as we noted, the lack of NATO membership did not prevent the Swiss from joining the international campaign against the cruise missiles. Alternatively, one might think of the fact that France, as a nuclear power, has chosen to maintain its own *force de frappe* and that the French, therefore, are generally little inclined to protest against nuclear weapons. But again there is a counterexample that casts doubt on this reasoning: Great Britain is also a major nuclear power, but that has not prevented the British from demonstrating massively against cruise and Pershing II missiles. One might still argue that maybe it was the combination of the two elements—France's being a nuclear power that had chosen to stay independent of NATO—that explains the exceptional behavior of its citizens. Elaborating this combined argument, a major difference between Britain and France in the 1980s was that Britain had, to all intents and purposes, abandoned its independent nuclear weapons capacity in favor of the cheaper option of buying American nuclear weapons. Moreover, it was U.S.-controlled cruise missiles that were to be sited on British soil (e.g., at Greenham Common). The French nuclear deterrent has thus been—and been seen to be—more truly independent than the British one. According to this more subtle argument,[3] the British could have been moved to oppose the stationing of U.S. missiles on their soil for nationalist reasons, whereas the French had no such incentive to mobilize.

Although we do not want to discard this type of argument, we believe that one should be skeptical about explanations of movement politics that do not take into account the more specific aspects of the national political context in which the mobilization of social movements takes place. There always are reasons enough to mobilize—in the absence of nationalist reasons, the French could, for example, have mobilized to manifest their international solidarity, just as the traditionally neutral Swiss have done. But mobilization is not always forthcoming and, if it is forthcoming, it takes different forms at different times and places. Our contention is that the mobilization of social movements is closely linked to conventional politics in the parliamentary and extraparliamentary arenas of a given country. We shall try to show that by paying attention to this crucial link, we will be better equipped to deal with the striking cross-national variations we find with respect to the mobilization patterns of social movements in Western Europe.

Given this perspective, we suspect, among other things, that it is no accident that there were two rival peace demonstrations in France in late October 1983, and we believe that the weak mobilizing capacity of the French peace movement at that time may well have had a lot to do with the split between its Communist and its new-left branches. We would also suggest that the lack of support of the movement by the Socialists in France—which contrasts sharply with the close alliance between the Socialists and the peace movement in countries like Germany, the Netherlands, and Switzerland—decisively contributed to its comparative weakness. Moreover, according to the perspective we have adopted for this study, we should also try to explain changes in the patterns of mobilization over time with changes in the national political contexts. Without recourse to such changes in the respective national political contexts, it would, for example, be quite difficult to explain why, by the early 1990s, the mobilization of the French peace movement no longer was exceptionally weak, but why it was now the turn of the Dutch peace movement to manifest a comparative lack of mobilizing capacity. In fact, in January 1991, the French peace movement mobilized comparatively strongly against the Persian Gulf war, as did the German movement. In contrast, the Dutch hardly mobilized at all, although their country was as much involved in the war as were Germany or France (Duyvendak and Koopmans 1991a).

Our emphasis on the political context for the explanation of the mobilization of social movements is in line with an important branch of recent theorizing in the area of movement research. Among the most recent developments in this field of study, the idea that processes of social change impinge indirectly, through a restructuration of existing power relations, on social protest has gained some weight. This idea, put forward by the political process approach to social movements (McAdam 1982), goes against the classical theories of collective behavior — such as the theories of "mass society" or "relative deprivation" — which stress a direct relationship between social change and protest. Recently, several authors have developed analytical tools for the analysis of the political context that mediates the effect of structural conflicts on overt mobilization. More particularly, the concept of political opportunity structure (POS) has become central to such studies. This concept was first introduced by Eisinger (1973), according to whom it was meant to represent the degree of openness of a political system to challenges addressed by social movements. Kitschelt (1986), Tarrow (1983, 1989b, 1994, 1995), Della Porta and Rucht (1991), Rucht (1993), among others, have contributed to elaboration of the concept, which has proved to be very useful for the study of collective action. In Tarrow's (1995: in press) apt phrase, the POS refers to all the "signals to social and political actors which either encourage or discourage them to use their internal resources to form social movements."

A Model for the Political Context of Mobilization

According to the conceptualization of the POS that we shall use in the present study, the POS is made up of four components: national cleavage structures, institutional structures, prevailing strategies, and alliance structures. First, we start from the idea that the mobilization capacity of social move-

ments is to a large extent determined by the country-specific political cleavage structures, which, in turn, are rooted in the social and cultural cleavages
of a given society. As Brand (1985: 321) has suggested, the existing configuration of political cleavages, or, if you will, of established political conflicts,
imposes important constraints on the mobilization of newcomers to the scene
of movement politics. Second, our concept of the POS includes the formal
institutional structure of political systems. This aspect of the POS has been
at the heart of Kitschelt's (1986) use of the term, which distinguished between formal "input" and "output" structures of the political system. In our
approach, the distinction between these two sides of the formal structure is
quite secondary, but we think that it is important to include the aspects of
what Tarrow (1994) has called the "statist" approach in our concept of the
POS. Third, unlike previous conceptualizations of the POS, we would like to
stress the distinction between the formal institutional setting for the mobilization of social movements and the prevailing informal strategies followed
by political authorities when dealing with them. Broadly defined, political
institutions not only include the formal rules governing politics in a given
country, but also the informal procedures and operating practices (Hall 1986:
19). We adopt such a broad conception of political institutions and shall make
use of the fact that formal rules and informal practices may vary quite independently between countries. Finally, our conception of the POS also includes
the less stable elements of the political context of mobilizing movements—
certain aspects of the configuration of power of a political system, which we
summarize under the term alliance structures. These are the elements underscored by the conceptualization of the POS by Tarrow (1989a, 1989b,
1994, 1995). He emphasizes the importance of the political conditions of the
moment, of short-term changes in political opportunities that may unleash
political protest and that may contribute to its decline. The elements of the
political context that may change in the short run include the opening up of
access to participation, shifts in ruling alignments, the availability of influential allies, and cleavages within and among elites. We shall concentrate on
two aspects of the changing political context that are of particular relevance
for the type of movements that constitute the major object of this study: the
configuration of power on the left and the presence or absence of the left in
government.

   These four components of the POS are more or less systematically linked
to each other. Thus, we maintain that the alliance structures are, in part at
least, determined by the three more stable components of the POS. As far

as the latter are concerned, we presuppose that cleavage structures constitute the most general and most stable aspect of the political context. They have contributed to the development of the prevailing strategies, which, in turn, have been to some extent formally institutionalized. The left-hand side of figure 1 summarizes these considerations.[4]

Authors using the POS approach have not always been very explicit about how the structural characteristics of the political context affect the mobilization of collective actors. In order to understand the impact of the POS on the mobilization of social movements, we need to specify the mechanisms that link the macrostructural level of the POS to the collective action of movement actors. Under the general heading of "interaction context," we propose a number of concepts designed to bridge the gap between the political context and the mobilization processes. According to our conception, the elements of the POS jointly determine the strategies of the members of the political system in general, and of political authorities in particular, with regard to the mobilization of social movements. These strategies imply a country-specific mix of facilitation/repression of the movements' mobilization, their chances of success, and the degree of reform/threat they have to reckon with. This specific mix defines the concrete opportunities of a given social movement. By specifying the costs and benefits of a movement's mobilization, these concrete opportunities in turn determine to an important extent the movement's own strategies, its level of mobilization, and the outcomes of the mobilization process.

However, we cannot expect to explain the whole process of mobilization on the basis of this "funnel of causality." At least three considerations limit the reach of the impact of the POS: First, the consequences of the concrete opportunities for the mobilizing strategies of a challenging movement depend on the extent to which the movement in question is acting instrumentally. As we shall argue in this study, there are different types of movements—instrumental, subcultural, and countercultural—which differ in the way they react to the concrete opportunities defined by the POS. Second, once the mobilizing process has been set in motion, the strategies adopted by the social movements will have a feedback effect on the strategies adopted by the authorities. An interactive system will be established with a dynamic of its own. Finally, as is especially emphasized by Tarrow (1994, 1995), depending on the magnitude of the mobilizing processes and the importance of the social movements involved, it is conceivable that the interactive dynamics will create their own opportunities, modify the POS—on the level of the

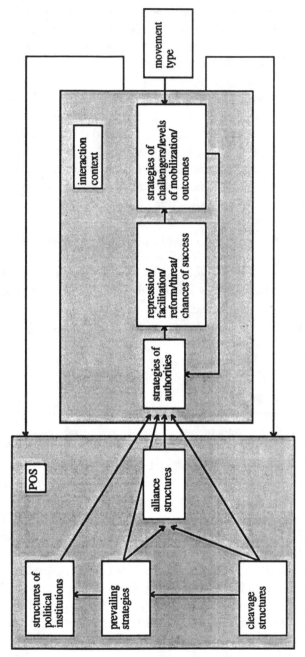

Fig. 1. Model of the political context and its impact on the mobilization of social movements

alliance structures, or even more profoundly, on the level of institutional structures, prevailing strategies, and cleavage structures. These considerations are summarized by the right-hand side of figure 1: the type of movement is introduced as an exogenous factor at the far right of this figure, while feedback processes are indicated by arrows pointing back to the POS and to the strategies of the authorities. This completes the presentation of our model of the political context and its impact on the mobilization of social movements.

We do not maintain that this model is applicable at all times and in all places. The present model presupposes a political system with a relatively stable structure and a certain degree of autonomy with respect to its environment. Both preconditions apply more or less well to the period and region of the world we propose to study in this book—Western Europe from 1975 to 1989. During this period, the national cleavage structures, the prevailing strategies, and the institutional framework of Western European countries have been relatively stable, certainly if compared to what has happened in Eastern Europe since the late eighties. It is true that the period in question was one of increasing integration of Western Europe into the supranational European community, or the European Union, as it is called since the ratification of the Treaty of Maastricht in 1993. Moreover, as our previous example of the massive demonstrations of the peace movement illustrates, the mobilization of social movements has come under the influence of the globalizing tendencies that have been manifest during this period, not only in Western Europe, but all over the world. But if, in an age of globalization, national political contexts are bound to become less and less important for the interpretation and explanation of the mobilization of social movements (Tarrow 1995), we maintain that the national contexts were still decisive for the understanding of the mobilization of social movements during the period under consideration. The cross-national variation in the example of the mobilization by the peace movement that we introduced at the outset provides us with a hint that national political contexts, indeed, still are quite important.

New Social Movements

While taking into account the protest events of all the movements that mobilized in the late seventies and eighties, our study focuses on a particular segment of the social movement sector in the Western European countries:

the so-called new social movements. These movements are of particular interest for a study of collective action since they have been responsible for the bulk of the mobilization that has taken place in Western Europe during the period in question. They constitute a specific "movement industry," according to the conceptualization by McCarthy and Zald (1977), or a specific "movement family," as Della Porta and Rucht (1991) prefer to call such clusters of movements. Most authors would probably agree that this family includes the ecology movement (with its antinuclear energy branch), the peace movement, the solidarity movement (solidarity with the Third World), the women's movement, the squatters' movement, as well as various other movements mobilizing for the rights of discriminated-against minorities (such as the gay movement). There have been numerous attempts to specify the common denominator of all the movements that constitute this movement family. Although we do not want to enter into the details of these theoretical discussions, we consider it indispensable to clarify our point of view before launching into the presentation of the different aspects of our study.

We agree with Raschke (1985: 413) that the basic characteristic of a social movement is constituted by the position of its main constituency in the social structure. Moreover, we agree with him that a theoretical understanding of a social movement requires that we go beyond a mere description of its social-structural characteristics and inquire into the transformation of the conflict structure within a given society that has given rise to its mobilization. We believe, indeed, that the rise of the new social movements was intimately linked to the slow, but profound, transformation of the society's conflict structure in the course of the macrohistorical process of modernization. This transformation implies, first of all, a weakening of traditional cleavages in which people are freed from traditional ties of class, religion, and the family. The result has been an unprecedented degree of individualization, but not the dissolution of structural and cultural bonds altogether.

The weakening of traditional structures is not equivalent to a lack of any structure. Nor does it necessarily have the disturbing consequences that were conjured up by theorists of the classical approaches to collective behavior, such as the theorists of "mass society," for whom the alienated citizens in modern society easily fall prey to mobilizing demagogues. The great structural transformation has brought with it new forms of control. Individuals now find they are dependent on new kinds of structurally determined circumstances, giving rise to conflicts between large groups in society. Some theorists have proposed to analyze these new conflicts in terms of processes of large-scale societal differentiation (Neidhardt and Rucht 1993). One of the present authors has preferred to interpret them in terms of class analysis (Kriesi 1987, 1989, 1993a)[5]. Thus, we have argued in some detail that there is an emergent "new class" cleavage traversing the new middle class, opposing the professionals whose work is mainly cued to organizational control (the "managers" and "technocrats") to those professionals whose work is mainly skills-oriented and cued to service to clients (the "social and cultural specialists").

According to this argument, the structural conflict between the two strata within the new middle class is a conflict about the control of work. In this conflict, the professionals whose control is based on expertise and skills are defending themselves against the encroachments on their work autonomy by colleagues who are primarily involved in the administration of the large private and public employers for whom the former work. Tending to lose out in this conflict, the skills- and service-oriented professionals constitute a crucial structural potential for the new social movements, all of which attack in one way or another the unrestricted reign of technocracy. A detailed analysis of the Dutch situation has, indeed, confirmed that social and cultural specialists are most heavily overrepresented in the avant-garde of the various movements that have been considered to belong to the family of the new social movements. Moreover, the activists of any given one of these movements also tend to be active in any given other one among them (Kriesi and van Praag Jr. 1987; Kriesi 1993a).

We would, of course, concede that the structurally determined conflicts of modern society cannot be reduced to this new class conflict about the control of work. This conflict is part of a larger struggle about the blueprint of modern society. As many analysts of new social movements have pointed out (Beck 1983, 1986; Brand 1987; Duyvendak 1992; Kriesi 1988; Offe 1985; Raschke 1985; Schmitt-Beck 1992; Touraine 1980b), these movements have been mobilized by new types of threats to individual autonomy exerted by corporate actors — "the colonization of the life world by systemic imperatives" of Habermas, or the "iron cage" of Weber — as well as by new, invisible risks affecting people in more or less the same way irrespective of their social position (radioactivity or AIDS, for example). These new threats have replaced the dependence on traditional bonds and the deprivation stemming from the inequality of resource distribution. The social and cultural service professionals are generally most sensitive to these kinds of threats, but their fears and motives are shared by large numbers of people who have, in part at least, been sensitized by the past mobilization processes of the very same new social movements for which they presently form a potential.

Like the social and cultural professionals, these people subscribe to the values and beliefs articulated most clearly by these professionals. These values and beliefs have often been described as "postmaterialist" (Ingelhart 1977, 1990a). Postmaterialist values include an emphasis on personal and political freedom, political and economic democracy, environmental protection, openness to new ideas, and a caring society. Flanagan (1987) has identified two major themes in this new set of values — a postmaterialist and a libertarian one.

One of the present authors has argued (Kriesi 1993a) that this new set of values is closely associated with the values traditionally defended by the left in Western Europe and includes at least three components: a social-democratic one referring to the set of goals of the Socialist reformers, a libertarian one directed against traditional authoritarian structures, and an emancipatory one oriented toward the implementation of an egalitarian society protecting both nature and individuals from the imperatives of large-scale organizations. In the same vein, Della Porta and Rucht (1991) propose to call the new social movements "left-libertarian movements." They adopt the term from Kitschelt (1990: 180), who uses it for the small parties of the new left and argues that "they are 'left' because they share with traditional socialism a mistrust of the marketplace, of private investment, and of the achievement ethic, and a commitment to egalitarian redistribution. They are 'libertarian' because they reject the authority of the private or public bureaucracies to regulate individual and collective conduct. Instead they favor participatory democracy and the autonomy of groups and individuals to define their economic, political, and cultural institutions unencumbered by market or bureaucratic dictates."

That the appeal of the new social movements has gone far beyond the narrow circle of the social and cultural professionals is evident from the level of mobilization they have attained throughout the last two decades. Moreover, these movements can count on the continued existence of enormous potentials for future political campaigns (Fuchs and Rucht 1992; Kriesi 1993a; Watts 1987). It is quite likely that not only the goals of these movements, but also their mode of doing politics — a participatory, issue-specific mode, oriented toward public opinion — have struck a responsive cord within the populations of the Western European countries. We would maintain, however, that these more procedural aspects of their mobilization pattern are no longer characteristic of the family of the new social movements. As is argued by Koopmans (1992a: 18), little is left of the initial differences in the action repertoires and the type of organization between the new social movements and other contemporary movements: on the one hand, certain innovations introduced by the new social movements, such as their informal organizational networks, have spread to the other types of movements; on the other hand, in the course of the eighties the new social movements have undergone a process of conventionalization that has contributed to the convergence of their formal aspects with those of the other types of contemporaneous movements. By the end of the eighties, most of the new social movements in Western Europe appeared to be pragmatic reformist movements (Küchler and Dalton 1990; Schmitt-Beck 1992), closely connected to established politics in various dimensions. As Nedelmann (1984) suggested some time ago, they are best interpreted as a differentiation of the system of political interest intermediation or, as Roth (1989, 1991, 1992) would say, as a new type of political institution. We hasten to add that if institutionalization has been the trajectory followed by the largest new social movements, others have developed along other lines to which we shall return.

In spite of the fact that the new social movements are no longer all that new, we shall use this label to characterize them throughout this study. Although the label is no longer all that appropriate, it has become so widespread and generally accepted to designate this type of movement family that we continue to use it in order to avoid possible misunderstandings. Focusing our attention on new social movements, however, does not make us typical representatives of what in the 1980s came to be called the "new social movements approach." Following the theme of Klandermans and Tarrow (1988) and Klandermans (1986, 1991), we are in fact trying to integrate the European and American approaches to social movement research. If the "new social movement approach" was mainly concerned with the structural origins of these movements, with the question of why they made their appearance in the first place, our approach also tries to address the question of why there are such enormous differences between Western European countries with respect to the timing, the capacity, and the forms of mobilization of the various movements belonging to this important movement family. We accept the idea of the European approaches that the new social movements are ultimately rooted in structural and cultural transformations that characterize all Western European countries to more or less the same extent. But we think that it is time to move beyond the generalizations of the European approaches and to introduce the more specific questions about the how and when of the mobilization of these movements in the various countries (Tarrow 1994, chapter 5). In trying to explain the cross-national differences by various aspects of the national political contexts of the countries compared, our analysis is also firmly grounded in the political process approach, which has its origins in the United States.

Research Strategy

As has already become apparent, we take a resolutely comparative perspective in this study. Cross-national comparisons are at its core. More specifically, we shall compare the family of the new social movements across four West European countries: France, Germany, the Netherlands, and Switzerland. Looking for differences between the mobilization patterns of Western European countries, we have adopted a "most similar systems design" (Przeworski and Teune 1970), which tries to control as large a number of explanatory variables as possible. The four countries selected are quite similar with respect to the level of their economic and social development, but they constitute quite different political contexts for the mobilization of the new social movements. In other words, they lend themselves to a systematic test of our political process model. The four countries, of course, differ not only with regard to their political context, and in this sense the differences in the mobilization patterns of the movements of interest to us shall be indeterminate, or, if you will, overdetermined. However, guided by the hypotheses we shall develop in each one of the following chapters, we shall be able to focus on the impact of specific aspects of the political context and render the relevance of these aspects more plausible.

Following the lead of other students of political protest (Kriesi et al. 1981; McAdam 1983; McCarthy, McPhail, and Smith 1992; Rucht and Ohlemacher 1992; Tarrow 1989b; Tilly, Tilly, and Tilly 1975), the present study is based on a quantitative analysis of protest events collected from newspaper sources.[6] Our notion of protest event is quite broad and includes an extensive list of various forms of unconventional political action. In addition, for five specific new social movements—the peace, ecology, solidarity, urban autonomous, and gay movements—we have also collected information on conventional political events, to the extent that the event was initiated by a social movement organization (SMO) or by a group of activists of one of these movements. For each event we coded a limited amount of information.

Compared to other quantitative sources such as official statistics, year-books, or archives, the most important advantages of daily newspapers for the study of the mobilization of social movements are perhaps that they provide a continuous, easily accessible source that includes the whole range of protest events produced in a given country. We have systematically analyzed one major newspaper in each of the four countries under study. The papers we selected are quite comparable with respect to their quality, their national scope, their political orientation, and the selectivity of their reporting on protest events. We chose *Le Monde* in France, the *Frankfurter Rundschau* in Germany, *NRC/Handelsblad* (NRC) in the Netherlands, and the *Neue Zürcher Zeitung* (NZZ) in Switzerland. For reasons of resource constraints, we have not coded all the issues of these papers for the entire period under study, but decided to concentrate on the Monday issues only. Monday issues were chosen because they cover two days of the week, and because a large number of unconventional events, on which our analysis is focused, are concentrated on weekends. The important category of strikes, which typically take place during the week, has been treated separately. More details about our analysis of the newspaper data as well as a discussion of the advantages and pitfalls of this type of analysis are given in the Appendix.

Our general position with respect to this type of data is well formulated by Rucht and Ohlemacher (1992: 101), who observe that "in a field which is marked more by speculation than by substantial knowledge," newspaper data provide a useful tool to arrive at more empirically grounded generalizations. The field of research concerned with new social movements abounds, indeed, with interpretations that, when confronted with the kind of empirical data we are providing here, can easily be shown to be highly misleading or just plain wrong. More specifically, although the use of newspaper data for the analysis of political mobilization has become quite common, this procedure has up to now hardly been used in a comparative perspective. The only study adopting a comparative approach and making use of this kind of data that we are aware of is the pathbreaking work of Tilly, Tilly, and Tilly (1975).

Building on our comparative set of data, we attempt to present a creative blend of theory and data analysis. In every chapter of this book, we develop a set of theoretical ideas which we then try to test on the basis of the comparative data from our newspaper sources. Our goal is to elaborate an empirically grounded theory about the impact of national political context structures on the mobilization patterns of social movements in general, and new social movements in particular.

Our study is divided into two main parts. Part I is devoted to the elaboration of our general concepts and to a presentation of the basic results of our research. The first three chapters of this part deal with the various aspects of the political opportunity structure. Chapter 1 presents an analysis of the impact of traditional cleavage structures on the mobilization of new social movements. Our data support the hypothesis that there is a zero-sum relationship between the mobilization capacity of traditional cleavages and the corresponding capacity of the new social movements to articulate a new cleavage. The pacification of the traditional cleavages allows for more "space" for new social movements to mobilize. By contrast, in countries where "old" conflicts are still not pacified, "new" conflicts turn out to be less likely to burst onto the political scene.

Chapter 2 introduces two further aspects of the political opportunity structure—the institutional structures and the prevailing strategies—which add to our understanding of why the level of mobilization and the action repertoire of new social movements vary substantially across the four countries. The country-specific mix of concrete opportunities derived in part from the combination of these two dimensions of the POS is shown to have an impact on the level of mobilization and the action repertoire of new social movements.

Chapter 3 deals with the more variable elements of the POS—the alliance structures. Two elements of these alliance structures are analyzed in detail—the configuration of power on the left and the presence or absence of the left in government. Facilitation of the mobilization of new social movements by established political actors, especially by organizations of the left, is an omnipresent phenomenon. But, as we shall see, depending on the character of the configuration of the old and the new left and on whether the left is in or out of government, the magnitude of the facilitation by the left varies considerably. Variable support from the left, in turn, goes a long way toward explaining variations over time in the country-specific capacity of new social movements to mobilize.

In chapter 4, the political opportunity argument is elaborated for different types of new social movements—instrumental, subcultural, or countercultural ones. Political opportunities are not the same for various movements within one and the same country; different movements face different constraints and opportunities. Thus, the reaction of the authorities to the challenges of social movements varies widely from one movement to the other, depending on the characteristics of the movements, and as a function of the types of issues they raise. The status of an issue raised by a challenging movement in turn depends to a large extent on how it is evaluated by the political authorities.

Finally, chapter 5 introduces interactive dynamics. According to the wave-like model presented in this chapter, shifts in the political opportunity structure are not sufficient to explain the development of protest waves once they have been set in motion. The interaction between different currents within social movements, the shifting balance of strategic resources, and the interaction between movements, adversaries, authorities, and allies give rise to an autodynamic of protest that is relatively independent of the more stable aspects of the political opportunity structure.

Part II is devoted to elaborations of the general themes introduced in the first part. Chapters 6 and 7 deal with the mobilization of two specific movements. The first of these chapters uses the example of the antinuclear movement to introduce framing processes into our analysis of the mobilization by new social movements. The main argument is that problems and grievances are not given, but depend on the political opportunities to "construct problems" in a way that "resonates" with concepts and discussions prevalent in established politics. Using the conspicuous example of Chernobyl — a suddenly imposed grievance of international scope — to illustrate and test our argument, this chapter tries to bridge the gap between structuralist and constructivist theorizing about processes of mobilization. Chapter 7 deals with the twin trajectories followed by our example of a subcultural new social movement — the gay movement. This movement has not institutionalized as suggested by the well-known Weber-Michels hypothesis, which applies well for instrumental movements. Nor has it radicalized as would be typical for a countercultural movement. Instead, the gay movement has followed the twin paths of commercialization and involution: movements commercialize as their SMOs increasingly become involved in commercial activities (like publishing, catering, or advertising); or they take the route of involution, if their SMOs and informal networks increasingly engage in self-help and social activities (Kriesi 1995).

The last two chapters address the questions of the diffusion of collective actions and their outcomes. Chapter 8 deals with the diffusion processes occurring among new social movements. The main argument is that collective action spreads across countries to the extent that (national) political opportunities are present in the country which are taking up the stimulus from abroad. Examples drawn from the antinuclear, peace, and urban autonomous movements provide some evidence that the political context also matters with respect to the cross-national diffusion of protest. Finally, chapter 9 adresses the difficult question of the outcomes of the mobilization by social movements. On the basis of examples drawn from the antinuclear, gay, and urban autonomous movements, this chapter argues that the outcomes of the new social movements in particular are largely influenced by the interplay of political opportunities and movement types.

Part I

General Concepts and Basic Results

Chapter 1

National Cleavage Structures

In this chapter we will analyze the way that traditional political cleavage structures facilitate or constrain the action space of new social movements. As already suggested in the Introduction, the new social movements tend to articulate a political conflict that is based on a *new cultural and social cleavage* in society. Not only in this case, but quite generally, political conflicts are ultimately rooted in structural and cultural cleavages. In other words, they have their origin in broad societal transformations that oppose social groups for structural and cultural reasons. However, "structure" and "culture" do not impinge directly on politics. Social and cultural dividing lines — societal cleavages — only result in political cleavages if they are politicized. As Bartolini and Mair (1990: 216) observe, political cleavages cannot be reduced simply to the outgrowths of social stratification; rather, social distinctions become political cleavages when they are organized as such.[1] If the social-structural basis of a political conflict emerges from social change, the conflict itself results from the coupling of these processes of social change with those of democratization, politicization, and mobilization. Thus, Bartolini and Mair continue, it is only through the historical processes of mobilization, politicization, and democratization that any specific political cleavage acquires its distinctive normative profile and organizational network (ibid.: 217). In short, political cleavages develop initially on the basis of a social stratification that sets the structural conditions for group identity, and only later do they become fully political, particularly with the development of mass democracies. Or, in other words, social change determines structural and cultural potentials for political mobilization that remain latent as long as they are not politicized. In order for such potentials to become politicized, they have to develop, on the one hand, a collective identity, a sense of solidarity, and political consciousness,[2]

3

and, on the other hand, an organizational infrastructure (Kriesi 1985: 30ff.; Klandermans 1988). The organizational infrastructure includes not only formal organizations, but also informal personal networks that allow for the micromobilization processes to take place that have been found to be so important in the mobilization for collective action.

Traditional societal cleavages constitute the basis of the political cleavage structure even today. Although Western European societies have undergone far-reaching social and cultural transformations, the impact of traditional societal cleavages on the political cleavage structure has proven to be very resistant to social change. Thus, according to the well-known "freezing hypothesis" of Lipset and Rokkan (1967), the political configuration in the party systems of the Western European countries of the late sixties still reflected the cleavage structures that had existed at the end of the First World War. If, in the meantime, the impact of the traditional cleavage structure on the voting behavior of Western European electorates seems to have considerably diminished in most countries (Franklin et al. 1992), the sediments of past political mobilization are still with us.

Given that the political mobilization by new social movements articulates a new societal cleavage, it seems obvious that the continuing strength of old cleavages, which is reflected in the national political conflict structure, has an impact on the possibility for the new cleavage to emerge. While the structural underpinnings of the new cleavage are present in all Western European countries, the relative strength of the old cleavages may be expected to restrict the possibilities of the mobilization on the basis of the new cleavage. The construction of new identities is only possible when old identities fade and lose their capacity to help people to interpret the world. Distinct existing identities provide, in other words, a shield against the framing attempts of rising collective actors. Moreover, the articulation of a new cleavage presupposes the mobilization of resources that may not be available if political mobilization on the basis of traditional cleavages is absorbing a great deal of the time, energy, and money of the relatively small part of the population that engages in political action. Organizations engaged in traditional political conflicts may even actively prevent potential supporters of new social movements from contributing to their mobilization. According to this line of reasoning, there exists a zero-sum relationship between the strength of traditional political cleavages and the possibility of new social movements to articulate a new societal cleavage.

Karl-Werner Brand (1985: 322f.) has already suggested that the mobilization of "new social movements" depends on the mobilization potential of traditional political conflicts. He maintained that there exists an inverse relationship between the mobilization potential of the traditional class conflict and the mobilization opportunities of new social movements. According to his hypothesis, the pacification of traditional class conflict by way of the expansion of the welfare state and by the institutionalization of the conflict over the distribution of the national product created "space" for the articulation of new conflicts. He did not propose the same substitutive relationship between the continued mobilization potential of other traditional conflicts and the mobilization of new social movements. He seemed to assume that, under certain conditions, these other traditional cleavages might serve as a catalyst for the mobilization of the new social movements rather than as a constraining factor.

The Mobilization Potential of a Political Cleavage

In order to get a clearer idea of the possible relationships between the traditional political cleavages and the new ones articulated by the new social movements, let us briefly discuss the concept of the *"mobilization potential" of a political cleavage*. The term "mobilization potential" was first introduced by Klandermans and Oegema (1987), who referred to the "potential of people in a society who could theoretically be mobilized by a social movement." Applied to a political cleavage, the term can be defined in an analogous way as the potential of people in the social groups involved in a political cleavage that could theoretically be mobilized by a social movement. In order to characterize the mobilization potentials of various cleavages in a more precise way, we propose to distinguish between two dimensions that we conceptualize by applying some ideas of Bartolini and Mair (1990). First, the mobilization potentials of political cleavages vary according to the degree to which the cleavages constitute social groups that are, at the same time, clearly segmented from each other and internally highly integrated. This dimension corresponds to what Bartolini and Mair call the *degree of closure* of the social relationship represented by the cleavage. Accordingly, a cleavage is structured by processes that restrict mobility in a number of ways (ibid.: 224): "through marriage, educational institutions, the urban and spatial setting of the population, social customs, religious practices and so on. And, as mass politics develops, these original forms of closure are extended to new kinds of behaviours, such as organizational membership and voting, which may then reinforce the original basis of the cleavage through an active defense of the community." Social homogeneity and cultural distinctiveness, on the one hand, and internal organizational integration and political encapsulation, on the other, are the parameters determining the degree of closure of social groups divided by a cleavage. The more socially and culturally distinct, and the more internally integrated and politically encapsulated a group, the greater is its degree of closure. Tilly's (1978) concept of "CATNET"(category + network) captures the same idea of closure of a social group.

This notion of closure is crucial, because, as Oberschall (1973) has argued convincingly, an internally highly integrated group in a segmented context — no matter whether it is integrated on the basis of traditional communal or more modern associational ties — constitutes a formidable basis for political mobilization. The members of a group that is closed in terms of a traditional cleavage will be readily mobilizable on the basis of their distinctiveness — that is, their collective identity and common interests, their loyalty to the group, and their shared consciousness of belonging to a distinct group — and on the basis of their integration into informal networks and formal organizations. However, the essential point in the present context is that they will only be mobilizable in terms of the traditional cleavage that defines their distinctive identity and their specific interests; that is, they will not be available for mobilization by new social movements.

The second aspect of the mobilization potential of a traditional cleavage is its *salience,* that is, the degree to which it dominates the conflicts in the political arenas. Bartolini and Mair introduce this term to assess the relative importance of a given cleavage with respect to other cleavages in the context of electoral competition. We propose instead to apply it to the significance of a given cleavage in the context of political competition in the extraparliamentary arena of movement politics. From this perspective, a cleavage is salient to the extent that it has not been institutionalized and, therefore, *pacified.* The institutionalization of a political cleavage implies that it becomes regulated by established procedures, that the groups involved are integrated into the political networks in the administrative and the parliamentary arenas, and that they abandon the challenging of authorities by unconventional means.

The institutionalization of a cleavage does not imply that it no longer gives rise to political competition. It only implies that the competition is no longer taking place in unconventional terms. By definition, a pacified cleavage no longer gives rise to political mobilization on a large scale outside of the parliamentary or administrative arenas. In contrast, it is rather likely that precisely this will happen in the case of a nonpacified cleavage. Moreover, it is essential for the present context not only that a nonpacified traditional cleavage is likely to give rise to political mobilization by unconventional means, but that it also tends to provide master frames for the interpretation of movement politics, that it tends to absorb the general public's attention and to occupy the political agenda of both conventional and movement politics to an extent that goes far beyond the more or less narrow confines of the social groups directly involved in the cleavage in question. Accordingly, a nonpacified traditional cleavage sets important constraints on the political opportunities for the mobilization of new social movements.

Note that this second aspect of the mobilization potential of a cleavage is quite distinct from the previous one. At first sight, a cleavage characterized by highly distinct and internally coherent groups is not likely to be institutionalized. But, if pacification of a closed cleavage is difficult to obtain, it is not impossible. It is conceivable that the strongly segmented groups maintain routinized, peaceful, and stable relationships with each other on the level of their representatives. Even if the ordinary members of the groups hardly have any contact with each other at all, their elites may be integrated into the political process and maintain good relations with each other. The Dutch system of "pillarization" provides the most prominent example of this configuration of a more or less pacified coexistence of segmented groups. Both the religious and the class cleavage constituted internally highly integrated groups in the Netherlands, which, nevertheless, maintained rather peaceful relationships with each other. The highly integrated character of the separate groups may actually be instrumental in the stabilization of the relationships on the elite level, since it allows the elites to control their grassroots base quite successfully. One may go even one step further, as do some authors in the debate on neocorporatism (e.g., Schmitter 1981), and suggest that the integrated internal structure of the groups involved in a given cleavage is a precondition for the institutionalization of intergroup relationships.

Combining the two aspects of the mobilization potential of a political cleavage, we arrive at four types of traditional cleavages with quite different mobilization capacities. Table 1.1 provides an overview of these types. First, take the case of a closed traditional cleavage that has been pacified. This is the case illustrated by the Dutch system of pillarization just mentioned. In this case, the traditional cleavage no longer gives rise to political mobilization outside of the conventional channels. Given its closure, however, the potential capacity for mobilization of the traditional cleavage is still important. The situation is one of "*latency.*" Although the members of the social

Table 1.1. Typology for the mobilization potential of traditional cleavages

Closure of the cleavage	Salience of the cleavage	
	Pacified	Not pacified
Closed	Latent potential	"Exclusively" mobilized potential
Open	Available potential for new mobilization	"Inclusively" mobilized potential

groups involved are not actively mobilized on the basis of the traditional cleavage, they will not be available for the mobilization by new social movements, given the closure of the traditional groups.

To the extent that the traditional elites lose their hold over their respective client groups—that is, to the extent that the closure of these groups weakens and they are opening up—their members may become available for the mobilization by new social movements. The acceleration of the process of "depillarization" of traditional Dutch society since the mid-sixties has, for example, increased the availability of Dutch religious groups for the mobilization by new social movements. If the traditional cleavage is open and pacified—our second type—the members of the groups involved become potentially available for the mobilization by new social movements. In such a situation, the extraparliamentary mobilization in terms of the traditional cleavage has ceased to be of any significance and the members of the groups involved become free for the mobilization in terms of new cleavages.

Third, if the traditional cleavage is closed and not yet pacified, the social groups involved tend to be highly politicized and mobilized in terms of the traditional conflict. The closure of the social groups involved in such a non-pacified traditional conflict proves to be particularly instrumental for their mobilization. Given a high degree of closure, the traditional political organizations, which typically mobilize "from above," can count on a preexisting consensus among their members and on elaborate recruitment networks among their respective social groups. In such a situation, the mobilization potential of the cleavage is highly visible, manifest, and activated, but—and this is the important point in our context—it is activated *exclusively* in terms of the traditional conflict. In other words, the social groups involved are not available for the mobilization by new social movements articulating new types of cleavages. Given the high degree of politicization in traditional terms, it is rather unlikely that the groups involved will open up to newcomers on the political scene.

Finally, if the traditional cleavage lacks closure, but is still highly conflictual and still gives rise to intense political mobilization, the situation is more complicated. The high degree of conflictuality implies a high degree of political consciousness among the members of the social groups involved, as well as a high degree of visibility of the symbols and ideologies linked to the traditional conflict. In this case, the lack of of closure is above all an organizational one. It implies, first, a greater amount of competition between the political organizations that mobilize their traditional client groups. Under these circumstances, some of the organizations associated with the traditional cleavage may try to outflank their competitors in the organizational field representing traditional social groups by trying to be different, that is, by appealing to new issues and new types of clients not catered to by their competitors (Duyvendak 1992: 115). If this is the case, the issues raised by new social movements may be interpreted in terms of the old identities and conflicts. The lack of organizational closure also implies the possibility of "mobilization from below" in the form of revolts against the organizational leadership or of direct challenges of the adversaries that bypass the organizational top. Such "mobilization from below" may be influenced by the interpretations of competitors from outside the traditional organizational field. In other words, lack of closure under conditions of high conflictuality gives rise to a great amount of competition not only within the traditional organizational field but also between traditional organizations and newcomers on the political scene. In this competitive space, the political organizations associated with the traditional cleavage are likely to make every attempt to mobilize their traditional potentials in terms of the traditional conflict and to impose the terms of this conflict on all the newly emerging conflicts in movement politics; that is, they will try to absorb new issues and new collective actors into the traditional conflict. This is why we propose to speak in this case of an *"inclusively"* mobilized traditional potential.

The extent to which traditional cleavages are "inclusively" mobilized also depends on the *proximity* of the traditional conflict in question to the concerns articulated by new social movements. The greater the proximity of the two conflicts, the greater the likelihood of competition between the collective actors that articulate the traditional conflict and new social movements. Proximate causes give rise to competition for scarce resources and conflicts of interpretation and strategy. However, proximity has ambivalent implications. It not only leads to competition, but it also implies the possibility of mutual support, facilitation — in short, alliances. We shall discuss alliances in chapter 3. For the time being, we wish to underline the first aspect of proximity, which suggests that, paradoxically, a traditional cleavage that is closely related to the cleavages articulated by new social movements may reduce the available mobilization potential for new social movements to a greater extent than a traditional cleavage that has nothing to do with the issues and concerns articulated by new social movements. The paradoxical character of proximity has already been pointed out by Simmel (1968: 205), who reminded us of the fact that the close relationship among kin tends to give rise to more profound antagonisms than we find among strangers.

The Mobilization Potential of Traditional Cleavages in the Four Countries

We can now turn to more specific questions concerning the mobilization potential of the traditional cleavages in each one of the four countries under study and the implications for the mobilization of new social movements. Following the lead of Rokkan (1970), we may distinguish between four traditional cleavages, which have been generally very important in the past: the center-periphery, religious, and urban-rural cleavages as well as the cleavage between the working class and the bourgeoisie. It will, of course, not be possible to study the strength of these cleavages in detail, but we shall nevertheless try to indicate the general makeup of each one of them in the four countries. Let us start with the conflict between the *center* and the *periphery*. This cleavage has traditionally given rise to regionalist or nationalist movements that have mobilized against the builders of the centralized nation-states. The defense of the periphery is typically linked to a specific territorial identity. In this respect, two elements play an especially important role — language and religion. Very often, language constitutes the crucial resource (Rokkan and Urwin 1983: 131). Religious and linguistic minorities in the periphery are particularly likely to mobilize if their territory is at the same time economically discriminated against. If a distinct regional identity is in any case conducive to mobilization, it is clearly reinforced by an unfavorable economic situation (Rennwald 1992: 171). We assume that the persistence of this conflict is closely related to the state structure and that it is much more salient in centralized states than in federalist ones. A federalist state may contribute to a certain degree of closure on the part of peripheral groups. But, by allowing the devolution of political power to the peripheral minorities, it goes a long way toward institutionalizing the conflict between the center and the periphery.

Of our four countries, France is the one where we would expect the most salient center-periphery cleavage. It is not only the most centralized, but it also has several ethnic and linguistic peripheries — in the Alsace, the Basque country, Brittany, Corsica, and Occitania—which are directly confronted with the discriminatory practices of the central state. On the other hand, we have the two federalist countries—Switzerland and Germany. Their federalism is, however, not of the same kind. Swiss federalism is what Lijphart (1984: 179) calls the "incongruent" type, whereas German federalism is "congruent"[3]: "Congruent federations are composed of territorial units with a social and cultural character that is similar in each of the units and in the federation as a whole. In a perfectly congruent federal system, the component units are 'miniature reflections of the important aspects of the whole federal system'. Conversely, incongruent federations have units with social and cultural compositions that are different from each other and from the country as a whole." Whereas congruent systems such as the German one are unlikely to produce strong territorial identities, and are, therefore, typically associated with open center-periphery cleavages, incongruent systems may preserve strong collective identities of a territorial kind, which implies the continued existence of rather closed groups defined in terms of the center-periphery cleavage, even if the federalism is likely to pacify the segmented groups.[4] In this case, the cleavage is not giving rise to large-scale mobilizations, but it is still present in the sense that it shapes loyalties and political consciousness; it influences the way political issues are conceived, and is liable to shut out from public attention issues that are entirely unrelated to it. In Switzerland, there is one more element to be considered: if its federalism allows center-periphery conflicts to be reduced, it may still be possible for a center-periphery conflict to develop within one of the member states of the confederation. This is especially likely if there are ethnic, linguistic, or religious minorities that are politically discriminated against by the majority within a member state. There is one Swiss region where these conditions have prevailed: the region of the Jura in the canton of Bern constituted both a linguistic (French-speaking) and a religious (Catholic) minority in a canton dominated by Swiss-German-speaking Protestants. The center-periphery cleavage has become particularly salient within this region throughout the postwar period, but especially since the late sixties (Rennwald 1994). The Netherlands, finally, is difficult to situate with respect to this cleavage. It is true that the Netherlands has a unitary state that is almost as centralized as the French, and there are also cultural minorities concentrated in specific regions of the country: the Frisians in the north and the Catholics in the south. However, the Frisians have never been a discriminated-against minority, and the Catholic south has been integrated into the pillarized system, which has served to considerably reduce the salience of the center-periphery cleavage at the same time as it weakened the religious one. In other words, we would not expect much mobilization along these lines in the Netherlands.

The *religious* cleavage takes different forms in predominantly Catholic countries, in Protestant countries, and in countries that are religiously mixed. Among our four countries, France is the only one that is predominantly Catholic, while the other three are all religiously mixed. In France, the religious cleavage refers to the conflict between the church and the secularized state, between practicing Catholics and those who are not affiliated with the church at all. This cleavage marks one of the constants of French politics, where the church has been associated with the political right since the ancien régime. The conflict has not definitely been pacified, but lingers on and erupts typically with respect to educational questions, which have been at its core since the nineteenth century. It has not given rise to stable patterns of political integration. There is, for example, no equivalent to a major Christian Democratic party in France that could integrate the practicing Catholics under one organizational roof. Similarly, the secularized part of French society is not organized in one clearly identifiable party. Although not pacified on the level of political representation, the mobilization potential of this cleavage is weakened by the fact that it crosscuts the predominant class cleavage.

In contrast, in the religiously mixed countries, the religious cleavage has traditionally opposed Catholics and Protestants. In all three of them, the Catholics have organized in defense against the dominant Protestants, who were the decisive builders of the nation-state. In all three, however, the religious cleavage was largely pacified by the mid-seventies. In Switzerland, federalism has allowed the Catholics to preserve their political power in the regions where they dominate. In the other regions, the creation of an organizational infrastructure reminiscent of the Dutch pillarized structures (Altermatt 1991; Righart 1986) has served to defend their interests. In several steps, the Catholics have then been integrated into national politics and the federal administration, which have carefully observed religious proportional representation for decades. The Dutch situation has traditionally been somewhat more complicated in that the Netherlands has known two types of religious cleavages — one between Protestants and Catholics, and a second one within the Protestant church, where orthodox dissenters broke off from the mainstream in the nineteenth century. Just as in Switzerland, however, the cleavage was pacified in several steps at the beginning of our century. Moreover, a process of massive "depillarization" took place in the late sixties, which implied that the various groups lost much of their distinctiveness, even if the organizational infrastructure of the pillars continues to exist. In the political arena, the parties of the various pillars have joined forces by creating one Christian Democratic party representing Catholics and mainstream and orthodox Protestants. The continued existence of pillarized organizations maintains some degree of closure of the system, but the pacification of the cleavage assures that the potential for mobilization in extrainstitutional channels remains largely latent.

In Germany, the traditional defensiveness of the Catholic minority, which still lived with the memory of Bismarck's Kulturkampf against the Catholic "state in the state," gave way to a much more open attitude after the Second World War. First of all, after the partitioning of the country, the Catholics no longer constituted a minority but approached 50 percent of the population. Second, their party was no longer a minority party but became the major party of the center-right, which was based on a double compromise (Smith 1986): even if the Catholics were the decisive element in the party, it represented an alliance of Catholics and Protestants. Moreover, it also became a party that cut across social classes and mobilized from all quarters of society. In other words, by its "catchall" character it not only weakened the mobilizing capacity of the old religious cleavage, but also that of the class cleavage to which we shall return shortly.

If the *urban-rural* cleavage, as Rokkan maintains, dominated the politics of the nineteenth century, it has generally lost much of its virulence in the course of the twentieth century. The main reason for the weakening of the mobilizing capacity of the urban-rural cleavage is that, by the end of this century, farmers have become a rather small, politically highly integrated minority in Western European countries. Although they have become a minority in the population even of France, farmers have maintained an important political position in all the countries under study. This is certainly related to the excellent political organization of the farming community and to the crucial electoral role played by the farmers in all these countries. Their firm integration into national politics has everywhere contributed to the pacification of the urban-rural cleavage. But, given their organizational infrastructure and their distinct identities, the farmers have everywhere retained a high mobilizing capacity. Due to the institutionalization of the cleavage, this capacity has remained latent for most of the period covered by our study. More recently, however, the political clout of the farmers has been declining in the context of the process of European economic integration. As a result, the farming population has been remobilizing, following an "exclusive" pattern. This remobilization has been especially strong in France.

The *class* cleavage — that is, the cleavage between the working class and the bourgeoisie — is the last and, from the point of view of the mobilization of new social movements, the most important of the traditional cleavages. The class cleavage is most closely related to the new cleavage articulated by the new social movements. In part at least, the organizations of the traditional and the new left, and those of the new social movements, address themselves to the same constituencies. Previous research has amply documented the close affinity between the constituencies of the parties of the left, on the one hand, and those of the new social movements, on the other (see, for example, Kriesi 1993a; Müller-Rommel 1984, 1985, 1990; Watts 1987). The details of the relationship between the left and the new social movements will occupy us in several of the following chapters. In the present context, the question concerning us more specifically refers to the extent of the comparative strength of the mobilizing capacity of the class cleavage in the four countries under study.

The mobilizing capacity of this cleavage depends, first of all, on the transformation of the class structure. As a result of the growing role of the service sector in the economy of Western European countries, the traditional working class is generally losing ground in the active labor force of these countries. This means that the traditional base of the labor movement is increasingly narrowing, which, in turn, implies that the mobilizing capacity of this cleavage, at least in its traditional form, is weakened. In addition, the increasing standard of living and the establishment of the welfare state equally weaken the cleavage in its traditional form in that they reduce the distinctiveness of working-class culture and working-class identities. As a consequence of the opening up of the class cleavage, its impact on the voting behavior of the Western European electorates has declined over the last twenty-five years. If the timing and the speed of this process is country-specific, Franklin et al. (1992) argue that it is taking place in a generalized way all over Western Europe.

The way the organizations of the labor movement have dealt with this process differs significantly between our four countries. In France, in particular, the opening up of the class cleavage has not implied its pacification.[5] In fact, this cleavage has continued to be highly conflictual and salient in French politics. In other words, the case of the class cleavage in France provides us with a particularly eloquent illustration of the pattern of "inclusive mobilization." A crucial factor explaining the continued salience of this cleavage is, as we shall argue in more detail, the split of the French left into a Communist and a Socialist or social-democratic branch. As a result of the repressive tradition of the French authorities with regard to the labor movement (Gallie 1983), and as a consequence of their record in the Resistance during World War II, the French Communists emerged as the major party on the left in the postwar period. Given the dominant position of the Communists on the French left, the political discourse in France continued to be cast in terms of class, and images of class struggle were continually reinforced until at least the early eighties. The French Socialists had no other choice but to compete with the Communists for the leading position on the left, and they had to do so on the latter's terms. The high mobilization potential of the class cleavage is also a result of the polarization between the left and the right, which in turn has been reinforced by the electoral system of the Fifth Republic (Duyvendak 1992).

The competition between the Communists and the Socialists in France extended to the union system, which again contributed to the mobilization potential of the class cleavage. A divided left prevents the unions from getting integrated into stable policy networks and from abandoning traditional notions of class conflict (Golden 1986). Moreover, as has been pointed out by Hibbs (1978: 169), the particular economic interventionism of the French state, which is oriented to the strengthening of market forces, prevents the pacification of industrial relations and contributes to the politicization of the strike. In the French situation, where the state is an important actor in the system of industrial relations, the strike is frequently used as a form of political action to exert pressure on the government. However, the French unions are organizationally weak. In fact, in terms of organizational density and structuration, the French union system is the weakest in Western Europe (Visser 1987; Rosanvallon 1988). The weakness of their organizational base implies that the mobilization tends to come from below and is likely to escape the control of the unions.

The French situation with respect to the class cleavage contrasts quite sharply with what obtains in the other three countries. In all three, the class cleavage has been largely pacified and depoliticized. By adopting the Bad Godesberg Program in 1959, the German SPD not only shed the remaining Marxist elements but also accepted the integration of West Germany into NATO. Following the lead of its successful competitor, it became a "catchall" party, or at least a "people's party" (Smith 1989). This shift in orientation was remarkably successful: by 1972, the SPD had become the largest party with 46 percent of the vote. Similarly, industrial relations were largely pacified in the Federal Republic. The German union system was completely restructured by the Allies after the war. It now follows the principle of industrial unionism. The new, comprehensive organizational structures as well as a number of restrictions in the realm of strike legislation, which the unions had to accept, facilitated the integration of the unions into the German policy networks. Although higher than in France, the organizational density of the German unions does not come close to the density rates of Scandinavian or even British unions. However, their comprehensive organizational structure reinforces their position. A highly encompassing, corporatist union system such as the German one is still a class organization "in the sense that it promotes and protects interests of workers that may be tempted by the advantages of pursuing particularistic interests" (Przeworski and Sprague 1986: 75). Moreover, such a union system tends to exert pressure on the Social Democrats to give priority to the traditional labor class concerns. But such a union system is also conducive to the institutionalization of industrial relations. Thus the German unions are highly integrated into institutionalized patterns of codetermination and political concertation (Schmidt 1987). Given its pacified character and the widespread lack of class identities reflected by relatively low union densities, the mobilization potential of the German class cleavage is rather limited. The overall conclusion is that the German situation with respect to the class cleavage is quite ideal for the mobilization of new social movements.

If, compared to France, the class cleavage has become rather inconspicuous in Germany, it is even weaker in Switzerland and the Netherlands. In these two consociational countries, the Social Democrats have been part of coalition governments throughout large parts of the postwar period. Moreover, their union systems have been integrated into corporatist policy networks. The union systems in both countries have been fragmented along religious lines, which has served to dilute images of class from the start of their development. The Socialist unions have never been able to represent the whole working class. Finally, the organizational density of the unions in both countries has been rather low throughout the postwar period, and the Dutch unions in particular have suffered important losses since the early eighties. Pacified, organizationally fragmented, and without distinct collective class identities, the union systems in both countries do not in any sense contribute to the mobilization potential of the class cleavage.

In order to corroborate these sketches of the mobilization capacities of the traditional cleavage structures in the four countries under study, we would like to present some data on the *electoral volatility* provided by Bartolini and Mair (1990) in their study on the closure and competition in Western European party systems.[6] Electoral volatility does not directly address our notion of

Table. 1.2. Electoral volatility in the four countries: 1945–89

Country	Total volatility (TV)		Class-specific volatility (CV)		% class-specific volatility (CV/TV)	
	1945–65	1967–89	1945–65	1967–89	1945–65	1967–89
Switzerland	3.1	6.5	1.3	2.3	40.1	34.7
Netherlands	5.2	10.1	2.4	2.5	46.3	28.2
Germany	12.4	5.7	3.8	2.5	30.4	41.6
France	16.3	10.4	2.4	5.0	17.8	44.1

Source: Bartolini and Mair 1990

the "mobilization potential," but it provides us with an indicator of both the degree of closure and the salience of traditional cleavages in a given society. Table 1.2 presents the relevant figures for the postwar period, which we have divided into two intervals of about equal length — 1945–65 and 1967–89. These intervals roughly correspond to the periods before and after the new social movements burst onto the political scene of the countries under study.

First, consider the *total volatility,* which is an indicator of the overall closure of the cleavage structure. During the first period, total volatility was much lower in the two smaller countries that have traditionally been known for their highly segmented — that is, closed — societies and their integrative politics. The high degree of volatility in the larger countries during this period is, however, not only a result of their more open cleavage structures but also a consequence of the restructuration of their party systems due to institutional changes. Thus the German party system was entirely reconstructed under Allied supervision after the defeat in World War II. In France, which had the highest total volatility in this period, the party system changed profoundly as a result of the transition from the Fourth to the Fifth Republic in the late fifties. During the second period, we note a certain convergence with respect to the total volatilities in the four countries, as a result of the opening up of the traditional cleavages in the smaller countries — the famous "depillarization" of the Netherlands, the weakening of the all-party coalition in Switzerland — and of the increasing institutionalization of the traditional cleavages and of the party systems in the larger countries.

Next, consider the *class-specific volatility.*[7] The most conspicuous aspect of this second comparison is the increase of the class-specific volatility in France from one period to the other. While, overall, the French system became less competitive, its class cleavage became more open for competition. In other words, the class cleavage became more salient in France. This is reflected in the last two columns of the table, which give the respective shares of the total volatility that can be attributed to the class cleavage in each country. If we add to this result the comparatively strong competition within the two blocks of the left and the right, which is included in the still rather high total volatility, we get a confirmation of the continued political salience of the various traditional cleavages in France.

The smaller countries provide a stark contrast to the French case. In Switzerland and the Netherlands, the redoubling in total volatility is not accompanied by a corresponding increase in class-specific volatility. As a result, the share of class-specific volatility decreases. In other words, the salience of the class cleavage in the context of electoral competition is reduced. It is quite likely that, in these two countries, the increase in the overall volatility is generally linked to an opening up of the traditional cleavages, as well as to the electoral repercussions of the mobilization of the new social movements. Finally, with respect to Germany, we would like to underline that its class-specific volatility is no longer higher than that in the two smaller countries, which reflects, in our view, the considerable pacification of the German class cleavage in the postwar period.

Although this test is far from rigorous, the data provided by Bartolini and Mair confirm the general sense of our previous discussion of the mobilization potential of the traditional cleavages in the four countries, independently of the actual mobilization capacity of the various cleavages in the arena of movement politics. Table 1.3 briefly summarizes this discussion. It points out quite clearly the specificity of the French case, in comparison with the other three countries. Given the largely nonpacified character of the French traditional cleavages, we expect that the "space" for the mobilization of the new social movements was particularly restricted in France, and that, therefore, the mobilization of the French new social movements has been weaker than that of the new social movements in the other three countries. Moreover, given our assessment that the French class-specific potentials in particular have been "inclusively" mobilized up to and including most of the period under study, we expect that the new social movements in France had to meet with particularly stiff competition from the organizations from the left. The only instance of another relatively salient traditional cleavage concerns the center-periphery cleavage in Switzerland. This implies that among the other three countries, the Swiss new social movements were experiencing somewhat greater competition for mobilizing space than the German and the Dutch ones. In other words, if anything, the Swiss new social movements should turn out to be somewhat weaker, in comparative terms, than the German and the Dutch ones.

Table 1.3. The mobilization potential of the traditional cleavages
in the four countries

Cleavages	France	Germany	Netherlands	Switzerland
Center-periphery	Exclusive	Available	Available	(Exclusive)
Religious	(Inclusive)	Available	Latent	Available
Rural-urban	(Exclusive)	Latent	Latent	Latent
Class	Inclusive	Available	Available	Available

Note: If a given pattern is present, but less pronounced, it is put in parentheses.

Some Tentative Empirical Results

Our newspaper data allow us to test this hypothesis in a first, rather tentative way. More detailed discussions of the relationship between traditional cleavages and the mobilization of new social movements will follow in subsequent chapters. For the time being, we have two rough indicators at our disposal for the analysis of this relationship. First, we shall consider the overall *distribution of unconventional events* over the different movements. As is discussed in more detail in the Appendix, "unconventional" events cover all actions of a demonstrative, confrontational, or violent type. Not included under this heading are conventional actions of a juridical (various kinds of lawsuits), political (lobbying, letter writing to politicians, participation in consultation procedures, etc.), or media-directed (leafleting, press conferences, public tribunals, etc.) nature, as well as direct-democratic events. The distribution of unconventional events is shown in table 1.4.

This table gives a rather detailed description of the distribution in question, but let us concentrate for the moment on the total share of events accounted for by the different new social movements, on the one hand, and the corresponding share accounted for by other mobilization processes, on the other. As a comparison of these shares across countries shows, our expectations about the impact of the strength of traditional cleavages on the mobilization of the new cleavage are largely confirmed. In France, where the traditional conflicts continue to be rather strong, the new social movements' share of the total number of events is much more limited (36.1 percent) than in the other three countries. The four traditional cleavages we discussed earlier account for almost 40 percent of the unconventional events in France, whereas their share varies between only 10.1 percent in Germany and 17.7 percent in Switzerland. The mobilization on these four cleavages is indicated by lines 14 to 18 in table 1.4, which refer to regionalist movements (center-periphery), education (religious), farmers (urban-rural), and to the labor movement and other left mobilizations (class cleavage). The remaining events

Table 1.4. Distribution of unconventional events by movement (1975–89)

	France	Germany	Netherlands	Switzerland
1. Nuclear weapons	.4	11.6	11.8	.7
2. Other peace movement	4.0	7.1	5.1	5.3
3. Nuclear energy	12.8	12.8	5.1	7.2
4. Ecology movement	4.4	11.3	8.0	10.6
5. Antiracism	4.8	8.7	4.5	.8
6. Other solidarity movement	4.4	6.3	13.2	15.2
7. Squatters' movement	.3	6.7	10.4	7.9
8. Other countercultural	2.7	6.7	3.7	10.5
9. Homosexual movement	.8	.3	2.0	.7
10. Women's movement	1.5	1.7	1.6	2.1
Total NSMs	**36.1**	**73.2**	**65.4**	**61.0**
11. Student movement	4.8	1.5	2.2	.2
12. Civil rights movement	1.5	1.3	.6	2.7
13. Foreigners	2.5	4.2	7.1	8.5
14. Regionalist movement	16.6	.1	.0	10.6
15. Education	4.0	1.5	1.0	.2
16. Farmers	6.6	.3	1.3	.8
17. Labor movement	10.1	4.3	9.2	3.7
18. Other left	2.0	3.9	2.4	2.4
19. Countermobilization	.9	1.3	3.0	.9
20. Right-wing extremism	3.3	3.8	.7	.6
21. Other right mobilization	2.6	1.9	1.0	2.0
22. Other mobilization	8.8	2.7	6.2	6.6
Total not-NSMs	**63.9**	**26.8**	**34.6**	**39.0**
All mobilization	100.0%	100.0%	100.0%	100.0%
N (number of events)	(2,132)	(2,343)	(1,319)	(1,215)

Note: The squatters' movement includes actions for autonomous youth centers, mainly to be found in Switzerland. The category "other countercultural" includes actions by groups like the Autonomen or terrorist organizations that are not directed at the goals of any of the other NSMs. "Countermobilization" refers to all actions directed against the new social movements listed in the table. Examples are demonstrations against abortion or in favor of nuclear energy. The category "civil rights" includes actions against repression and state control to the extent that they are not part of the campaigns of the other movements. The category "foreigners" refers to actions by residents of foreign origin, against both the regime in their country of origin and their treatment in the country of residence. The figures for the labor movement do not include strikes (see Appendix, the section titled "Why Monday Issues?"), but they do include any other actions that may take place around strikes (for instance, factory occupations or demonstrations).

were produced by mobilization processes that are not readily attributable to either the new social movements or movements associated with the four traditional cleavages.

According to this indicator, new social movements take the largest share of the overall mobilization in Germany. In Switzerland, the relative share of unconventional events attributable to new social movements is limited, as expected, by the moderate strength of the center-periphery cleavage. More detailed analyses show that, in this case, it is indeed the conflict in the Jura region that was responsible for the rather conspicuous presence of regionalist mobilizations (10.6 percent of the events as compared to 16.6 percent in France). The Jura conflict in the canton of Bern was of considerable importance throughout the postwar period. After many years of intermittent mobilization, it started to escalate in the late sixties and peaked in the course of the seventies. In 1979, the conflict was partially solved with the creation of a new canton, the canton of Jura (Rennwald 1994). The solution was only partial, however, because the new canton did not cover the whole territory claimed by the regionalist movement, which continued to mobilize throughout the eighties. In the Netherlands, the number of events produced by the labor movement is somewhat higher than we would have expected on the basis of the previous discussion (9.2 percent of events as compared to 10.1 percent in France). A more detailed analysis will have to show what accounts for this comparatively strong unconventional mobilization of the Dutch labor movement.

Our first indicator only takes into account one aspect of the magnitude of collective action — its frequency. Other aspects include its duration, its size (number of participants per event), and the intensity of the involvement required (Tilly 1978: 96). We propose a second indicator that takes into account the *size* of the events. We shall exclude from the calculations based on this indicator all demonstrative events that require only a minimal level of involvement; in other words, we exclude petitions and political festivals.[8] Table 1.5 presents the volume of participation in the various movements of the four countries. If we concentrate again, for the time being, on the relative weight of the mobilization of the new social movements, our expectations are once more confirmed. In France, the mobilizing capacity of the new social movements again turns out to be much weaker than that of the traditional movements, whereas exactly the contrary obtains in the other three countries. In fact, the weakness of the French new social movements turns out to be even more serious, if we evaluate them on the basis of this second indicator. These movements account for only 24.5 percent of the participation in unconventional events, compared to 64.7 percent in Switzerland, 72.0 percent in the Netherlands, and almost 80 percent in Germany. However, not all new social movements are equally constrained by the mobilization potential of the traditional cleavages in France. Thus, the mobilization for peace issues that do not concern nuclear weapons and the mobilization against racism reach a

Table 1.5. Volume of participation in unconventional events by movement (1975–89), in 1,000s per million inhabitants

	France	Germany	Netherlands	Switzerland
1. Nuclear weapons	0	92	89	10
2. Other peace movement	14	19	3	15
3. Nuclear energy	9	26	15	24
4. Ecology movement	2	11	5	16
5. Antiracism	10	7	4	1
6. Other solidarity movement	5	6	15	18
7. Squatters' movement	0	3	4	9
8. Other countercultural	0	3	1	5
9. Homosexual movement	1	0	4	0
10. Women's movement	2	1	3	3
Total NSMs	**43**	**168**	**143**	**101**
11. Student movement	23	4	7	0
12. Civil rights movement	0	2	0	3
13. Foreigners	1	2	3	8
14. Regionalist movement	4	0	0	11
15. Education	62	2	2	0
16. Farmers	3	2	1	1
17. Labor movement	33	19	19	15
18. Other left	1	3	14	4
19. Countermobilization	4	1	2	4
20. Right-wing extremism	1	0	0	0
21. Other right mobilization	1	7	2	4
22. Other mobilization	5	1	4	5
Total not-NSMs	**135**	**43**	**55**	**55**
All mobilization	**178**	**211**	**198**	**156**
N	(2,076)	(2,229)	(1,264)	(1,027)
23. Strikes	225	37	23	2
Total	**403**	**248**	**221**	**158**

Note: Sum of the number of participants in all unconventional actions per million residents (Germany 61.6 million; France 53.3; Netherlands 14.1; Switzerland 6.4; the figures for France are for 1979, and for the rest, 1980. Missing values have been replaced by the national median of the number of participants for a given type of event (e.g., a demonstration). Figures have been rounded to thousands, figures below 500 are given as 0. Petitions and festivals are excluded (see text). Strikes were not included in the newspaper sample (see Appendix). They are based on International Labor Organization (ILO) figures.

volume comparable to that of the other countries. As we shall argue in chapter 3, these mobilizations profited from the support of allies on the left.

With respect to the traditional cleavages, our second indicator shows that if the center-periphery cleavage gave rise to a particularly large number of events in France, it did not mobilize very many people. Instead, the religious cleavage (i.e., educational issues) and the class cleavage (i.e., the labor movement) were particularly mobilizing in France during the period under consideration.

If we add all *strikes* that took place in this period to the set of unconventional events we collected in our newspaper analyses (see line 23 in table 1.5), the relative mobilization potential of the French new social movements is further reduced. They now account for no more than roughly one-tenth (10.7 percent) of the total mobilization, compared to roughly two-thirds of the total mobilization in each of the other three countries. Adding strikes reveals the enormous strength of the class cleavage in France, which, on the basis of this indicator, accounts for no less than two-thirds of the people mobilized by unconventional events. Some readers may consider it inappropriate to classify strikes among unconventional events.[9] We believe, however, that it is justified to regard them as unconventional for the period and the countries we are dealing with here. On the one hand, one should not forget that for pacified union movements such as the Dutch, German, and Swiss movements, strikes are quite unconventional ways of pursuing their workers' interests. In Switzerland, for example, collective agreements between employers' associations and unions typically do not allow the workers to strike. On the other hand, as we have just seen, strikes are, indeed, quite frequent in France. But, as Schain (1980: 201) has pointed out, the style of the strike in France is often rather close to what we understand as a political demonstration: it takes the form of mass meetings, marches, and frequent attempts to mobilize the support of the broader public. Indeed, the style of the strike is to politicize, rather than to isolate, industrial conflict. We believe, therefore, that strikes are best categorized among demonstrative actions in all of our countries. But even if strikes are treated as less unconventional than we claim them to be, this result confirms the crucial importance the pacification of the traditional class cleavage has for the mobilization potential of the new social movements.

Finally, if we also take into account the *petitions and political festivals,* which we have excluded from the calculations presented in table 1.5, the overall results do not change very much: the mobilization potential of the French new social movements remains quite marginal, whereas these movements are still shown to be predominant in all the other three countries. If we add these two action forms, which require very little involvement, the new social movements turn out to be somewhat less prominent in Switzerland, because political festivals belong above all to the action repertoire of the regionalist movement and its countermovement in the Jura, which have mobilized large numbers of people for the festivals of the "people of the Jura." Table 1.6 pre-

Table 1.6. Summary of relative strength of the new social movements in the four countries (percentages)

	France	Germany	Netherlands	Switzerland
1. Relative number of unconventional events (table 1.4)	36.1	73.2	65.4	61.0
2. Relative size of mobilization capacity (table 1.5)	24.2	79.6	72.0	64.7
3. Relative size of mobilization capacity (as 2, but including strikes)	10.7	67.7	64.7	63.9
4. Relative size of mobilization capacity (as 3, but including petitions/festivals)	17.3	69.9	69.1	58.8

sents a summary of the different measures of the relative strength of the new social movements in the four countries.

The figures in table 1.5 also allow us to compare the *absolute* size of the mobilization capacity of new social movements and traditional mobilizations between the four countries. These figures are directly comparable, since they measure the number of people that have been mobilized per one million inhabitants. Excluding festivals, petitions, and strikes, we note that the new social movements in Switzerland have a mobilizing capacity roughly two and one-half times as important as that of their French counterparts, that the corresponding Dutch capacity is roughly three times and the German capacity roughly four times as large. On the other hand, strikes alone have had a greater mobilizing capacity in France than all the new social movements taken together in each one of the other three countries. If we exclude strikes from consideration, the four traditional cleavages have proved to be as mobilizing in France as the new social movements in Switzerland, but not quite as mobilizing as these movements have been in the Netherlands and in Germany.

The figures in table 1.5 also allow us to compare the overall level of mobilization in the four countries. This overall level is strongly dependent on the forms of action that we include in the analysis, as the differences between the totals including and those excluding strikes indicate. While it is true that the country-specific characteristics of the action repertoire are not wholly independent of a country's cleavage structure — the prominent place of political festivals in the Swiss regionalist movement is a case in point — action repertoires do not so much depend on the cleavage structure of a country as on its political opportunity structure. This is the subject of the next chapter, which shall also consider variations in the overall levels of mobilization between the four countries.

Conclusion

In this chapter, we have presented some concepts for the discussion of the relationship between the mobilization potential of traditional cleavages and the corresponding capacity of the new social movements to articulate new issues. We have found support for the idea that there exists a zero-sum relationship between the two. The French case has been particularly revealing in this respect. Our hypothesis that salient traditional cleavages can be quite constraining for the mobilization of new social movements has been confirmed by the French case. By contrast, where traditional cleavages are no longer closed and have been pacified, the new social movements seem, indeed, to find more "space" to mobilize. The availability of the social groups belonging to the constituency of the old and the new left—which are defined by the class cleavage—has turned out to be crucial in this respect, because these groups are most likely to form a constituency of the new social movements, too. The availability of some other groups, which are defined in terms of the three remaining traditional cleavages—farmers, orthodox Protestants or Catholics, ethnic minorities, or regional groups—is likely to be less significant for the mobilization potential of the new social movements, since these groups typically do not share their concerns in the first place. However, to the extent that these other three traditional cleavages are not pacified, they still dominate the political agenda in movement politics, absorb public attention, and provide master frames for the interpretation of political mobilization in general. Accordingly, we have found that, contrary to what Brand (1985) had expected, all nonpacified traditional cleavages impose important constraints on the mobilization potential of new social movements, even if they do not directly involve social groups that belong to their main constituencies.

Chapter 2

Institutional Structures and Prevailing Strategies

The analysis of cleavage structures in the preceding chapter allows us to understand why the goals for which people are most likely to mobilize differ from country to country, but it does not tell us much about the absolute levels and the action repertories of political mobilization. To explain these characteristics of political mobilization, we shall introduce two additional sets of elements of political opportunity structures (POS): the formal institutional structure of the political system and the informal procedures and prevailing strategies of political elites in dealing with challengers. Just like the national conflict structures, these two additional sets of elements constitute relatively stable elements of the political context of social movements. They are deeply embedded in the political heritage of a given political system and, from the point of view of the mobilizing social movements, they are essentially fixed and given. As such, these aspects of the political context are to be distinguished from the more volatile, conjunctural, or shifting ones, which will be the subject of the next chapter. The relevance of the conceptual distinction between more stable and more conjunctural elements of the political opportunity structure has been pointed out by several authors (Duyvendak and Koopmans 1989; Rucht 1990b; Della Porta and Rucht 1991; Gamson and Meyer 1995).

Moreover, we shall also elaborate upon our previous conceptualization of the more stable aspects of the POS by paying more attention to the different political arenas that exist within a political system. We keep, however, the basic distinction between formal and informal aspects of the POS, which we introduced earlier. In the first section, we shall discuss the formal institutional structure. The second section will deal with the prevailing informal strategies. In the next sections, we attempt to link the stable formal and informal aspects of the POS to the expected absolute levels of political mobilization and the action repertoires of the social movements. We shall do so by introducing a motivational theory, which will provide us with the mechanisms that translate the structures of the POS into individual and collective actions. Finally, we shall present an empirical test of our arguments.

Formal Institutional Structures

Formal structures determine to a large extent the openness of access to the state, as well as its capacity to act. Contrary to Kitschelt (1986), who makes a basic distinction between "political input structures" and "political output structures," we do not think that it is possible to separate these two types of structures clearly from one another. Open states tend at the same time to have only a limited capacity to act, whereas closed states tend to lack such a capacity. On the basis of their formal institutional structure, we shall make a distinction between strong states and weak ones: *strong states* are at the same time autonomous with respect to their environment and capable of getting things done, whereas *weak states* not only lack autonomy but also the capacity to act (see Badie and Birnbaum 1979; Krasner 1978; Zysman 1983: 298).

We are aware that the distinction between strong and weak states is a rather crude and overly schematic one. The strength of any given state varies, to be sure, from one policy domain or one period to the other (see, for example, Atkinson and Coleman 1989: 49; Lehmbruch 1991: 129). Strong states may turn out to be weak in a given policy domain, states that are weak under normal circumstances may momentarily gain in strength under exceptional circumstances, and vice versa. Nevertheless, we believe that the rough distinction on the macrolevel of analysis between strong and weak states is useful for conceptualizing the general outlines of the national political context in which social movements operate. As will become apparent, both aspects of the strength of the state are highly relevant for the mobilization of social movements.

In order to systematize the relevant input and output structures that determine the strength of the state, we shall distinguish between three political arenas: the parliamentary arena, the administrative arena, and the direct-democratic arena. According to the classic conception of representative democracy, there is a clear division of labor between the first two arenas: binding decisions are taken in the parliamentary arena, which are then implemented in the administrative arena. Citizens are essentially linked to the political process by the electoral process, which ensures that their demands are taken into account by the political parties in the parliamentary arena, and that the decisions taken by the political system are legitimate. In this model of representative democracy, the government straddles the two arenas, being, on the one hand, responsible either to parliament (in a parliamentary system) or to the people (in a presidential system), and, on the other hand, in charge of the direction of the public administration.

The reality of the political process, however, does not quite correspond to the classic division of labor between the two arenas that we find in the textbooks of constitutional law. Far from being the direct, linear result of parliamentary decision making, policy implementation also involves continuous negotiations, exchange processes, redefinitions, and reinterpretations of political objectives. In other words, once the legislature has taken its decisions, the political struggle continues in the administrative arena. Only the actors change, since interest groups take the place of the political parties as the primary links between the citizenry and the state. Moreover, the classic model does not take into account a third arena—the direct-democratic one—which constitutes a third channel of access to the state. In a few countries, access to this arena is institutionalized. In most countries, it is not regulated by formal rules.

The strength of the state is, first of all, a function of two general structural parameters that characterize not only each one of the three arenas separately but also their mutual interrelationship: the degree of the state's (territorial) *centralization* and the degree of its (functional) *separation of state power*. The greater the degree of decentralization, the wider is the degree of formal access and the smaller the capacity of any one part of the state to act. Decentralization implies a multiplication of state actors and, therefore, of points of access and decision making in each one of the three arenas. In federal states, such as those of Germany, Switzerland, or the United States, there are multiple points of relevant access on the national, regional, and local level. In centralized states, such as those of France, the Netherlands, or Sweden, regional and local access points are rather insignificant. In addition, the strength of the state is closely related to the (functional) separation of state power. The greater the separation of power between the different arenas—that is, between the legislature, the executive, and the judiciary—as well as within arenas, the greater the degree of formal access and the more limited the capacity of the state to act. In states with a relatively independent legislature, such as the Netherlands and Germany, or a strong judiciary, such as Germany or the United States, there are more points of access than in states with an all-powerful executive, as in the case of France. Switzerland can be considered as an intermediate case in this regard. These two general structural parameters operate, in our view, on both the input and the output side of the state.[1]

Next, let us look more closely at the parliamentary arena in particular. For Kitschelt, the openness of the state is above all a function of the institutional makeup of this arena: critical parameters are the number of parties, factions, and groups, as well as the formation of viable policy coalitions. As far as the number of parties is concerned, it is in turn a function of the national conflict structure and of the electoral system. The more complex the national conflict structure and the higher the degree of proportionality of the electoral system, the larger will be the number of parties. From the point of view of a challenger, proportional representation allows for easier access than plurality or majority methods. From the point of view of the already established parties, this means that they run a greater risk of competition from challengers in proportional electoral systems than in those with plurality or majority representation. Where there are large numbers of parties, social movements will be more likely to find allies within the party system. These allies may include challenging small parties as well as large established parties that adapt their positions under the impact of the competition by the smaller challengers.

Among the four countries of interest to us here, the Netherlands has by far the most far-reaching proportional representation. The country forms one single constituency in national elections, and the threshold for gaining a seat in parliament is lower than 1 percent. The German system for all practical purposes is also a proportional one, but one with a 5 percent threshold designed to keep out minor (radical) challengers. The relative openness of the German electoral system is further enhanced by the fact that any party that receives more than 0.5 percent of the vote is entitled to a very generous reimbursement of campaign costs by the state. The Swiss system is also a proportional one, with the cantons forming the constituencies in national elections. However, since the cantons vary greatly in size, the proportionality of the Swiss system differs from one canton to the other. In smaller cantons it is considerably more restrictive than the German system, while in the largest cantons it allows for more accessibility to challengers than the German one. Finally, the French two-ballot system is of the majority variety that gives challengers little opportunity to establish themselves within the party system.[2]

In three of the four countries, the electoral system simply serves to reinforce the impact of the two general structural parameters. In France, the two-ballot system contributes to the more general lack of access for challengers. Likewise, in Switzerland and Germany the relatively open electoral systems simply add one more channel of formal access to those already given by the first two aspects of the state's institutional structure. The very open electoral system in the Netherlands, however, significantly reduces the formal closure of the state resulting from its centralized character.

The number of parties determines, in part at least, the process of coalition formation. This process is, however, also dependent on the internal makeup of the parties — that is, on the number of factions and groups that exist within them (Laver and Schofield 1991). Very roughly, we can distinguish party systems with disciplined parties that can be considered as unitary actors from party systems with heterogeneous, undisciplined parties. In combination with the number of parties in a given system, we arrive at a typology of four different types of coalitions. The first type, of which Great Britain provides the classic example, is that of a single-party government, where the governing party is highly disciplined. Such governments generally have a strong capacity to act. Unlike either single-party governments based on heterogeneous, undisciplined parties, as we find them in the United States, which are often constrained by the need to find a balance among the interests of different constituencies, or multiparty coalitions, which are forced to make internal compromises, little prevents governments such as the British one from implementing radical policy changes.

Switzerland provides the clearest example of the opposite pattern, that of multiparty coalitions made up of undisciplined parties. Such a government is bound to be relatively weak. The broad range of parties represented in government reduces the government's capacity to act, since it can only implement policies for which a high degree of consensus exists. The undisciplined character of the parties implies that even a governing party may mobilize against the policy of the very government of which it is a member.[3] Germany and the Netherlands provide cases of multiparty governments with relatively disciplined parties. The Federal Republic of Germany was always ruled by coalition governments, but one of the coalition partners was always dominant, which implies that the German pattern is closer to the British than to the Swiss one. The Netherlands is closer to Switzerland in the sense that the governing coalitions have been less dominated by a single party as in the German case. The country has always been ruled by coalition governments of a more symmetrical kind, as none of the parties ever approached an absolute majority. Thus, the multiparty character of Dutch coalitions and the concomitant need for consensus also reduce the state's capacity to act, which, together with the formal openness of the electoral system, further relativizes the strength of the Dutch state. In the French case, finally, the Constitution of the Fifth Republic allows the government to put enormous pressure on the members of parliament from the governing parties. Even if the French parties are more heterogeneous and less disciplined than the parties in parliamentary systems, the French government still has an extraordinary capacity to act, given its constitutional prerogatives.[4]

In the administrative arena, formal access as well as the capacity to act are determined by the amount of resources at the disposal of the administration and its internal structure, by the structure of its interlocutors in the system of interest intermediation — primarily the interest groups — and by the structural arrangements that have been established between the two.[5] Turning first to the structure of the public administration, we may expect that the greater the amount of resources at its disposal, and the greater the degree of its coherence, internal coordination, and professionalization, the stronger it will be. Lack of resources, structural fragmentation, lack of internal coordination and of professionalization multiply the points of access and make the administration dependent on its private interlocutors in the system of interest-intermediation. This dependency will, however, not automatically open up the state to outsiders in the social movement sector; this will only be the case if the established interest groups are equally weak. On the contrary, a well-resourced, coherently structured, and professionalized system of interest groups may also be able to prevent outside challengers from having access to the state. Moreover, highly institutionalized, encompassing arrangements of policy negotiations between the public administration and private interest associations will be both quite inaccessible to challengers and able to act.[6]

France provides the prime example of a strong public administration, whereas the United States and Switzerland constitute the typical cases of weak administrations. In France, the administration is so strong that it largely dominates the policy process in the administrative arena. In the United States, the weak public administration is complemented by a fragmented system of interest groups and policy networks that tend to be pluralistic. In Switzerland, the public administration is weak. Policy networks may be strong in certain sectors, but they do not have an encompassing character allowing for linkages between different policy areas, and interest groups are quite fragmented, especially in the crucial domain of labor unions. The Netherlands and Germany are intermediate cases. In the Netherlands, the public administration is strong, given its high degree of centralization, its large amount of resources, its coherence, and its professionalization. The system of interest groups maintains highly institutionalized ties with the state, but it is structurally quite fragmented. Germany's "semisovereign state" (Katzenstein 1987) is relatively weak in terms of the conceptual distinctions made here. Its federalism, the strong position of its judiciary, and the autonomy of a large number of parastate institutions, such as the well-known Bundesbank, all contribute to the fragmentation of the German public administration. On the other hand, Germany has a coherent, centralized system of interest groups that is highly integrated into the policy-making process and thus contributes to the state's capacity to act.

Finally, formal access is a function of the degree to which direct-democratic procedures are institutionalized. From the point of view of challengers, the most important direct-democratic procedure is the popular initiative, which allows them to put an issue on the agenda of the political system and to ask for a vote of the whole electorate on the subject. Such procedures exist primarily in Switzerland, and in several states of the United States. The procedures of compulsory or optional referenda also give challengers an additional opportunity to intervene. They are, however, of less importance to them, because they only allow them to intervene after a decision has been taken by the political elite. Elaborate procedures of this type also exist in Switzerland, but not in the other three nations under study. In the Netherlands, however, citizens have elaborate rights of appeal (*inspraak*) in the course of the implementation of public policies (Duyvendak and Koopmans 1992: 46). These participation rights make up to some extent for their lack of direct-democratic rights in the decision-making process.

Table 2.1 allows us to summarize this discussion. For each arena we have tried to make a summary assessment of the state's institutional strength. For further discussion, we shall only retain the overall assessment, which gives a rough indication of the institutional strength of the different states. Switzerland clearly seems to have the weakest state among the four countries under study, France the strongest one. For its federalism, its independent judiciary, and its coalition government, the German state also tends to be rather weak, but because of its powerful parties, its strong system of interest groups,

Table 2.1. The institutional strength of the state

Country	Parliamentary arena	Administrative arena	Direct-democratic arena	Overall
Switzerland	weak	weak	weak	weak
Germany	intermediate	weak	strong	intermediate
Netherlands	intermediate	intermediate	strong	intermediate
France	strong	strong	strong	strong

its electoral system that bars access to small parties, and the absence of direct-democratic access on the federal level, we consider it to be an intermediate case. The Netherlands has a strong administration, no direct-democratic access in decision making, but a wide-open electoral system, relatively heterogeneous coalitions, and relatively elaborate access channels for citizens in the implementation of public policies, which makes it an intermediate case in the overall assessment, too. We do not want to exclude the possibility that there are other differences between the four states that contribute to their relative strength or weakness. We have insisted on the aspects that seem to us most relevant from the point of view of the opportunity structure of new or other social movements.

Prevailing Strategies

Organizational sociologists have long been insisting on the difference between the formal and the informal side of structure. Analogously, we should be aware of the distinction between the formal institutional structure and the informal ways in which it is typically applied. Scharpf (1984: 260) has used the concept of the "dominant strategy" to characterize the informal premises of procedure, the shared implicit or explicit understandings which emerge from the political process, and which guide the actions of the authorities. Contrary to Gamson and Meyer (1995), who suggest that we distinguish between institutional and cultural aspects of the POS, we prefer to stick to the distinction between formal institutional structure and informal strategies. Our concept of informal strategies is narrower than their concept of "political culture," since it is focused on the procedures that members of the political system employ when they are dealing with challengers, and since it does not make any reference to such excessively vague concepts as "zeitgeist," "civic culture," or "national moods." The informal procedures and prevailing strategies with respect to challengers are either *exclusive* (repressive, confrontational, polarizing) or *integrative* (facilitative, cooperative, assimilative). It is important to note that such procedures have a long tradition in a given country. According to Scharpf, they develop a powerful logic of their own. Efforts to change them are up against all the "sunk costs" of institutional commitments supporting them.

Given their long tradition, informal procedures and prevailing strategies have already had important consequences for the mobilization of the "old" labor movement. Thus, exclusive strategies that have typically been employed in southern European countries, but also in the Weimar Republic, led to an important split between the Social Democrats and the Communists within the labor movement. As is argued by Gallie (1983), the split in the French labor movement after World War I was the result of a particularly intransigent position of the French political elite at that time. While the British ruling elite chose to make important concessions to the radicalizing labor movement at the end of the war, the French ruling elite opted for a repressive strategy in similar circumstances. Gallie explains the difference in the reactions of the two ruling elites by earlier strategic decisions in an even more distant past. This illustrates the autodynamic of dominant strategies that makes for their reproduction across centuries. The split between Social Democrats and Communists has further radicalized the labor movement, which has again served to reinforce the dominant exclusive strategy of the authorities. In all the southern European countries, a strong Communist left has been excluded from power for decades. In Italy and France, the exclusion implied the delegitimation of the Communist Party; in Greece, Spain, and Portugal, the exclusion was the result of a long period of authoritarian repression (see Golden 1986).

Just as in the case of southern European countries, the German legacy is one of exclusion and repression. Although the formal institutional structure of the Federal Republic was completely rebuilt after World War II, and the labor movement has been to a large extent integrated, the dominant strategy of its ruling elites with regard to more recent challengers has continued to be marked by the experience of the past (Koopmans 1992a: 73ff.). In the context of the country's self-image of a militant democracy (*wehrhafte Demokratie*), the West German political elites compulsively sought to keep any trace of radicalism from the political stage. As a consequence of the Weimar trauma, tolerance with regard to challengers was interpreted as weakness and tough repression was seen as necessary to foreclose any possibility of another Weimar. In contrast to France, however, where the exclusive strategy is associated with a strong state, the exclusive strategy in the Federal Republic combines with a weaker state, which results in a different overall setting for social movements.

Likewise, integrative strategies toward new social movements have a history going back to a similar approach to earlier societal conflicts. We find them typically in small European countries with an open economy. Integrative strategies seem to be facilitated by the small size of a polity and its openness with regard to the world market (Katzenstein 1985). These countries have typically had weak absolutist or no absolutist regimes, which is one way to explain the relative absence of repressive strategies in the past. Some of these countries, such as Switzerland and the Netherlands, have learned to apply integrative strategies in dealing with their profound religious conflicts in the past. They all introduced proportional electoral systems after the First World War in order to accommodate their minorities. Finally, starting in the late thirties and continuing after the end of the Second World War, all of them applied integrative strategies to settlement of the class conflict as well. They have become known as "consociational democracies" (see, for example, Lijphart 1969; Scholten 1980; Steiner 1974) or as typical examples of "democratic corporatism" (Katzenstein 1985).

Just as in the exclusive case, integrative strategies are compatible with rather different formal institutional structures in the administrative and the parliamentary arena, which is also the reason why it is not possible to find a direct relationship between neocorporatist arrangements in the administrative arena and the development of new social movements (Wilson 1990).[7] A comparison of the Netherlands and Switzerland illustrates the point. The Netherlands has a strong unitary state with a relatively coherent bureaucracy, whereas the Swiss state is very weak because of its federalism, its fragmentation, and its direct-democratic institutions. The crucial difference between the Netherlands and Switzerland with regard to the state's autonomy and its capacity to act probably has its origin in the different approaches taken historically to the solution of the religious conflicts in the two countries. Swiss federalism and Dutch pillarization can be regarded as functionally equivalent solutions of the same problem of integrating diverse cultural minorities within the same polity—with very different implications for the institutional structure of the state. Whereas the territorial differentiation chosen by the Swiss implied a decentralization and fragmentation of the state, the social differentiation of the Dutch was compatible with a centralized and concentrated institutional structure (Kriesi 1990a).

In the parliamentary arena, in particular, the prevailing strategy has important repercussions on the politics of coalition formation. In countries with exclusive strategies, the governing coalitions tend to be ideologically rather homogeneous and the polarization between the government and the opposition tends to be rather acute. France is again the typical example. In contrast, countries with inclusive strategies have more heterogeneous coalitions, which include quite diverse ideological points of view, and the polarization between the government and the oppostion is less pronounced. Switzerland illustrates this pattern, which, of course, closely fits and further reinforces the weak and inclusive character of the Swiss political system as a whole. The Dutch and the German cases again provide intermediate examples.

Combining the distinction between strong and weak states, including an intermediate category, with the one between exclusive and integrative dominant strategies, we arrive at six distinct structural settings for political mobilization. We have situated our four cases with respect to this typology in Table 2.2. For illustrative purposes, we have also added some other Western European countries. It goes without saying that a more detailed study of these countries' political opportunity structures would be necessary in order to provide more solid ground for their categorization. The combination of a strong state with an exclusive dominant strategy we call a situation of "selective exclusion." This case is represented by France. Although challengers can be and are typically excluded from the political process in France, their exclusion is not absolute, as it would be in a nondemocratic state. Moreover, the strong French state can settle for substantive concessions if the social movements' demands happen to correspond to the political goals of the governing coalition. Under exceptional circumstances, movements may even be facilitated by governing parties in France. This is why we consider this situation as one of "selective exclusion."[8] At the opposite end, Switzerland constitutes a typical case of "integration," characterized by the combination of a weak state with an inclusive dominant strategy. Germany represents one of the two intermediate cases, the one coming close to what we shall call "formal inclusion." In the German situation, the challenger can count on some formal, but not on informal, access. Italy might provide an even closer approximation to this ideal type than Germany: its weak, "available" state has coexisted with an exclusive strategy with respect to the challengers, whether they came from the old Communist left or from the new left. The second intermediate case, the one of "informal inclusion," is represented by the Netherlands. It may apply even more specifically to the

Table 2.2. The general structural settings for political mobilization

Dominant strategy	Formal institutional structure: strength of the state		
	weak	intermediate	strong
Exclusive	*Formal inclusion* Italy	Germany	*Selective exclusion* France
Inclusive	*Integration* Switzerland	Netherlands	*Informal inclusion* Scandinavian countries, Great Britain, Austria

United Kingdom and to the Scandinavian countries. In such a general setting, challengers are faced with a state that is autonomous and has the capacity to act, but they can count on informal strategies, which make the state more accessible than one might have expected at first.

The Link between the General Structural Setting and the Mobilization of Movements: Concrete Opportunities

Like many "structural" theories of social behavior, POS theory has left unexplored the question of how structural characteristics of political systems enter the hearts and minds of movement organizers and participants. Kitschelt (1986), for instance, directly derives movement strategies from abstract categories such as "the strength of the state" or "open input structures," which obviously have little meaning for the average movement activist. Philosophers of social science have repeatedly emphasized that theories of social behavior should specify the mechanisms that translate social structures into individual and group actions (see, for instance, Harré and Secord 1972; Elster 1989). In our view, the issue is not just that POS theories that do not specify such mechanisms are not "complete," although completeness is a theoretical virtue in its own right. More important is the fact that by linking action directly to structure, current applications of POS often fail to appreciate the complex and sometimes contradictory ways in which political structures influence movement mobilization. The resulting explanations are therefore not only incomplete, but often overly simplistic, and sometimes plainly wrong.

Certainly, vague rational choice assumptions (social movements are "rational decision makers," who make "strategic choices"; Kitschelt 1986: 59–60) often figure in the background. This is, however, too little in two respects. First, stated in such general terms, rational choice theory does not constitute much of a bridge between political structures and movement action, since

it leaves us not much wiser with regard to the ways in which political opportunity structures translate into costs and benefits at the individual level.
Second, it is doubtful whether all forms of social movement action can be
adequately understood in purely instrumental terms. Adherents of the "new
social movements approach," in particular, have pointed to the expressive
nature of many forms of protest and to the importance of identity formation
in collective action. We shall treat this second problem in chapter 4. In this
chapter we shall, for the moment, make the simplifying assumption that social movements in general act instrumentally. In order to tackle the first problem, we shall ground our subsequent analysis of the relation between the
political opportunity structure and social movement action in a motivational
theory that consists of a set of derivatives of the general structural setting
that directly affect the costs and benefits of collective action.

For such an approach, we may distinguish between factors influencing the
costs and benefits of collective action itself (the "means" side), and factors
related to the goals of such action (the "ends" side). Among the factors determining "means," Tilly (1978) distinguishes between *facilitation,* standing
for any action by other groups that lowers the costs of collective action, and
repression, which includes any external action that increases such costs. With
respect to the "ends," Koopmans (1992a: 20ff.) adds *success chances,* which refer to the likelihood that collective action will contribute to the realization of
a movement's goals. However, collective action is not only affected by the answers people give to the question "What will happen if we act?" but also by
their expectations about "What will happen if we do not act?" The latter define the pair *reform/threat,* where "reform" stands for a situation in which collective benefits are expected even if no collective action is undertaken, and
"threat" refers to a situation in which collective "bads" are expected if the
movement does not act. We shall refer to these four factors as "concrete opportunities." Since they directly depend on structural characteristics of the
political context, and simultaneously have concrete meaning for movement
activists, they are well suited to serve as a bridge between the general structural setting and movement action.

Given that an instrumental actor may be expected to be very sensitive to
the costs and benefits attached to different options, each one of these factors is likely to have distinct effects on the absolute level of mobilization as
well as on the action repertoires employed. *Facilitation,* which lowers the
costs of acting, will therefore generally lead to increased levels of mobilization. It may take various forms. Among the most important of these are the
subsidization of movement organizations by the state or by other members

of the political system; the availability to social movements of direct channels of access to decision making, for instance in the form of formal or informal consultation, possibilities for juridical appeal, or direct-democratic procedures; and, finally, direct support by established actors such as political parties for movement campaigns. Since established actors and the state are its main sources, facilitation will generally be directed at relatively moderate organizations and actions, and will therefore lead to more massive, but also more moderate, forms of mobilization.

The effects of *repression* are less clear-cut, at least with regard to its impact on the level of mobilization. Although it is obvious that extremely high levels of repression will make collective action unattractive for the large majority of potential activists, it is less clear whether, at lower levels, increased repression will be able to reduce the amount of mobilization. In the literature, several examples of movements can be found that were actually stimulated by repression. A striking illustration of this point is provided by the civil rights movement, which deliberately chose a strategy of demonstrating in cities in the South of the United States, where an unmistakably repressive reaction to peaceful demonstrations could be expected (McAdam 1982: 178). The violent clashes that followed brought the movement more media attention than it would otherwise have received and conveyed the movement's message in a most powerful way, which consequently led to increased outside support. Another example concerns countercultural movements, which we shall introduce more systematically in chapter 4. Repression strengthens the collective identity that countercultural activists derive from conflictive interaction. Therefore, it stimulates rather than deters mobilization of these movements.

Although, at least in democratic regimes, repression may not reduce the level of movement mobilization, it can be expected to have a considerable effect on the action repertoire. Like facilitation, repression is typically selective. By focusing on more radical organizations and actions, it will reduce the amount of radical mobilization. Perhaps surprisingly, then, in democratic regimes the effects of facilitation and repression on the action repertoire tend to go in the same direction: high levels of each will lead to a moderation of movement strategies. As a corollary, the most radical action repertoire can be expected in those regimes that do not intervene in social movement activities at all, that is, neither in a facilitative, nor in a repressive way. However, in the special case of the countercultural movements, repression may lead to a radicalization of the action repertoire, for reasons to be explained in more detail in chapter 4. Adding this effect, it may be that high levels of repression lead to moderation and radicalization at the same time.

The net result may be a hybrid action repertoire, combining a moderate majority with a very radical, countercultural minority.

The relation between *success chances* and the level of mobilization may be expected to be curvilinear (see Eisinger 1973: 15; Kitschelt 1986: 62). If success chances are low, movement participants are likely to refrain from collective action, because the expected benefits will be too low to weigh against the costs. However, if success chances are very high, we will also generally find lower levels of mobilization, because in this case less collective effort is needed to realize a movement's goals. Rüdig (1990: 235) therefore concludes that partial success is "the condition which is crucial to a sustained development of protest groups." The effects of success chances on the action repertoire are more straightforward. If success chances are high, a movement will be able to reach a given level of goal attainment with less pressure on the authorities than is necessary in less favorable circumstances. In other words, where a petition may be sufficient, if success chances are high, disruptive strategies may be necessary in a less conducive environment. Since radical strategies are inherently more costly (even disregarding repression), social movements are likely to choose their action repertoire according to the rule "as moderate as possible, as radical as necessary."

Reform and threat, finally, will especially have an influence on the level of mobilization. Movement participants who do not value collective action as an end in itself, will only choose the relatively costly path of collective action if it is really necessary. In situations of reform, in which established political actors are already working in the direction of a movement's goals, collective action will not be necessary and it will, therefore, not be forthcoming. In situations of threat, where established actors are threatening to implement policies that considerably worsen a challenger's chances to get what he or she wants, we may expect the opposite effect. In such a case, the costs of collective action decrease relative to the now costly path of inaction. Mobilization becomes more attractive, even though it may be expected to accomplish little more than a continuation of the present situation or even a mere reduction of the expected deterioration.

The Implications of the Structural Setting for the Mobilization by Social Movements

We shall now apply these intermediate concepts and hypotheses to link the general structural settings in the four countries to the expected levels and action repertoires of mobilization in each one of them. Let us start with the role of *facilitation*. The first thing to note is that the structural openness of weak states provides a facilitative environment. This will lead to a high level of movement mobilization of a moderate type. Facilitation will also be more frequent in inclusive regimes, where social movement organizations are often co-opted in consultative bodies or are even subsidized by the state. This again implies a higher level of, generally moderate, mobilization. Facilitation is highest in Switzerland, with its generally weak and inclusive state. The elaborate system of direct democracy in particular provides a very strong institutional facilitation of movement mobilization. In the Netherlands, inclusive strategies, procedures of appeal in the implementation process, and the openness of the parliamentary arena provide a considerable amount of facilitation as well. In Germany, the federalist character of the state and the extensive opportunities for legal intervention in the process of policy implementation are particularly important with respect to facilitation. But otherwise, the German state is not very facilitative, given its exclusive informal approach, its relatively strong parties, and its strong interest groups. In France, facilitation by the state is even less likely to be forthcoming than in Germany.[9] Given these considerations on the effects of facilitation, the implication is that we may expect the highest and most moderate aggregate levels of mobilization in Switzerland and the lowest and least moderate levels in France. The Netherlands should be closer to the Swiss case, Germany closer to France.

For our present purpose, we may neglect the impact of the formal institutional structures on *repression*. The constitutions of the four countries studied here all guarantee basic human rights to every citizen, including the right to form political organizations. By contrast, the prevailing strategies may be expected to have a crucial impact on repression. Although inclusive strategies by definition imply relatively low levels of repression, it is not necessarily so that exclusiveness leads to strong repression. Precisely because of their strong position vis-à-vis challengers, political elites in strong states can normally afford to ignore protest. In weak, exclusive states, on the contrary, authorities will be tempted to resort to repression in order to counter the threat to their policies posed by social movements. This explains why the level of repression is highest in Germany, followed by Switzerland and the Netherlands (see Koopmans 1992a: 82–83). In France, the level of repression is on average rather low. But in exceptionally threatening situations, the French state may strike with full force. According to the argument made earlier about the possible contradictory effects of high levels of repression on the action repertoire of different types of movements, we may expect that the German action repertoire will display a primarily moderate tendency in combination with an extremely radical minority.

To assess the relation between state strength and *success chances,* it is important to make a distinction between two types of success. Success can either be "proactive"—implying the introduction of "new advantages," or it can be "reactive"—implying the prevention of "new disadvantages." In the first case, the challenging movement acquires policy-making power; in the second case, it is able to exert a veto. Characteristically, "reactive" success is more easily available in weak states than in strong ones (see Kitschelt 1986). "Proactive" success is quite difficult to get in any type of state. Weak states may sometimes be forced to grant proactive concessions, but are often unable to implement them because the movement's adversaries also have the possibility to exert a veto. Strong states, on the other hand, may have the capacity to act on behalf of a movement's demands, but they also have the capacity to resist any temptation to do so. Nevertheless, if a government is in power that is sympathetic toward a movement's goals, proactive demands may sometimes be realized in strong states. However, whether this happens depends more on the government's own priorities than on the pressure exerted by the movement. Therefore, such success is better viewed as a case of reform from above, which may lead to demobilization rather than to an intensification of protest. Taken together, these considerations imply that social movements are generally able to obtain a greater amount of success in weak states. Since, in the absence of much proactive gain, such success will be partial, we may expect higher aggregate levels of mobilization in weak states. Moreover, we may expect this mobilization to be more moderate than in strong states, where the pressure exerted by mobilization in the streets is virtually the only means by which opponents of government policies can make themselves heard.

With respect to the prevailing strategies, we may note that inclusiveness increases the chances of success of challengers, which implies higher levels of mobilization, of a more moderate kind, in inclusive systems. These considerations lead us again to expect the highest levels of mobilization with the most moderate action repertoires for the case of Switzerland. On the other hand, on the basis of success chances, France should again have the lowest level of mobilization and the most radical repertoire. Once again, the Netherlands should be closer to Switzerland, and Germany closer to France. In the Netherlands, the combination of a relatively strong state with an integrative strategy probably allows for more proactive success than in the other three countries.

This brings us to the final element of concrete opportunity: *reform and threat*. Because strong states have a greater capacity to implement policies either contrary to or in accordance with a movement's goals, situations of reform and threat will occur with greater intensity in such states. These situations will present themselves especially in relation with changes in government and will, therefore, be treated in more detail in chapter 3. Let us only note here that, whereas the effects of a change of government in weak states will be substantially moderated by institutional constraints and countervailing sources of political power, in strong states little stands in the way of drastic policy changes. This implies that we may expect greater fluctuations in the level of mobilization in strong states, with strong upsurges in times of threat and pronounced decreases in periods of reform. In weak states, on the contrary, the opportunities, and concomitantly the mobilization of social movements, will tend to be more stable. Finally, situations of reform and threat, and related fluctuations in the level of social movement activity, will be more pronounced in exclusive regimes, where governing elites are more likely to act on their interests without much regard for the concerns of societal forces outside their own constituencies.

On the basis of our expectations about the effects of these settings on the concrete opportunities available to social movements, we can summarize our hypotheses with regard to levels and forms of mobilization in each of the four countries (table 2.3). The French situation of exclusion clearly constitutes the most unfavorable setting for social movements. Lack of facilitation and success chances will lead to a relatively low aggregate level of mobilization. Formal social movement organizations will be particularly affected by this, and will have few opportunities to institutionalize, which renders them unattractive to prospective members. The Swiss situation of integration leads us to expect the exact opposite. Relatively high success chances and strong facilitation, particularly in the form of the system of direct democracy, will result in high aggregate levels of mobilization and a very moderate action repertoire. Social movement organizations will find plenty of opportunity to institutionalize, and may therefore attract a large following. Moreover, the social movement sector may be expected to be relatively stable, due to the relative constancy of formal and informal opportunities. The Netherlands and Germany represent two intermediate cases. In both countries, levels of mobilization are expected to lie between those in France and Switzerland, but the distribution over different strategies may differ somewhat. The strategies of subsidization and co-optation in the Netherlands are likely to strengthen the position of conventional mobilization by formal

**Table 2.3. The implications of concrete opportunities for the level of
mobilization and action repertoire of social movements**

Country	Facilitation	Repression	Success chances	Reform/ threat	Overall
Level of mobilization					
Switzerland	high	–	high	stable	high
Netherlands	high	–	intermediate	intermediate	intermediate-high
Germany	intermediate	–	intermediate	intermediate	intermediate
France	low	–	low	unstable	low
Action repertoire					
Switzerland	moderate	moderate	moderate	stably moderate	moderate
Netherlands	moderate	moderate	intermediate	intermediate	intermediate-moderate
Germany	intermediate	radical minority	intermediate	intermediate	intermediate-radical
France	radical	moderate	radical	radicalization/ moderation	radical

SMOs. In contrast, the high level of repression in Germany will provoke
strong countercultural identities among some activists, who may turn to radical forms of mobilization.

Levels and Forms of Mobilization

So far, we have used the term "level of mobilization" as if its meaning were
unambiguous. The term is, however, a quite tricky one. Depending on how
one delimits the action repertoire of mobilization, one may arrive at very divergent evaluations of the strength of social movement sectors in different
countries. In chapter 1 (table 1.5) we saw that with regard to unconventional
mobilization, France emerges as the country with the highest level of mobilization, a fact that runs counter to the hypotheses we have developed in
this chapter. However, the figures of the preceding chapter did not take into
account a number of other, more conventional, ways in which people may
become involved in social movements. The most important of these are
membership in SMOs, and participation in moderate forms of mass mobilization such as political festivals, petitions, and direct-democratic mobilization. Because such forms of mobilization often involve large numbers of people, their inclusion may significantly alter our evaluation of the aggregate level
of mobilization.

Table 2.4, which presents total levels of mobilization for different forms
of mobilization, measured in comparable terms (in 1,000s per million inhab-

Table 2.4. Levels of mobilization, in 1,000s per million inhabitants

Forms	Switzerland (includes official figures)	Switzerland (only newspaper data)	Netherlands	Germany	France
New social movements					
1. SMO membership	83	83	88	49	19
2. Direct democracy	534	67	–	4	–
3. Petitions	144	144	270	114	3
4. Festivals	9	9	2	13	33
5. Unconventional	102	102	144	171	41
Total	872	405	504	351	96
N = (2–5)	(763)	(765)	(863)	(1,770)	(737)
% Unconventional	12	25	29	49	43
Labor movement					
1. SMO membership	135	135	109	153	55
2. Direct democracy	262	1	–	0	–
3. Petitions	3	3	0	21	0
4. Festivals	1	1	0	0	0
5. Unconventional	15	15	19	19	33
5a. Strikes	2	2	23	37	225
Total	418	157	151	230	313
N = (2–5)	(57)	(47)	(121)	(101)	(216)
% Unconventional (including strikes)	4	11	28	25	82
Other movements					
2. Direct democracy	831	127	–	0	–
3. Petitions	56	56	21	1	19
4. Festivals	74	74	0	4	2
5. Unconventional	39	39	35	21	104
Total	1,000	296	56	26	125
N = (2–5)	(479)	(502)	(335)	(473)	(1,179)
% Unconventional	4	13	63	81	83
All movements					
1. Membership (NSM/ Labor)	218	218	197	202	74
2. Direct democracy	1,627	195	–	4	–
3. Petitions	203	203	291	136	22
4. Festivals	83	83	3	18	36
5. Unconventional	156	156	198	211	178
5a. Strikes	2	2	23	37	225
Total	2,289	857	712	608	535
N = (2–5)	(1,299)	(1,314)	(1,319)	(2,343)	(2,132)
% Unconventional (including strikes)	7	18	31	41	75

itants), demonstrates this point. The figures presented give the cumulative levels of participation over the fifteen-year period of our study. We propose to look first at the most global figures given at the bottom of the table, which include mobilization in all the different forms of all the social movements of each country. Since they are not affected by the different cleavage structures of the four countries (and the concomitant weights of "old" and "new" mobilization), these figures most clearly display the trends with regard to levels of mobilization and action repertoires. For Switzerland, two sets of figures are provided, which differ from each other only with respect to direct democracy. For technical reasons, our newspaper data tend to systematically underestimate the number of participants in direct-democratic mobilization processes. The first set of figures takes into account the much more complete official figures for the number of people who signed federal initiatives and referenda in the period covered by our research, whereas the second set is based exclusively on our newspaper data.[10] If the official figures are complete for the federal level, they do not take into account cantonal and local levels. It is, therefore, difficult to assess whether or not they over- or underestimate the Swiss level of mobilization in a comparative perspective.

The trends presented in table 2.4 confirm our expectation that the aggregate level of mobilization increases with the weakness of the state and the inclusiveness of elite strategies, and will be highest where both combine. The Swiss level of mobilization is the highest, with 857,000 persons mobilized per one million inhabitants, even if we limit ourselves to the newspaper data. The French level is the lowest, with 535,000 persons mobilized. The Netherlands and Germany take intermediate positions, with the Netherlands closer to Switzerland and Germany closer to France. If we also take into account the official figures for mobilization by direct-democratic procedures, we arrive at a total level of mobilization in Switzerland of as much as 2,289,000 per one million inhabitants. The differences between France, on the one hand, and Germany and the Netherlands, on the other, are not as large as one might have expected. As we shall see in the following chapter, established political actors are more frequently engaged in movement politics in France than in the other countries, which compensates in part for the rather unconducive institutional structures and prevailing strategies of the French political system.

Moreover, our hypothesis that radical action repertoires will be associated with precisely the opposite configuration of political opportunities is also corroborated. The bottom line gives the percentage of events that are unconventional (including strikes): this percentage is lowest in Switzerland (18 percent or even only 7 percent unconventional) and highest in France (75 percent), with the Netherlands and Germany again in intermediate positions (31 percent and 41 percent, respectively). It is worth noting that we would not have been able to draw this conclusion, had we focused exclusively on unconventional events. We would then have concluded that mobilization levels are highest in France, and that, apparently, strong, exclusive states are the most favorable setting for social movements. We now know that this only holds when one identifies social movements with unconventional mobilization, a view that ignores the fact that most SMOs and movement sympathizers will prefer other, less costly, action forms if the opportunities associated with these forms are favorable enough.

If we consider the different elements of the overall action repertoire in more detail, we first note the great importance of *direct democracy* in Switzerland, which distinguishes this country most from the other three. Direct-democratic forms are only available in Switzerland (except for four events in Germany), where they make a formidable contribution to the level of mobilization of all types of movements.[11] Of course, the involvement required for this form is quite low. As with petitions, the majority of participants provide no more than their signature. Moreover, direct democracy in Switzerland is a fully institutionalized form of political action and constitutes an important part of the action repertoire of political parties and institutional pressure groups. Nevertheless, to dismiss this form of mobilization as not radical enough to be considered as part of the social movements' action repertoire would not be wise. The peculiarity of the Swiss political opportunity structure lies precisely in its extreme formal openness. One may maintain that, as a result of this openness, Swiss social movements are less "movementlike" than their counterparts in other countries. But our point is that we are only able to note this particular aspect of Swiss movements if we do not focus exclusively on unconventional mobilization. Direct-democratic instruments are used massively—according to the official figures—by all types of movements.

Next, we see that *membership* in movement organizations—SMOs of new social movements, on the one hand, and unions, on the other—is much less widespread in France than in the other three countries. France not only has particularly weak unions (Visser 1987), but also particularly weak SMOs (Kriesi 1995). With respect to the other three, Germany has more union members, while the two inclusive states, Switzerland and the Netherlands, attract the largest number of members of SMOs of new social movements. Because of the strategies of informal co-optation in these countries, SMOs can more easily find access to decision makers, and are often directly facilitated by way of subsidization and incorporation into advisory bodies. The differences in SMO membership among the four countries can also be shown when we consider only the national branches of international movement organizations. For instance, the national chapters of Amnesty International and the World Wildlife Fund have, in absolute terms, a larger membership in the Netherlands and in Switzerland than in Germany and France, although the number of inhabitants of the latter two countries is much higher. The greater strength of the German union system (chapter 1) explains its greater number of members.

Petitions are more popular in the two inclusive countries, which also reflects the availability of informal opportunities. As the table shows in more detail, it is above all the new social movements, and, to some extent also the "other" movements, that make use of this form of action. Petitions are a very moderate action form, and are only worthwhile if the authorities can be expected to take such a polite appeal seriously. It is, therefore, not surprising that French new social movement activists in particular hardly take this strategy into consideration. *Festivals,* finally, are not indicative of any general trend, but can be found in specific movements only, such as the regionalist movements in Switzerland, and in the new social movements in France.

The figures for *strikes* in particular provide additional evidence for the general trends. Switzerland and France are again the two extreme cases. In Switzerland, we find a strike level that is very low. Together with the more general openness of the Swiss system, the availability of direct democratic access may explain why the strike level is exceptionally low in this country. It is illustrative of the nature of Switzerland's political system that many issues (social security, vacations, working hours, etc.) that elsewhere have been the object of labor disputes are contested by referenda and initiatives. In France, in contrast, the strike level is much higher than in the other three countries, despite the fact that union membership is very low. The Netherlands and Germany are again intermediate cases, but, with respect to the strike activity, both are rather close to the Swiss extreme. As a result of the pacification of the class conflict, labor relations are quite cooperative in Germany as well. This differs substantially from the more confrontational relations between the new social movements and the authorities, which are more in line with the expectations we have formulated in the theoretical sections. The pacification of the class conflict is, in fact, quite unexpected, given the exclusive heritage of the German dominant strategy. In our view, it can only be explained by the exogenous factor of the intervention of the Allies after World War II, who imposed a new union system and completely reconstructed the relationship between the "social partners."

For the assessment of national action repertoires, table 2.4 is still a bit crude. Particularly the category of unconventional mobilization is very broad, and includes anything from peaceful demonstrations to heavy violence. Table 2.5, which presents the distribution of protest events over different action forms, allows us to sharpen our view. Again, France and Switzerland emerge as the two most divergent cases. In Switzerland, we once more find a heavy reliance on moderate forms of action. Direct democracy is less important with regard to the number of events than with regard to the level of participation, but it still accounts for a sizable portion of events, although less for the new social movements (4.3 percent) than for the other movements (13.5 percent).[12] Switzerland is also distinguished by the relative popularity of another moderate form, the petition, which accounts for 8.1 percent of all events, three to six times more than in the other countries. On the contrary, confrontational forms, such as blockades and occupations, are used much less frequently in Switzerland (13.4 percent), and the same is true for heavy forms of violence such as bomb attacks and arson (4.7 percent). The only exception to this pattern of general moderation is the relatively frequent use of light forms of violence, mainly violent demonstrations, by the Swiss new social movements (10.8 percent). A closer look at these events reveals that the large majority of them were produced by the Zurich movement for autonomous youth centers at the beginning of the 1980s. This result is unlikely to be an artifact of our choice of a Zurich newspaper. Rather, it reflects a particularity of the local political opportunity structure in the largest Swiss city. Given the federal character of the country, the political context may vary a great deal from one region to another. The autonomous movement in Zurich has been one of unusual violence for Switzerland, for reasons that have to do with the specific interaction context of the development of this movement (Wisler 1993).

The French data confirm the radical tendency already apparent in the participation figures presented earlier. As a result of the general closure of the strong and exclusive French state, very moderate forms like petitions are not likely to bring any results, and are, therefore, rarely used (barely 1 percent). Conversely, heavy forms of violence are much more frequent in France than in the other countries. Among the new social movements, heavy violence accounts for nearly 18 percent of the events, and among the other

Table 2.5. Action repertoire of social movements per country
(percentages of the total number of protest events)

	Switzerland	Netherlands	Germany	France
New social movements				
Direct democracy	4.3	–	0.1	–
Petitions	8.7	2.7	2.7	2.0
Festivals	1.6	2.0	2.1	3.4
Demonstrative	58.3	52.1	61.8	55.1
Confrontational	12.6	30.9	19.1	17.0
Light violence	10.8	6.6	7.3	4.9
Heavy violence	3.9	5.7	7.0	17.6
N	(735)	(863)	(1,770)	(737)
Other movements				
Direct democracy	13.5	–	0.0	–
Petitions	7.3	3.1	2.8	0.8
Festivals	11.1	0.2	2.4	0.4
Demonstrative	44.4	45.4	57.1	34.6
Confrontational	14.5	42.5	19.9	28.5
Light violence	3.5	2.2	2.8	6.3
Heavy violence	5.8	6.6	15.0	29.5
N	(519)	(456)	(574)	(1,395)
All movements				
Direct democracy	8.1	–	–	–
Petitions	8.1	2.8	2.7	1.2
Festivals	5.5	1.4	2.2	1.4
Demonstrative	52.5	49.7	60.6	41.7
Confrontational	13.4	35.0	19.3	24.5
Light violence	7.7	5.1	6.2	5.8
Heavy violence	4.7	6.0	9.0	25.4
N	(1,322)	(1,319)	(2,343)	(2,132)

movements this proportion rises to nearly 30 percent, mainly due to the mobilization of the French regionalist movements, particularly those in Corsica and the Basque country. Apparently, many French activists feel that, given the general lack of opportunities, such radical means are necessary to attract attention and to publicize grievances. Moreover, the fact that the exclusiveness of the French state is not accompanied by particularly high levels of repression may make violence also a viable option for instrumental movements.

In line with our previous results, the Dutch and German action repertoires are neither particularly moderate nor very radical. There are some interesting differences of emphasis, however. The Netherlands is distinguished by a very high proportion of confrontational events that even surpasses that of France. Germany, on the contrary, is closer to Switzerland with regard to these forms of mobilization. But the level of heavy violence is quite high in Germany, especially among the other movements (15 percent, versus 7 percent for the new social movements). Moreover, a closer look at these events shows that they tend to have a very high intensity in Germany, virtually as high as in France; Germany has almost as many deaths by political violence—by both the left and the right—as does France. Although very few people died as a result of political violence in Switzerland and the Netherlands, in the period 1975–89, in Germany the number of deaths in the events included in our sample was 59, only slightly short of the number of deaths in France (74). In Germany, most of these deaths were a result of actions by terrorist groups related to the new social movements, such as the Rote Armee Fraktion (32), whose victims included a number of high-placed politicians, judges, prosecutors, and leading businessmen. In addition, actions by the extreme right also claimed a sizable number of deaths (24). In France, only a small proportion of the victims (seven persons) died in violent events related to the mobilization of new social movements.

The divergent patterns for Germany and the Netherlands can be related to the different opportunity structures of the two countries. Whereas the formal closure of the Dutch administrative arena does stimulate a certain degree of radicalism, the inclusiveness of dominant strategies to deal with challengers and the concomitantly low level of repression prevent the development of strong countercultural tendencies and an all-out escalation of political conflicts. The exclusiveness and repressive strategies of the German authorities, on the other hand, may succeed in pushing a majority of activists to more moderate strategies. However, repression will also strengthen countercultural tendencies and provoke a violent confrontation between the authorities and a minority of activists. In other words, whereas the Dutch opportunity structure allows social movements to choose a middle-of-the-road strategy between moderate, legal forms of mass mobilization and violence, the German movements face a configuration of opportunities that forces them to choose between one or the other of the extremes.

Conclusion

We may conclude, then, that our data generally confirm the expectations we had formulated on the basis of the four countries' general structural settings. The weak, inclusive Swiss state has given rise to a social movement sector characterized by a very high aggregate level of mobilization and a very moderate action repertoire. Formal SMOs tend to be strongly developed, as are moderate forms of mobilization such as direct-democratic campaigns, petitioning, and to some extent moderate unconventional forms like demonstrations. The strong, exclusive French state is associated with protest characteristics diametrically opposed to those of the Swiss movements. The overall level of mobilization is lower than in the other countries, but participation is heavily concentrated in unconventional forms. Within that category, moreover, violence occurs relatively often. On the other hand, formal organizations, and very moderate forms of mobilization such as petitions, are very weak in France. The moderately strong, highly inclusive Dutch state comes closest to the Swiss case. As a result, we also find strong SMOs and a relatively strong reliance on conventional forms of mobilization. However, due to the limited availability of formal access, unconventional forms play a more important role than in Switzerland, and the Dutch action repertoire does contain a substantial amount of more radical forms of (peaceful) civil disobedience. The comparatively weak, exclusive German state, finally, also occupies an intermediate position, but one a bit closer to France. Except for the strongly institutionalized labor movement, formal organizations, which lack informal access, tend to be weaker than in Switzerland and the Netherlands, but unconventional mobilization is more developed than in these countries. Although the radicalness of unconventional mobilization is, on average, more or less the same in the Netherlands and in Germany, the German repertoire turned out to be much more ambiguous. Because of the relatively high level of repression associated with the combination of a weak state and exclusive dominant strategies, unconventional mobilization in Germany tends to be either quite moderate or extremely violent.

Chapter 3

Alliance Structures

In this chapter, we shall turn to the less stable elements of the political opportunity structure—certain aspects of the configuration of power of a political system. These are the elements underscored by the conceptualization of the POS by Sidney Tarrow (1989a, 1989b, 1994, 1995). He insists on the importance of the political conditions of the moment, on short-term changes in political opportunities that may unleash political protest and may contribute to its decline. The elements of the political context that may change in the short run include the opening up of access to participation, shifts in ruling alignments, the availability of influential allies, and cleavages within and among elites. We shall concentrate here on two aspects of the changing political context of the mobilization by new social movements—the configuration of power on the left and the presence or absence of the left in government. At several occasions, we have already pointed out that the constituencies of the new social movements are closely related to those of the left. The implications of such a close relationship are quite ambivalent, as we already had occasion to note in chapter 1. Whereas we showed the restrictive implications of this proximity for the mobilization of new social movements in that chapter, in this one we shall put the accent on the other side of the coin: Given that the concerns of the left and those of the new social movements are closely related, we expect the mobilization capacity of the new social movements as well as their political success to depend closely on the support they receive from the organizations of the left.

The Old and the New Left

For the analysis of the relationship between the left and the new social movements, we shall distinguish between the old and the new left. The relative importance, the organizational and ideological makeup, as well as the strategies of these two parts of the left depend to a large extent on the institutional structures and prevailing strategies we dealt with in chapter 2. Thus, as we have already pointed out, the heritage of the prevailing strategies to deal with challengers has had a lasting impact on the strategies and the structuration of the *old left*. The heritage of exclusive strategies has contributed to its radicalization and to a split between the Communist and the Social Democratic/ Socialist currents. This split between Social Democrats and Communists has further radicalized the labor movement, which in turn has reinforced the dominant exclusive strategy of the authorities. In other words, the labor movement in exclusive states has a more militant tradition, and has had to rely more strongly on extraparliamentary mobilization to articulate its demands. This tradition of extraparliamentary action is likely to continue to affect the labor movement's strategies with regard to new social movements, in much the same way as the elites' strategies chosen to resolve earlier conflicts still affect the ways in which elites have dealt with more recent challenges. For this reason, we expect the parties of the old left and the labor unions to be more likely to support the actions of new social movements in exclusive regimes such as Germany and France than in inclusive ones such as the Netherlands and Switzerland.[1] This tendency will be reinforced by the fact that exclusive strategies affect not only the relations between new social movements and polity members but also those among polity members themselves. The latter, too, are more polarized in exclusive regimes, and, therefore, they are also more likely to confront each other by way of extraparliamentary mobilization. In political systems where exclusive strategies combine with a strong state, as in France, this tendency may be even stronger, because, apart from massive extraparliamentary mobilization, oppositional polity members have few other possibilities to press their demands (Duyvendak 1992). On the other hand, in inclusive regimes, where the relations between polity members are characterized by compromise, negotiation, and interdependence, such a confrontational course may actually weaken a polity member's strategic position, and is often considered as a serious breach of the "rules of the game."

If a militant old left in an exclusive regime is quite ready to support social movements that appeal to the concerns of a constituency closely related to its own, we should not forget that (*a*) the very presence of a nonpacified old left limits the action space of new social movements, and (*b*) a militant old left will only be ready to support new social movements on its own terms. As far as the old left is concerned, we are dealing with a typical case of an "inclusively mobilized potential" (see chapter 1). In the situation of a split old left,

the Social Democratic Party has traditionally been relatively weak in electoral terms, and it has been engaged in a contest with the Communist Party
for the hegemony on the left. This contest has above all been a contest for
the working-class vote, which means that the traditional class conflict between labor and capital and the concomitant Marxist ideology have always
played an important role in the strategy not only of the Communist Party but
also of the Social Democrats. In a context with a dominant Communist Party,
the discourse of all the actors on the left is shaped by the ideology of the Communists. Moreover, in the context of a split left, the union system is also split
along party lines with the Communist current typically taking the dominant
position. In such a context, the fundamental dilemma of Social Democratic
parties put forward by Przeworski and Sprague (1986) becomes particularly
acute. According to the reasoning of Przeworski and Sprague, the Social Democrats generally have to appeal to citizens other than workers in order to get
a majority at the polls, since workers do not constitute (and never have constituted) a numerical majority in their societies. An effective appeal to a middle-
class electorate, however, is likely to limit the Social Democrats' capacity to
get the workers' vote. In a situation where the left is divided into a Social
Democratic tendency and an equally or even more important Communist one,
the risk of losing the workers' vote to the Communists is obviously very serious. In such a context, one can expect the Social Democrats to subordinate
their support of new social movements, which characteristically have a new
middle-class core, to their struggle for hegemony on the left.

   In other words, in a country like France, where the left was dominated by
the Communist Party up to the late 1970s,[2] the Socialists could not become
unconditional allies of the new social movements. However, if the French
Socialists needed to appeal to the working class in traditional class terms to
ward off Communist competition, they also had to appeal to parts of the new
middle class in order to obtain the electoral majority required by the French
electoral system to defeat the parties of the right. For the French Socialists,
an alliance with the new social movements was, therefore, quite promising
for electoral reasons, as long as the concerns of these movements could be
reformulated in terms of the classic struggle of the labor movement. Moreover, as is pointed out by Duyvendak (1992: 105ff.), several factors facilitated
the alliance between new social movements and the left in France, as long as
the left remained in the opposition: on the one hand, the militant syndicalist
tradition of the old left as well as the Eurocommunist phase of the Communist Party during the period of the "common program" in the 1970s brought
the old left closer to the concerns of the new social movements. On the other

hand, dependent as they were on the old left, the French new social movements were forced to position themselves with respect to the PCF, and this in itself reinforced the influence of the old concerns in their orientation.

The German left was unified and pacified after World War II, in spite of the exclusive heritage of German politics. The destruction of the organized revolutionary working class during the Nazi period, the fact that many of the revolutionaries in exile returned to the "farmers' and workers' state" east of the Iron Curtain, the *Wirtschaftswunder*—the economic miracle—of the fifties and early sixties, and, above all, the new rules of the game imposed by the Allies contributed to a pacification of class conflict (Koopmans 1992a: 51f.). The Communist Party, which was one of the strongest in Europe before the Nazi takeover, disappeared as a relevant actor from the political scene even before it was declared unconstitutional in the fifties. The pervasive anticommunism and the idea of the militant democracy, which accompanied the Federal Republic from its very beginning, forced the SPD in turn "to demonstrate a gulf separating it from any movement further to the left. The demarcation had to be kept visible and complete" (Smith 1986: 231) until late in the seventies. The union system, which had been highly fragmented before the war, was entirely restructured as a result of Allied intervention, too. As we mentioned in chapter 2, the rebuilt union system was highly encompassing, organized according to the principle of industry-wide unionization. The unions were integrated into policy networks, and were able to enforce discipline on groups of workers that may have been tempted to pursue particularistic interests. They no longer relied heavily on mobilizing for radical strike action. Moreover, the unions tended to exert pressure on the Social Democrats to give priority to traditional labor class concerns, which means that the latter were less able to make concessions to, or to facilitate the mobilization of, new social movements than they might otherwise have been.

In other words, the German left is at first sight an unlikely candidate for support of the new social movements. However, a pacified old left such as the German one may become an ally of new social movements if it comes under competition of a new left or if it is captured by the new left. If confronted with a new left party, the fundamental dilemma of the Social Democrats presents itself in a rather different light. Since new left parties typically appeal to the new middle class, they do not pose a serious threat to mobilizing the working-class vote. They may, however, drain away some middle-class support from the Social Democrats. Challenged by a new-left competitor, the Social Democrats will, therefore, be likely to take some facilitative steps in the direction of new social movements. We may formulate the general hypothesis that the facilitation of the mobilization of new social movements by a pacified old left depends on the degree of competition the latter has to face from the new left, and on the extent to which the new left succeeds in gaining influence over the organizations of the old left. In opposition to a militant, split old left such as the French one, which tends to absorb the new left on its own terms, a pacified old left is more likely to be transformed under the impact of the mobilization of the new left.

The *new left* has generally been composed of two waves. The first wave concerns the political currents that emerged during the sixties. Whether these currents have crystallized into independent new parties and the extent to which these parties have become a relevant political force has mainly been determined by the degree of openness of the existing parties on the left with respect to these forces, and by the electoral system. The openness of the existing parties is itself likely to have been a function of the electoral system and of the inclusiveness of the strategy prevailing in the system with respect to challengers, as well as of the extent to which the new forces themselves have chosen to work through the old parties. New-left parties have generally remained rather small in electoral terms and they have — with few exceptions — not participated in governments. In spite of their limited scope, their presence may be expected to have played an important facilitating role for the action campaigns of new social movements. These parties appeal to the same constituency as the new social movements, and to a large extent they pursue the same goals as these movements. Moreover, they generally have a close affinity to the forms of political action preferred by the new social movements. Their militants may even be considered to constitute the "avant-garde" of the new social movements (Kriesi 1993a).

The second wave of the new left concerns the *Green parties,* which have emerged since the late seventies. While the first wave of the new left constitutes a precursor of the new social movements, the emergence of Green parties can be viewed as one of their structural impacts. The timing of the emergence of Green parties and the weight they have been able to acquire have again been a function of the openness of the existing parties on the left, including the parties of the first wave of the new left. It is obvious that the Greens play a facilitative role with regard to the mobilization of new social movements. Moreover, their presence is also likely to have an indirect impact on the major parties of the left, which is analogous to that of the new-left parties of the first wave. As a consequence of the increasing competition for the new middle-class vote, the Social Democratic Party is again pressed to take a more favorable stance with regard to the mobilization of new social movements.

A similar reasoning also applies to the two countries with an inclusive heritage, where the left was never seriously divided and where the class conflict had been pacified by the time of the emergence of the new social movements, just as it had been in Germany. In both of these countries, the Social Democrats have traditionally been the major party on the left. Moreover, both countries have fragmented and rather weak union systems that are split along religious lines. In spite of their fragmentation, these union systems have been pacified and integrated into policy networks. In both countries, the pacified old left has faced competition from a vigorous new left. Given the inclusive heritage of both countries, however, this competition has developed less fierce proportions than in the case of Germany.

Finally, we should add that, independent of the country-specific political context, the relationship between the left and the new social movements may vary from one movement to another. Two movements have traditionally been particularly close to the left in all the countries, and have therefore profited to a considerable extent from its support: the *peace movement* and the *solidarity movement*. Pacifism and international solidarity are two basic themes of the old left (Wijmans 1992). Both themes have been privileged rallying grounds for the Communists' internationalism. Moreover, all over Europe the new left has originally been mobilized with regard to international issues—aid to developing countries, the war in Vietnam, the Cultural Revolution in China, support of specific regimes in the Third World such as those of Chile, Nicaragua, or Cuba, and the struggle against repressive regimes such as apartheid in South Africa, fascism in Franco Spain, or the dictatorship of the Greek colonels. The new left has also long been critical of NATO. In opposition to the goals of other new social movements—the ecology movement, for example—the concerns of the peace and the solidarity movements were not incompatible with the economic and social policy objectives pursued by the labor movement. In supporting these movements, the left could hope to make inroads into the new middle-class electorate of the conservative parties. Therefore, the party-political polarization of these movements can be expected everywhere to be considerably greater than that of the ecology movement. In fact, Eurobarometer data of the mid-eighties confirm that, with the exception of France, the peace movement has been much more polarizing between socialist and conservative parties in European countries than the ecology movement (Watts 1987; Kriesi 1993a: 224ff.). The French exception is explained by the fact that the peace movement had hardly any mobilizing effect at all in France, which is again explained by the specificities of the French political context.

Government and Opposition

The support that the left may lend to new social movements also depends on whether it participates in government or not, and if it does so, on its position in government. If the Social Democrats in particular are in the opposition, they profit from the challenges new social movements direct at the government. This is especially true of moderate challenges that are considered legitimate by a large part of the electorate. Such challenges weaken their major opponents in the next elections. Moreover, since the supporters of new social movements also form a constituency of the left, the Social Democrats will appeal to them in the framework of a general strategy designed to build as broad an electoral coalition as possible. Being in the opposition, they will therefore tend to facilitate the mobilization of new social movements. However, being in the opposition, they have, of course, no possibility of making any material concessions to them.

If in government, the Social Democrats not only face electoral constraints but also operate under constraints of established policies and of pressures from dominant societal forces (industry, finance, technocracy). Given these constraints, they will have to make compromises with regard to their electoral promises. To maximize their chances for reelection, they will have to place a heavy emphasis on the economic concerns of their core electorate — that is, the working class. They will, however, also try to make secondary concessions to more peripheral groups of their electorate, among them the supporters of new social movements, or at least promise reforms taking into account the new social movements' point of view. A Social Democratic government may profit from a cooperative new social movement that articulates limited demands in a generally acceptable way. Such a moderate movement can serve as a driving force for Social Democratic reform politics. In a generally integrative setting, it is possible that a Social Democratic government will support the organizational infrastructure of such a movement, and will try to integrate it into established political channels. But even in this case, overt facilitation of action campaigns of new social movements by a Social Democratic government is unlikely, because of the risk that such campaigns might get out of hand (Kriesi 1993b).

These considerations imply decisive changes in the POS of new social movements, both when the left becomes part of the government and when it resigns from government. When the left takes power, the need for mobilization decreases for new social movements, because of anticipated chances of reform in their favor. At the same time, their mobilization is no longer facilitated by their most powerful ally. The net result predicted is a clear-cut decrease in the mobilization of new social movements, but not necessarily for other movements that are not dependent on the support of the left or that are not addressing demands directly to the government. Conversely, when the left resigns from government, the need for mobilization increases for new social movements, because the chances of reform in their favor become much more limited, while the threat that the government will implement policies that run counter to the concerns of new social movements assumes much more important proportions. Moreover, their mobilization is now likely to be facilitated by their most powerful ally. The net result to be expected in this case is a clear-cut increase in the mobilization of new social movements, but not necessarily of other movements that are not dependent on the support of the left or that are not addressing demands directly to the government. Let us add that the impact of the left's taking or losing power is particularly difficult to predict for the labor movement. While being dependent on the support of the left, it is often addressing demands directly to its adversary in industrial relations — the employers. Strikes in particular are typically used in the framework of industrial relations. The left's coming to power may reassure the unions and bring them to the bargaining table, as has been argued for the Scandinavian case in the 1930s (Castles 1978: 123f.). In a more polarized context, however, it may also stimulate their mobilization in industrial relations through an unwillingness to support the suppression of labor militancy, as has been argued by Tarrow (1994, chapter 5) for the French and the U.S. cases in the 1930s.

The impact of these changes in the political opportunity structure of new social movements may not exactly coincide with the change in government. We have to allow for some measure of anticipation or delay. For example, the deterioration of a government coalition in which the left participates may already improve the political opportunities of new social movements before the coalition's collapse. Similarly, prolonged coalition formation and unstable prospects of a newly formed right-wing coalition may delay the mobilization of the left against the new government. Moreover, the degree to which changes in the composition of government will affect the opportunities of new social movements will vary according to the strength of the state, the exclusiveness of elite strategies, and the details of the composition of the government.[3] Generally, the demobilizing impact of Social Democrats in power may be expected to be most pronounced in strong, exclusive states, especially when the Social Democrats govern alone. By contrast, in weak, inclusive states, where the Socialists participate in centrist, multiparty coalitions, the demobilizing effect may be very limited or may not exist at all. If the Social Democrats govern alone, they will be more able to make concessions than if they depend on a coalition partner. If they are only a minority partner in a coalition government, they may not be able to make any concessions at all. A Social Democratic party in a minority position in the governing coalition may, on the other hand, feel less constrained to support the mobilization of new social movements.

The Strategy of the Social Democrats in the Four Countries

We would now like to discuss briefly the strategies chosen by the Social Democrats in the four selected countries in the light of these theoretical expectations. Table 3.1 indicates the situation of the Social Democrats in the four countries over the course of the seventies and eighties. Let us first look at the French Social Democrats. In the early seventies, the Communists still were the dominant force on the left in France. It was at that time that President Pompidou predicted that, as a result of the bipolar dynamics of the presidential system, only two political forces would survive in French politics — the Gaullists and the Communists. He was, of course, wrong. By the early eighties, the Socialist Party (PS) had become the dominant force on the left. On the right, the Gaullists soon had to contend with a second major conservative force (French Democratic Union [UDF]), not to mention the rise of the Front National. To gain predominance on the left, the PS began in the early seventies to open up to various leftist militants. It attracted important groups of the new left — militants from the CFDT, the PSU — left-wing Catholics, and the new social movements. The PS gave itself an internal structure that permitted diverse tendencies to coexist — that is, it attempted to create a broad coalition movement. Simultaneously, it concluded an alliance with the Communists (common program), which strengthened the position of traditional tendencies within the party. Within the PS, the new left remained in a minority position. However, in spite of the contradictions inherent in the Socialists' strategy, the PS at that time appeared to be the best available alternative

Table 3.1. The situation of the Social Democratic parties in the countries under study

	Left pacified	Left not pacified
Left in government	Germany (seventies) Netherlands (until 1977, 1981–82) Switzerland	France (eighties)
Left in opposition	Germany (eighties) Netherlands (eighties)	France (seventies, 1986–88 "cohabitation")

for new social movement supporters and activists (Ladrech 1989). According to Duyvendak (1992: 108), it even constituted the only option the new social movements had in a polity polarized along the lines of the old class conflict.

The competition with the Communists never stopped. In late 1977, the common program was called off, and in 1978 the alliance was reduced to a simple electoral one. To prevent the Communists from exploiting possible internal divisions, the PS felt compelled to close ranks. Party decision making was recentralized, and the party became primarily oriented toward attaining an electoral majority. Given intense Communist competition, the PS had to stick to a position close to the common program, with only limited openings for the concerns of the new social movements. Finally, the centralization of power within the PS was enhanced by the general centralization of the French political system, and by the two-ballot system in particular. The party's strategy in the course of the seventies became less facilitative, although it remained generally favorable to the new social movements.

Not long after the PS came to power in 1981, its strategy has changed again, in line with what we would have expected. The party softened its support for new social movements in general and abandoned some of them completely. Thus, it gave up its — admittedly always quite limited — antinuclear position (von Oppeln 1989). With respect to cultural issues, however, the PS in power made some major concessions: for example, it substantially improved the status of homosexuals in France (Duyvendak 1992: 218–28). Depending on the type of new social movement, the PS in power, at its worst, followed a fully exclusive strategy, at its best one of preemption through reforms. The governing PS could afford to follow such a course because it was not threatened by a Green party from the left — another result of the French electoral system. In her fine analysis of the PS's strategy with regard to nuclear energy, von Oppeln (1989: 205) concludes that the party's strategy of early co-optation and later disappointment of the antinuclear movement contributed in a decisive way to the weakening of this movement. Two movements in the 1980s, however, did not suffer from this unconducive political situation: the student movement of 1986 and the antiracist movement. Especially the antiracist movement, which sprang up as a countermovement after the electoral successes of the Front National, received strong support from the Socialists. It is no accident, however, that the heyday of this movement coincided with the period of cohabitation — when the right was in government but the Socialists still controlled the presidency — between 1986 and 1988.

The German Social Democratic Party (SPD) traversed a trajectory exactly opposite to that of the French PS in the period under study. At the beginning of the seventies, the SPD had been open to the new forces of the left. The new openness of the old left under the government of Willy Brandt was summarized by its slogan "mehr Demokratie wagen" — the social-liberal government would dare to have more democracy. As Koopmans (1992a: 98) observes, this formula could perhaps only have been invented in the Federal Republic, where it reacted against the deep distrust the adherents of "militant democracy" felt with regard to popular participation in politics. Although the core of the extraparliamentary opposition (APO) still kept its distance from the SPD, the party was able to profit considerably from the politicization of the younger generation. Between 1968 and 1972, SPD membership rose by more than two hundred thousand. Half of the somewhat more than a million members in 1976, the peak year, had joined the party after 1967. These new members were predominantly young and members of a new middle-class background. The party's radicalized youth organization, the Jungsozialisten (Jusos) thus became increasingly important.

The reform euphoria did not last long, however. The reform coalition of Chancellor Brandt could not fulfill the hopes it had raised. The shift of the political climate became complete in 1974 when Brandt had to resign because an East German spy was discovered among his closest staff assistants, and Helmut Schmidt, leader of the party's right wing and an ardent Juso opponent, bercame the new chancellor. From now on, the SPD followed a strategy that came close to "selective exclusion" — just as the French Socialists in power did. To understand why, we should note first that the Social Democrats had to govern in coalition with the Liberals, which imposed a constraint on the amount of concessions they could have made to the new social movements. Second, the generally repressive legacy prevented the governing SPD from taking a more integrative stance toward the new social movements. Third, the terrorist attacks during the seventies, while being themselves in part a result of the generally repressive mood, reinforced the tendency of the governing SPD to resort to repression once again. Fourth, although there was no Communist competition in Germany, the SPD nevertheless was under pressure from the strong union movement to stick to the traditional goals of the labor movement, which particularly affected the party's policies with regard to nuclear energy. Finally, to the extent that the SPD did try to implement policies in favor of the new social movements, these were often blocked by the Christian Democrats, who controlled the majority in the Bundesrat (the second chamber of the German parliament, consisting of delegates of the member states of the federation) and who sometimes succesfully appealed to the Federal Constitutional Court, which, for instance, vetoed the liberalization of abortion (Koopmans 1992a: 97ff.).

However, contrary to the case of the French PS, the leadership of the SPD was not able to centralize the debate on the new issues and keep internal discussions under control. Von Oppeln (1989) attributes this greater openness of the German SPD in part to the federal structure of the German political system. In a federal system, she argues, the number of independent leadership positions is larger than in a centralized system, which increases the opportunity of persons with new ideas to enter into leadership positions within parties. She attributes the relative openness of the SPD to demands of the new social movements to the fact that many members of the Jusos were particularly close to these movements' concerns and introduced a number of their demands into the party's internal debate. A similar dialogue with the youth organization of the party did not take place in the French PS. Moreover, from 1977 onward on the regional level and since 1979 also nationally, the SPD has been confronted by the challenge of a vigorous Green party, which strengthened the position of new social movements' sympathizers within the party. Thus, increasingly, "the battle over conventional versus alternative politics was carried on within the SPD" (Pulzer 1989: 91). The SPD's internal dissension and programmatic disorientation in turn contributed greatly to the increasingly tense relations between the Free Democratic Party (FDP) and the SPD within the governing coalition, which eventually broke down in 1982. When the SPD had to join the ranks of the opposition, these factors had already resulted in a much more facilitative strategy with regard to the new challengers.

In line with the integrative strategy of the Dutch political system, the Dutch Social Democrats (PvdA) have been open to new social movements since the early seventies. Under the impact of the depillarization of the Dutch political system in the late sixties, the PvdA had radicalized and attracted many militants of the new left, which eventually gained control over the party (van Praag 1991). The fact that the PvdA was confronted by significant competition from new left parties—a result of the open electoral system—also contributed to its opening up. Since 1971, the party executive has accepted extraparliamentary activities as part of its action repertoire and since its 1973 congress the party has officially become an "action party," that is, a party oriented not only toward participation in government but also toward participation in movement activities. At the same time, the PvdA also became the dominant party in a coalition government that lasted from 1973 until 1977. At first sight, this configuration seems to be very promising for the mobilization of new social movements. However, the "action party" principles of the PvdA did not have much of an effect during this period, precisely because the party was in government, and its strategy of reform had more of a preemptive character. Moreover, the number of concessions made was also quite limited, because of the government's composition. On the one hand, the government included a new-left party (PPR) and a party of the center left (D'66), which were open to the demands of the new social movements. On the other hand, the Christian parties still held a strong position in the coalition. When it went into opposition in 1977, the PvdA came still closer to the new social movements, and increased its involvement in several movements. It joined the antinuclear power camp in 1979—after the Three Mile Island accident in Harrisburg (Cramer 1989: 66) —and, most important, it embraced the goals of the peace movement (Kriesi 1989). Except for its brief spell in government in 1981–82, one may describe the strategy of the PvdA with respect to new social movements during the first half of the eighties as one of strong facilitation.

This situation changed radically, however, after 1985. The Christian Democrats had been able to stabilize the electoral base of the various denominational parties (which had been eroding all through the sixties and seventies) after their merger in 1980. Moreover, the internal left-wing opposition within the Christian Democratic Party, which was still a powerful force at the beginning of the eighties, was silenced once the party had entered a stable coalition with the right-wing liberals in 1982. These developments seriously affected the Social Democrats' strategic position and their chances of participating in government. In 1985, the PvdA's liaison with the peace movement finally proved to be a failure when the government decided to deploy cruise missiles after all. Subsequently, the Social Democrats' close link to the new social movements was almost completely severed as a result of a new party strategy (finally successful in 1989) designed to regain acceptance by the Christian Democrats as a coalition partner. This example shows that there may be conditions under which an oppositional Social Democratic Party may refrain from supporting the new social movements. This Dutch example is

complementary to the case of the French Socialists who supported the mobilization of the solidarity movement even when they controlled the presidency. The two "deviant cases" indicate that tactical considerations of the Social Democrats may lead to changes in the opportunity structures for new
social movements that do not coincide with the left's moving from the government to the opposition or vice versa.

The Swiss Social Democrats (SPS/PSS), finally, had an ambiguous position with regard to new social movements. Having been part of the grand
coalition that has governed Switzerland since 1959, they shared the formal
responsibility for the government policies against which the new social movements mobilized. Having always been in a clear minority position within the
governing coalition, they have, at the same time, opposed the government on
specific issues, including several issues of concern to new social movements.
The ambiguity of the party's position is reflected by its internal division in a
party left and a party right. The party left consistently favored the demands
of new social movements throughout the period under consideration; the
party right, which is close to the unions and to the party's representatives
in government, has consistently been skeptical of new social movements.
Given the highly fragmented character of the Swiss party system, the specific configuration of power within the party has varied from one canton to
the other. There is a considerable difference between the two major linguistic regions in this respect. In the most developed cantons of German-speaking
Switzerland, the SPS has experienced a strong influx of new left militants,
and has been confronted with vigorous competition from new-left parties
since the early seventies. At the end of the seventies, the party left has been
able to take power within the party in several of the Swiss-German-speaking
cantons. As a consequence, in these cantons — notably in Basel and Zurich —
the SPS has become a major alliance partner of new social movements. This
has led to serious internal tensions with the party right, and finally to splits
in both Basel and Zurich in the early eighties. In French-speaking Switzerland, the PSS has not so much been challenged by new left parties as by the
traditional Communist Party (PdT/PdA). This may explain both why it has
been less facilitative for new social movements in these parts of the country
and why the Swiss Green party developed first in the French-speaking cantons (Ladner 1989).

In line with the preceding considerations about the effect of the Social Democrats' acceding to or resigning from government, we expect that in France
a clear decline in the level of mobilization of new social movements occurred

from 1981 onward, that is, from the moment the left came to power. The mobilization of the other French movements is less likely to have been affected by this change. Conversely, for Germany we expect an increase in the level of mobilization of new social movements starting in the early eighties. The left lost power in 1982, but the coalition had already started to get into difficulties before that date and the competition from the Greens set in as early as 1977. No corresponding increase is expected for the other movements—with the possible exception of the labor movement. In the Netherlands, the mobilization of new social movements, but not necessarily of other movements, should have begun to increase in 1978 and to decline again after 1985. Due to the coalition character of Dutch governments, and to the inclusive dominant strategies, the changes in the level of mobilization of the Dutch new social movements may be somewhat less immediate and pronounced than in Germany. For Switzerland, predictions are more difficult, because there has never been an explicit change in the federal government as in the other countries, and because of cantonal differences. However, one might argue that the takeover of the Social Democratic Party organization by its left wing in some cantons during the late seventies may have had a clear mobilizing effect on the new social movements in the regions concerned.

Level of Facilitation of the New Social Movements by the Left

We shall first consider the overall level of facilitation of new social movements by the old left (unions, social-democratic, and communist parties) and by the new left (new left and Green parties) for the whole period under study; that is, we shall, for the time being, disregard the question of the left's participation in government. For each protest event, we have coded whether or not the different organizations of the left facilitated it by participating in the event. We are aware of the fact that this is quite a demanding measure of facilitation, but more indirect forms of facilitation cannot be coded reliably on the basis of our newspaper data. A first indicator of the level of facilitation by the left is provided by the share of protest events of new social movements that were supported by the direct participation of various external allies. Since the number of participants mobilized varies widely from one event to the other, we have also calculated a second indicator, which corresponds to the percentage share of people mobilized in protest events in a given country during the period under study who were mobilized in events facilitated by various

Table 3.2. **Facilitation of new social movements by allies in the four countries (percentages of supported protest events)**

Type of ally	France	Germany	Netherlands	Switzerland	Total
1. Old left	15.9	16.0	5.6	7.4	12.2
unions	9.0	8.8	2.9	1.4	6.2
social-democratic party	8.5	8.2	3.2	4.3	6.5
communist party	6.3	5.6	4.3	3.5	5.1
2. New Left	5.7	11.0	3.9	5.8	7.6
new left parties	5.4	.6	3.9	5.4	3.1
Green parties	.8	10.6	.1	.6	4.8
3. Old and new left	17.9	20.2	6.4	9.8	15.0
4. Others	5.4	11.8	7.2	2.1	7.8
5. All	21.2	24.9	10.9	11.5	18.8
Share of left (3:5)	84.4	81.1	58.7	85.2	79.7
N	(775)	(1,770)	(863)	(772)	(4,180)

Note: The percentages do not add up, since various actors could have jointly supported one and the same event.

allies. This second indicator gives us a more precise idea of the mobilizing capacity of the facilitation by allies.

Tables 3.2. and 3.3 present the data concerning the facilitation of all forms of protest events—including direct-democratic forms, petitions, and festivals—for the two indicators.[4] As table 3.2 shows, the share of protest events of new social movements that were facilitated by allies of any kind of persuasion is rather small. Overall, only 18.8 percent of these events found such allied support. In the two countries with an exclusive heritage—France and Germany—facilitation was, as expected, generally more frequent than in the countries with an inclusive tradition. But even in these countries, no more than a fourth of the protest events of our movements could count on external support.

If facilitation is not forthcoming very frequently, the predominant facilitating role of the left is quite evident from the figures presented in this table. Almost 80 percent of the events that were supported at all profited from facilitation by the left. The role of left facilitation is equally prominent in France, Germany, and Switzerland (see last line of the table). Only in the Netherlands did other allies such as the churches, the moderate right (the dissidents within the Christian Democratic Party, for example), or even the authorities play a relatively important facilitative role. Facilitation by the left and facilitation by other allies do not, of course, exclude each other. There are many instances where facilitation was forthcoming from various quarters at

Table 3.3. **Facilitation of new social movements by allies in the four countries (percentages of people mobilized in protest events supported by allies)**

Type of ally	France	Germany	Netherlands	Switzerland	Total
1. Old left	70	41	56	11	37
2. New left	4	32	54	10	27
3. Old and new left	71	46	57	15	39
4. Others	4	29	26	1	16
5. All	73	51	59	16	43
Share of left (3:5)	97	90	97	94	91

Note: The table presents the percentages of people who were mobilized in protest events supported by a given type of ally. These percentages do not add up. The total number of people mobilized in a given country during the period under study is equal to 100 percent.

the same time. This is why the percentages in the table generally do not add up.

According to table 3.2, facilitation by the old left turns out to be much more frequent in France and Germany than in the other two countries, but, as we have argued, for quite different reasons. In France, where the traditional class cleavage is still highly conflictual (see chapter 1), the old left still has a strong mobilizing capacity. Accordingly, it dominates the new left, which is reflected in the much smaller share of events supported by the parties of the new left. In Germany, by contrast, the far-reaching pacification of the traditional class cleavage has implied the rise of a new left competing vigorously with the old left for the support of the political potentials represented by the new social movements. This is illustrated by the fact that the share of events facilitated by the German new left turns out to be much larger than the corresponding share in any of the other three countries. In the Dutch and the Swiss cases—the other two countries with a pacified left—the competition between the old- and the new-left parties for the support of the new social movements appears, indeed, to have been less intense, since in these two countries both the old and the new left have less frequently facilitated their mobilization. Thus, the general hypothesis that the facilitation of the mobilization of new social movements by a pacified old left depends on the degree of competition from the new left receives some support.

These results confirm what we found in an analysis of the alliance structures of the most important SMOs of the new social movements in the four countries (Kriesi 1995). Except for the Netherlands, a majority of the SMOs turned out to be allied to parties on the left. Only two SMOs in our sample said they were allied to a party on the right—one in the Netherlands and one in Switzerland. Moreover, we found that virtually all the SMOs in all four countries have a membership that prefers parties on the political left. In addition, some SMOs also said they recruited sympathizers of parties on the political right. It comes as no surprise that, on the one hand, these SMOs are most numerous in Switzerland, and that, on the other hand, there exists not a single SMO recruiting sympathizers of parties on the right in France. The strong party-political polarization forces all the participants in French politics to take sides, whereas the less conspicuous character of the opposition between left and right in the more inclusive countries allows for crossing the fault lines.

Turning now to our second indicator — the share of people mobilized in events facilitated by allies — we notice that, from this point of view, the facilitation of new social movements is much more significant (table 3.3). Overall, 43 percent of all the participants were mobilized in events that were facilitated by allies. In other words, if allied support is forthcoming, it adds considerably to the mobilizing capacity of new social movements. Or, to put it in yet another way, allies facilitate mainly large-scale protest events. As a more detailed analysis shows, these large events are at the same time of a relatively moderate kind. However, the mobilizing capacity of allied support varies greatly between countries. It is largest in France, where 73 percent of all the participants in the new social movements' events were mobilized in events facilitated by allies, and lowest in Switzerland, where the corresponding share amounts to no more than 16 percent. Germany and the Netherlands are located in between, with shares of 51 percent and 59 percent of the participants mobilized with the support of allies.

The role of the left turns out to be even more crucial if we take into account the number in participants in the facilitated events. In all the countries, 90 percent or more of the participants that were mobilized with allied support were mobilized with the support of the left. In the case of France, the large contribution of the mobilizing capacity of the left is almost entirely attributable to the old left. This confirms the extensive dependence of the French new social movements on the old left, which illustrates once again the "inclusive" character of the mobilization potential of the traditional class cleavage in France (see chapter 1). In Germany and the Netherlands, in contrast, the old and the new left jointly contributed to the mobilization of some of the new social movements' large-scale campaigns. The Swiss movements, finally, seem to be particularly independent of the left — new or old. This result may, however, be somewhat artificial. Large-scale campaigns of the Swiss new social movements often take the form of a popular initiative. Although these initiatives are launched by the movements themselves without external support, the campaigns preceding a vote on an initiative of a new social movement are generally supported by all the parties of the left. Since, in collecting our data, we coded an initiative only at the time of its launching, we did not take into account the support by allies at the time of the vote.

As we have pointed out, not all new social movements are equally close to the left. Accordingly, we expect the *peace and solidarity movements* to profit most from its support. The following two tables, which allow us to compare the external facilitation of these two movements with that of the other new social movements, confirm this expectation. With respect to the first indicator, the share of events supported by allies, table 3.4 shows that, overall, almost a third (30.5 percent) of the events of the peace and the solidarity movements were supported by allies, compared to only one-tenth (9.8 percent) of the events of the other new social movements. We find analogous discrepancies, although at varying absolute levels, in all four countries. The left bears the brunt of the facilitation of the events of all the new social movements, but it was most prominent in the case of the peace and the solidarity movements. In the exclusive countries — France and Germany — the left facilitated as much as one-third of the events of these two movements, compared to one-sixth (17.6 percent) in Switzerland and only one-tenth (10.7 percent) in the Netherlands. With respect to the other new social movements, the left's support almost vanishes in the two inclusive countries and amounts to no more than one-tenth of the events in the exclusive ones. As far as the number of people mobilized is concerned, table 3.5 indicates that the left overwhelmingly contributes to the mobilization of the peace and solidarity movements, whereas its facilitation of the other new social movements is quite insignificant. The dependence of the peace and solidarity movements on the support by the left is almost total in France, where 88 percent of their participants were mobilized with left support. In Germany and the Netherlands, the corresponding percentages still amount to about two-thirds of all the participants mobilized by these movements. Only in Switzerland were these movements relatively independent of the left, with roughly one-third of their participants having been mobilized in events facilitated by the left. Finally, in France, it is above all the old left that mobilized for the peace and the solidarity movements, while in the three other countries, the new left contributed almost as much to their mobilization capacity.

Table 3.4. Facilitation of two types of new social movements by allies in the four countries (percentages of supported protest events)

Type of ally	France	Germany	Netherlands	Switzerland	Total
Peace and solidarity movements					
1. Old left	27.9	26.4	10.1	13.5	20.7
2. New left	7.8	16.0	6.1	10.5	6.8
3. Old and new left	31.3	31.8	10.7	17.6	24.4
4. Others	9.5	19.5	10.5	3.0	13.2
5. All	37.4	39.1	16.7	20.6	30.5
Share of left (3:5)	83.6	81.3	64.0	85.4	80.0
N	(294)	(806)	(456)	(267)	(1,823)
Other new social movements					
1. Old left	8.5	7.3	.5	4.2	5.7
2. New left	4.4	6.7	.2	.8	1.7
3. Old and new left	9.8	10.5	1.5	3.4	4.6
4. Others	2.9	5.3	3.4	1.6	3.7
5. All	11.2	13.0	4.4	6.7	9.8
Share of left (3:5)	87.5	80.7	34.0	50.7	46.9
N	(481)	(964)	(407)	(505)	(2,357)

Note: The percentages do not add up, since various actors could have jointly supported one and the same event.

Table 3.5. Facilitation of two types of new social movements by allies in the four countries (percentages of people mobilized in protest events supported by allies)

Type of ally	France	Germany	Netherlands	Switzerland	Total
Peace and solidarity movements					
1. Old left	87	56	67	31	60
2. New left	3	43	64	27	44
3. Old and new left	88	63	67	34	63
4. Others	2	40	33	2	27
5. All	89	70	76	37	69
Share of left (3:5)	99	90	88	92	91
Other new social movements					
1. Old left	14	11	6	5	7
2. New left	8	11	6	5	6
3. Old and new left	16	13	6	8	10
4. Others	8	6	1	1	2
5. Total	20	16	7	9	11
Share of left (3:5)	80	81	86	89	91

Note: The table presents the percentages of people who were mobilized in protest events supported by a given type of ally. These percentages do not add up. The total number of people mobilized in a given country during the period under study is equal to 100 percent.

The Left in and out of Government

Figure 3.1 allows us to test our expectations with regard to the impact of a change in the left's participation in government. It contains four diagrams, one for each country. In each diagram, the development of the number of protest events caused by new social movements and that caused by all the other movements are shown. In addition to the unconventional events, direct-democratic forms, petitions, and festivals are again included in the analysis. Let us first look at the two larger countries. The contrasting development of the number of new social movement events in the two countries starting in the early eighties is striking: whereas Germany experiences a surge of new social movement activity after 1980, France sees a decline. This contrast corresponds to our hypothesis about the impact of the loss of power of the left in Germany, and of its access to power in France. The level of mobilization of the other movements has hardly been affected at all by this change in the configuration of power, which also corresponds to our expectations. Here, however, the aggregation of all other movements obscures important differences, particularly in France. Whereas left-wing mobilization follows the same, declining pattern as the new social movements, mobilizations from the right increase after the Socialists come to power. This strong polarization of the trends for left-wing and right-wing mobilization in France confirms our idea that the effects of situations of reform and threat will be particularly pronounced in strong and exclusive states.

Turning to the two smaller countries, the case of the Netherlands confirms the general hypothesis once again. After the Social Democrats lost power in 1977, the level of mobilization of new social movements began to increase and reached impressive peaks in the early eighties. The reaction to the change in power has not been as rapid as in France or Germany, but the general pattern conforms to our expectations. As we expected, after 1985 the Dutch new social movements experienced a relatively sharp decline, which coincides with changes in the strategy of the Social Democrats. As in France and Germany, the other movements were not affected by such changes in the configuration of power. In the Swiss case, we also find a substantial increase in the mobilization of new social movements in the early eighties. However, this increase cannot be explained by a change in the composition of the federal government. The upsurge of the Swiss new social movements was mainly the result of the mobilization of the urban autonomous movement in Zurich, which lends some support to our hypothesis that the change in power within the regional and local Social Democratic

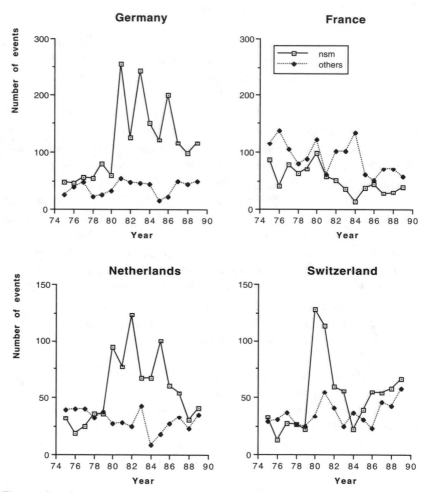

Fig. 3.1. Development of the number of events caused by new social movements and other movements in the four countries between 1975 and 1989

Party may have contributed to the enormous increase in the overall level of mobilization. In a highly decentralized, weak state, the local or regional alliance structures may be more important for the mobilization of new social movements than those of the national political context. The pattern of mobilization of the Swiss new social movements has also been affected by processes of diffusion from one country to another, which we shall consider in more detail in chapter 8.

If, instead of looking at the development of the number of events, we consider that of the number of participants in the protest events of new social movements, the previous results become even more pronounced for Germany and the Netherlands (fig. 3.2). In these two countries, it was above all the *peace movement* that mobilized enormous numbers of people during the first half of the eighties against the stationing of cruise missiles in Western Europe. In both countries, the peace movement's campaigns were strongly facilitated by the left. In the German case, mobilization by the peace movement had already set in before the collapse of the left-liberal coalition in October 1982. In September 1981, 80,000 people demonstrated against the visit of U.S. Secretary of State Alexander Haig, and on October 10, the largest demonstration to date in the history of the Federal Republic (300,000 participants) was staged by the peace movement in Bonn. This demonstration was joined by one-quarter of the SPD members of parliament. After the fall of the Schmidt government in 1982, the huge demonstrations of 1983 were fully backed by the SPD and the unions (Koopmans 1992a: 202). The Dutch peace movement's mobilizing capacity was equally impressive. To influence the deployment decision that was to be taken by the Dutch government in December 1981, the Dutch movement organized a large demonstration in November. Although they were a member of the governing coalition, the Social Democrats joined the organizing committee for the demonstration. At that time, their ambiguous position as a governing party and an action party became more apparent than ever. Many of the 400,000 participants in the demonstration were well aware of this: the speakers from the Social Democrats and D'66—a left-liberal party that was also participating in the governing coalition—were both hissed off stage. In May 1982 the Social Democratic ministers stepped down. The tensions about matters of social and economic policy, but also about the question of the cruise missiles, had become too great. Having no longer been considered part of the coalition formation following the elections that year, the Social Democrats' position on the peace movement from then on became unambiguously supportive. By the time of the people's petition in 1985, the Social Democrats, even more so than the small parties of the new left, had become a core element of the organizational infrastructure of the peace movement in the Netherlands (Kriesi 1989).

The Swiss and French patterns are less dependent on the mobilization of the peace movement. In both countries, the campaign against the deployment of cruise missiles was less prominent, given that neither is an active member of NATO. Although the Swiss pattern in figure 3.2 still resembles that of

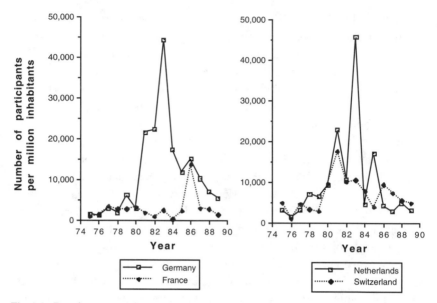

Fig. 3.2. Development of the number of participants mobilized by new social movements in the four countries between 1975 and 1989

figure 3.1, the French pattern turns out to be quite different. Compared to the upsurge in the number of people participating in new social movement events around 1986, the decline at the beginning of the eighties is quite negligible. This peculiarity of the French pattern displayed in figure 3.2 has at least three origins: first, the demobilization of the French new social movements with the coming to power of the Socialists is primarily a result of the *demobilization of the ecology movement,* and of its antinuclear branch in particular. This movement, which did not have a very large mobilizing capacity to begin with but which had produced a relatively large number of events during the seventies, completely demobilized with the coming to power of the Socialists. Overpoliticized and too dependent on the Socialists, it did not survive their "betrayal" once they were in government (Duyvendak 1992: 211). Contrary to what Touraine (1980b) maintains, we would point out with Duyvendak that the antinuclear movement in particular did not retreat after the events at Creys-Malville (violent confrontations between the antinuclear movement and the police near the site of the future fast-breeder reactor of the French nuclear energy program) but after it was abandoned by its own ally, the PS—which, as a governing party, had become its new adversary. A more detailed analysis of the development of the ecology movement in the different countries indicates that the development of the French ecology movement contrasts quite sharply with that of its German and Swiss counterparts. Only the Dutch ecology movement also declined throughout the eighties — less precipitously, if we compare the number of events, but quite abruptly, too, if we also take into account the number of people who participated in its events.

Second, the French pattern also results from the fact that the French *peace movement*, as already noted, did not mobilize in the early eighties. Although, together with regionalist forces, it had led a vigorous campaign against the planned enlargement of a military training ground in Larzac during the seventies, the French peace movement did not take part in the international campaign against the stationing of cruise missiles that took on such huge proportions in the Netherlands and in Germany. The absence of the French peace movement in the early eighties may in part be explained by the fact that the French Socialists not only did not facilitate the movement but actively campaigned against it (Duyvendak 1992: 176ff.). The French left, in other words, in no way joined the international campaign against the cruise missiles.

However — and this is the third specificity of the French pattern — the French left largely facilitated the *antiracist movement*. This movement mobilized in two waves. At the beginning of the eighties, it mobilized against the increasing number of violent attacks against immigrants and against the (right-wing) government's legislation. Then the movement grew quite spectacularly, as a reaction to the equally spectacular rise of the Front National since 1983. Although the number of events was not greater than in the earlier wave, the number of people mobilized was now much more impressive: 500,000 people responded to the call of SOS-Racisme for a demonstration in 1985 at the Place de la Concorde; 200,000 in 1986 at the Place de la Bastille; 250,000 in 1987 and 300,000 in 1988 at the Esplanade de Vincennes. SOS-Racisme, by far the most important French SMO of the late eighties, was strongly supported by the Socialist Party (Duyvendak 1992: 191). This support was forthcoming because, given the change in the electoral system introduced by the Socialist government, which had adopted the proportional system for national elections, the Front National became a real electoral threat — not only for the right, but also for the left — in the 1986 elections for the National Assembly. Moreover, once Jacques Chirac had come to power during the period of "cohabitation" (1986–88), the antiracist movement succeeded in destabilizing his right-wing government. After Chirac reintroduced the majority system, and after the left returned to power in 1988, SOS-Racisme found mobilization much more difficult.

For these reasons, the French pattern does not entirely conform to our general expectations with respect to the impact the left's participation in government ought to have on its support for the mobilization of new social movements. In a polity such as France, where the social movements are completely dependent on the political parties, the latter instrumentalize them for their own purposes whether they are in or out of government. Accordingly, the clear-cut relationship between the left's participation in government and the level of its support of new social movements does not hold for France. This is illustrated by table 3.6. For three of our four countries,[5] this table presents the *differences* between the share of events that are facilitated by a given type of actor during the period when the left is in opposition, and the corresponding share for when it forms (part of) the government. According to our hypothesis, facilitation from the left should mainly be forthcoming when the left is in the opposition—that is, we expect to find only positive differences for actors from the left. In the French case, however, table 3.6 actually contains a lot of negative differences. In this case, the share of events facilitated by the left was in fact much lower during the period when the left was in opposition than when it was in power. It is above all the support given to SOS-Racisme by the ruling Socialists that accounts for this deviation in the general pattern.

The German case, in contrast, is much more in line with our hypothesis. As expected, the German left facilitated protest events of new social movements to a greater extent when it was part of the opposition. The German figures are quite consistent, apart from the fact that the old left—but not the new one—facilitated the mobilizations of the peace and solidarity movements to virtually the same extent whether the left was in the government or not. This exception calls for a more detailed analysis of the German situation. As we have already noted, the competition between the old and the new left has been intense in Germany, especially since the formation of the national Green party in 1979. This challenge, combined with the internal dissension and programmatic disorientation of the SPD that preceded the breakdown of the left-liberal coalition in 1982, had, as we have observed, already resulted in a more facilitative party strategy with regard to challengers prior to the change in power. We should make a distinction between three periods in the German case: the seventies, when the left was in government; a transition period (1980–82), when the left-liberal coalition came under increasing pres-

Table 3.6. Support of new social movements and government by the left (differences between percentages of facilitated events when the left is in the opposition and when it is in government)

Type of ally	France	Germany	Netherlands
All new social movements			
1. Old left	−12.6	+8.2	−1.4
2. New left	−2.3	+10.0	+3.1
3. Old and new left	−13.5	+10.7	+3.5
4. Others	+1.4	+9.1	+3.6
5. All	−10.8	+14.0	+3.2
Peace and solidarity movements			
1. Old left	−32.6	+0.1	−3.1
2. New left	−3.9	+11.3	+4.1
3. Old and new left	−31.6	+1.5	−3.1
4. Others	+6.2	+11.5	+2.6
5. All	−25.0	+4.0	+0.7
Other new social movements			
1. Old left	+1.4	+5.5	+0.7
2. New left	−1.1	+6.2	+2.2
3. Old and new left	−0.5	+7.9	+2.2
4. Others	−1.3	+3.2	+5.0
5. All	0.0	+9.8	+6.5

Note: A plus sign indicates that the left facilitated a given type of movement more frequently when it was in the opposition; a minus sign indicates the opposite.

sure; and the rest of the eighties, when the SPD had joined the opposition. If we do this, we find an even clearer picture for Germany. In fact, as a more detailed analysis shows, support for the various new social movements by the left already began to increase during the transition period. This increase was tremendous for the new left, but the old left to some extent followed suit, especially with respect to the peace and solidarity movements. Once the left was out of government, left support generally continued to grow, except for the facilitation of the peace and solidarity movements by the old left, which had already reached a particularly high level during the transition period.

The Dutch pattern is much less clear-cut than the German one, but it is nevertheless in general agreement with our hypothesis. The major exception to the expected pattern in the Dutch case concerns the facilitation of the peace movement by the old left. The peace movement was even more frequently facilitated by the old left when the latter was in power. Our earlier discussion of this movement indicated, however, that the quality of this facilitation — at least as far as the Social Democrats are concerned — changed considerably when they found themselves back in the opposition. In other words, we suggest that, in this case, our rough indicators are not quite sensitive enough to the quality of the facilitation of protest events by the left.

Conclusion

Facilitation of the mobilization of new social movements by established political actors, especially by organizations of the left, is an omnipresent phenomenon. But, as we have seen, depending on the character of the configuration of the old and the new left and on whether the left is in or out of government, its magnitude varies considerably. Facilitation has also been shown to be a function of the type of movement. Thus the peace and the solidarity movements have been shown to be particularly close to the left. From the point of view of the new social movements, facilitation by the left may turn out to be as much a handicap as it is an asset. The Dutch and German peace movements, as well as the French solidarity movement, illustrate this point. Although the support they received from the left made it possible for these movements to mount unprecedented mobilizations, their close association with the left at the same time limited their possible influence. Thus, as Koopmans (1992a: 202) points out, the identification of the German peace movement with the left opposition in parliament allowed the government in November 1983 to ignore this movement as easily as it could ignore the votes against missile deployment cast by the Green and Social Democratic parliamentary opposition. Similarly, as van Praag (1991: 118) observed, the close alliance between the peace movement and the Dutch Social Democrats turned the people's petition against the deployment of cruise missiles in fall 1985 into a referendum for or against the cabinet of the Christian Democratic Premier Ruud Lubbers. The alliance with the Social Democrats made it impossible for the Christian Democrats to support the petition. As a consequence, van Praag reaches the paradoxical conclusion that facilitation by the established left, when it is in the opposition, may increase the mobilizing capacity of a new social movement, but at the same time it is also likely to reduce the possibility for the movement to have any effect on government policy.

Pursuing his discussion of the German peace movement, Koopmans (1992a: 206) is somewhat less pessimistic about the implications of its alliance with the old and the new left. In his view, in the long run the defense policy of the conservative coalition did not remain unaffected by the concerns of the peace movement—even if it had decided in favor of deploying the cruise missiles in 1983. Moreover, as Koopmans points out, the massive mobilization of the peace movement contributed to transforming the configuration of the left. Thus, it contributed not only to the electoral breakthrough of the German Greens but also to strengthening the new left within the SPD. In other words, it is not only the new social movements that are transformed if they conclude alliances with the left, but the left as well may be strongly affected by these alliances. The impact of the alliance of the peace movement on the German left is just one case in point. The case of the Social Democratic Party in the canton of Zurich provides another example. Its support of the urban autonomous movement in the early eighties accentuated the internal conflicts between the old and the new left within the party. Finally, it came to a break between the new-left majority of the party and its old-left representatives in the city government.[6] The social-democratic city councillors who had fought the movement were eventually excluded from party membership, and representatives of its new-left wing ran against them in the following elections (Kriesi 1984).

In a more general way, these examples suggest that in a polity with a pacified old left, the new social movements strengthen the new left within and outside of the established parties. It appears that this reinforcement of the new left has been one of these movements' main latent functions. However, in a polity where the old left has not yet been pacified and where the polarization between the old left and the old right still dominated politics in the eighties, the new social movements could not hope to have such an effect on the configuration of the left. Under such circumstances, rather than transform the left, they were transformed by a left that exploited them for its own political purposes. This is the lesson we draw from our analysis of the French case.

Chapter 4

Social Movement Types and Policy Domains

In this chapter, we analyze the relationship between social movements and their political context in a somewhat different perspective. Whereas in the preceding chapters we focused on differences between the NSMs of the four countries in relation to differing national political contexts (POSs), in this chapter *similarities across countries* and *differences within countries* command our attention. Until now, we have dealt with the impact of political opportunities on a whole social movement sector. The general idea to be investigated in this chapter, however, is that the POS does not influence a whole social movement sector in the same way and to the same extent. In what follows, we would like to introduce two sets of concepts related to the idea of POSs specific to the different components of the NSM sector and offering an explanation of the remarkable variations between movements within countries.

First, we take into account the different reactions of challengers to political opportunities, depending on some of the challengers' characteristics. In this regard, the distinction between *instrumental movements, countercultural movements,* and *subcultural movements,* introduced by Koopmans (1992a), emerges as a powerful analytical tool. Due to characteristics *inherent* to the movements — their logic of action and their general orientation — movements of the same type follow comparable interactive dynamics, that is, the same reaction pattern to concrete opportunities. Since authorities and allies, in their turn, have movement-type specific (re)action patterns as well, similarities will occur across countries among movements of the same type and, as a consequence, differences among movements of the same country will appear.

Second, we consider the relation of the POS to different issues raised by social movements, causing different interactive dynamics *within* movement types as well. We adopt the terms *high-profile* and *low-profile* (Duyvendak 1992) in order to distinguish between issues according to their relation to the POS. Whereas movement types' dynamics are primarily dependent on characteristics of the challengers, an issue's profile is a function of the evaluation by political authorities. What is crucial is the priority of an issue on the political agenda, which is determined by its relevance in the perspective of dominant cleavage structures (see chapter 1) and by the authorities' conceptions of the core tasks and interest of the state. Since issues are generally connected, forming larger issue areas, we would like to introduce the idea that the impact of the POS on social protest differs according to *policy domains.* Some policy domains are seen as more crucial than others by established actors. Hence issues raised by social movements that concern such policy domains are potentially more threatening for the authorities, who in this case would be less responsive/accessible to challengers. In contrast, movements that raise potentially less threatening issues concerning less crucial policy domains would find the political system to be more open.

This perspective is also the one followed by the so-called agenda-building approach (Cobb and Elder 1983), according to which political issues have varying patterns of entrance or access to the agenda of decision makers. Yet this approach has mostly dealt with a bottom-up process, looking for factors that enable political issues to reach the systemic or the institutional agendas, focusing on the definition of issues by those who raised them, and stressing such factors as the issue definition, the symbol utilization, and the expansion to a relevant public. Here we would like to underline the evaluation of issues by established actors, above all by political authorities, and to show how this top-down process influences the mobilization by NSMs.

We will first show how variations between movements within a given political context can in part be explained in terms of the different reaction of movement *types* to the set of concrete opportunities deriving from the structural characteristics of the political context. Then we will elaborate on the idea of *policy domain*-specific POSs in the search of an explanation of variations within movements of the same type.

Types of Movements

In chapter 2, we introduced four motivational factors—facilitation, repression, success chances, and reform/threat—which form the set of concrete opportunities for the mobilization of NSMs. Yet the model was confined to an instrumental conception of social movements, in which means and ends can be neatly distinguished. Although we agree with the resource mobilization perspective that this assumption is adequate enough to serve as a basis for analyzing the strategic decisions of most movements and participants, we think the new social movement approach makes a valid point in arguing that some movements follow a much more expressive logic in which collective action and the identities it produces become ends in themselves (Hirschman 1982). Because of such differences among movements, several authors have proposed a distinction between strategy-oriented and identity-oriented movements[1] (Cohen 1985; Pizzorno 1978; Raschke 1985; Rolke 1987; Rucht 1988). Koopmans (1992a) has refined this typology by proposing an additional distinction between two types of identity-oriented movements. Subcultural movements, such as the gay movement, the new women's movement, and many ethnic movements, are primarily directed at collective identities that are constituted and reproduced in within-group interaction. In contrast, countercultural movements, such as terrorist organizations or sections of the squatters' movement and, again, many ethnic movements, derive their collective identity from conflicting and confrontational interaction with other groups.

Thus we can classify (new) social movements according to their logic of action (identity/instrumental) and their general orientation (internal/external). Figure 4.1 illustrates the position of each movement type in the conceptual space formed by the combination of these two criteria for the definition of movement types. Subcultural movements are predominantly internally oriented and identity-based. Instrumental movements are in some way their antithesis since they have an external orientation. Finally, countercultural movements are in between, for they combine their identity basis with a strong external orientation. The fourth combination has no logical foundation. If a social movement is instrumental, it cannot have an internal orientation, since instrumentally acting refers by definition to the pursuit of goals in the environment. Here we consider the ecology movement, the peace movement, and the solidarity movement as predominantly instrumental, the homosexual movement and the women's movement as predominantly subcultural, and the autonomous movement as predominantly countercultural. Yet this characterization is a relative one, in two ways. On the one hand, the position of each movement type may differ from one country to the other. For instance, countercultural movements may be more confrontational in one country than in another. As we have seen in the preceding chapters, such differences can easily be explained by the POS approach. On the other hand, within a given

	Logic of action	
	Instrumental	Identity
Internal		Subcultural movements
External	Instrumental movements	Countercultural movements

General orientation shown at left spanning Internal/External rows.

Fig. 4.1. The three types of movements

political context, the position of each movement type may change over time. For instance, instrumental movements may become more identity-based and subcultural movements more externally oriented. In other words, one and the same movement may shift from one type to the other, at least as a general tendency. As a consequence, the evaluations and reactions by authorities and allies with regard to a given movement change accordingly, generating new interactive patterns.

The importance of this typology for our present purpose lies in the fact that movements of different types react differently to their environment. First of all, this follows from the fact that in identity-oriented movements the distinction between means and ends largely disappears. Since for these movements "the medium is the message," success chances and reform/threat — which are the two factors related to the goals of collective action (the "ends" side) — are of relatively minor importance to them. On the other hand, because in the identity-oriented logic collective action itself occupies a central place, repression and facilitation — which are the two factors influencing the costs and benefits of collective action itself (the "means" side) — become more important as determinants of collective action. A second important implication of the typology is that, due to their strong internal orientation, subcultural movements will, on average, be less affected by external opportunities, whereas the mobilization of both instrumental and countercultural movements strongly depends on external reinforcement (Koopmans 1992a).

But what are the effects of concrete opportunities on these different movement types? In chapter 2, we discussed the relationship between POS and social movement action as mediated by these motivational factors in the case of *instrumental movements.* Here we shall discuss the two identity-oriented types of movements. As far as they are concerned, we can concentrate on the effect of the opportunities that have an impact on collective action itself — that is, facilitation and repression. For *countercultural movements,* we can restrict our attention to *repression,* because these movements are so radical that hardly any established actors will be ready to facilitate them. Furthermore, even if any were ready to do so, countercultural movements would be unlikely to accept such support, which they generally see as an attempt by "reformists" to tame them and to prevent them from attaining their revolutionary goals. Repression, however, will have a strong impact on the mobilization of these movements. Interestingly, these effects will be exactly opposite to those described earlier for instrumental movements. Repression strengthens the collective identity countercultural participants and activists derive from conflicting interaction. Therefore it stimulates rather than deters mobilization and will provoke a radicalization rather than a moderation of the action repertoire (Koopmans 1992a: 40–44).

With regard to *subcultural movements,* we have indicated that they do not depend to the same extent on external opportunities as the other two types. Nevertheless, to the extent that they interact with their political environment, even subcultural movements are affected by political opportunities. Because subcultural movements have elements in common with both countercultural movements (the identity orientation) and instrumental movements (conflict is not sought for its own sake), we can expect their relations to *repression* and *facilitation* to combine elements of both logics. When facilitation is forthcoming, the externally directed activities of subcultural movements tend to take on an instrumental character. Under conditions of repression, a more countercultural attitude may come to predominate (Koopmans 1992a: 44–45). However, both instrumental and countercultural tendencies will be limited because of the predominant orientation toward within-group interaction. Facilitation may lead to assimilation and a blurring of the boundary between subculture and dominant culture, and may thereby undermine the movement's raison d'être. This will result either in the movement's disappearance or in a reaffirmation of the movement's identity and a relaxation of ties with the dominant culture and politics. Similar limits apply to countercultural tendencies in more repressive circumstances: at higher levels of repression that threaten the movement's subcultural basis, conflict-aversive strategies are likely to gain the upper hand (Koopmans 1992a; see also chapter 7).

To sum up, the discussion of the relationship between concrete opportunities and movement types shows that variations in the patterns of mobilization may be explained, at least in part, by the fact that different movement types react differently to the POS. We may distinguish between two aspects covered by this idea, related to the two criteria for the definition of movement types. On the one hand, political opportunities are of variable *relevance* for different types of movements. Whereas for instrumental movements all four motivational factors may have an impact on their mobilization, for countercultural movements repression is the dominant factor, and subcultural movements are relatively independent from their political environment. On the other hand, the *consequences* of a given structural set of political opportunities vary from one movement type to the other. Thus, instrumental, countercultural, and subcultural movements do not respond in the same way to the formal openness or closure of the system, to a given strategy of the political authorities, or to a given configuration of power. In order to support these claims, we shall briefly present and discuss some data with regard to the level of mobilization, the action repertoire, reactions and alliances, and the dynamics of these three types of movements.

Level of Mobilization

Why have subcultural and countercultural movements been acting and mobilizing less than instrumental movements in all countries, even in the field of NSMs? If we consider the effect of the POS on the three types of movements, we can explain this. *Subcultural* movements can be expected to mobilize the least frequently, because of their strong internal orientation. This in itself implies a withdrawal from (external) political activity, particularly when the political system is not very open. Their identity-based logic of action, however, produces rather strong ties within the movement. Thus, although mobilization will not be very frequent, it can be massive.

Countercultural movements are also identity-based, but externally oriented. As a consequence, they can be expected to show a higher frequency of mobilization, especially where repression is strong. Yet their level of mobilization can hardly reach that of instrumental movements, because of the kind of protest events they produce. Radical actions are always less facilitated and more easily repressed than moderate ones. Hence, compared to instrumental movements, countercultural movements always face higher mobilization costs. For this reason, instrumental movements are expected to attain the highest level of mobilization. Table 4.1 gives some empirical support to the hypothesis linking the level of mobilization to the type of movement.

As we can see from the table, which reports (*a*) the percentages of unconventional protest events produced by each type of movement and (*b*) the percentages of people mobilized by each type in the four countries, the data confirm our expectations. It is clear that important and interesting differences

Table 4.1. Level of mobilization of the three movement types per country (unconventional events)

	France	Germany	Netherlands	Switzerland
a) Level of activity (percentages)				
Instrumental	89.7	79.8	72.9	66.8
Countercultural	8.1	17.6	21.5	28.9
Subcultural	2.2	2.6	5.6	4.3
Total	100%	100%	100%	100%
N	(737)	(1,770)	(863)	(772)
b) Volume of participation (percentages)				
Instrumental	99.0	96.7	93.7	91.7
Countercultural	0.0	2.3	2.5	6.6
Subcultural	1.0	1.0	3.8	1.7
Total	100%	100%	100%	100%
N	(737)	(1,770)	(863)	(772)

among movement types occur regarding both the number of protest events and the number of participants. In all countries, instrumental movements predominate by far among NSMs with respect to the level of activity as well as the volume of participation: the majority of people mobilized participate in instrumental movements. This may be surprising, given that a number of authors of the so-called new social movements approach (Melucci 1980; Offe 1985; Pizzorno 1978; Raschke 1985; Touraine 1978) argue that a shift has occurred away from the old "instrumental" paradigm toward a new paradigm in which identity-oriented action has become predominant. This new paradigm is considered to be absolutely predominant in NSMs.[2] Our data clearly contradict the claim of such a paradigm shift toward identity-oriented movements. Subcultural movements mobilize much less than instrumental movements. For their participants, the process of identity construction is the collective good and the predominant motivation for their action. The access to these movements is *exclusive* (Zald and Ash 1966): one has to possess or develop specific characteristics in order to participate in the movement. This has important consequences on the mobilization capacity of these movements, in contrast to instrumental movements, which can include more or less everybody. Whereas an individual's tie to instrumental movements is loose and inclusive, and many such ties may exist, the tie to the subcultural movement is exclusive but strong. Although the group involved in subcultural movements will be small, the participation rate can be relatively high. Although countercultural protest events rank second in frequency in all countries, few people participate in these often radical, exclusive actions. This largely confirms our expectation that countercultural movements mobilize less than instrumental movements. We may thus conclude that all identity-oriented movements are by and large relatively small.

Action Repertoire

The general orientation and the logic of action of movement types have probably the most important consequences on the action repertoire of NSMs. In other words, the action repertoire of social movements is not only dependent on the country-specific mix of opportunities, as we have shown in detail in the preceding chapters, but also on the type of movement. According to our general hypothesis, the three types of movements would use different forms of action when acting in the political space. Instrumental movements are influenced by all four motivational factors, and particularly by success chances. These movements aim primarily at changing existing politics without, however, seeking conflict as a goal in itself. Being oriented to obtaining political goals, they try to adapt their action repertoire to the external conditions. This, of course, explains why we find important variations across countries. But it also seems plausible to hypothesize the existence of strong cross-country similarities, if we compare this movement type to the other two.

In the four countries under study, the level of repression is usually low compared to some situations outside Western Europe. It is possible to make political demands through unconventional actions, which is not always the case outside Western Europe. As a consequence of such "democratic" conditions, instrumental movements are expected to adopt quite a moderate action repertoire in all four countries. Subcultural movements are also expected to act rather moderately, due to their relatively strong internal orientation. This characteristic provokes a withdrawal from political action when the outside conditions become too unfavorable. In this situation, participants prefer to avoid confrontations with political authorities. Thus subcultural movements make political demands generally when the conditions are not too bad — that is, when repression is low and some chances of success are present — leading to the use of moderate forms of action. These parameters change fundamentally with countercultural movements, which are expected to adopt a rather radical action repertoire. As we have defined them, countercultural movements reproduce their collective identity through interaction with adversaries, most notably with political authorities. Hence they often seek conflicting interactions with authorities. Such a confrontation can be reached only

Table 4.2. Action repertoire of the three movement types per country (percentages, unconventional events)

	France	Germany	Netherlands	Switzerland
Instrumental				
Demonstrative	64.8	73.8	65.6	88.0
Confrontational	17.7	16.8	24.6	6.6
Violent	17.5	9.4	9.8	5.4
Total	100%	100%	100%	100%
N	(661)	(1,413)	(629)	(516)
Countercultural				
Demonstrative	5.0	30.9	18.3	29.6
Confrontational	11.7	31.2	58.6	30.5
Violent	83.3	37.9	23.1	39.9
Total	100%	100%	100%	100%
N	(60)	(311)	(186)	(223)
Subcultural				
Demonstrative	93.8	84.8	91.7	97.0
Confrontational	6.2	8.7	6.3	3.0
Violent	0.0	6.5	2.0	0.0
Total	100%	100%	100%	100%
N	(16)	(46)	(48)	(33)

through quite radical forms of mobilization; otherwise the movement is left without a response. Table 4.2 shows the action repertoire of the three types of movements in the four countries.

In this table, we have reported the percentages of demonstrative, confrontational, and violent protest events produced by the three movement types in the four countries under study. Everywhere countercultural movements are the most radical ones. Indeed, most of the protest events they produce are confrontational or violent, and in none of the four countries do their demonstrative actions exceed one-third of the total number of actions. The confrontational character of these movements is certainly responsible for the fact that political authorities treat them in a more repressive way than other movements. Of course, participants in countercultural movements react to these often tough responses to their demands with more radical and violent actions. This results in a spiral of violence from which there is no easy way out. On the opposite side, subcultural movements are the most moderate in each country. In all four countries, demonstrative protest events prevail by and large. Instrumental movements also have a rather moderate action repertoire, but in general a less moderate one than that of subcultural movements. As we will see, this is caused by the different political status of many issues instrumental movements deal with as compared to the issues raised by subcultural movements, causing a more repressive reaction toward instrumental movements than toward subcultural ones, which in turn evokes somewhat more radical actions from the instrumental movements.

Reactions and Alliances

In line with our general hypothesis, we expect to find movement-type specific patterns of reactions by authorities and allies. The reactions of political authorities to social movements' actions can be illustrated by the level of repression in general and by the number of arrests per event in particular. We hypothesize that in all four countries the level of repression by the government will be highest for countercultural movements, even if these movements use the same action repertoire as the other types of movements. As we have seen, countercultural movements react strongly to the authorities, and vice versa: both sides seem more interested in conflict than in cooperation. Problems dealt with by countercultural movements represent no "positive" value for the authorities, and therefore we may expect repression to be strong in their case. The opposite holds for subcultural movements. These movements do not represent a "threat" for political authorities and, as we have seen, they do not act in a radical manner, so the level of repression they undergo should be quite low. We expect to find instrumental movements in between, for the same reasons we mentioned with regard to the action repertoire. Table 4.3 shows the level of repression of the three movement types by political authorities in the four countries. The table includes two kinds of data: (a) the percentages of demonstrative protest events that were repressed and (b) the average number of arrests for demonstrative protest events.

The results show that, according to both indicators, our expectations are largely confirmed. In each country, countercultural movements are more strongly repressed than instrumental and subcultural movements, and instrumental movements are more repressed than subcultural movements, even if these latter differences are less clear-cut in the Netherlands.[3] Thus governmental reactions to protest events show that political authorities value and treat the various types of movements differently. As table 4.3 shows, even if the countercultural movement acts in a demonstrative and peaceful manner, government reactions are more repressive.

Political allies have been said to form a principal component of the POS (see chapter 3 and Tarrow 1989b). We expect different types of movements to receive varying degrees of support from established allies. Both instrumental

Table 4.3. Level of repression of movement types per country
(unconventional demonstrative events)

	France	Germany	Netherlands	Switzerland
a) Percentages of repressed demonstrative events				
Instrumental	9.8 (428)	16.7 (1,043)	7.0 (412)	4.2 (454)
Countercultural	–[a]	39.6 (96)	29.4 (34)	16.7 (66)
Subcultural	0.0 (15)	10.3 (39)	6.8 (44)	0.0 (32)
b) Average number of arrests per demonstrative event				
Instrumental	0.2 (428)	4.1 (1,043)	0.1 (412)	0.0 (454)
Countercultural	–	14.6 (96)	1.2 (34)	0.4 (66)
Subcultural	0.0 (15)	0.0 (39)	0.4 (44)	0.0 (32)

Note: Number of cases in parentheses
[a]Fewer than ten cases

and subcultural movements are likely to enjoy the support of established allies, whereas the radical countercultural movements are expected to be more
isolated. This is largely due to the fact that established political actors, like
parties, cannot support too radical a social movement without running the
risk of losing part of their electoral support. Two kinds of external support
can be distinguished. First, there is organizational support: established political actors provide material (money, members, etc.) and symbolic (public
recognition, organizational skills, etc.) facilitation. Second, support may take
the form of common participation in protest events. Table 4.4 shows some
results with respect to the second kind of support for each movement type,
again for demonstrative events only.

   Support may come from political parties or from interest groups. In the
table we have merged them into a single category. In all four countries, countercultural movements are much less supported by external established actors than instrumental and subcultural movements, even if they use the same
action methods. The radicalism of the goals of the countercultural movements and their negative image in the general public contribute largely to
their isolation. We may note that in all countries, but in particular in Germany,
subcultural movements obtained a lot of support. This indicates that subcultural movements deal with particular types of issues. On the one hand, their
issues are not questions of state interest asking for (repressive) reactions
by the side of authorities. On the other hand, the "symbolic" character of the
issues makes them attractive for parties to express their solidarity; these
movements provide opportunities to allies to profile themselves without many
costs involved. Parties that address themselves to groups with strong identities ("communities") may hope for a positive electoral effect.

Table 4.4. **External support to movement types per country**
(percentages of supported unconventional demonstrative events)

	France	Germany	Netherlands	Switzerland
Instrumental	30.8 (428)	34.8 (1,043)	18.7 (412)	16.5 (454)
Countercultural	–	17.7 (96)	2.9 (34)	3.0 (66)
Subcultural	6.7 (15)	35.9 (39)	13.6 (44)	6.3 (32)

Note: Number of cases in parentheses

Hence, when political allies want to support unconventional political action, they have different patterns of behavior depending on the type of movement. This is bound to have important consequences on the development of NSMs.

The Dynamics of Movement Types

Changes in the POS are largely responsible for variations in the level of mobilization and for shifts in the action repertoire of NSMs in a country. In this chapter, we show that within a country, the development of these NSMs may also vary depending on their movement type. Changes in POS—more specifically, in the power configuration—do not affect all NSMs in the same way, regardless of their general orientation and their logic of action. Let us assume that there is a change in the configuration of power. More specifically, we assume changes in the position of the Socialist Party—from the government to the opposition and vice versa. As we saw in chapter 3, when Socialist parties are in the opposition, they tend in most countries to facilitate NSMs, whereas when they are in government, facilitation diminishes. On the basis of our previous discussion, we would expect instrumental movements to be most affected by a change of the Socialist Party from the government to the opposition and vice versa. If the Socialists are in government, these movements experience a situation of "reform"—they will not mobilize as long as the government is working in their direction. Countercultural movements, on the contrary, will not demobilize since for this type of movement nothing changes; Social Democrats never support them, either in opposition or in government, and success chances are by definition of little relevance for them. Subcultural movements, finally, will be less active regarding their explicitly political aims when the Socialists are in government; in general, however, they will be more stable than instrumental movements since identity production always remains one of their tasks. When the Socialists are in opposition, facilitation will support the mobilization of both the instrumental and the subcultural movement types, whereas the mobilization pattern of the

Table 4.5. Changes in the configuration of power—Socialists in government or in opposition—and level of activity of movement types in France, Germany, and the Netherlands (average number of protest events per year per period, unconventional events)

	Instrumental	Countercultural	Subcultural
France			
1975-81 (opposition)	61.5	4.5	1.3
1981-89 (government)	32.4	3.6	0.8
N	(661)	(60)	(16)
Germany			
1975-82 (government)	56.5	26.5	2.1
1982-89 (opposition)	127.0	15.2	3.9
N	(1,413)	(311)	(46)
Netherlands			
1975-77 (government)	14.4	9.5	2.0
1977-81 (opposition)	28.8	15.1	4.5
1981-82 (government)	80.5	18.4	0.0
1982-89 (opposition)	45.3	10.0	3.7
N	(629)	(186)	(48)

countercultural movement will not change that much since facilitation will not occur. Table 4.5 shows the relative level of activity of the three movement types in periods based on changes in the position of the Socialist Party (in the government or in the opposition).[4]

The table reports the average number of protest events per year for each period that Socialists were in government or in opposition. In France, the coming to power of the Socialist Party indeed seems to have had dramatic consequences on instrumental and subcultural movements. As expected, countercultural movements felt the consequences of this change to a lesser extent: countercultural movements do not seem to have been heavily influenced since they were not supported by the Socialists anyway. In Germany as in France, the Social Democratic Party's move into the opposition facilitated instrumental and subcultural movements. Countercultural movements, however, declined during right-wing government, which may be an indication that the mobilization logic of the countercultural type is the inverse of the other two: whereas instrumental and subcultural movements are largely dependent on the support of the Socialists, radical movements consider the Socialists "enemies" when they are in power for allegedly "betraying" their left-wing ideals. The situation in the Netherlands partly confirms the German picture. Subcultural movements, and to a lesser extent instrumental movements, profited from the Socialist Party's exit from government. This does not apply, however, to instrumental movements in the exceptional and short period of 1981–82, when the peace movement was successfully mobilizing against a split center-left government. The countercultural movements did not follow the exact inverse pattern either, since their mobilization increased somewhat in the period 1977–81 when the Socialists were in opposition, whereas we would have expected an increase during periods of left-wing government (1975–77), as was the case in Germany. The development in 1981–82 is more in line with the idea that countercultural movements mobilize against (center-)left governments: Dutch countercultural movements peaked in these years and declined when the left again went into opposition.

Hence, changes in the configuration of power have different consequences on the level of mobilization of different types of movements. Instrumental movements respond to such changes with an increase (Socialists in opposition) or a decrease (Socialists in government) in activity, whereas countercultural movements are either less affected by these changes or show the inverse pattern: mobilization against the left in government. The fact that countercultural movements are less affected by changes at the national level is also due to the local character of the squatters' movement.

The results with regard to subcultural movements enable us to understand the results of the previous section: these movements only act politically in favorable circumstances. The fact that their level of mobilization modified in important ways when changes in the configuration of power occurred during the period under study seems to contradict to our hypothesis that subcultural movements are less influenced by external conditions than instrumental and countercultural movements. Perhaps we should reformulate this idea, because subcultural movements also depend on political opportunities to the extent that they act in the political arena. In their case, just as for instrumental movements, the Socialist Party becomes a powerful ally when it is in the opposition. We may thus think of positive changes in the configuration of power as a means for subcultural movements to develop their movement side, whereas in unfavorable circumstances the subcultural side becomes predominant. This "double face" guarantees subcultural movements more continuity than the other movement types: the impact of changes in the power configuration upon subcultural movements seems to be mitigated by their subcultural underground.

Social Movement Issues in Policy Domains

So far we have discussed the role of movement types for explaining differences between movements within countries and similarities across countries. Yet variations are also observable within movement types, most notably within instrumental movements. Neither the general POS argument put forward in the preceding chapters nor its elaboration based upon the distinction of movement types outlined in this chapter can explain such variations in a satisfactory manner. Here we would like to indicate a possible way of going beyond such limitations. The general idea is that varying political opportunities exist that act specifically upon different components of NSMs: to a certain extent, different parts of the social movement sector have a specific POS. This derives from the fact that not all issues movements deal with have the same relevance within the political arena. Across countries, however, many similarities in the "position" of issues come to the fore. For instance, nuclear energy is considered a crucial issue by members of all political systems sharing a faith in technological progress as a fundamental source of welfare. Similarly, there is rather general agreement in considering national defense and security as crucial tasks of the state.

High-Profile and Low-Profile Policy Domains

Since issues are linked to each other according to various criteria, we can adopt the concept of *policy domain* in order to delimit sets of issues.[5] A policy domain may be defined as "a basic policy-making subsystem within a larger polity" (Pappi and Knoke 1991: 184). Policy domains include "all arenas into which governmental authority has intruded" (Laumann and Knoke 1987: 10). Hence many of them are crucial concerns of social movements and, more specifically, of NSMs. The various issues reaching the political agenda concern different policy domains. Usually a social movement raises issues concerning more than one policy domain. The ecology movement is the most typical example in this regard.

Social movements are confronted with various reactions of political authorities and allies in different policy domains. As far as these reactions are concerned, we can make a distinction between *high-profile* and *low-profile* policy domains (Duyvendak 1992: 248–50). Whether a policy domain is considered to be high-profile or low-profile depends on how authorities and allies define it on the basis of their conception of the core tasks and the core interests of the state. According to the way they are defined by members of the system, some issues and the corresponding challengers find the political system to be less accessible than others. The relevance of an issue in the dominant cleavage structure, as well as its perception by authorities and allies, are both factors that determine its priority on the political agenda. Some issues do not even penetrate into the political arena at all. According to the political agenda-building approach, the openness and closure of the political arena is determined by the views of the members of a polity: "In the interest of their own political survival, leaders and organizations must make sure that issues which threaten their existence, their own allocations of political space, are not admitted to the political arena. Toward some species of conflict they must remain impenetrable" (Crenson 1971: 23). As we saw in chapter 1, organizations representing old cleavages either organized new issues out of the political arena or admitted "new" issues on the condition that they were formulated in old terms. Here we make the point that among NSMs there also exist differences as to the degree to which they are "acceptable" for both political authorities and allies, depending on the policy domain's profile, that is, the type of issues the movement deals with and the potential threat they represent for the authorities.

The notion of the status of a policy domain in the system—high-profile or low-profile—implies a hierarchy of political issues. We may select a number of criteria that enable us to distinguish high-profile from low-profile policy domains. First, the amount of material resources involved in the policy domain strongly influences its profile. The more resources are involved, the more threatening a social movement may be for political authorities. As a consequence, the high-profile character of the policy domain increases. The amount of resources is not limited to past expenses, but concerns future investments as well. Second, the power at stake is one of the crucial factors contributing to a policy domain's profile. Thus a high-profile policy domain is one in which, if challenged by a social movement, the power held by established actors is the most endangered or in which the power they may potentially acquire is fundamentally contested. Third, a policy domain's profile is also determined by its electoral relevance. This factor refers to the possibility that a challenge could threaten the survival of the government. A fourth factor influencing a policy domain's profile is the extent to which the policy domain concerns the "national interest." The more the national interest is concerned, the more a challenge is seen as a threat.

Depending on whether the issue at stake concerns a high-profile or a low-profile policy domain, established political actors—authorities and allies—behave differently and, consequently, political opportunities vary accordingly. With regard to high-profile policy domains, challengers face a rather closed political system. Political authorities tend to follow a more exclusive strategy and to concentrate their efforts on defeating challengers. In doing so, they are often supported by the lobbying activity of economic interests. Because of the large amount of resources involved in high-profile policy domains, pressure by lobbies and interest groups against the challengers' goals becomes more important. Indeed, in such policy domains we find the most powerful interest groups, which are able to prevent challengers from gaining access to the system. Moreover, the public administration is willing to invest a large amount of resources in the struggle against challenging groups. As a consequence, high-profile policy domains offer a relatively unfavorable mix of concrete opportunities to challengers deriving from the closure of the system in such policy domains. Facilitation is rather limited; repression may be present when challengers use radical action forms and success chances are rather low. Even when direct-democratic procedures are at the challengers' disposal, success chances deriving from the use of this institutional possibility are expected to be quite low. On the other hand, low-profile policy domains tend to be more open to challengers. The opposite arguments may be put forward to show how in this case concrete opportunities represent a more favorable setting to a social movement's mobilization. The administrative arena tends to be more open and more responsive. Therefore facilitation is larger, repression practically absent, success chances higher, and so on. Moreover, when direct-democratic procedures are present, the chances of a positive result are higher than in high-profile policy domains.

As a consequence of the relative closure of high-profile policy domains and the relative openness of low-profile policy domains, we expect the level of mobilization with regard to the former to be low and radical, and, with regard to the latter, to be high and moderate. But, as we have already pointed out, the question of the status of new issues concerns not only political authorities but potential *allies* as well. At first glance, the allies of the NSMs—parties of the left—should support SMOs and actions within high-profile policy domains more strongly and more frequently, for the latter can be more "lucrative" in electoral terms than low-profile policy domains.[6]

In what follows, we shall try to identify policy domains within the NSM sector. We shall mainly discuss the instrumental movements, because differences in profile within the two other types are, generally speaking, small: countercultural movements deal with high-profile issues, subcultural movements with rather low-profile ones.

Policy Domains within Instrumental NSMs

We earlier distinguished between three instrumental movements within the NSM sector: the peace movement, the ecology movement, and the solidarity movement. Each of these movements can be further subdivided into policy domains. Here we would like to propose a distinction between seven policy domains that treat issues raised by NSMs. With regard to the concerns of the peace movement, we may distinguish between nuclear weapons policy and national defense policy. With regard to the concerns of the ecology movement, we have identified three policy domains: energy policy, transport policy, and environmental protection policy. As to the concerns of the solidarity movement, we make a distinction between the immigration policy field and the domain of international solidarity. Let us take a closer look at these seven policy domains.[7]

Nuclear weapons. This is a single-issue policy domain that is related to the international security system and that is part of the foreign policy of a given country. Since the emergence of the NSMs in the 1970s, their mobilization within this policy domain has mainly concerned the stationing of cruise missiles in some West European members of NATO, among them Germany and the Netherlands. Even if the protest did not seem to seriously threaten the institutions and the established political actors, the trustworthiness of these countries as members of NATO was at stake, as well as the credibility of NATO policy in general. In the other countries, which include France and Switzerland, the question of the stationing of cruise missiles was almost a nonissue. The fact that mobilization around nuclear weapons was almost absent in France — one of the two European nuclear powers — does not imply, however, that in France the maintenance of the *force de frappe* is considered a state task of minor importance. On Swiss territory, nuclear weapons were not installed, nor were any plans developed to do so. This suggests that we consider the nuclear weapons issue as a high-profile policy domain in Germany, the Netherlands, and France, and as a low-profile policy domain in Switzerland.

National defense. With respect to issues other than nuclear weapons, the peace movement is the best example of a social movement that raises issues of national interest. These are typically considered by political power-holders as their own affair. Movements mobilizing on the basis of such issues will, at the outset, often be depicted as antinational forces supporting the interests of other countries and ideologies. Peace issues normally only manage to enter the political agenda temporarily, under exceptional circumstances, when conflict among members of the political system can no longer be "hidden." Formal integration of movement organizations in advisory boards, co-optation of movement members within bodies of public administration, subsidies of national or local governments — these measures are rarely taken with respect to the peace movement. This formal closure is, however, not necessarily linked to exclusive or repressive informal strategies. As long as movements do not pursue radical goals with radical means, and to the extent that they mobilize massively but peacefully, governments will not react violently. In contrast to other issues, however, the chance that governments will respond positively to the demands raised by the movement is very small. Thus national defense policy is a typical high-profile policy domain.

Energy. The national interest is at stake in other policy domains as well. The antinuclear energy movement is often confronted with the argument that the energy supply is not a matter for the street, but that it only concerns scientists and politicians. In all countries, movements that challenge the state's nuclear power policy run the risk — as long as they are small — of encountering quite repressive government strategies, absence of facilitation, and limited chances of success. But they are "assured" of some form of reaction; these movements cannot be "ignored" as easily as movements dealing with (nonnuclear) ecological or solidarity issues. Since it is a rather new movement, the antinuclear movement has fewer historical bonds with the main left-wing parties than do, for instance, the peace movement or the solidarity movement. The result is that state repression is not tempered by facilitation on the part of allies. Because of the threatening character of the issues related to nuclear energy, energy policy clearly is a high-profile policy domain.

Transports. Whereas neither the peace movement nor the antinuclear movement have actually received state subsidies, the moderate parts of the ecology and the solidarity movements are often (partially) co-opted by authorities. This happens, for instance, within the transport policy domain, which treats all problems related to the construction and management of road, rail, and water networks in a given country. The nonthreatening character of most of the movement's goals within transport policy suggests that we are dealing with a rather low-profile policy domain. The construction of airports is, however, an exception to the rule that transport is a rather low-profile area. In all countries, airport construction and management is a top priority, resulting in harsh confrontations between challengers of these projects and authorities. Therefore, the overall conclusion should be that transport is an issue somewhere in between high- and low-profile.

Environment. What we have said with respect to most of the transport issues holds even more for another part of the ecology movement: the one acting within the policy domain of environmental protection. In this case, the ecology movement is not so threatening for political authorities. This fact leads us to consider this policy domain to be low-profile.

Immigration. The solidarity movement is a broad movement in which there are many non- or less conflicting issues, clustered in subunits such as human rights, Third World activism, and support to specific political regimes. Generally speaking, the solidarity movement as a whole seems to be rather non-threatening for political authorities, and therefore rather low-profile, for its protest is generally addressed to foreign political authorities or supranational institutions. Nevertheless, one of its components may be thought to have more of a high-profile character, since it deals with an issue of national interest, one that has important consequences on the whole political system. We are referring to the immigration policy, which concerns all problems having to do with foreigners living or aspiring to live in a given country. More precisely, this policy domain includes problems having to do with political refugees, with immigrants in general, and with racism. Although this policy domain is less high-profile than, for instance, the national defense policy or the energy policy, it seems to deal more with questions of national interest ("Who is a citizen?") than the rest of the solidarity movement.

International solidarity. Another component of the solidarity movement is concerned with issues pertaining to the international aid policy. This is clearly a low-profile policy domain, because the issues raised by the movement are not very threatening for national political authorities. Such a relative lack of threat stems from the fact that these national authorities have less of a say in matters of this policy domain, although we should not forget that any mobilization related to this policy domain is very heterogeneous and includes many different issues.

Before turning toward an empirical illustration of our argument, we would like to add two important qualifications. First, the suggested classification of policy domains within NSMs is rather vague. A policy domain's borders are not as clear-cut as our description presupposes. On the contrary, we have to take into account the interdependence between political issues. Therefore, an issue is not easily placed into one policy domain or the other. Second, the relevance of an issue or of a policy domain varies from one country to another. This is a result of the fact that political authorities do not have the same priorities or interests in the different countries, as the example of nuclear weapons illustrates. Moreover, such priorities may change over time.

Policy Domains and Mobilization by Instrumental Movements

Next we shall present some data in order to provide an empirical illustration of our argument. It is important to stress that what follows has to be considered only as a tentative test of our main argument. Moreover, the fact that the definition of policy domains as high-profile or low-profile may change across countries as well as over time prevents us from obtaining a clear-cut empirical picture.

Since our ideas about high- and low-profile policy domains presuppose divergent reactions of authorities toward challengers on the various fields, we should first look at data regarding the level of repression of instrumental movements within the seven policy domains in the four countries. As table 4.6 shows, our idea that important differences exist in the reaction of authorities regarding specific topics makes sense.

The table gives (*a*) the percentages of protest events repressed by political authorities within each policy domain and (*b*) the average number of arrests that occurred during those events. Some interesting results indicate a rather clear relationship between a policy domain's profile and the level of repression. Overall, challengers acting within high-profile policy domains seem, indeed, to be more repressed than challengers acting within low-profile policy domains. In all countries, the percentages of repressed events and the average number of arrests are higher for high-profile topics than low-profile ones. It appears that, on average, challengers acting within policy domains like national defense or energy have faced a more hostile context than, for instance, challengers acting within the policy domains of transports or environmental protection. This tendency is particularly evident when we look at the average number of arrests. These data make clear that it makes sense to distinguish between nuclear energy and environmental issues in an analysis of the ecology movement: across all countries, nuclear energy is more "defended" by authorities. The results pertaining to the peace movement show that in Germany, the Netherlands, and France, the profile of nuclear weapons is indeed much "higher" than in Switzerland. The issues of the solidarity movement are more difficult to classify. Nonetheless, the hypothesis that "immigration" is a high-profile issue whereas "international solidarity" is low-profile seems to find some support in the data. Mobilizations around immigration issues were quite strongly repressed in all four countries, especially in Germany—though not in terms of arrests—compared to other issues. Hence concrete opportunities really seem to be more favorable within low-profile policy domains, where the political system is more open.

Since the concrete opportunities, such as repression, vary across policy domains, the action forms used by NSMs are also expected to vary according to the policy domains. High-profile policy domains are expected to lead to

Table 4.6. Level of repression of instrumental movements regarding their unconventional actions in seven policy domains per country

	France	Germany	Netherlands	Switzerland
a) Percentages of repressed events				
National defense	15.5 (58)	19.2 (120)	55.0 (40)	6.1 (33)
Energy	18.1 (282)	27.7 (310)	34.3 (67)	11.0 (91)
Immigration	9.4 (127)	37.0 (235)	14.3 (77)	12.5 (48)
Nuclear weapons	11.1 (9)	24.9 (273)	16.1 (155)	–
Average high-profile	13.5 (476)	27.2 (938)	29.9 (339)	9.9 (172)
Transports	8.3 (36)	27.2 (136)	14.3 (28)	1.4 (74)
Environment	11.4 (44)	4.0 (125)	12.0 (75)	2.1 (47)
International solidarity	16.7 (36)	24.0 (125)	10.9 (147)	6.6 (136)
Nuclear weapons	–	–	–	0.0 (12)
Average low-profile	12.1 (116)	18.4 (386)	12.4 (250)	2.5 (269)
b) Average number of arrests				
National defense	0.5 (58)	4.8 (120)	1.9 (40)	0.2 (33)
Energy	0.2 (282)	12.0 (310)	1.5 (67)	0.8 (91)
Immigration	0.2 (127)	5.1 (235)	1.2 (77)	0.0 (48)
Nuclear weapons	0.0 (9)	10.6 (273)	0.7 (155)	–
Average high-profile	0.2 (476)	8.1 (938)	1.4 (339)	0.3 (172)
Transports	0.0 (36)	2.9 (136)	0.1 (28)	0.0 (74)
Environment	0.2 (44)	0.3 (125)	0.1 (75)	0.0 (47)
International solidarity	0.1 (36)	7.8 (125)	0.2 (147)	0.0 (136)
Nuclear weapons	–	–	–	0.0 (12)
Average low-profile	0.1 (116)	3.6 (386)	0.1 (250)	0.0 (269)

Note: Number of cases in parentheses

a more radical mobilization than low-profile policy domains. Table 4.7 presents some data showing the action repertoire of NSMs within each of the seven policy domains in the four countries in order to test this hypothesis.

The table gives the percentages of (*a*) confrontational and violent protest events and (*b*) conventional protest events. If we compare the action repertoires across countries and across policy domains, we find some empirical support for the hypothesis mentioned above. In all countries, proponents of high-profile issues use more confrontational and violent action methods, whereas low-profile issues are predominant among the conventional events (with the exception of Switzerland, where 40 to 50 percent of both high- and low-profile events are conventional). In particular, mobilization within the national defense and the energy policy domains, which we have defined as high-profile, is more radical than mobilization relative to the other categories (except for Germany, where "national defense" is less confrontational and violent than,

Table 4.7. Action repertoire of instrumental movements in seven policy domains per country

	France	Germany	Netherlands	Switzerland
a) Percentages of confrontational and violent events				
National defense	51.6 (64)	12.1 (182)	58.4 (48)	10.5 (86)
Energy	34.7 (311)	22.3 (422)	35.8 (81)	6.7 (223)
Immigration	16.7 (168)	15.6 (303)	17.7 (118)	8.0 (100)
Nuclear weapons	36.4 (11)	20.5 (346)	17.2 (197)	–
Average high-profile	34.8 (554)	17.6 (1,252)	25.2 (444)	8.4 (407)
Transports	25.6 (43)	22.7 (215)	15.8 (38)	0.0 (325)
Environment	17.3 (81)	7.7 (297)	31.5 (130)	1.6 (182)
International solidarity	36.7 (49)	17.8 (191)	21.5 (195)	5.5 (200)
Nuclear weapons	–	–	–	0.0 (12)
Average low-profile	26.5 (173)	16.1 (703)	22.9 (363)	1.8 (719)
b) Percentages of conventional events				
National defense	9.4 (64)	34.1 (182)	16.7 (48)	50.0 (86)
Energy	8.4 (311)	26.5 (422)	17.3 (81)	44.8 (223)
Immigration	24.4 (168)	22.4 (303)	34.7 (188)	51.0 (100)
Nuclear weapons	18.2 (11)	21.1 (346)	21.3 (197)	–
Average high-profile	15.1 (554)	26.0 (1,252)	22.5 (444)	48.6 (407)
Transports	16.3 (43)	36.3 (215)	26.3 (38)	35.1 (325)
Environment	45.7 (81)	57.9 (297)	42.3 (130)	59.9 (182)
International solidarity	26.5 (49)	34.6 (191)	24.6 (195)	31.0 (200)
Nuclear weapons	–	–	–	33.3 (12)
Average low-profile	29.5 (173)	42.9 (703)	31.1 (363)	39.8 (719)

Note: Number of cases in parentheses

for instance, "transports" and "international solidarity"). We may conclude that the less facilitative situation of these issues really seems to have some influence on the action repertoire of NSMs. Yet there are important exceptions to this rule. They result in part from the difficulty of giving a clear-cut definition of the policy domains concerned by demands of NSMs. But they are above all due to the varying character and meaning of certain issues across countries, which is the main obstacle to an empirical analysis like the one we are trying to make. Nevertheless, at least in the case of the peace and the ecology movements, the hypothesis of a link between a policy domain's profile and the degree of radicalism of the mobilization occurring within it seems to find some support.

The level of repression of instrumental movements in seven policy domains and the action forms used by movements have, of course, effects upon the mobilization level of movements. Table 4.8 shows the level of mobilization within each of the seven policy domains in the four countries.

Table 4.8. Level of mobilization of instrumental movements in seven policy domains per country (conventional events, direct-democratic events, and petitions excluded)

	France	Germany	Netherlands	Switzerland
a) Level of activity (percentages)				
National defense	9.9	8.7	6.9	8.2
Energy	47.4	23.6	11.8	22.7
Immigration	21.5	18.2	12.7	11.3
Nuclear weapons	1.5	21.0	25.9	–
Total high-profile	80.3	71.5	57.3	42.2
Transports	5.8	10.0	4.8	14.5
Environment	7.5	9.1	12.7	10.3
International solidarity	6.3	9.5	25.4	31.1
Nuclear weapons	–	–	–	1.8
Total low-profile	19.6	28.6	42.9	57.7
High-low-profile ratio	4.1	2.5	1.3	0.7
Total	100%	100%	100%	100%
N	(586)	(1,279)	(568)	(379)
b) Volume of participation (percentages)				
National defense	4.3	6.1	1.8	7.1
Energy	23.7	17.2	11.2	32.1
Immigration	67.5	4.9	5.3	8.4
Nuclear weapons	0.8	61.6	68.0	–
Total high-profile	96.3	89.8	86.3	47.6
Transports	0.8	4.4	2.5	7.9
Environment	1.6	2.1	1.5	12.8
International solidarity	1.1	3.7	9.5	18.7
Nuclear weapons	–	–	–	13.0
Total low-profile	3.5	10.2	13.5	52.4
High-low-profile ratio	9.7	2.5	5.4	0.2
Total	100%	100%	100%	100%
N	(727)	(1,956)	(807)	(1,128)

The table shows (*a*) the percentage of protest events and (*b*) the percentage of participants mobilized. In this table, we observe once again important differences within the same country and, parallel to them, important similarities across countries. The level of mobilization varies greatly from one policy domain to the other, especially when it is measured by the volume of participation. But such differences are also striking with respect to the level of activity. Whereas (nuclear) energy is very mobilizing in all four countries, environment and transports attract fewer participants; whereas nuclear weapons is a highly mobilizing issue in Germany and the Netherlands, it attracts fewer people in a country like Switzerland where it is a low-profile issue.

However, table 4.8 also shows that the high-low-profile ratio varies greatly from country to country. The differences among countries are striking. Switzerland in particular seems to deviate from the general trend that mobilization around high-profile issues is more frequent and massive than around low-profile issues. How to understand that in Switzerland, at least in terms of mobilization, the distinction between high- and low-profile issues seems to lose its relevance? In countries where either the formal institutional structure, the prevailing strategies of political authorities, or both are closed — the Netherlands, Germany, and France, respectively — NSMs have mobilized more with respect to high-profile policy domains than in low-profile ones. By contrast, in Switzerland, where the political system is open according to both dimensions of the POS, they have mobilized most with respect to low-profile policy domains. Moreover, it does not seem accidental that the two most different cases in our POS typology (France and Switzerland) are located at the extremes, whereas the two intermediary cases (Germany and the Netherlands) stand in between. These results suggest that the more closed the political system, the more the protest tends to concentrate on a few specific, highly politicized and central issues (central in the view of the members of the system). By contrast, the more open the system, the more the protest addresses rather "apolitical" and secondary issues. This is a very interesting result, which calls for an explanation. In closed political systems, political authorities concentrate their (hard) reaction on the most threatening issues. Mobilization addressing low-profile policy domains is often left without a response, since the state can afford to ignore it. This different treatment, combined with the low degree of access to the system, stimulates mobilization directed at high-profile policy domains and discourages mobilization addressing low-profile policy domains, for, in the former case, challengers are called to action through the increasing threat to which they are subject, whereas in the latter case they would abandon the action because of the low chances of success. This is what happens in France, for instance. By contrast, in open political systems like Switzerland, mobilization directed at low-profile policy domains is high, because authorities cannot ignore issues (since challengers have the capacity to put issues on the political agenda), and consequently, allies facilitate low-profile issues as well. This may explain why, with regard to the mobilization data, the cleavage between high- and low-profile issues is less clear-cut in Switzerland.

High-Profile and Low-Profile Movements

Policy domains, as our results generally attest, are a good way to show how political authorities behave differently according to whether the challengers are addressing more threatening, or less threatening, issues. In fact, challengers that address issues concerning policy domains considered crucial by the authorities and other members of the political system are confronted with a more closed POS than other, less threatening ones. Yet at this point it is important to go back to single movements within the NSM sector. Political issues concerning specific policy domains are carried by social movements or parts of them, like SMOs. Parallels in movement development from country to country can be explained if we take into account the fact that the importance of different movements for politics varies in a more or less comparable way within each country; that is, political agendas concerning policy domains addressed by NSMs resemble each other across countries (apart from the nuclear weapons issue in case of Switzerland). On the basis of the more or less threatening character of the different issues raised by NSMs, as it results from our discussion about policy domains, it appears that of the *instrumental* movements the peace movement and the antinuclear movement have to be considered as high-profile. As we have already said, the peace movement is the best example of a movement that addresses issues of national interest, and such issues are often considered by political authorities as their affair. As we have also pointed out, national interest is also at stake in the case of the antinuclear movement. The *countercultural* squatters' movement also attacks one of the state's fundamental responsibilities: the protection of private property. Conversely, the other parts of the ecology movement, the solidarity movement, and the *subcultural* gay, lesbian, and women's movements can be considered as low-profile, which do not threaten in such a dramatic way the core interests and tasks of the state.

The fact that high-profile movements face a more closed POS than low-profile movements does not necessarily imply a lack of political allies. Thus, as we have seen, although the peace movement does not have much access to the system, it is frequently supported by allies. Indeed, the peace movement is a typical example of a movement that is supported by allies, on the one hand, while, on the other hand, the state remains closed, even when its political friends are in power. The ecology movement, in contrast, has a high degree of access to the system, but does not have at its disposal a comparable support by allies. The concrete opportunities of the ecology movement—with the exception of the antinuclear movement—are the exact opposite of those of the peace movement: the former is normally confronted with an open state and little support by the traditional left-wing parties, whereas the latter is not facilitated by the state but by allies. This results in a different relationship between the level of mobilization and the organizational infrastructure of these two movements. The peace movement is expected to have a weaker organizational infrastructure than the ecology movement, because it lacks formal access to the system; the ecology movement is expected to have a more restricted mobilization capacity than the well-facilitated peace movement. Table 4.9 shows two indicators of the organizational infrastructure (the number of members and the level of resources) of some important SMOs and the mobilization capacity of five NSMs.

The difference between high-profile movements and low-profile movements with regard to the number of members, the mobilization capacity, and the level of resources is quite striking. The latter have many more members and far greater financial resources than the former, but fewer participants in action. In particular, the contrast between the ecology and peace movements—the two most important movements of the eighties—shows that similar instrumental movements may be very different with respect to their organizational infrastructure and the number of people mobilized during the last decade.

Conclusion

This chapter represents an attempt to apply the political process model to a level of analysis other than the one usually adopted. In general, researchers trying to show how the political context influences social movements and their mobilization check for differences between single movements or clusters of movements—as, for instance, the NSM sector—in different national contexts. Thus they can stress some structural factors that have an impact on the level of mobilization, the action repertoire, the movement's organization, and so on. Such an endeavor is also the main purpose of this book. Yet, in this chapter we have tried to add a new element to the theory of POS, with the intention of improving our knowledge of the mechanisms that regulate collective action. More precisely, we took into account not only regularities across countries but also across sets of movements and across parts of movements. In doing so, we have put forward two main arguments. First, we have

Table 4.9. Constituency, level of resources, and level of mobilization of five new social movements in four countries

	Ecology	Peace	Solidarity	Autonomous	Gay
a) Average level of membership of SMOs in four countries in 1989 per movement					
Per SMO	91,800	5,300	15,500	880	5,000
Per million inhabitants	5,450	270	1,020	110	170
N	(27)	(15)	(32)	(6)	(16)
b) Average level of financial resources of SMOs in four countries in 1989 per movement (thousands of dollars)					
Per SMO	4,390	330	1,850	170	720
Per million inhabitants	235	8	144	24	14
N	(31)	(12)	(31)	(6)	(9)

c) Total level of mobilization of five social movements in four countries 1975–89[a]

	Absolute level
Peace movement	9,099,079
Ecology movement	3,383,546
Solidarity movement	2,024,453
Autonomous movement	515,368
Gay movement	118,497

Note: Parts (*a*) and (*b*) are taken from Kriesi 1995.
[a]Petitions and festivals excluded

tried to show that the way in which movements perceive and react upon concrete opportunities is determined by their typical logic of action and by their general orientation. As has been shown, political authorities, in turn, have a specific reaction pattern to each movement type as well: authorities are well aware of the different degree to which the types of movements pose a direct challenge. Countercultural movements are always considered a threat, resulting in repressive reactions, whereas subcultural movements are either ignored or appeased. Second, focusing on instrumental movements, we have related differences within this type to the more or less challenging character of political issues raised by these movements. The concrete opportunities of each instrumental movement vary according to the political evaluation of its issues. Here we have proposed to cluster the issues raised by NSMs according to the policy domain they deal with. Challengers acting within high-profile policy domains—that is, raising threatening issues—are confronted with a rather closed system, whereas challengers acting within low-profile policy domains face a rather open system; with regard to the former, the strategies of political authorities will be exclusive; with regard to the latter they will be inclusive. Moreover, not only do the authorities' strategies vary from policy domain to policy domain, but allies' strategies vary across domains as well, which adds a further element of variation within a given political context.

All this results in rather different settings for social movements, dealing with several policy domains. These differences in the political context can help to explain contrasts in movement development within countries and similarities across countries.

Chapter 5

The Dynamics of Protest Waves

In the preceding chapters, we have discussed differences and similarities in the mobilization of new social movements across countries and across movements. We now focus on a third dimension: the dynamics of NSMs over time. This dimension was touched upon in chapter 3, where we analyzed the impact of discrete changes in political opportunity structures on the level of mobilization of NSMs. However, this analysis remained confined to a static comparison of mobilization levels before and after changes in POS, and leaves us with a number of questions as to the subsequent development of NSMs. We have, for instance, shown that there are important differences among countries in the action repertoires of NSMs. But are these repertoires constant within each country, or do they also fluctuate over time in systematic ways? Another question concerns the sudden character of the expansion of NSMs at the beginning of the 1980s in Germany, the Netherlands, and Switzerland. After all, the POS changes that triggered this expansion were relatively gradual. And, perhaps most important, why did the level of mobilization in these countries decline again after a certain period of time? Again, POS provides an insufficient explanation. The conservative backlash within the Dutch Social Democratic Party may explain why decline was relatively pronounced in the Netherlands. However, this leaves unexplained why protest also declined in West Germany after 1986, even though, with the opening up of the Social Democrats and the increasing success of the Green party, the NSMs' opportunity structure seemed more favorable than ever before.

The dynamic analysis of mobilization that these questions call for is not an easy task. Tarrow has called this "the largest current problem in collective action research" (1988: 435), and McAdam, McCarthy, and Zald (1988: 728) cited "our relatively underdeveloped knowledge about the dynamics of collective action past the emergence of a movement" as being among "the most glaring deficiencies in the literature" (see also Rucht 1990b: 168; McAdam 1983: 735). To keep the problem manageable, we will therefore focus in this chapter on one specific — but very important — object of analysis, which has commanded appreciable attention in the recent literature: the phenomenon of protest waves or cycles.

Protests tend to be strongly clustered in large waves that wash over a country and sometimes even have a worldwide character. The 1960s, for instance, saw a more or less simultaneous increase in the level of mobilization of a wide variety of social movements across the industrialized countries. Interestingly, despite strong cross-country differences in political opportunities and protest themes, the trajectories followed by the different national protest waves during this period displayed several remarkable similarities. For instance, the waves tended to emerge outside established organizations, among loosely structured organizations, subcultures, and networks. The action forms employed by pioneer activists across the Western world also shared many features. The initial action repertoire did not consist of mass demonstrations, lobbying, or violence, but of disruptive actions like bus boycotts, faculty occupations, or sit-ins. In many countries, moreover, processes of institutionalization, on the one hand, and radicalization, on the other, accompanied the decline of the 1960s protest wave. Everywhere, the 1960s wave gave rise to the emergence of new professional SMOs, lobby organizations, or — especially in Europe — new-left political parties. Moreover, the protests did not leave established politics unaffected. They led to programmatic renewal within institutions like political parties, labor unions, universities, and churches, and in many cases helped to bring reform coalitions to power. Of course, the degree to which the activists of the 1960s succeeded in bringing about such changes differed considerably from one country to another, but on the whole the link between protest and subsequent institutionalization and reform is unmistakable. The same holds for the contrary but simultaneous radicalization of some of the 1960s activists. Thus, the late 1960s and early 1970s saw a worldwide surge of left-wing terrorism. Again, it is not that there were no significant differences among countries in the extent and forms of radicalization. But whatever the differences between the short-lived Weathermen in the United States, the amateurism of the Dutch Rode Jeugd, or the deadly fanaticism of the German Rote Armee Fraktion, the simultaneity of their emergence remains striking. This synchronous appearance of terrorism led many commentators to conclude that some kind of global conspiracy was going on. The argument advanced in this chapter will be that there was as much conspiracy to this wave of terrorism as there was to the simultaneous wave of political reforms. What looked like a coordinated effort in fact sprang from a common dynamics underlying the development of the different national protest waves.

What Constitutes a Protest Wave?

But how do we know a protest wave when we see one? Sidney Tarrow defines protest cycles as "periods of generalized disorder" and of "heightened conflict across the social system" (1989b: 46–48).[1] We propose to specify this definition with four criteria: Protest waves

1. are characterized by a strong expansion and contraction of the magnitude of protest;
2. extend over a longer period of time;
3. encompass large parts of the social movement sector; and
4. affect most of the national territory.

This definition implies that not every increase and subsequent decrease in the overall magnitude of protest in a country constitutes a protest wave. Short-term fluctuations are an inherent consequence of the noninstitutionalized character of protest, and are therefore excluded following the second criterion. Here, the minimal requirement will be that the magnitude of protest remain above the average for the fifteen-year period under study for at least three subsequent years. Similarly, fluctuations that are caused by one or a few movements or campaigns, or that remain limited to a few regions or cities, fail to meet the third and fourth criteria. It may be that some of the patterns that can be found in genuine protest waves are also relevant for short-term or localized fluctuations, or for the development of single movements, and subsequent chapters indeed point in this direction (see also Koopmans 1992b: 167–228). In this chapter, however, we will focus on large-scale protest waves, whose intensity, scope, and longevity force members of the national polity to take sides. In that sense, protest waves occupy an intermediary position between routine protests and revolutions: unlike routine protests, protest waves shake the foundations of the polity; unlike revolutions, they ultimately cause only limited damage (see also Tarrow 1989b: 42). The intense and protracted interaction that takes place within a protest wave among a variety of social movements and polity members forms the basis for the specific dynamics we will now analyze.

The first question we have to address is whether, according to the four criteria just enumerated, any protest waves occurred in the four countries in the period 1975–89. In chapter 3 (fig. 3.1) we saw that in all four countries the levels of activity of NSMs and other movements were not systematically correlated. Therefore, we will limit our search for protest waves to the NSMs. Table 5.1 shows that the peak years of NSM mobilization in the four countries were unquestionably clustered in time. This is most clearly the case in Germany, where both the number of events and the number of participants reached above-average levels in six successive years from 1981 to 1986. Moreover, this surge of NSM activity was not limited to a few movements, but involved all the major NSMs, which all reached peak levels of events and participants somewhere between 1981 and 1986. The fact that some movements reached their peaks earlier than others suggests that processes of diffusion were at work. The German protest wave was also fully developed in terms of its geographical extension: in each of the four regions distinguished, the level of protest peaked during these six years. Again, the results are compatible with a diffusion hypothesis, and display a remarkable center-periphery pattern: the strongholds of the 1960s new left — Berlin and Hesse (particularly the Frankfurt region) — led the way with peaks in 1981; the North followed with a peak in 1983, and in the conservative and rural South protest reached its heyday as late as 1986. Finally, the German protest wave's amplitude was particularly impressive: the number of protests per year between 1981 and 1986 increased more than threefold compared to the period 1975–80, and the average number of participants per year increased to 1.4 million — more than eight times as many as in the preceding period.

In the Netherlands we can distinguish a protest wave that peaks from 1980 to 1985. The results displayed in the table show that the intensity and coherence of this protest wave were not as high as in Germany, which may be related to the more gradual and less spectacular nature of the changes in political opportunities in the Netherlands (see chapter 3). Thus, the amplitude of the Dutch wave, both relative to the preceding period and in absolute terms, falls somewhat short of the German level. Moreover, the Dutch pattern is not as fully perfect as the German pattern: there is a dip in overall participation in 1984, and the peak in the number of people mobilized by the solidarity movement occurs in 1988 — long after the wave's crest.

Table 5.1. Characteristics of fluctuations in the level of activity of NSMs in the four countries

	Germany	Netherlands	Switzerland	France
Years with above-average number of NSM events	1981–86	1980–86 1986–89	1980–83 1977–81	1975
Years with above-average number of participants in NSMs	1981–86	1981–83 1985	1980–84 1986–87	1977; 1980 1986–88
Peaks in number of events of:				
Peace movement	1983	1985	1983	1975; 1978
Antinuclear energy movement	1986	1980	1978; 1979	1980
Ecology movement	1981	1982	1986	1975; 1977
Solidarity movement	1983	1982	1988	1980
Autonomous/Squatters' movement	1981	1980	1980	1982
Peaks in number of of participants of:				
Peace movement	1983	1983	1983	1986
Antinuclear energy movement	1986	1981	1981	1977
Ecology movement	1981	1982	1984	1989
Solidarity movement	1983	1988	1975	1986
Autonomous/Squatters' movement	1981	1980	1980	1982
Regional peaks in number of events (4 regions)[a]	1981; 1981 1983; 1986	1982; 1982 1982; 1985	1980; 1980 1980; 1981	1975; 1977 1980; 1980
Regional peaks in number of participants (4 regions)	1981; 1983 1983; 1986	1981; 1982 1983; 1985	1980; 1981 1981; 1982	1977; 1977 1986; 1986
Candidate wave period	1981–86	1980–85	1980–83	1975–80
Length in years	6	6	4	6
Scope: number of movement and regional peaks in wave period (max. = 18)	18	17	13	11
Wave amplitude				
Average number of events per year in wave period (prewave period = 100) (for France postwave period = 100)	333	293	352	181
Average number of participants per year in wave period (prewave period = 100) (for France postwave period = 100)	815	444	346	69
Absolute number of participants in wave period in thousands per year per million inhabitants	22	18	14	2

[a]For each country the peak years of four regions or cities were computed. For Germany: Berlin, Hesse, the North, and the South; for the Netherlands: Amsterdam, The Hague, the remaining western Netherlands, and the South, East, and North; for Switzerland: Zurich, Bern, remaining German-speaking regions, and French- and Italian-speaking Switzerland; for France: Paris, the East, the South, and the North and West.

The Swiss pattern deviates much more from our criteria. To begin with, there are two separate peaks of NSM activity—one from 1980 to 1983,[2] and another from 1986 to 1988. Moreover, in both periods the increase in activity levels did not extend to the whole NSM sector. The period 1980–83 saw peaks of the autonomous and peace movements, and, as far as the number of events is concerned, of the antinuclear movement. The increase of protests in the period 1986–88 was even less encompassing, and only saw peaks in the number of events of the ecology and solidarity movements, but no participation peaks at all. The timing of regional mobilization peaks in Switzerland confirms that the period 1980–83 is the most likely to deserve the label protest wave: each of the four regions had its event and participation peaks in this period. Nevertheless, overall it is doubtful whether we can really speak of a protest wave in Switzerland between 1980 and 1983. Not only did five out of ten mobilization peaks of the major NSMs occur outside this period, the amplitude of the increase in protests was relatively limited, especially as regards participation. Moreover, the increase in 1980 in the number of protests was strongly related to the mobilization of one NSM, the movement for autonomous youth centers, which was concentrated in a few urban centers. Finally, it is doubtful whether the mobilizations of the two main constituents of the 1980–83 wave—the autonomous and peace movements—were significantly linked. The rise of the autonomous movement was related to changes in the local POS in cities like Zurich (see chapter 3), whereas the Swiss peace movement—whose demands were not directed at any Swiss authority—was a result of international opportunities and the influence of mass peace protests in neighboring countries. Therefore, it may well be that the proximity in time of these two movements was largely coincidental.

In France, finally, we find no evidence of a protest wave at all. The most likely candidate would be the period from 1975 to 1980, but five out of ten movement peaks and two out of eight regional peaks occurred outside this period. Moreover, the average number of protests was not very much higher than in subsequent years, and the average number of participants was hardly impressive. In fact, average participation from 1975 to 1980 was lower than the average for the following years, and compared to the other three countries the absolute number of people mobilized was very low.

Summing up, in Germany, and to a somewhat lesser extent in the Netherlands, we can identify well-developed protest waves, with strong increases in the level of protest of all the major NSMs, extending over more than half a decade and over the entire national territory. Whether the rise in protests in Switzerland in the early 1980s constituted a genuine protest wave is much more doubtful. This is perhaps not so surprising if we realize that no major changes in POS occurred during this period. Nor is it unexpected that we do not find an NSM protest wave in France: the marginal position of these movements within the French political system makes it impossible for the NSMs to produce a challenge of established politics that even approaches the intensity of a protest wave. In what follows, we will therefore focus on Germany and the Netherlands. Before turning to the analyses of the dynamics of the protest waves in these countries, we will discuss two theories that provide a promising starting point.

Karstedt-Henke: The Counterstrategies of Authorities

In her analysis of the emergence of terrorism in West Germany, Karstedt-Henke (1980) argued that protest waves typically pass through four phases. In the initial phase of mobilization, the authorities overreact to the emergence of protest. In an attempt to quell unrest, they follow a strategy of repression, but because they are caught off guard they do so in an inconsistent and undifferentiated way that provokes public outrage and leads to further protests (1980: 200–209). Their initial strategy of repression having failed, the authorities, in the second phase, combine continued repression of some actions and organiz: ions with efforts to appease other parts of the protest movement through concessions or facilitation. However, this double strategy cannot yet be implemented effectively because the authorities still have difficulty differentiating between "good" and "bad" protesters, and sometimes apply the wrong measures to the wrong group (ibid.: 209–13). Thus the radical and moderate wings of the movement continue to grow, but become increasingly distinguishable. In the third phase, this differentiation among activists, which often provokes internal conflicts, offers the authorities opportunities to exploit the double strategy. Moderate wings are integrated into the political system and will gradually abandon protest activities, while radical wings are not satisfied with the gains that have been made, and decisions about further protest activities increasingly become their exclusive domain. This radicalization of a movement's actions is reinforced by the authorities' reactions. Robbed of their moderate allies within and outside the movement, radicals are now confronted with full-scale repression. The result is spiraling violence and counterviolence, which produces terrorist organizations (ibid.: 213–17). Ultimately, integration and radicalization lead to a decline in protests — moderates are no longer interested in protest activity as their attention shifts to conventional channels of political participation, while the extreme actions of radicals become too costly for most social movement participants. Moreover, radical groups become closed to new participants because they are forced underground and because they develop an exclusive ideology and organizational structure. The combined result of these tendencies is the fourth phase: latency of the potential for protest (ibid.: 217–20).

Tarrow: Competition among Organizations

Tarrow's (1989a, 1989b) theory of protest dynamics is more complex than Karstedt-Henke's model. According to Tarrow, social movements emerge "when new opportunities are at hand — such as a less repressive climate, splits within the elite, or the presence of influential allies or supporters." Subsequently, protests spread through the diffusion of tactical innovations developed by early protesters to other themes, groups, and locations. Such diffusion is not a spontaneous process, however, but "follows an organized logic through competition and tactical innovation within the social movement sector.... Competition intensifies the evolution of the repertoire toward more radical forms, as movements try to show they are more daring than their opponents.... At the peak of mobilization the increased propensity to engage in disruptive collective action leads to the formation of new movement organizations and draws old organizations into the social movement sector. The competition between these SMOs for mass support leads to a radicalization of tactics and themes. The resulting intensification of conflict reduces the audience for social movement activity and triggers a spiral of sectarian involution, on the one hand, and of goal displacement, on the other." As a result, "the cycle declines through a symbiotic combination of violence and institutionalization" (1989b: 8, 54; 1989a: 14, 16).

Tarrow thus shares Karstedt-Henke's belief that violence and institutionalization are linked products of protest waves, and that the combination of these processes is the main cause of their decline. However, the explanations for these developments differ. In Karstedt-Henke's model, factors external to the social movement, particularly the shifting counterstrategies of the authorities, determine the development of protest. Tarrow, on the contrary, emphasizes internal factors, and sees competition among social movement organizations and between SMOs and established political organizations as the crucial mechanism.

The Development of the Action Repertoire

From the available studies of protest development, a remarkably regular pattern emerges that conforms to Karstedt-Henke's and Tarrow's hypotheses about the shifts in action repertoires that occur over the course of protest waves.

In his study of the Italian protest wave between 1965 and 1975, Tarrow found that nonviolent, confrontational actions like blockades and occupations peaked early in the wave. More moderate, demonstrative actions peaked a few years later and they increasingly involved established allies like unions. Violence, finally, was most common in the late stages of the wave, after other forms of action had begun to decline (1989a: 70). Moreover, mass violence was increasingly replaced by more extreme forms of violence by small groups (Della Porta and Tarrow 1986: 618–19; Tarrow 1989a: 306).

McAdam's (1982) study of the American civil rights movement provides additional evidence for these basic trends. Here too the wave started with confrontational actions like bus boycotts and sit-ins, gradually took on a mass character, and subsequently began to disintegrate as radicalization (e.g., ghetto rioting) and institutionalization (e.g., increased external support for the more moderate NAACP) set in (McAdam 1982: 209, 222, 253).

Similar patterns can be found for the German and Dutch protest waves of the 1980s. Figure 5.1 presents the development of the number of protests for four main strategies. As in the Italian and American cases, confrontational actions, such as blockades and occupations, were heavily concentrated in the early phases of the German and Dutch protest waves, around 1981 and 1980, respectively. As McAdam (1983) and Tarrow (1989a, 1989b) noted, these strategies often included important tactical innovations that enabled movements to transcend the constraints attached to traditional repertoires of contention (Tilly 1986b: 4). Partly, the innovations that helped launch the German and Dutch protest waves had been introduced already in the 1960s, when teach-ins, sit-ins, occupations of universities, and a more general strategy of nonviolent civil disobedience diffused from the United States to Western Europe. However, in the 1960s, the use of such strategies remained limited to a very small section of the population — namely, the student milieu of a few large cities. In the 1970s, the use of these forms of political action spread to much wider sections of the public, which in itself constituted an important innovation. In addition, new tactics were invented, such as squatting and site occupation[3] (Koopmans 1992b: 132–36). The authorities were generally

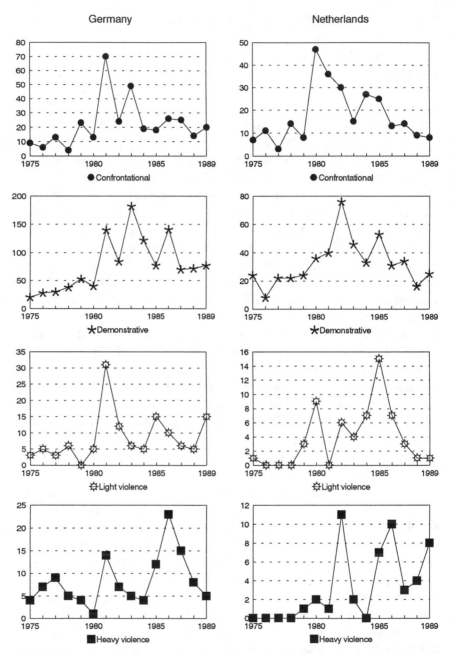

Fig. 5.1. Development of the number of protest events, by strategy, Germany and the Netherlands, 1975–89

unprepared for such strategies, whose novelty and spectacular nature en-sured wide coverage in the media. Thus, these innovations partly offset the unequal balance of power between challengers and authorities, and their ini-tial success contributed to the rapid diffusion of protests in the early stages of the two waves.

However, as their novelty waned and the authorities learned to respond more effectively, confrontational actions declined. They were increasingly replaced by more moderate, demonstrative actions (e.g., legal and nonvio-lent demonstrations, petitions, rallies), which peaked two years after con-frontational protests—in 1983 in Germany and in 1982 in the Netherlands. Demonstrative actions not only increased in frequency in this period, but also in size: many of them were mass demonstrations mobilizing thousands of people. As we will see, this trend toward moderate mass actions was re-lated to the growing involvement of professional SMOs and external allies in protests.

For protests involving light violence (e.g., limited property damage, vio-lent demonstrations), the German and Dutch patterns differ somewhat. In Germany, the pattern for light violence resembles the development of con-frontational protests, with a strong peak in 1981 and rapid decline afterward. In the Netherlands, on the contrary, protests involving light violence were concentrated in the late stages of the protest wave, with a peak in 1985. Thus, the development of light violence in the Netherlands resembles the pattern for heavy violence. This difference may be related to the nature of the 1960s protest wave in the two countries. Whereas in Germany violence had already occupied an important place in the action repertoire of the 1960s and 1970s (Koopmans 1993), the Dutch protest wave of the 1960s and early 1970s had remained very peaceful, due to the fact, among others, that the Dutch move-ments of this period were much more successful, both substantively and in penetrating established politics, than their German colleagues (Koopmans 1992c). Thus, the use of violence in the Netherlands implied a clear break with previous protest traditions, which explains why radical activists did not immediately turn to violent action forms once the efficacy of confrontational tactics waned and repression against these tactics became more intense. Within the German situation, on the other hand, the step from nonviolent confrontation to protests using light violence was easier and almost imme-diate. In Germany, both strategies peaked in 1981, but confrontational ac-tions declined sharply during the second half of the year, while the number of protests involving light violence reached a maximum intensity in late 1981 and early 1982, after the authorities started an offensive against squatters (resulting in the death of one activist) and violently cleared an occupied runway construction site near Frankfurt (Mulhak 1983; Rucht 1984; Koopmans 1992a: 178–94).

Thus, the seeds of institutionalization and radicalization were planted by the growing involvement of professional SMOs and external allies on the one hand, and the increasing repression of confrontational actions on the other. In the late stages of the waves, these trends became increasingly prominent. Thus, heavy violence was most common during the second half of the 1980s, when the aggregate number of protests had already declined substantially. Not only the number of protests involving heavy violence increased, but so did their intensity. Of the German protests involving heavy violence between 1980 and 1984, only 4 percent involved violence against people, whereas from 1985 on, 25 percent involved violence against people. Not coincidentally, the terrorist Rote Armee Fraktion made a comeback in the second half of the 1980s. Within the less polarized Dutch context, radicalization did not extend to violence against people, but over the course of the 1980s there was a clear intensification of heavy violence against objects. Thus the amateurish Militant Autonomen Front that was active in 1982 gave way to the professionalism of RARA (Radikale Anti-Rassistische Aktie), which was responsible for a series of spectacular acts of arson against firms with connections to South Africa. Radicalization extended further beyond the period of our data: in 1991 and 1992, RARA was responsible for bomb attacks against the house of the state secretary responsible for refugees, and against the interior and social affairs ministries.

Whether this tendency toward radicalization in the late stages of the two protest waves was accompanied by a trend toward institutionalization can be answered only to a limited extent by the protest event data. The increasing dominance of demonstrative actions in the period around 1983, and the increasing involvement of established allies in these actions, are the first signs of institutionalization. After these years, however, the relative importance of demonstrative actions and the involvement of allies in protests declined again. Yet the German and Dutch movements did not deinstitutionalize. At first, institutionalization may lead to a shift toward more moderate goals and actions and increased involvement of established allies and professional SMOs in unconventional protest. As institutionalization proceeds, however, movements increasingly turn toward conventional strategies and exit from the protest scene. This may take several forms. Institutionalization may find expression within the party system, either in the emergence of new parties or in increased support for established reformist parties. During the 1980s, this form of institutionalization was particularly pronounced in West Germany, where the Green party succeeded in penetrating first local and regional politics and then the national political arena. In addition, the NSMs and the pressure exerted by the Greens brought about important changes in the program and leadership of the social-democratic SPD.

SMOs themselves may also institutionalize by substituting a reliance on access to the media and the conventional policy process for mobilization of their constituency, and by replacing the active involvement of adherents with that of a few professionals, who are paid with the membership contributions of an otherwise passive constituency. Figure 5.2 shows that in both Germany and the Netherlands the membership of national SMOs of the NSMs increased throughout the period. In other words, the evidence points to a long-term, secular trend toward institutionalization of the NSMs. What is striking in the figure, however, is that periods of strong membership growth do not coincide with the peak periods of unconventional protests: in the Netherlands, the growth rate of SMOs even declined from 1980 to 1985 — the heyday of the protest wave. In both countries, however, SMO membership increased spectacularly in the second half of the 1980s, that is, in the declining phases of the two protest waves.

As a theoretical aside, we may note that this incongruence between SMO development and the development of unconventional protest casts serious doubt upon the common research strategy — especially within the resource mobilization perspective — of investigating a social movement through its SMOs. Moreover, the results undermine the basic tenet of the resource mobilization approach — the idea that increases in social movement activity are explained by a rise in the amount of resources available to the movement. A comparison of figure 5.2 with the mobilization curves of the German and Dutch NSMs suggests an opposite relation. The spectacular increase in resources (finances, staff, etc.) available to SMOs in the second half of the 1980s did not lead to any increase in mobilization, but was accompanied by a clear decline in the number of protests. The increase in resources, therefore, did not cause mobilization, but, quite to the contrary, was a result of the preceding protest wave.

Summarizing, we find striking parallels between the development of the action repertoire in the German and Dutch protest waves of the 1980s, which largely coincide with results of earlier research with regard to the development of the Italian protest wave of the 1960s and early 1970s and of the American civil rights movement. Moreover, elsewhere we have shown that very similar trends occurred in the German protest wave of the 1960s and early

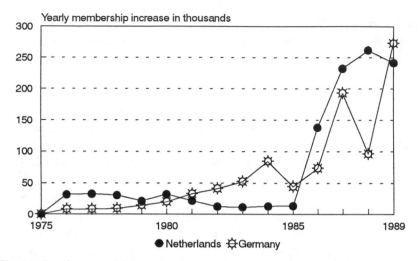

Fig. 5.2. Development of the membership of national new social movement organizations, yearly increases in thousands, Germany and the Netherlands, 1975–89

1970s (Koopmans 1993). In all these waves, protests started with disruptive but nonviolent confrontational actions, subsequently entered a phase dominated by more moderate mass mobilization, and ended in a twin process of institutionalization and radicalization.

Repression and Facilitation

Although Karstedt-Henke's model may hinge too much on a single explanatory factor — the reactions of political elites — and is somewhat deterministic in that it sees terrorism as an inevitable outcome of protest waves, it nonetheless offers valuable insights that may help to provide an explanation for the similarities we have found among different protest waves. Her explanation for the seemingly contradictory development of protest waves toward institutionalization and radicalization, although perhaps incomplete, is quite convincing. Political elites can choose between two basic reactions to protest: confrontation or integration. Both repression and facilitation typically are selective: activists with radical goals and strategies are more likely to be subjected to repression, whereas moderate wings are more likely to receive facilitation. Thus, different wings of social movements receive different strategic cues.

Radical wings, which disproportionately confront repression, are likely to be further radicalized and develop antisystemic identities that may escalate violence on both sides. Moderates, on the other hand, receive cues that work toward further moderation. Political parties may support the moderate sections of a movement conditional upon deradicalizing demands and the strategies used to advance them. State facilitation or co-optation of social movement organizations may occur as well, but again, it is unlikely to be granted unconditionally. Thus the reactions of established political actors typically reinforce divisions among the activists, which leads to a twin process of moderation and radicalization. This development need not be the result of a conscious "divide and rule" strategy by the authorities, as is suggested by Karstedt-Henke. Members of the polity may themselves be internally divided — for example, among government parties, between government and opposition, or between political authorities who prefer integrative strategies and law enforcement authorities who prefer more repressive strategies.

Nevertheless, the data suggest that repression and facilitation are also employed strategically in attempts to create or reinforce divisions among protesters. Figures 5.3 and 5.4 show the percentage of protests using each of three main social movement strategies that were repressed or facilitated (actions involving light violence or heavy violence are combined).[4]

An obvious conclusion that can be drawn from figure 5.3 is that repression increases with increasingly radical strategies used by protesters. More interesting here, however, is the development of repression over time. In both countries, the percentage of violent protests and demonstrative protests that encounter repression remains relatively stable throughout the period[5] — about 60–80 percent of violent protests and between 10 percent (the Netherlands) and 20 percent (Germany) of demonstrative protests.[6] However, repression against confrontational protests changes considerably — and in a strikingly similar way — over the course of the two protest waves. Initially, the level of repression against such actions is similar to that for demonstrative actions, but it then increases substantially to end up at a level close to that for violent protests.

Thus, instead of a general rise or decline in repression over the course of the German and Dutch protest waves, only repression against confrontational but nonviolent protests increases. This strategic increase in repression is perfectly suited to the creation of divisions within movements. That in Germany such a strategy was at least partly deliberate is indicated by a "New Internal Security Strategy for the 1980s" that was unfolded by a leading police theorist in an article in the journal of the German police and in a book published in early 1982. Although this strategy envisaged a more tolerant

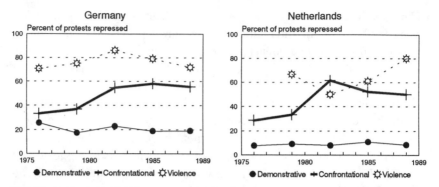

Fig. 5.3. Percent of protests repressed for three types of protest, Germany and the Netherlands, 1975–89

approach to moderate sections of the NSMs, a tougher line was recommended against militant minorities to isolate them from the rest of the movements (Brand 1988: 212).

Thus, as nonviolent disruption becomes more costly and its practitioners are depicted and treated as criminals, protesters who use such strategies are increasingly forced to choose sides. The increased costs of nonviolent disruptions favor a turn to more moderate actions, a trend that is often reinforced by the involvement of established actors in the protests. Figure 5.4 shows that both in Germany and in the Netherlands the percentage of facilitated protests was very low at the beginning of the protest wave. The subsequent increase in facilitation by established political actors during the course of the 1980s wave was heavily concentrated on the more moderate demonstrative protests. Between 1984 and 1986, the percentage of demonstrative protests that were supported by political parties, labor unions, or churches reached a maximum of 35 percent in Germany and 17 percent in the Netherlands.[7] By contrast, external support for confrontational protests increased only slightly in Germany, and not at all in the Netherlands. Not surprisingly, external support for violent protests was negligible throughout the period in both countries. Thus, intensified repression increased the relative costs of nonviolent disruptions over the course of the wave, while facilitation by established actors decreased the relative costs of moderate protests. McAdam (1982) found similar patterns in the reactions of authorities and external supporters to the civil rights movement. Repression focused on the more radical organizations like SNCC and CORE, whereas the NAACP received more benevolent treatment. The sharp increase in external support after 1964 ben-

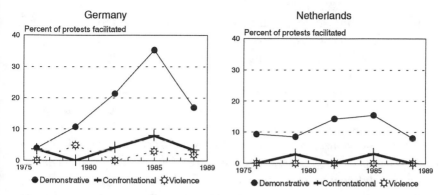

Fig. 5.4. Percent of protests facilitated for three types of protest, Germany and the Netherlands, 1975–89

efited the NAACP, while support for the other groups declined (McAdam 1982: 209–17).

On the other hand, increased repression may have provoked some activists to turn to violence. Repression against nonviolent protest delegitimizes the state's monopoly on violence and strengthens the position of those activists who see reactive violence as legitimate. Moreover, the shift to violence is facilitated because the cost of violence compared to the cost of nonviolent disruption decreases. The final result of these countervailing pressures is an erosion of the middle ground of the action repertoire—nonviolent confrontations—and the simultaneous development of moderation and radicalization as hypothesized by Karstedt-Henke.

Two Views on the Role of Organizations

Tarrow's explanation for the changing repertoire of protest emphasized the role of organizations and the competition among them. In the early phase of a protest wave, competition among SMOs, which try to outbid each other in radicalness and determination, still plays a positive role, and accounts for the diffusion of disruptive tactics: "The expanding phase of the cycle is the result, not of pure spontaneity, but of the competition between movement organizations and their old competitors for mass support" (Tarrow 1989a: 10; see also 186, 193). However, as new organizations are attracted by the successes of pioneer SMOs, the social movement sector becomes increasingly crowded and organizers are forced to adopt more radical strategies in order to maintain their organization's positions or to create a niche for themselves. "In a competitive social movement sector, when the most extreme groups adopt violent stands, it is difficult for any group to come out against violence" (ibid.: 284). This violence turns people off and ultimately draws the protest wave to a close.[8]

Tarrow's view of SMOs as sources of disruption and violence differs sharply from the view of Piven and Cloward (1977), who argued that "whatever influence lower-class groups occasionally exert in American politics does not result from organization, but from mass protest and the disruptive consequences of protest.... Protest wells up in response to momentous changes in the institutional order. It is not created by organizers and leaders" (36). Thus, organizations are not the driving force behind protest expansion and disruption, but, on the contrary, take the disruptive sting out of protests by diverting resources into more conventional—and, in the view of Piven and Cloward, less effective—channels.[9]

These two diametrically opposed views of the role of organizations cannot both be true. Tarrow's interpretation implies two hypotheses: (1) disruption should be highest when organizational competition is strongest; (2) protests in which organizations are involved should be more disruptive than "unorganized" protests. The first hypothesis is proven wrong by Tarrow's own data: nonviolent disruptions peaked early in the Italian protest wave, in 1968 and 1969 (Tarrow 1989a: 81). However, in those same years, unorganized protests peaked as well (ibid.: 65–66). In other words, organizations declined in importance at a time when protests spread spectacularly and their disruptiveness peaked. It is hard to see how competition can be strongest at a time when the "market" expands dramatically and the number of competitors is at its lowest point relative to the size of the market.

With regard to the second hypothesis, however, the Italian evidence seems to confirm Tarrow's expectation: protests that involved no organizations were the least disruptive; protests in which a union was involved were slightly more disruptive; protests in which an "external group" was involved were much more disruptive; and protests involving a union *and* an "external group" were even more disruptive. Therefore, Tarrow concluded that "competition for worker support was a direct cause of disruption and thus of the high point of social movement mobilization" (ibid.: 186). However, apart from the fact that this conclusion contradicts Tarrow's other findings, other reasons cast doubt on this conclusion. Tarrow's claim would have been strong if his data referred only to attempts to mobilize a worker constituency. However, Tarrow combined all protests, including the many protests in which "extreme left- and extreme right-wing groups attacked one another's headquarters or engaged in physical confrontations in the streets" (ibid.: 232). In other words, not all protests between 1966 and 1973 were designed to mobilize workers. In fact, a sizable number of the "external groups" were mobilizing against that constituency. Violent conflicts between left-wing and right-wing groups can hardly be interpreted as competition for a single "market".[10]

Organization and Spontaneity in the German and Dutch Protest Waves

What is the relation between the spread of protests, organization, and the radicalness of the action repertoire in Germany and the Netherlands? Is the diffusion of protests the work of SMOs, or is it spontaneous? Are disruption and violence a result of competition among organizations or does organization lead to a moderation of the action repertoire? Figure 5.5 shows the development of the number of protests that involved particular organizations. Consistent with Tarrow's data, in both countries the start of the protest wave was associated with particularly strong increases in the number of unorganized protests, whose share of total protests peaked at 64 percent in Germany in 1981 and at 69 percent in the Netherlands in 1982.[11] These years were also characterized by a particularly high level of confrontational events (fig. 5.1). In other words, as in Italy, the involvement of organizations and the competition among them cannot account for the rapid spread of protests or their disruptive character.[12]

This does not imply, however, that organizations did not play important roles in other phases of the two protest waves. To allow for a more detailed view of the development of organizational involvement in NSM protests, the figure displays the development of four types of organization: three types of social movement organization—terrorist, professional, and other[13]—and external allies (e.g., political parties, unions, churches). The figure makes clear that the four types of organization did not all follow the same trajectory. In both countries, the relative importance of professional SMOs and external allies increased toward the end of the protest wave, which, as indicated earlier, is related to tendencies toward the institutionalization of protest. However, the involvement of these organizations meant more than just a channeling of activism into institutional channels. Because of the resources these organizations controlled, they were also an important vehicle for extending protests to a mass public: actions supported by allies or professional SMOs tended to mobilize much larger numbers of people than other protests. The other side of the coin was that once professional SMOs and external allies

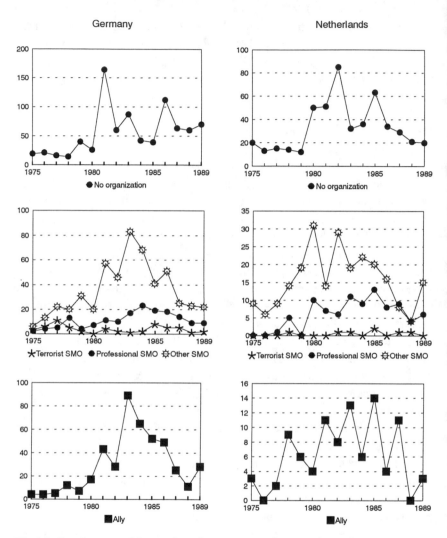

Fig. 5.5. Development of the number of protest events, by type of organization, Germany and the Netherlands, 1975–89

had succeeded in finding new constituencies through their involvement in unconventional protests, they quickly returned to their normal habitus (i.e., conventional interest-group politics for the professional SMOs and the parliamentary arena for external allies), drawing along with them many former movement participants as voters, funders, or members.

Terrorist SMOs followed a similar trajectory, reflecting the accompanying trend toward radicalization. Although the absolute number of protests organized by terrorist SMOs was quite low, especially in the Netherlands, the extremely radical nature of their actions made their impact on the development of the larger protest wave much more important than their number might suggest. Moreover, much of the violence of the second half of the 1980s was produced by small, nameless circles of activists, as reflected in the revival of unorganized protests around 1985–86. In that respect, the radicalism of the 1980s differed from that of the 1970s, which was heavily dominated by Communist vanguard organizations and terrorist groups. The figure for Germany, in fact, shows the tail of the radicalization process of the 1960s protest wave, with a peak in terrorist activity around 1977. Consistent with the argument advanced here, it was only in the declining phase of the 1980s protest wave that new violent groups arose and old terrorist organizations like the Rote Armee Fraktion and the Revolutionäre Zellen were reinvigorated by an influx of new members and sympathizers.

Thus, the involvement of professional SMOs, external allies, and terrorist groups was a product rather than a cause of the increase in protests. On the other hand, the relative importance of protests organized by "other SMOs," a category primarily consisting of loosely structured, often short-lived, and locally or regionally based organizations with relatively few resources (e.g., *Bürgerinitiativen* (civic initiatives) in Germany and *actiegroepen* in the Netherlands), tended to decline as the wave progressed (even though in absolute numbers they remained the most important type of organization of the NSMs).[14] As the figure suggests, protests involving these loosely structured organizations played an important role during the initial stages of the two protest waves. In fact, this was the only category of protests that was already substantially increasing *before* the spectacular eruptions of the number of protests in the early 1980s. Indeed, *Bürgerinitiativen* and *actiegroepen* were important trailblazers for subsequent protests. During the 1970s they experimented with new forms of action and organization, mobilized heretofore acquiescent sections of the population, and obtained a number of important successes that heightened the public's belief in the efficacy of protest.[15] Nevertheless, in doing so, they opened up space for protests that to a large extent was filled by others—initially by relatively spontaneous actions (e.g, the squatters' movement), and later by political parties, professional SMOs, and countercultural radicals.

Summarizing, we may conclude that the role of organizations varies over the course of a protest wave. Informal, loosely structured organizations that rely more on the commitment and imagination of activists than on other resources are important at the beginning of a protest wave. In this initial phase, protests require strategic planning and patience. However, once early protests have shown the way, the costs and difficulties of staging subsequent protests decrease. Actions that might require months or even years of preparation in less conducive circumstances may be accomplished almost instantaneously during these times of general arousal. Leaflets, rumors, intensified media coverage, or brutal police repression may then do the job of movement organizers, who often are unable to control the energies their pioneer actions have unleashed. In that sense, the diffusion of protests is neither spontaneous nor organized, but rather an often uneasy combination of the two.

After disruptive protests have peaked, the importance of organizations increases again. However, the organizations that dominate in this period often differ from the organizations that started the wave. Basically, these later organizations reflect the twin tendencies toward radicalization and institutionalization. External allies try to profit from the mobilization by entering the social movement sector, which extends protests to a wider public and exerts a moderating influence on goals and actions. In addition, preexisting or newly founded professional SMOs may try to get a slice of the protest pie. Radicalization may be accompanied by the formation of new organizations, too, although the high degree of organization characteristic of the radicalism of the 1970s seems to be a result of the Marxist theories and Leninist models of organization that predominated at the time.

Table 5.2 shows the relationship between the involvement of organizations and the action repertoire. Contrary to Tarrow, both in Germany and in the Netherlands the involvement of organizations declines with more radical strategies. The only partial exception to this rule is that in Germany the relation between the degree of organization and type of protest seems to change at the far radical end of the action repertoire. Protests involving heavy violence were more organized than protests involving light violence. Moreover, among protests involving heavy violence, those directed against people involved a (terrorist) organization in two-thirds of the cases, a level similar to that for demonstrative protests. This is, of course, related to the conspiratorial nature of such protests, which require careful planning: kidnappings or political murders do not happen spontaneously.

If we look next at the involvement of different types of organizations in different types of protests, we see that the moderating effect of the involvement of organizations is most pronounced for external allies, whether acting on their own or in combination with an SMO. As was already indicated by figure 5.4, the NSMs' allies within established politics are generally not prepared to support actions that go beyond the confines of legality. To a some-

Table 5.2. Percentage distribution of protests by involvement of organizations, for types of protest: Germany and the Netherlands, 1975–89

Type of organization	Demonstrative protests	Confrontational protests	Protests using light violence	Protests using heavy violence	Total protests
A. *Germany*					
No organization	37.7	63.1	80.3	60.2	47.1
Terrorist SMO	0.0	3.9	3.1	30.1	3.1
Professional SMO	5.9	3.6	0.0	0.0	4.7
Other SMO	22.8	18.6	12.6	7.3	20.2
External ally	14.0	4.8	0.8	1.6	10.4
SMO + external ally	19.6	6.0	3.1	0.8	14.5
Total	100%	100%	100%	100%	100%
N	1,174	333	127	123	1,757
B. *The Netherlands*					
No organization	52.9	62.2	61.4	71.4	57.4
Terrorist SMO	0.0	0.0	0.0	12.2	0.7
Professional SMO	6.1	6.4	1.8	0.0	5.6
Other SMO	23.9	27.7	36.9	16.4	25.4
External ally	6.7	2.2	0.0	0.0	4.5
SMO + external ally	10.4	1.5	0.0	0.0	6.4
Total	100%	100%	100%	100%	100%
N	490	267	57	49	863

what lesser extent, this is also true for professional SMOs, although in the Netherlands their involvement does extend to confrontational protests. The more radical character of Dutch SMOs is clearer still for other SMOs. Although in Germany the involvement of these organizations is strongly biased toward moderate strategies (though less so than for professional SMOs and external allies), in the Netherlands there is no systematic relation between the involvement of loosely structured SMOs and the type of protests. This may be related to the greater tolerance of the Dutch authorities for radical protests, which allows SMOs to go further than their German counterparts, who have to reckon with serious repression and outlaw status if they engage in illegal protests.

The results for Germany and the Netherlands are confirmed by other studies on the role of organizations in protest. Killian's (1984) analysis of two campaigns of the civil rights movement in Tallahassee, Florida, also found that the initial phase of a protest wave is characterized by a "mixture of planning and spontaneity.... Spontaneity is especially likely to be important in the early stages of a social movement and during periods of transition from one type of action to another" (777–80). Oberschall (1978), studying the role of SMOs in the American protest wave of the 1960s, concluded that "created hastily and expanding rapidly, SMOs controlled but a small part of their total social interaction field. Only a small fraction of the total resources expended upon movement activity by transitory teams and the wider circles of sympathizers actually passed directly through a central leadership group with a resource allocation capacity. The communications network between the leadership and rank and file was rudimentary, and relied heavily on the mass media over which SMOs had little direct control" (267). McAdam's (1982: 147–48) study of the civil rights movement found that the grassroots organizations that dominated the movement's early phase gradually became less prominent, while the involvement of formal movement organizations and external support increased.

These findings support Piven and Cloward's argument that the involvement of organizations has a moderating influence rather than a disruptive influence as Tarrow suggests. The squatters' protests of the early 1980s, for instance, were more a result of spontaneous imitation and the mobilization of preexisting networks of activists than of careful planning and organization. Nevertheless, the role of spontaneity in the spread of disruptive protests should not be overemphasized. These episodes would never have occurred without the groundwork laid by organizations like the civic initiatives, which successfully experimented with new strategies and introduced new issues into the political agenda. Only after the peak of disruption do organizations become a moderating force, as professional SMOs and established allies join the movements to exploit the pool of members, adherents, and voters revealed by the eruption of protests. Thus, Piven and Cloward's stress on the spontaneity of disruptions and the moderating influence of organizations, and their critics' emphasis on the importance of organizations in preparing the ground for disruption, both contain an element of truth. The main difference between these interpretations is their focus on different types of organizations and different periods in the mobilization process.

Determinants of the Rise and Fall of Protests: A Synthesis

The findings point to striking regularities in the development of protest waves that are independent of the particular themes addressed and movements involved, and that can be found in countries as divergent as Germany, the Netherlands, Italy, and the United States. Karstedt-Henke's explanation for these regularities, which emphasizes the effects of repression and facilitation by established political actors, finds more support in the data than does Tarrow's focus on competition among organizations.

Nevertheless, Karstedt-Henke's explanation is not wholly satisfactory: it assumes that the fragmentation of social movements into moderate and radical components and the ensuing decline in protests are the result of cunning counterstrategies devised by the authorities, and that social movements are powerless victims in their hands. Although repression and facilitation can have powerful effects on the relative costs and benefits of different strategies open to social movements, Karstedt-Henke's explanation ignores the fact that authorities cannot *force* activists to institutionalize or build terrorist organizations. The theory must consider why, within the constraints set by their environments, social movement activists consciously choose one strategy and not another.

What are the basic strategic options available to social movements in their efforts to change existing policies? Different answers to this question have been proposed. Some authors, especially those working in the classical tradition, stress violence as the basic resource available to social movements (Gurr 1970). De Nardo (1985), on the other hand, emphasized the "power of numbers," although he acknowledged that "violence can be used to compensate for inadequate support" (200). Tarrow (1989b) argued that "the power of protest lies neither in its numbers ... nor in its level of violence, ... but in its threat to burst through the boundaries of the accepted limits of social behavior" (7; Piven and Cloward [1977] argued in a similar vein). Rochon's (1990: 108) view that all three elements of movement power—which he labels *militancy, size,* and *novelty*—are important seems more realistic than a reductionist emphasis on one of these elements. These three elements are particularly relevant here because they can easily be linked to the three main action strategies: demonstrative protests aim primarily to mobilize the power of numbers; confrontational protests are most suited to capitalize on the advantages of novelty; and violence clearly aims to change policies through a display of militant force and determination.

Social movements derive power from large *size* because the more people who are mobilized, the more the legitimacy of the authorities and their policies is called into question. Moreover, in democracies, participants in social movements and their sympathizers are also voters, so that size can become a considerable electoral factor.

The power of *novelty,* apart from the media attention it attracts, lies in its unpredictability and the insecurity it provokes among established actors about the limits and consequences of protests (Tarrow 1989a: 59). Moreover, novelty gives protesters a strategic advantage—authorities are unprepared for new strategies, political actors, and themes. Given the inertia of institutional politics, effective responses develop slowly, whereas in the early phase of rapid diffusion, social movements are highly flexible—they appear and disappear in ever-changing guises at unpredictable times and places.

Militancy is the most direct source of power available to social movements. Radical protests, especially when they involve violence, almost invariably attract media coverage. Moreover, the authorities are forced to react to serious disturbances of law and order that challenge their monopoly on the use of violence. However, violence employed by social movements is a risky tool. The individual costs are likely to be steep for those arrested, and the probability of backlash is high. Nevertheless, if the violence is sufficiently enduring and massive, it may succeed. Repression can backfire, especially when it is excessive and badly directed. Moreover, repression is costly, and in some situations these costs may induce authorities to give in to the movement's demands.

These three sources of power for social movements are also associated with specific phases in the development of protest waves. Clearly, in the initial phase of a wave, novelty is the most important basis of power. Because the public at large is not yet mobilized, pioneer movements attract few participants, which rules out strategies that depend on large size. Violence is also not an attractive option because the public and the media have serious moral objections and will consider violence only as a last resort. Moreover, in the initial phase, protesters can attract attention with less militant and less risky actions. Thus, pioneer activists are likely to opt for actions that are novel and unconventional enough to attract media attention and militant enough to concern authorities, but that do not depend for effectiveness on large numbers of participants. Confrontational protests like occupations, sit-ins, and blockades satisfy these criteria and thus are important in the expansive phase of a protest wave.[16]

Similar considerations affect the organizational support for protests. Formal, professional movement organizations do not play dominant roles in the initial phase of a protest wave. Such organizations, if they exist when protests start, tend to suffer from the same structural inertia as do established political actors. Therefore, they are unlikely to spawn tactical and thematic innovations. Also, in the face of insecurity about the outcomes of such "experiments," they are reluctant to risk their resources (e.g., access to decision makers or to the media, mass membership, subsidies, salaried staff). Nor are the pioneers of protest waves likely to opt for formal organizations because such organizations require an already mobilized mass constituency that offers members and funding. Oberschall (1979) argued that in a group that is not yet represented by an existing SMO or political organization, "the first individuals to attempt organization run high personal risks as a result of innovator-loss dynamics; there are free rider tendencies; and the sheer length of time that would pass before SMO efforts might bring relief, even if they could get under way, also make[s] an organized challenge unlikely" (63). Moreover, formal organization would not be fruitful strategically. Unpredictability, novelty, and fluidity are an emergent movement's main resources, whereas the involvement of formal organizations makes a movement's boundaries clearer, its leaders identifiable and accountable, and its strategies more predictable.

However, this initial strategic model is inherently instable and alternative strategic options gradually become more attractive. Tactical innovations like site occupation and squatting lose their ability to surprise, are no longer attractive to the media, and authorities learn to deal with such actions more effectively (Freeman 1979: 186; Hilgartner and Bosk 1988: 62–63; Rochon 1988: 186).

Similarly, the initial model of loosely structured organizations is difficult to sustain (Oberschall 1979: 67). In the initial phase of a protest wave, such organizations often have the field to themselves. However, as the wave progresses, they are increasingly faced with competition from professional SMOs and external allies on the one hand, and from radical groups on the other. Because they lack the resources and internal coordination to compete effectively with professional SMOs and established allies for media access and mass support, and because they lack the strong identity that underlies the mobilization capacity of radical groups, these organizations become increasingly marginal. As Oberschall (1978) argued, this marginalization will be reinforced by the reactions of the media and the authorities, who are interested in "structuring" protests by focusing on a few identifiable leaders and organizations — "the media contributed in making leaders out of some who otherwise might not have been, and created more structure in the movements than they actually possessed" (272). When protests begin to decline, the positions of the loosely structured parts of social movements become even more precarious. To survive declining participation, social movements must have either an enduring organizational structure with resources that do not depend on mass participation (McAdam, McCarthy, and Zald 1988: 716ff.) or a strong identity that allows them to continue to mobilize even under unfavorable circumstances. The organizations and spontaneous collectives that dominate the initial phase of protests possess neither of these traits and are therefore likely to be the first victims of decline (Jenkins and Eckert 1986: 816).

Social movements must compensate for the loss of novelty with increased numbers or increased militancy. A strategy to increase numbers is favored if established political actors, preexisting SMOs, and social movement entrepreneurs are interested in allying themselves to movements. However, support from these groups is often accompanied by a moderation of strategies and goals, which may lead to friction with the more radical activists who do not wish to compromise on the original strategies and demands. Since these radicals are unable to outstrip the moderates and their allies in numbers, they resort to increased militancy, and some of them ultimately to violence, to make themselves heard. The presence of a radical minority may in turn strengthen the moderate faction's tendency toward moderation and institutionalization. "The presence of 'extremist' SMOs can actually help to legitimate and strengthen the bargaining position of more moderate SMOs [and may encourage] funding support for the 'moderates' as a way of undercutting the influence of the radicals" (McAdam, McCarthy, and Zald 1988: 718–19).

Thus, over the course of a protest wave social movements split over strategy, and the moderate and radical wings are increasingly separated. This division need not have immediate negative consequences on the protests. Initially, the involvement of allies may broaden public support for the movement's activities and enhance the media presence of the movement. Nevertheless, if institutionalization and radicalization continue, protests will ultimately decline. When established allies incorporate a movement's demands into their programs, when "movement parties" like the German Green party enter parliaments or governments, and when professional SMOs gain acceptance as representatives of a movement's demands in the media and in policy making, many movement sympathizers find protests less urgent. Because participation in social movements is relatively costly and time-consuming compared to voting for a sympathetic party or joining an SMO, institutionalization leads many to shift to such alternatives.

Increased radicalism may also lead to a decline in protests. Few activists are prepared to endure the repression that radical actions entail. Moreover, the increasingly hostile reactions of the authorities and the increased efficiency of repressive measures push radical groups toward covert actions involving a small activist core. The repression and marginalization of these groups also stimulate sectarian conflicts and distrust among activists, which diverts energy from external activities and discourages outsiders from participating (De Nardo 1985). Finally, if radicalization escalates to extreme violence or terrorism, it may provoke a backlash that undercuts the general legitimacy of protests.

A decline in protests may be reinforced by a decline in the chance of success of protests, which makes participation less attractive. One may hypothesize that the chance of success erodes over the course of a protest wave. Social movements tend to succeed first when opportunities are most favorable—for example, by focusing on issues with large public support and on which elites are divided. Being rational actors, activists focus on such "ripe apples" first. As a guide for movement organizers stated, "It is desirable to make the first organized project of the group a short term one that has a high probability of success. Your first issue should be an attainable goal which will provide you with your first victory" (as quoted in Fireman and Gamson 1979: 30). Once success has been attained or a compromise has been reached on these initial demands, the movement must continue mobilization on issues for which opportunities and public support are less favorable. Thus, subsequent successes are increasingly difficult, which gradually erodes the motivation to participate.

The increasing lack of success may reinforce tensions between moderates and radicals. While the prospects for success are favorable, different factions may find a common ground or at least agree to a "peaceful coexistence." Once things go wrong, however, strategic debates often erupt with full force, and these internal conflicts can substantially weaken a movement. This happened to the German peace movement, for instance, after the government decided to deploy cruise and Pershing missiles in 1983.

Summarizing, the explanation for the dynamics of protest waves advanced here combines external and internal factors. The progress of a protest wave is the outcome of the interplay between the external constraints of facilitation, repression, and success chances, and activists' choices among the strategic options of novelty, size, and militancy.

Switzerland and France Revisited

With the German and Dutch results in mind, we will now briefly return to the French and Swiss cases. Because in France no protest wave occurred in the period under study, the French case can only figure as a counterfactual test of the validity of the argument advanced here. If the strategic and organizational trajectories we found in the German and Dutch cases are indeed specific to protest waves, we should not find comparable developments in the mobilization of the French NSMs. If we did, the similarities would have to be attributed to some other mechanism — for example, cross-national diffusion. However, the development of French NSM protests does not reveal many similarities with the German and Dutch cases. As regards the action repertoire, all strategies declined more or less simultaneously after 1981, although the decrease in violent protests is somewhat more gradual than the decrease in other strategies. This relative radicalization may well have been a result of the almost total failure of the French NSMs, but the fact that this tendency was very weak supports the idea that radicalization is a product of the interactive dynamics within protest waves and not merely a response to frustrations about lack of success. In a similar manner, the fact that few French SMOs were able to increase their membership during the 1980s, during which many of them experienced a decline, shows that the institutionalization of social movements is not an autonomous process, but is equally a product of protest waves.

The only significant development that can be traced in France is a gradual increase in the percentage of demonstrative NSM protests that were facilitated by external allies, from about 15 percent in the second half of the 1970s to 35–40 percent after 1984. However, because this increase in facilitation was accompanied by a decline in the number of NSM protests, it can hardly be compared to the increase in facilitation in Germany and the Netherlands. In these countries, the increase in facilitation was a reaction to spectacular increases in protest activities initiated from below. In France, on the contrary, facilitation can more aptly be characterized as a form of "domestication" (Duyvendak 1992) of the weakened NSMs by political parties. The increase in facilitation was very selective and limited to themes that were instrumental to the political parties in their mutual competition. Thus the peace movement came under exclusive control of the Communist Party, while the antiracist movement served as an extension of the Socialist Party in the context of the latter's opposition against the right-wing cabinet during the period of cohabitation.

For Switzerland, the evidence examined at the beginning of this chapter was inconclusive as to the question of whether the mobilization peaks in the early 1980s constituted a genuine protest wave. However, a number of parallels between the Swiss and the German and Dutch cases suggest a positive answer to this question, although there are also a few differences. Thus the development of the action repertoire of the Swiss NSMs is similar to the German and Dutch cases in that the initial rise of protests was particularly strong for confrontational actions. Moreover, as in Germany and the Netherlands, the decline of protest activity was accompanied by institutionalization in the form of strong membership growth of professional SMOs. The involvement of organizations also followed the by now familiar pattern: unorganized protests were heavily concentrated in the wave's initial stages, and loosely structured organizations declined in importance relative to professional SMOs and external allies over the course of the wave. As in the other two countries, the increase in facilitation by external allies was heavily concentrated on moderate demonstrative protests, and followed rather than preceded the rise in the number of protests.

Thus the institutionalization side of the Swiss protest wave was well developed. Radicalization, on the contrary, was virtually absent: the second half of the 1980s did not see the emergence of terrorist organizations or an increase in heavy violence. This absence of radicalization may be related to a second deviation—the absence of an increase in repression against confrontational protests. In Switzerland, the percentage of confrontational protests that were repressed remained at a relatively low level, comparable to the prewave levels in Germany and the Netherlands (i.e, about 25–35 percent). In fact, the only significant development in Swiss repression was a steady *decrease* in the level of repression against demonstrative protests from almost 20 percent in the period 1975–77 to less than 5 percent from 1981 to 1989. Thus, the asymmetric development of Swiss protests (institutionalization but no radicalization) is mirrored by a comparable one-sidedness in the reactions of established political actors to the NSMs. Whereas in Germany and the Netherlands the moderation of protests was a result of a combination of push (increased repression against confrontational protests) and pull (increased facilitation of moderate actions) factors—with the radicalization of a minority of the activists as a side effect—the Swiss movements experienced only pull factors, both in the form of increased facilitation and of decreased repression of demonstrative protests. In addition, there was a strong structural component to the Swiss movements' institutionalization, in the form of the availability of direct democracy. Not coincidentally, the 1980s saw a steady increase in the use of referenda and initiatives by the NSMs, reaching a maximum in 1989. Thus, the deviating development of the Swiss protest wave perfectly mirrors the general opportunity structure of the Swiss state, which we characterized as full integration.

The Swiss pattern is not unique, however. The Dutch protest wave of the 1960s followed a comparable trajectory, with virtually no radicalization and a decrease rather than an increase in repression over the course of the wave (see Koopmans 1992b, 1992c). These two cases thus point at important mechanisms of variation among protest waves. Although, as a general tendency, we may hold on to the idea of the twin processes of institutionalization and radicalization, the relative weight of these two trends may differ substantially among protest waves, depending on variations in the reactions of political elites to the rise of protest. Germany and the Netherlands in the 1980s may represent the most common pattern, in which political elites react to protests by using a combination of carrot and stick. Switzerland in the 1980s and the Netherlands in the 1960s, however, show that elites sometimes also employ an all-out integrative strategy, which results in strong institutionalization of social movements in the absence of radicalization. Conversely, we can hypothesize that protest waves that occur in strongly exclusive regimes may follow a third trajectory. In such regimes, the reaction of political elites to rising protests will be full-scale repression, and challengers are unlikely to find allies within the political system. Provided that repression is not so effective that the continuation of protests becomes impossible, the likely result of this elite strategy will be a strong radicalization of protests, possibly in the form of an armed insurrection. Examples of such outcomes of protest waves can be found in many Third World countries, but also in Northern Ireland, where the repression of a wave of peaceful protests by Catholics in the late 1960s and early 1970s resulted in the armed struggle of the Irish Republican Army. Within the domain of the NSMs, such extreme examples do not exist, although the outcomes of the German and Italian protest waves of the 1960s tended in this direction.

Part II

Elaborations

Chapter 6

The Political Construction of the
Nuclear Energy Issue

The question of the relation between social movements and social problems is perhaps the most hotly debated theme in the social movement literature. Conventional wisdom has it that the explanation for protest behavior lies in intolerable circumstances, unbearable deprivations, and intense grievances. Classical theories of collective behavior have generally followed this line of argumentation, and saw social movements as a direct result of the frustrations and anomie caused by large-scale social-structural change. Adherents of the resource mobilization model have taken a diametrically opposed position, arguing that "there is always enough discontent in any society to supply grass-roots support for a movement if the movement is effectively organized and has at its disposal the power and resources of some established group" (McCarthy and Zald 1977:1215). This position is generally shared by adherents of political process models, although their alternative to the grievance model emphasizes external political opportunities for mobilization rather than the internal resources that are central to the resource mobilization approach (for instance, McAdam 1982).

Thus far, we have only dealt occasionally with alternatives to the political opportunity explanation for international differences. In this chapter, we will discuss two other explanations in a more systematic way: the grievance model and the frame alignment model. These two alternative models share a focus on the relevance of the intensity of social problems for the mobilization of social movements. The difference between the two alternative models is that the grievance model tends to see social problems as given, objective facts to which social movements react, whereas the frame alignment model emphasizes the active role played by social movements in defining and constructing social problems. By focusing on the intensity of social problems to account for differences in social movement mobilization, these models challenge the basic tenet of the opportunity model, which holds that what matters for mobilization is not the availability of problems but the opportunity to do something about them—which may well be greatest where the intensity of the problem is relatively low.

We will first briefly discuss recent grievance-oriented explanations, and put these to a test by investigating the impact of the Chernobyl disaster on the mobilization of the antinuclear movements of Germany, France, the Netherlands, and Switzerland. Subsequently, we turn to the frame alignment model and discuss whether this model is able to provide an explanation for differences in public support, mobilization, and success of antinuclear movements in Western Europe.

Grievance Explanations

Although the classical tension-release model is now almost extinct, grievance-oriented explanations of social movements have recently made a comeback in the literature. A few quotations from studies of the ecology movement in Europe may illustrate this:

> The actual course of ecological movements varied strongly between countries. Most importantly, it depended on the particular ecological problems of each individual country and the specific issues which happened to be raised, often precipitated by environmental disasters and scandals. (Rüdig 1988: 28)

> Rates of participation in the ecology movement are highest in Greece, and it is significant that metropolitan Athens probably has the most severe pollution problems of any major city in the European community. (Inglehart 1990b: 52)

> In West Germany, the construction of nuclear energy plants and pollution damage to the Germans' beloved forests served to mobilize public support for the environmental movement. In France, however, there was no such mobilizing issue.... The absence of such a central cause retarded the development of all social movements. (Wilson 1990: 80)

Although such explanations may seem plausible at first sight, closer examination casts some doubt upon their validity. Why, for instance, did the construction of nuclear power plants in Germany "serve to mobilize public support for the environmental movement," whereas the construction of far more plants in France provided "no such mobilizing issue"? And do mobilizing issues simply "happen to be raised"?

These questions notwithstanding, a strong case has been made in the recent literature for a reevaluation of discontent as a cause of mobilization by studies of protest reactions to "suddenly imposed grievances." In his study of protests in the wake of the Three Mile Island nuclear accident of 1979, Walsh (1981), for instance, demonstrated a strong increase in antinuclear energy mobilization in the Harrisburg region after the accident, which suggests a strong link between the appearance of new grievances and the level of mobilization.

For our present purpose, suddenly imposed grievances with an international scope are of particular relevance. Such occurrences can provide a powerful test of the grievance argument, because they allow us to compare social movement mobilization in different settings, which are confronted with a similar "problem." The grievance model would then predict similar protest reactions in the different settings, whereas the alternative models would predict different reactions as a result of variation among the settings with regard to the prior level of mobilization of the movement in question (resource mobilization) and/or the available political opportunities (political process).

Chernobyl[1]

The Chernobyl disaster of April 26, 1986, provides a unique opportunity to test the grievance explanation of political mobilization since it affected many countries in a similar way and at the same point in time. Of course, the most immediate and serious consequences of the accident—in the form of death, illness, and evacuation—were limited to a relatively small area around the damaged reactor. Outside this area there was no way in which people could have noticed anything without the mediation of the authorities and the news media. Radiation was invisible and intangible and its consequences lay in the future and would only be detectable statistically.

One may argue that because it required such mediation, the Chernobyl accident is exceptional, and therefore not very suited for a test of the merits of grievance-oriented explanations of social protest. However, in this respect the Chernobyl accident resembles many modern social problems, and especially those addressed by the NSMs. Whether one takes acid rain, the decay of the ozone layer, the disappearance of tropical rain forests, the threat of nuclear war, Iraqi aggression against Kuwait, or poverty in the Third World, none of these problems is immediately felt by the populations of the industrialized countries and all of them have to be made "visible" by the media and have to be defined, interpreted, and framed by politicians, scientists, and social movements.

The degree to which the different Western European countries suffered objectively from increased levels of radiation differed considerably. Organization for Economic Cooperation and Development (OECD) figures cited by Rüdig (1990: 331) show that the average dose of radiation in the first year after the accident was highest in countries such as Austria, Finland, and Italy. Germany, Switzerland, and Sweden occupied an intermediate position, while France, the United Kingdom, and the Netherlands received relatively small doses. However, these figures hide even larger differences between regions within countries and over time. In the weeks immediately after the accident it was hardly possible for the authorities, let alone for the public, to make a reliable assessment of its impact. No one knew when the reactor fire would be under control, and areas that were lightly affected one day might be severely hit the next day, simply because of a change in wind or rainfall. As a result of the dependency of radiation levels on local weather conditions, regional variation was extremely high, and hot spots could be found all over Europe, even in countries that were on average only lightly affected (Hawkes et al. 1986: 207–8; Rüdig 1990: 331, 342). In some regions of France, for instance, radiation levels of up to four hundred times the normal level were measured (Hawkes et al. 1986: 154).

Given the complexity of the situation and the importance of local and regional differences, it seems warranted to conclude that, certainly in the period immediately following the accident, there were no substantial differences in the degree to which the different Western European countries were affected. The degree to which the events in Chernobyl led to a revival of antinuclear protest nonetheless differed immensely, even among neighboring states like Germany, France, the Netherlands, and Switzerland. As figure 6.1 shows, of these four countries only Germany witnessed a spectacular rise in the number of antinuclear protest events, whereas in France and Switzerland only a small increase took place and in the Netherlands no change at all was detectable.[2] The participation figures displayed in figure 6.2 reveal similar cross-national differences. Germany again shows the largest increase in mobilization, while in the Netherlands Chernobyl did not cause any change in the (low) level of antinuclear protest. The figure also makes clear that the modest increase in the number of protest events produced by the French antinuclear movement did not imply any significant increase in the volume of

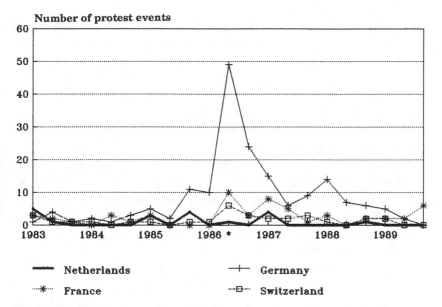

Fig. 6.1. Number of protests of the antinuclear movement per trimester in the four countries, 1983–89

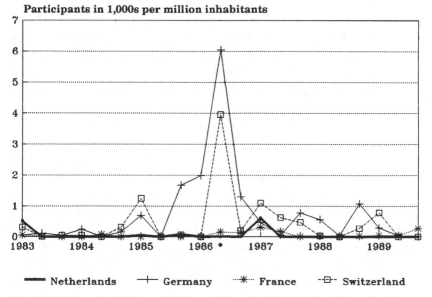

Fig. 6.2. Number of participants in actions of the antinuclear movement per trimester, per million inhabitants in the four countries, 1983–89

participation. In Switzerland, however, the Chernobyl accident was followed by a substantive increase in participation, although the level reached did not match the German level. Summing up, in Germany the accident brought about a surge of actions—radical ones such as sabotage of electric-power pylons and blockades, as well as massive demonstrations. In Switzerland the Chernobyl effect was more modest, and was limited to a few mass demonstrations. The French and Dutch movements, however, were unable to profit from the political fallout of the disaster.

Thus, while people demonstrated in German Saarbrücken against the nuclear power station in French Cattenom, the same station remained unchallenged in France itself; and while the power station in North German Brokdorf—in an area only lightly affected by radiation—became the object of mass demonstrations, all was quiet around the two Dutch nuclear power stations.

The reactions of the authorities were equally divergent: "On one side of a Rhine Bridge, at Kehl, in West Germany, the children were forbidden to play on the grass and the lettuces sat uneaten in the ground. On the French side of the bridge, around Strasbourg, very similar lettuces were declared harmless" (Hawkes et al. 1986: 154). As the German weekly *Der Spiegel* concluded, although several other countries (at the time of writing, particularly Sweden and Finland) were more seriously affected by the "immediate" consequences of the disaster, "the Federal Republic has been stricken most by the mediated consequences of the cloud—measured in fear becquerels and radiation-scare REM" (May 20, 1986: 97).

Should we see the particularly strong reaction in Germany as a result of a typically German proclivity toward hysteria, or is even fear mediated by political circumstances? There is good reason to believe that the latter is the case with regard to the German reaction to Chernobyl. To begin with, as figures 6.1 and 6.2 show, the rise of antinuclear protest in Germany did not appear out of thin air, but had begun in 1985. This increase was due particularly to the rise of a massive protest movement against the construction of a nuclear reprocessing plant in Wackersdorf, Bavaria. The fact that the Chernobyl accident occurred in the middle of this vigorous campaign, which had attracted national attention and had reached a peak with a demonstration of eighty thousand people less than a month before the events in Ukraine, must be considered an important explanation for the intensity of the German reaction to Chernobyl (Koopmans 1992b). Public opinion had already been mobilized around the issue of nuclear reprocessing, the movement was well prepared organizationally, and it had a concrete object to focus its mobilization upon.

In addition, the antinuclear movement was strengthened by the reactions of the West German political parties. The Social Democratic Party (SPD) had already declared itself against the nuclear reprocessing plant in Wackersdorf in 1984. After the Chernobyl accident, the SPD government of North Rhine-Westphalia refused to license the fast-breeder reactor in Kalkar, and in the autumn of 1986 the party's federal congress adopted a resolution calling for the phasing-out of nuclear power within ten years (Rüdig 1990: 341). Moreover, even within the ranks of the governing parties, nuclear energy was no longer uncontested: several state branches of the liberal Free Democratic Party (FDP) spoke out against the Wackersdorf project, and a number of prominent members of the Christian Democratic Union (CDU), among them Federal President Richard von Weizsäcker, expressed their doubts with regard to nuclear energy (*Der Spiegel,* July 29, 1986: 73). In combination with the staunch pronuclear position maintained by the federal government, and the Bavarian government's determination to complete the plant in Wackersdorf at any cost, this provided for a very favorable mix of opportunities for mobilization, making protest both necessary, possible, and potentially successful.

In France and the Netherlands, on the contrary, the antinuclear movement was in a rather desperate state at the time of the accident. The formerly impressive French movement had been reduced to marginal proportions after the Socialists took office in 1981, and even after Chernobyl all the major parties remained firmly behind nuclear power (Duyvendak 1992: 203–13). In the Netherlands, the movement had largely demobilized after its campaign to force the closure of the country's two operating nuclear plants failed in 1981. By the time of the Chernobyl accident, however, the designation of a site for two new nuclear power stations was due. This could have given the movement some opportunities for mobilization, although its lack of combat readiness would certainly have been a formidable barrier to the kind of mobilization successes achieved in Germany. As it was, even this opportunity was taken from the movement. Because the Chernobyl accident occurred shortly before national elections, the right-wing government swiftly moved to postpone the decision on new nuclear stations, and ordered renewed investigations into their safety and necessity (van der Heijden 1993). As a result, at the few antinuclear rallies that were organized in the Netherlands after Chernobyl, only a few dozen people showed up.

In Switzerland, finally, the conditions for an increase in protest were somewhat more conducive, since the construction of the country's most controversial nuclear project—the power station at Kaiseraugst—was about to begin. This may explain why the level of participation in the first trimester after the accident was higher in Switzerland than in France and the Netherlands. However, the government's October 1986 decision to postpone the Kaiseraugst project, much in the same way as the Dutch government's move, prevented a further reinvigoration of protest (Giugni 1992: 276–91).

Interestingly, it seems that even German federalism contributed to the intensity of post-Chernobyl mobilization in that country. Whereas the French authorities' claim that the radioactive clouds had somehow halted at the French borders could go virtually unchallenged, the German federal government was faced with a much more difficult task. Although it claimed, like its French counterpart, that there were no acute health risks and that the German nuclear power stations were not comparable to their Russian counterparts, it lacked the power to impose this view on local and regional authorities and thus was unable to convince the public. Much to the annoyance of the responsible federal minister, several state and local governments prohibited the consumption of fresh vegetables, closed children's playgrounds and swimming pools, and even canceled sports events (Hawkes et al. 1986: 149–50; Joppke 1991: 182).

We must conclude, then, that the political impact of the Chernobyl disaster cannot be adequately understood as a simple reaction to a "suddenly imposed grievance." Certainly, to some extent the accident brought about protest reactions in all Western European countries, and it may be that without Chernobyl the rise of antinuclear protest in Germany would have been less spectacular. Nevertheless, the results show that the effects of a suddenly imposed grievance such as the Chernobyl disaster are conditioned by situational factors such as the state of the antinuclear movement at the time of the accident, the political situation in which it occurred, and the outcome of the interpretive struggle between the antinuclear movement and pronuclear authorities.

Frame Alignment

The Chernobyl case shows not only the importance of political opportunities but also that prevailing definitions and interpretations of similar events can differ widely from one setting to another. Processes of definition and interpretation occupy a central place in the "framing" perspective on protest (Snow et al. 1986; Snow and Benford 1988, 1992). Snow and his colleagues to a large extent share our criticism of the traditional grievance perspective, and point out that "too much attention is focused on grievances per se and on their social psychological manifestations (e.g., relative deprivation, alienation), to the neglect of the fact that grievances or discontents are subject to differential interpretation, and the fact that variations in their interpretation across individuals, social movement organizations, and time can affect whether and how they are acted upon" (Snow et al. 1986: 465). At the same time, they criticize the resource mobilization perspective for skirting interpretive issues altogether, by assuming that grievances are ubiquitous and therefore do not merit investigation (ibid.: 466).

We do not want to contest the view that framing processes are important, but we do think it is necessary to inquire as to what their precise status is. As Snow et al. have pointed out, an important issue to be resolved concerns the success or failure of framing efforts by social movements:

> In arguing that one or more varieties of frame alignment is a necessary condition for movement participation, we have proceeded as if all framing efforts are successful. But clearly that is not the case. Potential constituencies are sometimes galvanized and mobilized, on other occasions framing efforts fall on deaf ears and may even be counter-productive. This obdurate fact thus begs the question of why framing processes succeed in some cases but not in others. (Ibid.: 477)

The basic question, in our view, is whether the success of framing efforts depends on the argumentative power of the discourse as such (which would imply that frame alignment may have an independent effect on movement participation) or whether framing functions primarily as a mechanism that translates structural conditions, constraints, or opportunities into articulated discontent and dispositions toward collective action (which would imply a more modest status for frame alignment as a transmission belt) —which, it should be stressed, does not make it unimportant, since any sound explanation should specify the mechanism that links causes and effects (Harré and Secord 1972; Elster 1989).

Snow et al.'s position on this issue is not entirely clear. On the one hand, they claim that frame alignment provides an independent contribution to the explanation of the success or failure of mobilization efforts (Snow et al. 1986: 478). On the other hand, when Snow and Benford discuss factors influencing the potency of framing efforts they suggest that the success of framing efforts depends on their "empirical credibility" and "experiential commensurability" (Snow and Benford 1988: 208), which brings the frame alignment model closer to the grievance-oriented explanations discussed earlier. Empirical credibility refers to "the fit between the framing and events in the world": "By empirical credibility, we refer to the evidential basis for a master frame's diagnostic claims . . . to the extent that there are events or occurrences that can be pointed to as documentary evidence . . . a master frame has empirical credibility" (Snow and Benford 1992: 140). Experiential commensurability refers to whether a frame fits "the personal experience of the targets of mobilization" (Snow and Benford 1988: 208). As an example, the authors give an explanation for the greater mobilizing capacity and more radical program of the Western European peace movements compared to their American counterpart:

> In Western Europe, in contrast to the United States, . . . movement activity appears to be more constant and intense. To the extent that these observations are empirically accurate, we think they can be explained in part by differences in the nature of cross-national experience with warfare and nuclear weaponry. Experience with warfare and nuclear weapons has been less direct and immediate in the United States than it has in Japan and Europe. Although the United States has been involved in numerous wars and skirmishes, none have taken place on its soil since the mid-1800s. Additionally, U.S. nuclear weapons installations tend to be located greater distances from dense population settlements than is the case in Western Europe. Given the Europeans' direct experience with warfare and the closer proximity of nuclear weapons installations to population masses, it follows that the threat of nuclear war has far greater experiential commensurability for citizens of European countries than for Americans. (Ibid.: 209)

To be sure, in a footnote in a later article Snow and Benford emphasize that what is at issue "is not whether diagnostic and prognostic claims are actually factual or valid, but whether their empirical referents lend themselves to being read as 'real' indicators of the claims. When they are, then the claims have empirical credibility." However, they immediately take the edge off this radically constructionist position, by stating that "although this is obviously an interpretive issue, *we suspect that it is easier to construct an evidential base for some claims than for others*" (Snow and Benford 1992: 140–41; emphasis added). Gamson has accurately diagnosed the ambiguity of Snow and Benford's model: "The authors have their feet planted solidly in a conventional positivist epistemology while their heads are in the clouds of a post-positivist, constructionist world. The very term 'empirical credibility' suggests the unresolved conflict" (1992: 69).

We now propose to take a closer look at the struggle over nuclear energy to see if, and to what extent, the frame alignment model—in either of its versions — may help to explain the differential impact on public opinion and the diverging levels of mobilization of antinuclear movements in different Western European countries.

The Struggle over Nuclear Power

Not only in the specific case of the Chernobyl disaster, but also more generally, the conflict over the use of nuclear power has given rise to diverging dominant interpretations. In some countries, such as the Netherlands or Denmark, the antinuclear movement's viewpoint that nuclear energy is both dangerous and unnecessary has become the dominant one among the general public, the news media, and a majority of the political parties. In other countries, such as West Germany, no clear winner has emerged from the debate between pronuclear and antinuclear interpretations, and the fight for hegemony continues. In still other countries, with France as the best-known example, antinuclear forces have clearly lost the discursive struggle, and have been marginalized by a discourse that emphasizes the safety of the national nuclear industry and the need for nuclear power as a guarantee of economic independence and as a source of national grandeur.

The differential success of the framing efforts of antinuclear movements is reflected in the figures displayed in table 6.1 about public opinion toward nuclear energy in eight Western European countries. The table shows that support for the antinuclear movement's view that the risks of nuclear energy are unacceptable generally increased since 1978. In 1978, those who found nuclear energy worthwhile still formed a majority in half of the countries, but by 1987 opponents of nuclear energy were in the majority in seven out of eight countries. However, there are two exceptions to this pattern of increasing support for the antinuclear movement's views: France, where in 1978 opponents of nuclear energy still formed a slight majority, but which by 1987 was the only country with a pronuclear majority; and Belgium, where the size of the antinuclear majority decreased from 12 to 6 percent. On the other side of the spectrum, we find two countries, Italy and Denmark, that have seen particularly spectacular increases in the number of opponents of nuclear energy, who in 1978 still formed a minority in both countries.

Thus, it is evident that framing efforts by the antinuclear movement have had differential success across countries. The question to address now is where these differences come from. One possibility is that antinuclear movements in countries like France have constructed less convincing frames against nuclear energy than their counterparts in Italy, the Netherlands, or

Table 6.1. Public opinion toward nuclear energy: size of antinuclear majority (percentage who find risks of nuclear energy unacceptable minus percentage who find nuclear energy worthwhile)

	1978	1987	Change 1978–87
France	2	−3	−5
Switzerland	−2	10	12
Germany	11	19	8
Netherlands	26	27	1
Belgium	12	6	−6
United Kingdom	−32	1	33
Italy	−24	46	70
Denmark	−3	49	52

Note: The answering categories "of no interest," "don't know," and "no answer" have been disregarded. For Switzerland, no *Eurobarometer* data are available. As a substitute we used the percentage difference between antinuclear and pronuclear votes in two national referenda held in 1979 and 1990 (the antinuclear majority in the latter referendum led to a ten-year moratorium on the construction of new nuclear power stations). We have displayed information only for those countries for which *Eurobarometer* data are available for both 1978 and 1987 (which led to the exclusion of all non-EC countries (except Switzerland), as well as Spain and Portugal, for which no 1978 data are available). In addition, we excluded those EC countries that do not have nuclear power stations, and never had plans to build them either (Luxembourg, Ireland, and Greece). The latter decision follows from our consideration that attitudes toward nuclear energy are only meaningful in countries where nuclear energy has been a matter of political decision making and public debate.
Source: Eurobarometer, cited in Rüdig 1990: 346

Denmark. This explanation is not very plausible. To begin with, to an important extent the antinuclear frame was an international discourse, with relatively little cross-country variation, resulting from intensive international diffusion of arguments and symbols (just think of the laughing sun as the antinuclear symbol, or of the slogan "Nuclear Energy? No, Thanks!") (van der Heijden, Koopmans, and Giugni 1992). Moreover, this interpretation cannot explain why, for instance, the idea that nuclear energy would lead to a police state was unconvincing in a strong state like France—where the idea had first come up (*électrofascisme*) — whereas in Germany it became a major discursive weapon for the movement (*Atomstaat*).

An alternative explanation along the same lines would be that crossnational variation can be explained by the fact that *pro*nuclear forces were able to construct more convincing frames in some countries than in others. For example, it may be argued that appeals to national independence and grandeur struck a responsive chord in France, whereas in other political cultures with a less pronounced sense of national identity such appeals would be much less effective (this form of frame resonance is called "narrative fidelity" by Snow and Benford [1988: 210–11]). The problem with this explanation, which emphasizes the role of relatively stable national political cultures, is that it is unable to account for the fact that in 1978 public opinion was still compara- tively favorable to the French antinuclear movement, which, moreover, ful- filled a pioneering role in the early 1970s, and achieved mobilization levels far higher than any other European antinuclear movement at that time (see Rüdig 1990). This is illustrated in an exemplary way by the history of anti- nuclear protest in the French-German border region. In the early 1970s, the French movement served as an example for German civic initiatives across the border, and French protesters were actively involved in the 1975 site oc- cupation in the German village of Wyhl that brought about a breakthrough for the German movement. By the end of the 1980s, this situation had com- pletely reversed. While German protesters had been strengthened by their ultimately successful campaign against the Wyhl station, their French col- leagues had demobilized almost completely, and the few protests that were still organized against the French nuclear stations at Fessenheim and Cat- tenom were dominated by German activists (Koopmans 1992b:169-71; see also chapter 8 on diffusion in this volume). These remarkable shifts clearly can- not be explained by relatively stable national political cultures and identities.

Thus, we will have to look outside the discursive realm for the causes of the diverging success of antinuclear movements in convincing the public. Fol- lowing Snow and Benford, we should investigate whether the claims of the antinuclear movement had more "empirical credibility" or "experiential com- mensurability" in some countries than in others. A factor that is likely to play a role in this respect is the size of a country's nuclear industry. Follow- ing the argumentation of the frame alignment model and as an analogy to Snow and Benford's explanation for the divergent mobilizing capacities of the Western European and American peace movements, it may be argued that in countries with a large number of nuclear plants, in which many people have direct experience with nuclear reactors in their immediate surround- ings, the antinuclear movement's views will more easily find a sympathetic hearing.

Table 6.2 shows, however, that this is not the case. On the contrary, France and Belgium, the countries where the antinuclear movement has been least successful in convincing the public, are also the two countries with the largest share of nuclear energy in total electricity production. Moreover, in the coun- tries with the largest antinuclear majorities—the Netherlands, Italy, and Denmark—nuclear energy is least developed.[3] (See chapter 9 for a discussion of the reasons behind the variable degree of substantive success of antinu- clear movements.)

Table 6.2. Planned and realized shares of nuclear energy in total
electricity production (percentages)

	Planned 1974	Realized 1988	Percentage of plan realized
France	68	70	103
Switzerland	44	37	84
Germany	47	34	72
Netherlands	43	5	11
Belgium	50	66	132
United Kingdom	43	19	44
Italy	43	0	0
Denmark	23	0	0

Source: Rüdig 1990: 102, 348

Another explanation that is sometimes suggested is that pronuclear forces find it easier to influence public opinion in countries with limited natural energy sources. This would indeed account for the high percentage of supporters of nuclear energy in France, but it fails to explain why in Denmark, which has the highest dependence on energy imports of the eight countries (Rüdig 1990: 355), opponents of nuclear energy are firmly in the majority. Moreover, the two countries with large national energy sources at their disposal—the Netherlands and the United Kingdom—occupy very divergent positions as regards the public's attitudes toward nuclear energy.

The results displayed in table 6.2 suggest that an explanation that focuses on political opportunities, and more particularly on success chances, is better able to make sense of cross-national variations in public attitudes toward nuclear energy. The last column of the table presents the percentage of planned nuclear capacity in 1974 that had been realized by 1988, which may serve as an indicator for the success of the antinuclear movement in limiting the expansion of nuclear energy.

Before we discuss results presented in the table, we would like to emphasize that it is not a necessary condition for our argument that reductions of nuclear energy programs be wholly attributed to the antinuclear movement's efforts. In fact, the political process model suggests that the opportunities provided by the movement's opponents—governments and nuclear industries—will be a more important determinant of success than the mobilizing capacities or strategies of antinuclear movements. What matters here is whether we may counterfactually suppose that without pressure from the antinuclear movement the nuclear programs of the 1970s would have been implemented to approximately their intended extent. This presupposition is plausible in most of the countries under study. The only exception might be Great Britain. As Rüdig has noted, the reductions of the British nuclear program have had little to do with pressure from the—very weak—British antinuclear movement: "Throughout the history of nuclear power in Britain, many delays were *not* due to anti-nuclear opposition but due to problems located within the industry. The British anti-nuclear movement found itself largely unable to exploit the difficulties in the nuclear sector" (Rüdig 1990: 352; emphasis in original). This may also explain why, as we will see, the development of the mobilization of, and public support for, the British antinuclear movement deviates to some extent from the pattern found in the other countries.

If we compare tables 6.1 and 6.2, we note striking similarities in the positions different countries occupy in the two tables. Thus, the failure of the French and Belgian movements to influence public opinion is linked to an even greater failure to influence nuclear energy policies: in both countries, nuclear energy's share in electricity production in 1988 was even larger than the share envisaged by the authorities in 1974. In Italy, Denmark, and the Netherlands, on the other hand, the antinuclear movement not only achieved a discursive victory, but also succeeded in either preventing any expansion of nuclear energy beyond the level already attained in 1974 (the Netherlands), blocked plans to embark on nuclear energy (Denmark), or even forced the closure of all existing nuclear power stations (Italy). Furthermore, Switzerland and Germany occupy intermediary positions in both tables: the antinuclear movements of these countries were moderately successful both in convincing public opinion and in influencing nuclear energy policies. The only partial exception to this pattern is the United Kingdom, which in 1988 had the second-most unfavorable public opinion climate for the antinuclear movement, despite a sizable reduction of the country's nuclear program. On the other hand, the strong increase in the number of opponents of nuclear energy since 1978 is again in line with the pattern for the other countries.

Thus we find that discursive success and substantive success are intimately related. This cannot be interpreted as a logical consequence of the responsiveness of authorities to public opinion. As table 6.1 shows, in 1978 French and Belgian public opinion was comparatively favorable to the antinuclear movement, whereas the Italians and the Danes were far from staunch opponents of the nuclear option at that time. If the degree of expansion of nuclear energy was simply a function of an initially antinuclear public opinion climate we would have expected the French and Belgian movements to have been more successful in substantive terms than their Italian or Danish counterparts. The results therefore suggest that the direction of causality is reversed: antinuclear attitudes have followed rather than caused substantive movement successes. Apparently, in order to solve the problem of "cognitive dissonance," people have changed their definitions of nuclear energy as problematic in countries where they found no opportunities to influence the development of nuclear energy (Duyvendak 1992: 240–44). As Cobb and Elder put it: "We normally think of policy problems as having their origins in events and circumstances. These create difficulties, which prompt a search for solutions. Often, however, this is not the case.... Situations defined as inevitable and unalterable, however lamentable, are not likely to be considered policy problems, but rather just hard facts of life" (1983: 177, 174). Conversely, in countries where the development of nuclear energy has come to a standstill or has been abandoned altogether, the public seems to have interpreted this as proof of the problematic nature of this form of electricity production.

Seen from this perspective, it is no longer surprising that opponents of nuclear energy in France, with its strong, exclusive state and predominance of traditional socioeconomic cleavages, resulting in few opportunities for success, have largely given up their struggle and to some extent have even bent their viewpoints to the inevitable. The weak Swiss and German states provided the antinuclear movement with more successes, although the more limited degree of state control over the nuclear industry has prevented a victory of the extent achieved in the strong, inclusive Dutch state.

Variations in movement success offer a plausible explanation for variations in public attitudes toward nuclear energy, but what about mobilization? A comparison of the mobilization levels reported in table 6.3 with the public opinion figures in table 6.1 makes clear that grievances again do not predict levels of mobilization: the two countries that share a low level of mobilization — France and the Netherlands — are each other's perfect antipoles with regard to the level of antinuclear grievances.[4] But a comparison of tables 6.2 and 6.3 makes clear that there is no linear relation between success and mobilization either, since both the highly successful Dutch movement and the highly unsuccessful French movement have a relatively low level of mobilization for the period 1975–89. Rather, moderate levels of success, as in Germany and Switzerland, seem to offer the best conditions for a high level of antinuclear mobilization. This result is in line with the conclusions drawn from earlier investigations into the relation between success and movement

Table 6.3. Level of mobilization of the antinuclear movement:
total participation, 1975–89 (per million inhabitants)

France	9,000
Switzerland	24,000
Germany	26,000
Netherlands	15,000

mobilization. Eisinger (1973: 15) and Kitschelt (1986: 62) both arrive at the conclusion that the relationship between the degree of "openness" of a political system and movement mobilization is curvilinear: both very open and very closed regimes have lower levels of mobilization, whereas regimes that are neither very open nor very closed tend to display the highest level of movement activity. Rüdig similarly concludes that partial success is "the condition which is crucial to a sustained development of protest groups" (1990: 235).

As we saw in chapter 2, this curvilinear relation between success and movement mobilization results from a combination of counteracting factors. On the one hand, success stimulates further mobilization because it enhances belief in the efficacy of collective action. On the other hand, further mobilization after a success has been achieved often necessitates a reorientation of the movement, which requires effort and time and may cause the movement to lose momentum and initiative. Moreover, subsequent successes tend to become harder and harder to obtain, since movements tend to pick the ripest apples—those parts of the nuclear program against which public opposition is strongest and institutional resistance weakest—first (Koopmans 1992a: 30–33). This happened, for instance, to the Dutch antinuclear movement, which was very successful in blocking construction plans for new nuclear power stations but was unable to sustain its level of mobilization when it subsequently had to focus on the closure of the two already existing stations, a goal that was much more difficult to achieve, and for which the movement found little political support.

Conclusion

Taken together, the results of our comparative analysis of antinuclear energy movements provide little support for grievance-oriented approaches to social movements. Despite the fact that the nuclear accident in Chernobyl confronted different countries with the same event, the intensity and content of protest differed widely, from a surge of antinuclear protests in Germany to virtually no reaction in the Netherlands and France. This result points to a fundamental problem attached to the concept of "suddenly imposed grievances"—namely, that it equates objective conditions with the sentiments attached to them, and therefore presupposes much of what we need to explain. Labeling nuclear accidents as "suddenly imposed grievances" is taking one important step too far, and may lead one to focus only on those accidents that did lead to mobilization by antinuclear activists, ignoring both the fact that many nuclear accidents have provoked little, if any, protest (or may even have remained unknown to us),[5] and, as the Chernobyl case demonstrates, that the same accident may be a major political event in one country while provoking as little controversy as the weather report in another.

Our data on the struggle over nuclear power confirm this absence of a direct relation between objective conditions, grievances, and mobilization. The objective extent of the nuclear energy "problem" was found to be unrelated to the level of mobilization of the antinuclear movement; nor could it explain public attitudes toward nuclear energy (i.e., grievance levels). Grievances, in turn, provided no explanation for levels of mobilization. Of course, we do not deny the trivial truth that the existence of antinuclear energy movements depends on the discovery and development of nuclear energy, just as peace movements do not develop in absolutely peaceful societies. In other words, the very existence of the objects movements focus upon is indeed a necessary—but far from sufficient—condition to give birth to grievances and protest. But any mobilization asks for "facts" to be considered as "problems." As adherents of the constructionist perspective on social problems have stressed time and again, these facts do not speak for themselves (Blumer 1971; Spector and Kitsuse 1973; Schneider 1985; Hilgartner and Bosk 1988). The appearance that they do speak for themselves (as reflected, for instance, in the concept of "suddenly imposed grievances") is only created after they have been given meaning by human agents.

Processes of meaning-giving are central to the second approach we have scrutinized in this chapter: the frame alignment model. The Chernobyl case and the struggle over nuclear power more generally provide ample evidence of cross-country differences in the dominant discourses in which nuclear energy has been framed. The importance of processes of collective definition and interpretation is therefore not at issue. Our attention has instead been directed toward the factors that determine the potency of framing efforts by antinuclear movements and their opponents in different countries. As we have pointed out, Snow and Benford's position on this issue is somewhat ambiguous and oscillates between a purely constructionist position in which the potency of frames is determined by factors internal to the discursive process, and a focus on a frame's "empirical credibility" and "experiential commensurability," which links the frame alignment model to grievance-oriented explanations. The latter interpretation of Snow and Benford's position shares the general failure of explanations focusing on supposedly aggrieving conditions in accounting for differences in the mobilization of antinuclear movements.

This does not mean, however, that the construction of grievances or social problems is a self-contained process, with no "external" foundation whatsoever, as is supposed in the alternative reading of Snow and Benford's position and in many versions of the constructionist view on social problems. Our findings indicate that the construction of grievances and social problems, and the degree to which they give rise to social movement mobilization are rooted not in aggrieving conditions but in political power relations. Such political opportunities determined the degree of success of challenges to the ambitious nuclear programs formulated in the 1960s and 1970s, and in turn, success proved to be a powerful determinant of both antinuclear grievances and mobilization. Therefore, instead of focusing exclusively on discourse and meaning, it seems necessary to look also at the political conditions under which specific discourses become imaginable. The cases discussed here provide ample evidence of the influence of opportunities on the perception and definition of events as grievances. In the Chernobyl case, the strong French state even successfully denied the existence of a problem, and, in the absence of any competing version among the country's political elites, was able to convince the population that radiation had somehow halted at the country's borders, and that the unsafe nature of Soviet reactors was of no relevance to superior French nuclear technology. This interpretation of the problem may have been unreal, but it was perfectly real in its consequences.

Conversely, antinuclear movements that were confronted with more favorable opportunity structures and were able to successfully block or slow down the construction of nuclear power stations were also able to win the discursive battle, and to convince a majority of the public of the problematic nature of nuclear energy. In that sense, Mauss is correct when he states that "social movements generate social problems" (1975: xvi–xvii). However, he is also right in adding that "social unrest, social problems, social movements, and the like are more likely to occur under some social conditions than under others. One important and rather obvious example of such a contingency

is whether the political system permits the collective expression of new con-
structions of reality by interest groups" (ibid.: 38–39; see also Schneider 1985:
224–25; McAdam 1990: 12). Social movements are sometimes victorious in
their efforts to frame situations as problematic, but only when they operate
in a political context that offers them the opportunities to do so.

Chapter 7

Gay Subcultures between Movement and Market

Understanding the gay and lesbian movement is, to a certain extent, more complicated than grasping an instrumental movement like the environmental movement. Whereas the latter's goal realization depends almost 100 percent on the external world—adversaries, authorities, and allies— in the history of the gay and lesbian movement, campaigns directed toward authorities and against adversaries alternate with internally oriented activities. These internal activities in particular confront us with the following conceptual problem: how do we draw the boundary between movement and subculture if both their activities are aimed at identity construction? In order to comprehend the gay and lesbian movement, we propose to distinguish between politicized identities (constituting a movement) and purely subcultural identities—often formed in the commercial subculture—that do not challenge the outside world.[1]

This introductory discussion makes clear that for the sake of a better understanding of the dynamics of the gay and lesbian movement, a precise analysis of the relation between movement and subculture is necessary. How crucial this relation is can be illustrated by the following two examples. The first shows that, in order to "survive," this movement should not take too much distance from its subcultural basis; the second shows that it should not identify with the (commercial) subculture either.

1. During the 1970s, the COC (Cultural and Recreational Center), the main Dutch gay and lesbian organization, was opposed to its local chapters using dances primarily oriented toward a gay and lesbian public. The organization held the opinion that places exclusively accessible to gay men and lesbian women were an obstacle to the integration of homosexuality in Dutch society: everybody should feel welcome. In those days, the COC focused on social

and political changes, which, in its view, implied openness toward the outside world. The underlying idea was that the interests of gays and lesbians were best served by the dissolution of homosexual identities as such. This implied the disappearance of separate, pleasure-oriented recreation that produced these identities. It was only at the end of the 1970s that its opinion changed:

> The COC is moving away from its rather negative attitude toward "recreation" of the first half of the 1970s. Considering it as "ghetto" activities obstructed the view that separate recreation offers many opportunities for the construction of gay identities. (Cited in Jansen 1983: 101; translated by the author)

Subcultural and political activities were no longer considered to be contradictory, but rather complementary: strong identities became a prerequisite for the emancipation of gays and lesbians. Separate, pleasure-oriented recreation was now even stimulated because it was considered a support to the liberation struggle.

2. In 1985, in a letter published in *Gai Pied,* a French gay weekly, the most significant gay entrepreneur of those days (David Girard) wrote, a few days before the gay pride parade:

> Everyone to the demonstration! What is certain is that we are not going to demonstrate in the same spirit as the people of CUARH [Comité d'Urgence Anti-Répression Homosexuelle—a highly politicized SMO]. They march in order to denounce antihomo racism. That is their right. But allow me to say that taking up a banner and marching under it chanting "No to antihomo racism" will not change a thing; it will not even attract sympathy. It is sad. It is gray. All of us, we come to celebrate. And what we shall defend is the right to celebrate. It is surely more communicative (and communicating), more of a tonic for the participants, and consequently more impressive and attractive for onlookers and media. (*Gai Pied,* April 27, 1985: 61; translated by the author)

This letter highlights a turning point in the history of French homosexuality. Although it shows that in 1985 Girard and others were still of the opinion that the newly acquired sexual freedom should be expressed and shown to the outside world, later it turned out that the drive to show just how "gay" gay life was no longer generated sufficient incentive for mobilization. The number of participants of the French gay pride parade declined from ten thousand at the beginning of the 1980s to two or three thousand by the second half of the decade. Whereas in earlier days political demands were expressed, as time went by the element of fun became more important. Increasingly, political and recreational goals were not experienced as complementary but as contradictory: the creation of gay identities by "recreation"—more precisely, by a *commercial* subculture—became a "stone wall" for the development of a *political* gay identity.

This chapter aims to analyze this ambiguous relationship between subculture and movement in order to understand the dynamics of the subcultural movement type. In chapter 4, the gay movement was introduced as the subcultural movement par excellence: because a positive gay or lesbian self-identity is formed through subcultural activity, the common sexual orientation is an incentive for individuals to mobilize and organize collectively. This implies, however, that gay and lesbian movements are obliged to walk the line between *desires* and *interests:*[2] the French example shows that when desire prevails over political struggle, the movement may become a pure subculture; the Dutch example may teach that when the representation of political interests becomes too dominant and the link with the subculture too loose, such movements will not survive in the long run, since identity production—the reason why most people participate—will no longer take place.

As long as movement organizations are the only ones providing "positive" identities, this problem is still limited. A subcultural movement whose collective good can only be shared by its members does not suffer from free-riding. This is only true in the short run, however. Although at the start of the emancipation process, participation is a sine qua non for sharing in the collective good, later on "parasitic behavior" becomes an option. "Over time, the very success of ... movements may result in the transformation of these collective identities into public goods available to everyone. That is, movements may produce collective identities of such salience ... that they cease to be exclusive property of the movement, thus losing their power to compel participation" (Friedman and McAdam 1992:157–58). This is particularly the case for the gay movement: when subcultures become more *commercial,* people can share collective identities outside the movement, purely on the basis of pleasure (Duyvendak 1990). In this situation, many SMOs can only survive by becoming more pleasure-oriented and less political. Gay journals in particular will show the tendency to *commercialize,* by publishing more erotic pictures and less political information (Duyvendak and Duyves 1993).

Both these processes of *involution* and *commercialization* may take place when social and political discrimination have begun to diminish. Although organizations of all types of movements can commercialize—irrespective of whether they were originally instrumentally, counter- or subculturally oriented—this trajectory is the most frequently "chosen" by subcultural organizations. The same holds with regard to involution: since internal activities constitute the basis of subcultural organizations, the involutionary step toward an exclusive internal orientation is rather small for a gay organization.

The French example provides evidence for these processes. In France, the movement showed a real involution process. The gay movement finally even disappeared due to a boom in the commercial subculture that provided the common identity many people were looking for. However, this identity was not very politicized or oppositional to the straight world anymore—the political struggle seemed over and the party had begun.

The shifts in the relation between subculture and movement are not endogenous processes but depend on the broader social and political context. Since the Dutch gay movement saw opportunities for social acceptance of homosexuality in the 1970s, it urged members to come out of the closet and to participate in hetero/homosexual mixed activities. The very concept of an autonomous subculture was considered backward and superfluous, and a collective gay identity as self-repressive. The social and political circumstances were so inviting that the maintenance of a proper subculture was seen as being at odds with the integration of homosexuality into society. In time, however, the COC realized that creating collective identities is a necessity for a movement of the subcultural type—both in order to attract members and to enable it to act as an organization that represented an identifiable group. A gay organization that moves too far into an instrumental direction runs the risk of eroding its proper basis.

The situation in France in the 1980s also proves that a one-sidedly instrumental path, as chosen by the CUARH in the conducive political situation after May 1981, indeed creates a fatal imbalance between interests and desires. This is especially the case in combination with sudden and total political success, as happened when the left-wing government abolished many discriminatory laws (Duyvendak 1992: 223). Its fixation on interests left room for other organizations to satisfy desires. The demand for identities was effectively met by the booming commercial subculture, and political activity seemed more and more superfluous and obsolete.

In theoretical terms, these examples seem to confirm that the development of the gay movement depends to a large extent on the "concrete opportunities" discussed in chapters 2 and 4: not only the relations between the pure subculture and SMOs of the gay movement are heavily influenced by the degree of facilitation and repression, and to some extent by the chances of success provided by the political system, but so are the collective identities of the subculture. Political circumstances codetermine whether these identities are more political or more commercial. Of course, this is not to deny that, in case of subcultural movements, cultural factors also play an important, independent role. In many Western European countries, with rather divergent political systems, since the 1960s more liberal attitudes toward sexual issues have evolved (Inglehart 1990a), clearing the way for both gay movements and gay subcultures.

It is one step too far, however, to suggest—as do supporters of the so-called New Social Movements approach—that "new" movements are beyond the reach of politics. And, although the gay movement may be considered the prototype of an NSM, with its emphasis on identity production, it is not exclusively oriented toward "the control of a field of autonomy or of independence vis-à-vis the system" (Melucci 1980: 220) either. In order to weigh the importance of "autonomous" versus politically oriented activities, and to evaluate the influence of cultural and political factors, I will sketch the development of the gay movement and subculture in the Netherlands, Germany, France, and Switzerland.[3]

The Movement

After the leading gay movement in Germany and its branches in surrounding countries had been wiped out by the Nazis, emancipation had to make a fresh start after World War II. Succeeding gay journals published in Weimar Germany, *Der Kreis* (The Circle) (1933–67) was exceptional in surviving the war. In the 1950s this international cultural journal, edited by Karl Meier in Switzerland and obtainable only by subscription, appeared in German as well as in French and English.

For gay men and lesbians in Europe, the 1950s were a period of repression. Male homosexuality was still illegal in several states. In West Germany, where the Nazi law on homosexuality was not repealed, the number of legal prosecutions for homosexual offenses and "public indecency" even increased compared to the prewar period. In some other countries, such as the Netherlands, the age of consent for same-sex activity was higher than for heterosexual activity. In general, the media reinforced the moral consensus by caricaturing homosexuals as immoral corrupters of youth and potential or actual traitors. They had to live a double life and could only express themselves in the underground subculture.

Before the 1960s, reformist organizations advocating equal rights had to operate cautiously and discreetly so as not to offend the authorities and public opinion. The most successful was the Dutch COC, founded in 1946. By approaching leading figures of several political and religious groupings, it tried to influence the outside world, while at the same time offering support and recreation to individual gay men and lesbians (Tielman 1982; Warmerdam and Koenders 1987). The COC's strategy was typical for homophile organizations, which were also founded in West Germany (1949) and France (1954). Politically, these organizations upheld a neutral position and by endorsing dominant values they tried to improve the image of "homophiles" as respectable citizens—apart from sexual orientation, no different from heterosexuals. At the beginning of the 1950s, the COC took the initiative to establish the International Committee for Sexual Equality, in which several national organizations participated. By the early 1960s, however, this international committee withered away, mainly because most national organizations were too weak to survive.

During the second half of the 1960s, the gay movement received new impetus in many European countries. Attitudes toward homosexuality changed, not so much because of the impact of gay activism but more as a consequence of a relaxation of the moral climate in Western European welfare states. Puritan moral codes began to crumble as a result of a long period of economic expansion and growing affluence. Possibilities for geographical and social mobility were increasing and facilitated individualism and alternative lifestyles. Changes in family life and the increase in birth-control facilities stimulated the supersession of procreation by affection and pleasure as the main purpose of sex. Around 1960 more and more professionals, politicians, and clergymen began to doubt the effects of the criminalization and oppression of homosexuality and argued for a humanitarian attitude.

After 1965, in several Western European states liberal-humanitarian reforms in the field of the family and sexuality were introduced, with only France— under the authoritarian Gaullist regime—showing a different trend. An important legal reform concerning homosexuality took place in West Germany (1969). Much publicity was given to the issue of homosexuality, and self-organization was stimulated by the decriminalization. Next to the appearance of new homosexual journals, more radical gay groups came into being.

The early 1970s were a turning point in the gay movements of many European countries. The reformist homophile organizations that had tiptoed through the liberal 1960s by stressing the need for discretion and respectability were superseded by militant and more radical gay groups. Like the American Gay Liberation Front, which sprang up after the Stonewall Riots in New York City, they advocated openness, defiance, gay pride, and self-activity, and linked personal exploration with political activism. Liberationist organizations came to the fore in all four countries. Although a lot of inspiration and rhetoric was drawn from the American example, all were rooted in the specific traditions of their national political culture. In France, the revolutionary climate of 1968 gave birth to the Comité d'Action Pédérastique Révolutionnaire (Committee for Revolutionary Faggot Action). In 1971, the FHAR (Front Homosexuel d'Action Révolutionnaire — Homosexual Front for Revolutionary Action) was established, which in turn stimulated the development of the liberation fronts in other countries. All these fronts were dominated by students involved in activities of the extreme left. The more the political climate they were working in was polarized, and the more their parties were used to thinking in terms of revolutions (as in France), the more politically radical homosexuality became. In the southern European countries dominated by machismo, the revolutionary attack against "normal" gender roles followed the strategy of "inversion": "our asses are revolutionary," wrote Guy Hocquenghem, one of the founders of the FHAR.

In Germany and in German-speaking Switzerland, the contested film *Nicht der Homosexuelle ist pervers, sondern die Situation in der er lebt* (It is not the homosexual who is perverted but the situation in which he lives; 1971) by Rosa von Praunheim gave rise to several local groups — many of them, such as Homosexuelle Aktion Westberlin (Homosexual Action West Berlin), Marxist in orientation. In the Netherlands, already in the late 1960s radical student groups defied the reformist COC, followed in the 1970s by Red Faggots and radical lesbian-feminist groups. The Dutch COC finally adapted its policy to the new trend and survived the wave of radical gay activism, but many other old organizations and newspapers, such as *Arcadie* (France) and *Der Kreis* (Germany/Switzerland), which refused to adapt to new social and political circumstances, disappeared.

In the 1970s, in many countries the expansion of the gay movement was accompanied by fragmentation. Internal conflicts about the priority of cultural activities versus political activism and lobbying, and about political strategy (integration versus separatism), took place. These, and disputes about feminism, transvestism, pedophilia, and sadomasochism, resulted in dispersal. At the same time, increasing specialization and institutional integration took place: gay groups sprang up in political parties, churches, trade unions, social work, and universities. European cooperation was stimulated by the International Gay Association, founded in 1978.[4] In many countries, including Switzerland, France, Germany, and the Netherlands, annual gay parades were institutionalized in the late 1970s. Although most gay liberation groups were small and short-lived, they had a big impact on homosexuals themselves and on society. In addition to the expansion of the gay community and a commercial, pleasure-oriented subculture, homosexuality had become a public and political issue; increasingly the idea gained ground that homosexuality itself was not the problem, but rather society's attitude toward it.

The Subculture

Since no serious research on the gay subculture in the four countries has been carried out—perhaps because of its "exclusive" character—we can only present a very general "social map" of the gay subculture in them, without quantitative or temporal parameters. In the "map," sports, social, cultural, religious, and health activities are included.[5] It is most striking to discover that in many ways the subcultures of the four countries resemble each other: often hidden from the outside world, the following subcultural activities and organizations exist(ed) *in all four countries*:

- commercial places such as bars, cafés, discos, restaurants, hotels, saunas, partner agencies, gay travel agencies, gay dance schools, gay campsites, gay libraries, gay publishing houses (for journals, revues, erotic and pornographic materials, and literature);
- sports activities, the most popular being swimming, hiking, driving motor cars, playing volleyball, going to the gym together, and practicing self-defense;
- cultural activities such as singing in choirs, playing in gay theater, talking Esperanto with each other, holding film festivals, setting up art galleries, keeping gay archives and documentation centers, spreading information by switchboards, publishing noncommercial journals and revues, broadcasting gay radio programs;
- social groups of gay youngsters, of gay elderly, of gay fat people, of children with a homosexual parent, of parents with gay and lesbian children, of married homosexuals, of disabled homosexuals, of foreign gays, of gays with psychological problems (therapeutic and self-help groups), of homosexuals within denominational organizations (within almost all Christian churches, within humanistic organizations, and in the Jewish community), of gays and lesbians within unions (in particular teachers and health workers), at universities and high schools, of doctors, theologians, and lawyers;
- AIDS health groups, both self-help and semiprofessionalized (for people with AIDS, for people who are HIV positive, for surviving relatives), AIDS prevention activities, and so on.

A conclusion must be that there is, almost unnoticed, an enormous "pillarization" process taking place among gay men, leading to very similar "pillars" in different countries:[6] during the 1970s and 1980s, the subcultures of the four countries became quasi-identical.

However, the kinds of collective identities produced in these subcultures range from hyperpoliticized to apolitical. This is due to the fact that, whereas the subcultural infrastructures closely resemble each other across countries, each country has its own typical field of SMOs. Therefore, if we want to understand a subcultural movement, we should look at the precise relation between movement and subculture in the four countries.

The Countries

The movement is by far the most developed in *the Netherlands*: this is the only country with a strong national organization (COC) (10,000 members), a national weekly (circulation: 20,000), a peak organization responsible for the annual gay parade (the Pink Front), many interest groups (even in traditionally homophobic professions like the military and the police), gay and lesbian studies departments at several universities, and so on. The Dutch movement is very professionalized — not only in the AIDS sector, as is the case in the other three countries as well, but in many fields. This professionalization is the result of relatively massive subsidies and other facilities provided by local, regional, and national governments. Repression is almost absent, and success chances are rather favorable: a liberal majority in the parliament is strongly in favor of equal rights for gays and lesbians. This is, however, not yet a situation of reform (which would lead to demobilization) since the rather traditional Christian Democrats play a pivotal role in Dutch government, causing delays on the way to equal rights (Duyvendak et al. 1992).

Until now, the movement has survived the competition of the flourishing subculture precisely because of the external support of both allies and the authorities: a professional movement attracts members if success chances and facilitation are present. The very fact, however, that the interest-oriented movement is so strong in the Netherlands also accelerated the depoliticization of the subculture. In Amsterdam in particular — famous for being the "gay capital of Europe," where discrimination is almost absent — a combative attitude seems unnecessary. This fact, together with the existence of a strong movement that was vigilant to what happened in politics, made the collective identities of the commercial subculture rather apolitical.

Both the mobilization capacity of the Dutch movement (a gay pride parade with fifteen to twenty thousand participants in recent years) and the very developed subculture may be surprising in a country where homosexuality is accepted by more than 75 percent of the population — one of the highest percentages in the world (see table 7.1). First of all, why should people demonstrate if discrimination against homosexuals is marginal? And second, linked to this question, why do people build their own subcultural "pillar" at a time when they seem welcome in the outside world? In response to the first question, we have to recall that mobilization and repression are not linearly related, as was explained in chapters 2 and 4. The mobilization process of a subcultural movement seems to have its own logic, in that repression may be the trigger (for instance, in the Stonewall Riots), but this only leads to continued participation if success chances and facilitation by third parties are present. A situation of pure repression does not evoke any mobilization — as it would in the case of countercultural movements — but stimulates "sheltering" behavior as in the 1950s; a situation of complete, sudden success and lack of facilitation demobilizes, as French history teaches.

Regarding the second question, although organization indeed takes place on a segregated basis, the identities created in this separate world are not very different from identities in society at large (see Duyvendak 1991). In chapter 1, the idea was put forward that in the case of sociopolitical groups distinctiveness implied "collective identity and common interests, loyalty to the group, and shared consciousness of belonging to a distinct group," but in a commercial subculture, highly distinct groups do not necessarily produce group loyalty, and common, even very similar ("cloned") identities do not immanently go hand in hand with the feeling of belonging to a community, as long as these identities are not politicized. In the Dutch commercial subculture, being distinct implies less and less being "different": apolitical gays find their place within the subculture, stressing their "sameness" rather than their pride in being "different." The Dutch situation suggests that the trend toward organizing life according to sexual orientation, tells us more about the importance of sexuality in present-day culture (Foucault 1976; Giddens 1992; Seidman 1992) than about the presence of discrimination. The all-embracing sexualization of society implies a potential proliferation of places that can be domesticated as "gay": next to bars and other traditional meeting places, new meeting points develop (Duyvendak 1994a).

In *France,* the development of the gay movement and the unfolding of the commercial gay subculture did not keep up with each other, as they did in the Netherlands. Whereas the support by the Socialist Party at the end of the 1970s was still an impetus to both the movement and the subculture, differences occurred following successes of the movement. Although the left-wing government kept its promises with regard to gay issues, it decided not to subsidize any interest-oriented gay organization. This implied the slow death of almost all of these groups (Duyvendak 1993a). Subsidies given to pleasure-oriented clubs were shown to be superfluous in any case: this terrain was covered by the developing commercial subculture. National organizations focusing on interests disappeared, leaving the floor to subcultural and *local* groups, offering all kinds of divertissements to their members. As in the Netherlands, the collective identities created in the subculture became depoliticized. In contrast to the Netherlands, however, any appeal to political identities fell on deaf ears: no independent interest-oriented organizations existed anymore, that could have defended gay interests or mobilized if necessary. A distinct network of pleasure institutions developed without any political commitment. Moreover, the visibility of the subculture was lower than it was in the Netherlands due to the fact that openness is risky in a country where almost half the population holds a rather negative opinion of homosexuality (see table 7.1) (Copley 1989; Duyvendak 1995).[7]

In *Germany* and *Switzerland,* at first sight, many parallels with the French situation seem to obtain: a weak movement at the national level and many different groups at the local level. But whereas in France the decentralization of activities was the result of political success on the national level, in Germany and Switzerland the local focus of interest groups was linked to the weakness of the central state[8] (see, for Switzerland: Trüeb and Miescher 1988; Walser 1991; for Germany: Salmen and Eckert 1989). This local orientation fitted very well into the overall bias of subcultural movements, which is "proximately" oriented by nature, based on face-to-face activities. In Germany and Switzerland, journals are often the only *visible* national "organizations" (for instance, *Magnus* in Germany; in Switzerland, *Anderschume/Kontiki* [German-speaking] and *Dialogai* [French-speaking]). In contrast to France, in both Germany and Switzerland there are also interest-oriented groups at the local level. Although rather small, due to a lack of subsidies,[9] they do influence the types of gay identities. In these countries, collective identities are more politicized than in France, thanks to a certain overlap between the local movement and the local subculture. In terms of chapter 1, the gay "communities" of these countries have not only distinct group identities but rather integrated structures as well. Their visibility is, however, still lower than in the Netherlands, owing to the fact that public opinion is less favorable toward homosexuality.

The social map of the gay subculture in the four countries showed that a flourishing (commercial) subculture can be combined with a strong national movement (the Netherlands), with a rather strong local movement (Switzerland and Germany), or with no movement at all (France). Whereas in the first and the last cases, collective identities in the commercial subculture tend to be rather apolitical, in Switzerland and Germany the overlap of subculture and movement produces politicized identities. In the Netherlands, the situation in the smaller cities and villages can be compared with Germany and Switzerland, while in the big cities, the professional movement produces politicized identities, often competing with the "pleasure" identities created in the commercial subculture. In the French situation, gay people, lacking political identities, do not even consider themselves as being part of one and the same community.[10]

Explaining the Movement, the Subculture, and Collective Identities

In this book, we stress the decisive influence of *political* opportunities on the development of both instrumental and countercultural movements. Although the sketch of the subcultural gay movement in the four countries shows that the political context is relevant for this type of movement as well, the history of the gay movement indicates that, in the case of subcultural movements, *cultural* factors play their own, independent role: the trend toward more liberal opinions regarding homosexuality cleared the way for both the commercial, visible subculture and the "new" gay movement. Table 7.1 shows this transnational trend: it turns out that in all countries listed conservative opinions are related to the age of the respondents, implying that the group that rejects homosexuality is fading away.[11]

Apart from the overall converging trend toward liberalization, we find striking differences among countries as well. This shows that the transnational cultural process of "liberalization" itself is conditioned by *national* traditions. Of all possible factors that may explain diferences in the national "speed" of the liberalization process, *cultural* and *political* ones seem to be most relevant; *economics* (read: the level of welfare) seems in fact to be relatively unimportant since the richest country in the world (the United States) is the most conservative of the "modern" countries (see D'Emilio 1992). Welfare may be a necessary condition for the individualization of lifestyles, but it is not a sufficient condition for the emancipation of homosexuality.

Table 7.1. Rejection of homosexuality by age group (percentage saying homosexuality can *never* be justified)

Age	Netherlands	Denmark	Germany	Britain	France	Belgium	Spain	Ireland	Italy	U.S.
18–24	11	18	26	31	28	42	38	41	50	55
25–34	13	28	31	30	29	43	41	48	51	57
35–44	19	32	40	38	53	47	57	54	65	64
45–54	23	45	43	40	62	53	67	76	72	77
55–64	39	47	58	67	67	62	67	79	81	78
65+	52	54	70	72	76	66	80	87	81	78
Total	22	34	42	43	47	51	56	59	63	65

Source: World Values Survey, 1981–82; cited in Inglehart 1990a: 194

Among the cultural factors, *religion* seems to be important. Although Catholicism is perhaps not by definition an obstacle for sexual liberation (see, for instance, the progressive impetus by parts of the Roman Catholic Church in a religiously mixed country like the Netherlands [Oosterhuis 1992]), opinions about gays and lesbians seem particularly negative in countries dominated by this belief system: next to the southern European countries, Ireland and Belgium may serve as clear examples. The United States, however, shows that the relevant question is perhaps not to *which* belief system one adheres— Roman Catholic or Protestant—but whether people adhere to *any*; in those countries where many people indicate that they are religious, tolerance toward homosexuality is significantly less developed than in countries where people are less likely to describe themselves as religious: "The ... American public is not only more religious than those of most West European countries, but also less tolerant of homosexuality" (Inglehart 1990a: 194).

At first sight, *political* factors do not seem related to opinions regarding homosexuality: although Spain suffered from right-wing dictatorship until the mid-1970s, Italy shows itself to be even more repressive toward homosexuality. However, at the end of the 1970s and the beginning of the 1980s, France is proof that if political opportunities are favorable, not only may changes in the legal position of gays and lesbians occur but prudent shifts in the opinion of the population at large may come to the fore as well. The cultural climate is not per se an insurmountable problem. It may change, even in a "macho" country, making room for a more visible subculture and a mobilizing movement.

Although the example of France shows that the national political context may play an important role through the opportunities it provides the gay movement and the subculture, we should not overestimate the liberalizing force of politics in domains such as sexuality. In liberal democracies, politics will never be very much ahead of the cultural *communis opinio* with regard to sexual issues. Politicians who are too permissive in the view of the electorate run the risk of ruining their political careers. Thus, the combination of a positive political climate for gay issues and a negative public opinion, as it occurred in France at the beginning of the 1980s, is a rather rare exception. The opposite is unlikely as well: a favorable cultural climate and negative political attitudes (the Weimar Republic is perhaps an exception to this rule). In most cases, a liberal cultural climate will go hand in hand with political openness (for instance, the Netherlands [see Kriesi 1993a]), and cultural rigidity will be mirrored in, and strengthened by, political closure (France in the 1970s [see Mossuz-Lavau 1991], as in the United States in the 1980s [see D'Emilio and Freedman 1988]).

The mutually reinforcing effects of political and cultural factors can also be illustrated by reactions to the AIDS epidemic. In the 1980s, AIDS caused a moral panic in the Western countries in which the "political" position of gays was still weak, and in those countries it was an occasion for right-wing backlash as well.

In conclusion, whether a gay movement and subculture develop depends above all on the dominant opinions regarding homosexuality. The more liberal climate of the 1960s and 1970s had a direct effect upon both the evolution of the gay ("homophile") movement and the unfolding of the (commercial) subculture. Politics generally follows societal developments regarding sexual norms and values. Under exceptional circumstances, however, political authorities may have an emancipating effect upon society and the values it maintains (in France, for instance, in the early 1980s).

The *cultural* change toward more liberal opinions concerning homosexuality, caused by broad social and economical trends, is a necessary condition for the initiation of the movement and the visible subculture. For the further development of the gay movement, *political* openings are indispensable. Although cultural factors still play their role—in particular in relation to the unfolding of the subculture—politics (repression, facilitation, and success chances) seems to be of decisive influence.

But that is not all. Analyzing the gay movement by placing it in a broader cultural and political context seems to suggest that the movement itself does not play a role in the emancipation of homosexuality—a suggestion that contrasts with the picture sketched by authors who link the liberation of homosexuality to the rise of the gay and lesbian movement itself (see, for instance, Cruikshank 1992). Although we think that the claim of "self-liberation" is often too strong, and we want to stress that the start of the movement *followed* rather than preceded the liberalization of opinions within society and politics, we do not deny that the very moment a movement is established it may have some influence upon the further transformation of dominant values in both politics and society. In a dynamic model of movement development, the impetus of "the actors" themselves should also be taken seriously.

Moreover, in a subcultural movement like the gay movement, the internal interaction between subculture and movement is, as we have shown, of the greatest importance: the type of identity dominant within the subculture is influenced by the movement, just as the development of the movement is strongly linked to the expansion or decline of the commercial subculture. In other words, apart from external cultural and political factors, the development of the movement is influenced by the subculture, and vice versa.

A model integrating these external and internal factors increases our understanding of the diverging mobilization capacity of the gay movement in the four countries. Whereas all countries have a "segmented," developed commercial *subculture,* the type of prevalent identities in the subculture and the degree of internal integration by *movements* diverge. When we recall the dimensions of the model presented in chapter 1, we see that in France, following the political success gained in 1981, the subculture commercialized and the movement did not have any integration capacity. On the basis of a pacified, relatively open cleavage, we may predict a weak mobilization capacity for the gay movement, which is corroborated by the facts (see table 7.2). In the Netherlands, on the other hand, the integration capacity remained strong thanks to the professionalized movement. This did not imply strong "exclusive mobilization" for gay issues, however, since people in the commercial subculture in the big cities were not mobilizable on the basis of political identities: the cleavage was, in their view, at least partly pacified. Notwithstanding this, the existence of a professional, national movement predicts a rather strong mobilization capacity, in particular of gays who live in small villages. This prediction fits with the facts as well. Germany and Switzerland, finally, are characterized by a developed distinct subculture in combination with a rather fragmented movement. Although the movement and the subculture do overlap at the local level, this implies that the mobilization capacity remains rather weak. In this situation of a distinct subculture, a fragmented movement, and a cleavage that is to some extent pacified, mobilization will be more limited than in the Netherlands, but stronger than in France in the 1980s.[12] In table 7.2 only data regarding the mobilization level of the gay pride parades of France and the Netherlands are included because the num-

Table 7.2. Absolute number of participants in French and Dutch gay pride parades

Year	France	Netherlands
1979	–	5,000
1980	3,000	6,000
1981	10,000	6,000
1982	8,000	4,500
1983	8,000	8,000
1984	3,000	8,000
1985	4,000	4,000
1986	1,000	5,000
1987	5,000	6,000
1988	1,500	7,000
1989	4,000	15,000
1990	1,500	10,000
1991	5,000	15,000
1992	5,000	15,000
1993	10,000	20,000

bers of the two other, federal states are not comparable: in Germany no national gay parade is organized, and in Switzerland the "national" gay parade does not attract people from all over Switzerland. We know, however, that the sum of all local mobilizations in these two countries shows a more impressive mobilization capacity than the French movement possesses.

In the 1990s, we observe an increase in the mobilization capacity of the gay movement. We think that the AIDS crisis is the main cause of this rather impressive rise in the number of people involved in gay pride parades. Although AIDS policies vary from country to country—as was argued in chapter 6, reactions of national authorities toward transnational "events" are often surprisingly different—in all the countries researched homosexuality became through the AIDS crisis a public and political topic. In this process, sooner or later, the gay movement got a kind of recognition by the authorities, often in the form of subsidies. This combination of a threatening "social" situation and some political support turned out to be conducive for the annual mobilization of the gay movement.

Although the AIDS epidemic caused some comparable trends within the movement and the subculture across the countries being studied, differences among the countries are more eye-catching. This chapter has shown that the type of collective identities dominant in the subculture, the relation between subculture and movement, and the development of the movement itself are still highly colored by the national cultural and political context.

Chapter 8

The Cross-National Diffusion of Protest

Social movement activists know very well that what they are doing relates to what other people, sharing the same willingness to struggle for a common cause, are doing. They also know that what they constantly see about other people struggling for the same or similar causes strongly influences their political activism. In other words, social movement participants implicitly acknowledge the fact that their actions are subject to external influences and that the external environment is subject to their actions. Students of social movements, on the contrary, often seem to have forgotten this apparently simple fact. By neglecting the links among activities that social movements carry out, they have treated them as discrete entities instead of "multipolar action systems" (Melucci 1980). Eventually, proponents of the resource mobilization approach acknowledged the relational nature of social movements. Yet they have done so mainly in terms of networks of organizations or activists to describe the complex exchange system existing within the social movement sector, explaining movement mobilization by means of such a system. Few authors have tried to link the exchange system that one can observe within the social movement sector with the idea of diffusion. As a consequence, we suffer from a lack of studies on the diffusion processes taking place among social movements. Such a theoretical gap sharply contrasts with the suggested empirical evidence on influence patterns among social movements. We all remember the almost simultaneous rise of student unrest in the late sixties, when protest erupted at the Free University of Berlin and soon spread to the rest of Europe, especially France and Italy. Moreover, European student protest came in the wake of the Free Speech Movement in Berkeley in 1964, which, by all evidence, had been influenced by the civil rights movement in the United States. The numerous influences of the civil rights movement on other social movements have been pointed out by McAdam (1988, 1994), among others. Similarly, Oberschall (1993: 302) mentions several examples of "transnational convergence of collective action": 1848–49, 1917–19, and 1968. More recent instances include the international antinuclear opposition in Western Europe in the seventies, the concomitant protest by the urban autonomous movement in 1980 and 1981, and the simultaneous mass mobilization against NATO's cruise missiles at the beginning of the eighties.

These are all examples of international protest waves that imply an almost simultaneous rise of protest. Two factors may account for such international protest waves. First, certain issues may transcend national borders and hence provoke simultaneous reactions resulting from independent dispositions in different countries. In this case, an international theme represents the stimulus for reactions in different contexts. Second, protest waves may be the result of a chain of country-specific mobilizations that mutually influence each other. In this case, a process of diffusion is set in motion. Although in the former situation we cannot attribute the rise of protest in one country to the influence of a similar mobilization occurring elsewhere, in the latter this would seem to be the most plausible explanation, since no stimulus common to all countries is present. Thus diffusion is likely to play a role in such situations. This is all the more true if the mobilizations follow each other in quick succession. Moreover, a combination of independent dispositions and diffusion processes may occur in certain circumstances. The collapse of Communist regimes in Eastern Europe is probably a relevant example. Expanding political opportunities at the international level—that is, the weakening and subsequent demise of the Soviet Union—provoked country-specific situations of turmoil, while, at the same time, a chain of protest events spread from one country to the other in a relatively short period of time, at least reinforcing the process. The same combined effect may have been at work in the case of the Chernobyl nuclear accident.

Yet if cross-national diffusion is crucial to explaining mobilization by social movements that is clustered in time and takes place in different countries, it does not have to be seen as an ineluctable process. Protest often spreads across countries, but often it does not. The main argument that we would like to make in this chapter is that cross-national diffusion of protest occurs to the extent that the political opportunity structure is favorable to a movement's mobilization. In other words, protest is unlikely to spread to a country in which political opportunities for a given movement are weak. Yet,

THE CROSS-NATIONAL DIFFUSION OF PROTEST   183

political opportunities, although necessary, are not sufficient for diffusion to take place; other conditions also have to be met. Here, although we focus on political factors, we shall point to organizational and cultural factors.

We aim in this chapter to accomplish three tasks. First, we shall discuss the applicability of classical diffusion theory to the field of social movements and try to provide a conceptual clarification for the study of diffusion of collective action. Second, we shall sketch a general model of cross-national diffusion of protest that stresses the importance of political conditions, above all political opportunities. Third, we shall provide some illustrations of the model by drawing from some relevant examples of international protest waves involving new social movements. Our discussion should give at least provisional answers to whether diffusion is involved and to the conditions for its occurrence. Given the relative lack of studies about diffusion of collective action, our purpose is not to empirically test a model of diffusion, but rather to suggest some ideas about how to approach diffusion among social movements and to illustrate our arguments in a plausible way.

Diffusion Theory

When approaching the study of diffusion of collective action, a number of questions arise to which answers are crucial for understanding such a process: What does the general and rather abstract term "diffusion" mean? What is to be diffused? Through which channels does diffusion take place? What is the result of such a process of diffusion? Most important, why does diffusion occur in certain places and at certain moments? Unless we give at least a partial and provisional answer to these and other related questions, we can only recognize the existence of a process of spreading protest without being able to explain it. Yet, since the sociological literature includes many studies about diffusion processes in general, perhaps the first question to be answered is, Can classical diffusion theory be useful for the analysis of diffusion of collective action?

Diffusion theorists generally agree on the definition of the concept. For instance, Katz (1968) sees diffusion "as the acceptance of some specific item, over time, by adopting units — individuals, groups, communities — that are linked both to external channels of communication and to each other by means of both a structure of social relations and a system of values, or culture." In a similar vein, Rogers (1983: 14) states that there is diffusion when "an innovation is communicated through certain channels over time among the members of a social system." More recently, Michaelson (1993: 217) defines diffusion as "the process by which an innovation (any new idea, activity or technology) spreads through population." Diffusion theorists have generally used such a definition to study the diffusion of information and opinions (e.g., Berelson, Lazarsfeld, and McPhee 1954; Fisher 1978; Katz and Lazarsfeld 1955; Lazarsfeld, Berelson, and Gaudet 1944) or innovations and techniques (e.g., Coleman, Katz, and Menzel 1966; Hagerstrand 1967; Mahajan and Peterson 1985; Rogers 1983). In the former case, diffusion has often been considered as a means of influence. In the latter case, mathematical models of diffusion of innovations have often been presented.

Although we have to acknowledge the "usefulness of diffusion theory to our field of study" (McAdam and Rucht 1993: 58), at least as a starting point and a source of conceptual clarification, the uses of the concept within sociological diffusion theory and in anthropology have to be somewhat modified in order to be applied to the field of collective action. On the one hand, diffusion theorists would seem to be more interested in modeling the rate of diffusion of an idea, technique, or innovation than in determining the social conditions under which diffusion occurs. On the other hand, they are most concerned with direct channels of diffusion, and hence neglect indirect channels, which would also seem to be important for the flow of information among social movements.

Several authors have questioned the applicability of the classic model to the field of collective action. For instance, Pitcher, Hamblin, and Miller (1978: 25) have remarked that "the nature and mechanisms of the diffusion of collective violence are not isomorphic with those of general cultural diffusion, and that an alternative model is needed." As these authors have stressed, the arguments against the logistic model of cultural diffusion (Dodd 1953, 1955; Griliches 1957; Coleman, Katz, and Menzel 1966) result from several serious problems that it raises. Among other things, some authors have pointed out that in the case of violent protest the probable mechanism is not direct communication, but rather an indirect learning process based on mass media (Archer and Gartner 1976; Spilerman 1976; Pitcher, Hamblin, and Miller 1978). Yet these authors probably overlook the role of direct links in the diffusion of protest. Indeed, one of the most important discoveries of recent research on social movements is that social networks are a major source of mobilization.

Classical diffusion theorists were well aware of the existence of two major *channels of diffusion*: direct interpersonal links and indirect transfers of information through mass media. This is a first fundamental distinction one has to make to study the diffusion processes within the field of collective action. The diffusion of protest from one movement to another or across countries can follow two distinct paths. The transfer of information can be either *direct* or *indirect*. First, a direct transfer of information may follow an organizational path. This path can be formal (communications from one social movement organization to another) or informal (participants talk about a previous experience to other people). Previous participation of people in protest actions is an important possible direct channel of diffusion. In this case, activists that have participated in protest events bring their experience to other situations and to other political struggles. Second, the transfer of information is indirect when it is filtered through media reports about a given action, organization, or movement. This channel, obviously, becomes increasingly important in the present-day information society.

A second basic distinction concerns the *content of diffusion*. We would suggest that at least five different contents can be spread from one movement to the other or from country to country. First, the content of diffusion may cover the very *content of mobilization*. Specifically, what is spread may be a particular goal, issue, theme, idea, slogan, and so on, which is adopted by new actors and articulated in a different context. In this respect, McAdam and Rucht (1993) have pointed to cross-national diffusion of some ideas between American and German new left. This kind of diffusion allows a social movement to introduce new goals in its "issue repertoire" in a different context. A second kind of content of diffusion is the *form of organization*. In this case, what is adopted is a particular feature of the internal structure of a social movement organization, such as the division of tasks, the administrative form, or the degree of centralization or professionalization. A well-known example is the early diffusion of the *Bürgerinitiative* (citizens' action group) as the typical form of organization among new social movements. Later on, more institutionalized forms of organization—sometimes approaching the structure of an interest group—have emerged and expanded within the new social movement sector, especially within the ecology movement. Third, the content of diffusion may be a *form of action*. Besides tactical innovation (McAdam 1983), a challenging group can display new forms of action by adopting them from other groups. In this way, a social movement is able to widen its action repertoire by incorporating strategies that have shown their efficacy in other contexts. One of the most typical examples of this process is the sit-in. This form of action, which consists of a protest camp usually held

at the center of a conflict, was pretty much "invented" by the civil rights movement in the United States during the fifties. Since the sit-in turned out to be
an effective tactic, other social movements subsequently adopted it—the student movement in particular. The new social movements—especially the
peace and the antinuclear movements—have also been capable of learning
from the experience of others and have incorporated this form into their action repertoire. Fourth, at a more abstract level, diffusion may spread a *model
of action*. In this sense, a social movement's mobilization becomes an example for other actors, organizations, or movements. For instance, the eruption of the urban autonomous movement, first in the Netherlands and later
in Switzerland, provided a model for mobilization by its counterpart in Germany. Finally, also at the abstract level, diffusion may involve the *likely effects of collective action*. This is a crucial element, which can have a fundamental impact on the level of mobilization of a social movement. Indeed, as we
have seen (see chapter 2), the chances of success are one of the most important motivating factors for people participating in political actions carried
out by social movements. According to several authors (Eisinger 1973; Kitschelt 1986; Rucht 1990a), there is a curvilinear relationship between the
chances of success—or the openness of the political system, which has a
direct impact on them—and the level of mobilization; a lack or an excess of
chances of success is less conducive to protest than an intermediary level.
Thus, we expect information or beliefs about the likely effects of collective
action to have an impact on the chances of success of a challenging group,
and therefore on its mobilization.

   We may group these five kinds of content of diffusion into two main categories. First, the content of the mobilization, forms of organization, and forms
of action are all specific features of a social movement or of its mobilization.
In this case, diffusion consists of the *adoption of particular features* of a challenging group by another group, either within the same country or in another country. Second, a model of action and the likely effects of collective
action concern the mobilization itself and imply that the latter works as an
example or a stimulus to other actors, organizations, or movements. In this
case, diffusion consists of the *spread of collective action itself* from one area
or sector to another; a challenging group mobilizes or remobilizes because
of the example provided by the mobilization of another challenging group.
Diffusion in its two main forms—the adoption of particular features and the
spread of protest itself—may take place *across movements* or *across countries*. Often, both processes occur at the same time.

Of course, these are only analytical distinctions, which are intended to facilitate the study of diffusion processes that take place among social movements. At the empirical level, these types of diffusion largely overlap and often combine to produce a protest wave. In the remainder of this chapter, we shall focus on cross-national diffusion of protest itself.

The Conditions for Diffusion

If it remains mere taxonomy, a simple conceptual clarification such as the one we just proposed is obviously not sufficient to understand diffusion and its mechanisms. Indeed, "the real challenge is not so much in demonstrating the mere fact of diffusion ... but to investigate systematically the conditions under which diffusion is likely to occur and the means by which it does" (McAdam and Rucht 1993: 58). Authors drawing from the collective behavior tradition have suggested some mechanisms for the diffusion of collective behavior, such as contagion, suggestibility, circular reaction, identification, and imitation.[1] Nevertheless, these works share a psychological bias and are often based on the idea of the irrationality of such behavior. Moreover, they do not make any real attempt to integrate these notions into a general theory of collective action or to estimate the extent to which they have an impact on protest. More recently, some authors have begun to deal with diffusion of collective action in a more straightforward way, by abandoning the flaws of the collective behavior approach and often drawing from the large body of sociological literature on diffusion.[2]

The most well known attempt to build a theory of collective action on the concept of diffusion has been that of Tarrow (1983, 1989b). In chapter 5 we saw that, in its early stages, social protest tends to spread from the place where it emerged to other places and from a specific group or movement to other groups or movements. This process results in the shaping of a protest wave that involves many movements in many places. Moreover, during such a wave, new collective frames and new forms of action emerge and spread to other actors within the wave. Tarrow (1983, 1989a, 1989b) has theoretically stressed and empirically tested the role of diffusion within protest cycles. He has pointed out that "protest cycles resemble politics in general in their uneven and irregular diffusion across time and space" (Tarrow 1989b: 46). He has also stressed the "recurrent paths of diffusion from center to periphery" (ibid.) that are a typical feature of protest cycles. Yet Tarrow does not systematically distinguish between different types of diffusion — geographical, sectorial, and so on—and, above all, does not specify the conditions under which collective action is likely to spread across space and across movements. The underlying assumption would seem to be that diffusion takes place automatically once a protest wave has been triggered. This is already hard to maintain for diffusion of protest within a country, since not all sectors of society mobilize during a given protest wave, but it is even more tenuous when one deals with cross-national diffusion. In the case of protest within countries, the political context remains constant (unless we consider locally oriented movements such as the urban autonomous movement), but we expect variations in the political opportunities to occur across countries. Thus cross-national diffusion of protest takes place under certain conditions. Moreover, we expect such conditions to vary according to the content and the channel of diffusion. Although here we would like to stress the political conditions for diffusion, other conditions should be taken into account as well. Figure 8.1 shows the outline of our general model of cross-national diffusion of protest.

We could think of diffusion as a process that may be facilitated by three kinds of conditions. Once information about events abroad is available through direct or indirect channels, organizational, political, and cultural factors may facilitate the diffusion of protest from one country to the other. First, and most obvious, organizational conditions have to be met. A necessary one is the presence of a movement subculture. If no political potential is available for mobilization, diffusion cannot take place. McAdam (1994) has put forward another "organizational" condition by stressing the relevance of "initiator" movements in setting in motion a protest cycle, which is the result of diffusion processes involving "derivative" movements. Thus, the presence of a strong movement that initiates a protest cycle may facilitate the diffusion of protest to other sectors of society.

Second, some authors have stressed the importance of cultural conditions for diffusion. Strang and Meyer (1993), for instance, have emphasized the social construction of cultural categories and the process of theorization of actors and practices as ways of facilitating the flow of social elements. According to them, such cultural linkages are particularly strong in "modern" social systems, and shape and accelerate diffusion by creating "culturally analyzed similarities among actors." At the same time, these linkages allow diffusion to take place even in the absence of direct relational ties. McAdam and Rucht (1993) have drawn on these ideas to explain cross-national diffusion of social movement ideas, but have tried to avoid a clear-cut division between direct and indirect channels of diffusion. According to them, these

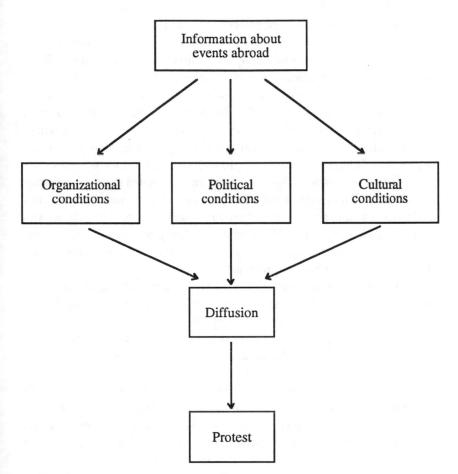

Fig. 8.1. General model of cross-national diffusion of protest

two types of channels combine to spread movement ideas across countries:
"Early relational ties encourage the identification of adopters with transmitters, thereby amplifying the information available through non-relational
channels" (McAdam and Rucht 1993: 74). Thus, the "social construction of
similarity" creates the minimal identification that is necessary for diffusion
to occur. Some degree of identification between transmitters and adopters
has to be established. A similar argument is put forward by McAdam (1994)
in relation to the rise and development of protest cycles.

   We agree that the attribution of similarity between adopters and transmitters may facilitate the diffusion of protest. As McAdam and Rucht (1993), as
well as McAdam (1994), have suggested, such a process of attribution is

encouraged by the presence of direct relational ties. This process may be further enhanced by certain "objective" similarities. We can mention two such similarities. On the one hand, since direct contacts are more likely within a short geographical distance, *spatial proximity* increases the network of direct ties, hence enhancing the process of attribution of similarity. On the other hand, the type of collective actors involved has an impact on diffusion. Tarrow's model of protest cycles implies a generalized situation of mobilization, in which there is diffusion of protest among movements that may be very different (Tarrow 1983, 1989b). In chapter 5, we gave some indications that we had better leave out such an assumption in favor of another one, stating that only movements that have certain common characteristics are involved in this generalized situation of mobilization. Similarly, we can posit that diffusion is more likely when it takes place between two movements that are similar in regard to their goals or their constituencies. This is what we might call *cultural proximity.*

Third, political conditions are crucial for diffusion among social movements. We would like to stress political conditions since they have largely been neglected in the literature. As we said earlier, the main argument of this chapter is that in presence of weak political opportunities, diffusion is unlikely to occur. Accordingly, diffusion depends on the concrete opportunities — chances of success, repression, facilitation, reform/threat — which in turn are constrained by the political opportunity structure. This idea is in line with the general argument of this book, which stresses the importance of political opportunities for the mobilization by new social movements. Here, we introduce a further way for social movements to mobilize in response to external stimuli, provided the internal political opportunities are favorable and offer a fertile ground for diffusion to occur. By doing so, we reject the idea of diffusion as a totally independent variable, which models about protest waves or cycles seem to suggest. Such models imply that diffusion is ineluctable once information is available, regardless of the specific structural constraints faced by potential adopters. Yet, when we look at cross-national diffusion, we have to take into account the impact of the political opportunity structure. This is another way of saying that a protest wave can expand beyond national borders only to the extent that it finds favorable political opportunities. The political opportunity structure may constrain or facilitate the diffusion of protest, because it may either improve or worsen the chances of success of a movement, make its mobilization easier or more difficult through facilitation and repression, and make collective action necessary or unnecessary through a situation of threat or reform. As we know, these are all direct consequences of the political opportunity structure. Thus, we have to consider certain aspects of the political context and their impact on mobilization by social movements as crucial factors in constraining or facilitating the diffusion of protest.

As far as the channels of diffusion are concerned, we would like to add a further argument. Although we agree with McAdam and Rucht (1993) that direct and indirect channels combine to spread movement ideas (as well as other movement features) across countries, we think that the contribution of each one of these channels is different. Short of being able to provide evidence, we would like to advance the hypothesis that direct channels — that is, informal personal ties and formal organizational networks — contribute above all to the diffusion of specific features of the mobilization, such as a theme, a form of action, or a form of organization. These items are brought from one context to the other by activists who have participated in previous actions and who try to apply their experience in a new situation. The effect of diffusion through direct channels consists of redefining a social movement's mobilization or modifying some of its characteristics by adopting other movements' features. Of course, diffusion through direct channels may also have an indirect impact on the level of mobilization, because it may be the source of tactical innovation, which, provided the political conditions are propitious, may trigger an active phase of the movement. Indirect channels — that is, the mass media — may, in contrast, lead directly to the diffusion of protest itself. Information that movement participants or sympathizers obtain through the mass media concerns primarily the model of action and the likely effects of collective action. Thus, if the political conditions are favorable, diffusion has the effect of spreading the protest from one context to another.

Diffusion within the Antinuclear Movement

Let us now look at some examples, drawn from the new social movements, in which diffusion processes have been involved, starting with the antinuclear movement. As Rucht (1990a) and Rüdig (1990) have pointed out, the first European antinuclear movement emerged in France. Opposition to nuclear energy plants had begun in 1969, although massive mobilization took place only in the second half of the seventies, as it did in many other European countries. During those years, the French government was trying to develop a strong nuclear energy program. In 1969 it decided to build two nuclear reactors in Fessenheim, a site that had first been chosen for a gas reactor in 1967. This change of reactor type was a stimulus for the opposition

(Rüdig 1990). A regional antinuclear committee—perhaps the first in Europe—was formed in 1970 and, on April 12, 1971, the first antinuclear demonstration took place: fifteen hundred people gathered in Fessenheim to protest the planned nuclear plant. Many actions took place in this area during that same year, including a large demonstration of fifteen thousand, a camp and a sit-in near Bugey, a protest march from there to Lyons, and a press conference in Strasbourg supported by forty-seven antinuclear groups (Rucht 1990a). The French—and European—antinuclear movement was born.

What is interesting for our purposes is the location of Fessenheim, the center of protest at that moment. This village is located in Alsace, close to the German border. On the other side of the Rhine, in Germany, is a place—Wyhl—that was to become the scene of one of the strongest antinuclear oppositions ever. In Wyhl, antinuclear protest received national attention when, on February 18, 1975, the site for the planned construction of a nuclear plant was occupied by a few hundred people. This occurred about one month after the granting of the construction license by the state government (January 22, 1975). After the police had evicted the occupiers, about twenty-eight thousand people took part in a demonstration on February 23 that resulted in a reoccupation of the site that lasted several months. What is the link between Fessenheim and Wyhl? What happened between the two mobilizations? Many things happened.

For one thing, protests against the planned nuclear plants in Fessenheim continued. For instance, in May 1972 a demonstration took place in the village. Most important, people from the region around Wyhl participated in the event. Meanwhile, the government of Baden-Württemberg—the competent authority in this respect—decided to build a nuclear power plant in Breisach, another small town in the region located on the border with France. From 1971 to 1973, opposition against this decision grew rapidly. German activists established contacts with French activists who were struggling against the plans for a power plant in Fessenheim. Eventually, this strong opposition—among other things, sixty-five thousand signatures were collected—led to the abandonment of the project in 1973. More precisely, the utility decided to build the plant elsewhere: in Wyhl, which is about ten kilometers from Breisach. During 1973 and early 1974, protest against this new project was not very strong. Those were the months of the great energy crisis. Yet, in the second half of the year something happened that would influence subsequent events in Wyhl: in July, the French government decided to allow the construction of a lead factory in Marckolsheim, located in the area under discussion. Opposition arose quickly in this village, but on the French side.

People from both sides of the Rhine united to struggle against the decision, aided by the fact that they all spoke German. As Rüdig (1990: 132) observes, "the lead factory plans were perceived as further evidence of the planned industrialization of the entire area which had to be stopped." Among other things, the following events took place: a joint demonstration with about two thousand participants (July 28), another with about three thousand participants that led to the formation of an "international committee" including twenty-one *Bürgerinitiativen* from the regions of Baden and Alsace, and the occupation of the site by several hundred people (September 20). Events in Larzac (France), where farmers successfully employed such a form of action against the extension of an existing military training range, inspired the occupation in Wyhl. As happened several months earlier in Breisach, the struggle in Marckolsheim was successful: the French government withdrew the construction permit on February 25, 1975.

Thus, the successful mobilizations in Breisach and Marckolsheim, together with the protests in Fessenheim and Larzac—the former unsuccessful, the latter successful—provided visible examples for the antinuclear protest that took place in Wyhl. As a result, protest in Germany, to an important extent, had been imported from France. Yet this was not sufficient to provoke an outburst of protest. Governmental insensitivity to the demands of the opponents, as well as to the results of the hearing required by the German law and to the decisions of the courts, provoked a tactical change by the movement. Therefore, after the state government issued the first construction licenses, the site occupation took place and lasted until November 7, when the citizens' action groups left the site after being reassured that no construction would be begun until the courts had ruled on the legal challenge under way (Rüdig 1990).

The story is not over. The Swiss antinuclear movement began to mobilize not long after its French and German counterparts had already entered the public space. Where? Not incidentally, in Kaiseraugst, a small village on Swiss territory but located near Fessenheim and Wyhl. This place had been chosen for an oil-fired power station in 1962 and for a nuclear plant in March 1967. At first, the local political authorities were favorable to the project and there was practically no opposition, but around the turn of the decade people began to worry about it. Several social movement organizations formed and soon the local population understood the danger it would face if the project was carried out. A change in the movement's tactics took place with the formation of a new local organization, the Nonviolent Action Kaiseraugst (GAK), on November 1973.

The change to direct action from conventional and institutional forms of actions — which were mainly conducted under the leadership of the North-West Swiss Action Committee against Nuclear Plants (NWA), a regional organization formed on May 1970 — opened up a new era in the Swiss antinuclear struggle. Influenced by the French and, especially, the German experiences, the opponents decided to undertake a "trial occupation" of the construction site during the week of December 25 to December 31, 1973. This occurred about one and a half years after the first antinuclear demonstration to be held in Switzerland took place in Rheinfelden — a village located in the same region — on May 12, 1972. After a rather low level of mobilization in 1974 — a year devoted to efforts by the GAK to develop a consensus among the population — the organization planned to occupy the site for a longer time. The beginning of work on the site, on March 24, 1975, provided the rationale for the occupation. Several authors agree on the fact that there is a link between the events in Wyhl and those in Kaiseraugst. For instance, Rüdig (1990: 137) observes that "the successful occupation of the Wyhl site just a few dozen miles to the north in February 1975 certainly provided a major boost for the GAK" and that "it proved that a site occupation was actually possible, a major facilitating factor without which, arguably, the Kaiseraugst events which were to follow could not have happened," or "at least, the crucial local and regional support for the occupation might have been much weaker."

Thus, in view of the threat represented by the beginning of work on the site, a week later, on March 31, 1975, a group of about two hundred activists occupied it. The mass demonstration that took place the following Saturday brought out fifteen thousand people, and at another demonstration, this time in Bern (April 24, 1975), about eighteen thousand turned out. From that moment on, nuclear energy became a national issue and the antinuclear movement was able to mobilize in many parts of the country. In other words, in addition to cross-national diffusion, a process of national diffusion also occurred. Because of the important impact of the events in Kaiseraugst on the mass media and the general public, the persistent work of "consensus mobilization" (Klandermans 1984, 1988) by highly committed activists, and the increasing politicization of nuclear power, the protest expanded from a local and regional one to one of national scope. The same process was happening in Germany.

The case of antinuclear opposition in the "Regio Basiliensis"[3] suggests some preliminary ideas about how different types of diffusion can operate and under what conditions cross-national diffusion of protest is likely to occur. First, and most important, diffusion did not take place everywhere. Specifically, antinuclear protest spread from France (Fessenheim and Marckolsheim) to Germany (Breisach and Wyhl) and to Switzerland (Kaiseraugst). Not incidentally, political opportunities for antinuclear protest were present in Germany and Switzerland. Hence, not only could opponents of nuclear energy in those two countries easily adopt the theme but nuclear energy could become a political issue, with the events triggering a process of national diffusion that led to mass mobilization in many parts of the two nations. Second, the German and Swiss movements imitated forms of action used by the French movement. Specifically, the opponents decided to make use of direct action in their struggle against nuclear energy. The fact that these tactics were sometimes successful, as in Wyhl, facilitated their transfer from one country to the other. Chances of success increased as a result of previously successful mobilizations. Thus, the German and Swiss movements gathered positive information about the likely effects of antinuclear protest, more particularly of direct action. Third, they obtained this information directly as well as indirectly. On the one hand, previous common participation in protest events had functioned as a social learning process. On the other hand, the fact that such events had been widely publicized represented a channel of diffusion for the protest. The result of these processes was diffusion of protest across countries, which increased the level of mobilization of the antinuclear movement in Germany and Switzerland. Finally, the networks of contacts between activists in the different countries provided a channel for diffusion of certain features of antinuclear protest, such as specific forms of action, not only within the same movement but between different movements as well. Thus, the proximity between the antinuclear and the peace movements with regard to ideology and the issues they raised facilitated the diffusion of certain characteristics of the mobilization from one country to the other. For instance, seminars on nonviolent tactics given by German peace movement activists could have influenced the adoption of such tactics by Swiss antinuclear activists.

Diffusion within the Urban Autonomous Movement

During 1980 and 1981, some West European countries witnessed a wave of urban youth protest. This was typically a local phenomenon. Young people mobilized after years of silence to struggle for alternative cultural codes. They addressed their demands to local political authorities—more precisely, to city legislative and executive powers. Youth mobilization of the eighties, in contrast to that of the sixties and seventies, abandoned universalistic claims in favor of more pragmatic and concrete demands about free spaces. The Netherlands, Switzerland, and Germany were the most affected by this wave of youth protest; Amsterdam, Zurich, and Berlin were centers of awakening youth in Western Europe. This follows the chronological order of the protest, which began in Amsterdam, spread first to Zurich, and then to Berlin. Obviously, the mobilization also spread within the individual countries, but, as with the previous example, let us concentrate on cross-national diffusion. Some evidence might be helpful. Table 8.1 shows the development over time of the number of protest events of the urban autonomous movement during 1980 and 1981 in the four countries studied.

As the table illustrates, the wave began in the Netherlands. While France, Germany, and Switzerland saw almost no actions during the first quarter of 1980, during the same period the number of protest events of the urban autonomous movement in the Netherlands was already rather high. The second quarter saw an upsurge of the Swiss urban autonomous movement and the beginning of an intense protest season, especially in Zurich, which was eventually to have heavy consequences on the local political system (discussed in chapter 9). Although the movement in Switzerland gradually increased the number of protest events during the rest of the year, it was not until the beginning of 1981 that the German urban autonomous movement suddenly took off, particularly in Berlin. By then, the Dutch movement was already in decline and the Swiss movement was experiencing such strong repression in Zurich that it was soon defeated across the board. There was an almost total absence of a French counterpart; diffusion practically did not take place in France. A possible explanation may lie in the internal conditions for mobilization at the time the protest wave was taking place in other West European countries.

Many factors linked to the specific political context in the Netherlands, especially at the local level, might explain the fact that the protest began there. However, rather than seek to account for that, we are interested here in the subsequent development of the movement in other countries. The mobilization by the urban autonomous movement soon spread to Switzerland, specifically to Zurich. In this city, some signs of effervescence in the form of illegal actions and of demonstrations around the housing issue had already appeared in 1979, as well as in early 1980. Thus, the movement had to some extent already mobilized before its sudden upsurge, which was to occur on May 30, 1980. That was the day of the "opera riot," as the bourgeois press called it. Through a peaceful demonstration, the movement wanted to protest the decision of the city council to grant a credit for rebuilding the opera. The

Table 8.1. Number of protest events of the urban autonomous movement by quarter in the four countries

	Netherlands	Switzerland	Germany	France
1/1980	11	0	1	0
2/1980	11	21	3	2
3/1980	8	33	3	0
4/1980	14	40	3	0
1/1981	16	22	45	0
2/1981	1	28	32	0
3/1981	5	11	34	0
4/1981	1	6	7	2

movement wanted some of the money to be invested in creating an autonomous youth center. The repressive reaction by the police and by the bourgeois parties triggered a spiral of violence that eventually led to the destruction of the movement after several months of intense struggle. The so-called "city hall riot" on June 18, 1980, attests to this sudden disruptive upsurge of the urban autonomous movement in Zurich. These events consisted first in a large peaceful demonstration demanding discussions with the local executive power, and later, following a repressive response, in violent clashes between the movement and the police.

One had to wait until 1981 to observe a similarly strong mobilization by the urban autonomous movement in Germany. More precisely, the rise of the squatters' movement in Berlin coincides with the riots that occurred in this city in December 1980. However, the greatest number of protest events took place during the first three quarters of 1981. In fact, before the Berlin events, the movement had already mobilized in other parts of the country. Specifically, a series of conflicts around squatted buildings had taken place in Göttingen and, most important, the first large-scale confrontation between squatters and the police had occurred in Freiburg in June 1980. We can easily see the proximity in time between the start of the protest in Zurich and the Freiburg events. There is also, to some extent, geographical proximity between the two situations. One might conclude that diffusion played a role in those circumstances. Protest could have spread from Switzerland to the region of Germany close to the Swiss border and, later on, to Berlin as well as to other cities, following a sort of two-step process in which the Dutch and Swiss urban autonomous movements provided important examples to the German.

The fact that the movement was stronger in Berlin than in other German cities allows us to reiterate our main contention: internal political conditions are crucial to understanding why diffusion occurs. The strength of the move-

ment in Berlin is closely related to the specific political situation at the moment of its emergence at the beginning of 1981 (Mulhak 1983). Political opportunities were most favorable for the movement between December 1980
and June 1981. Extreme political instability in Berlin characterized this period. Moreover, the political authorities were not able to react in a clear and
decisive way to the movement's mobilization. Two problems of the city government (Senate) were at the origin of the instability. First, a financial scan-
dal led to the Senate's resignation on January 15, 1981. Second, the Senate—
the old as well as the new one—was unable to impose its policy regarding
the movement upon the judiciary or the police, and tried instead to seek a
compromise with it. This may have provided fertile ground for diffusion to
occur. Indeed, the Zurich movement was still very active during the first
months of 1981, although the number of protest events was already declining, as table 8.1 indicates. Thus, temporary internal political weaknesses
combined with external stimuli to facilitate diffusion processes from Amsterdam and, especially, Zurich to Berlin.

International Themes and Diffusion within the Peace Movement

Let us consider a third, and final, example. The strong mass mobilization
that took place at the beginning of the eighties, in opposition to NATO's decision in December 1979 to station cruise missiles in some West European
countries, represented both the heyday and the beginning of a certain decline of the peace movement. In late 1981, protest against the imminent implementation of this decision arose rapidly in several West European countries, beginning with Germany, where a demonstration of 250,000 people took
place during the weekend of November 10–11, 1981. Two weeks later, similar
demonstrations occurred in Belgium (300,000 participants), France (60,000),
Great Britain (200,000), and Italy (300,000). Mobilization was particularly
strong in the Netherlands, where 400,000 people joined a demonstration in
Amsterdam on November 21, 1981.

Thus, a huge international protest wave was triggered whose focal point
was opposition to NATO's decision, although the movement took advantage
of its momentum to address general peace issues as well. Unlike the two
previous examples, this protest wave had an external, international input.
The origin of this protest wave lies in the fact that the issue transcended national borders, since a transnational institution made the decision to station
the missiles. Therefore, all West European countries were simultaneously

facing a threatening situation. To be sure, not all countries had to deal directly with NATO's decision. Finland, Sweden, and Switzerland are neutral countries, while Denmark and Norway did not give permission for nuclear weapons to be stationed on their territory. Yet protest also arose in those countries. Given the highly destructive nature of the missiles, even people living in neutral countries or in countries whose governments did not accept the missiles on their territory felt threatened and concerned by the issue.

Thus, the peace movement mobilized almost everywhere in Western Europe, although to varying degrees. In the presence of an international stimulus, the distinction between an account in terms of simultaneous reactions to the stimulus or in terms of diffusion processes becomes problematic. The diagnosis of diffusion is not as straightforward as in the case of independent national issues. The protest wave could be the result of simultaneous reactions to NATO's decision occurring independently in different countries, but we think that similar patterns of mobilization in different countries also have to be linked to processes of diffusion. Certainly the protest wave initially arises in response to the international input, but its subsequent development also results from diffusion from one country to the other. An explanation that combines both factors is, in our view, the most plausible.

A simple way to test this is to look at the temporal sequence of protest. Among the four countries in our study, Switzerland is a case in point. On at least three occasions, the Swiss peace movement mobilized massively against cruise missiles: during fall/winter 1981, spring 1982, and fall/winter 1983. Before discussing the Swiss case in greater detail, let us first provide a picture of the mobilization by the peace movement in the first three years of the eighties. Table 8.2 shows the development over time of the number of protest events of the peace movement in the four countries.

The table points to some possible patterns of diffusion. The wave began in Germany because, on the one hand, it was the country most affected by NATO's decision (more than a third of the missiles were to be stationed there) and, on the other hand, the German peace movement was already in an ascending phase prior to 1979 as part of a larger protest wave that included the antinuclear movement as perhaps its most important collective actor. At that time, both the Communist and the Christian segments of the movement were already acting in the social movement arena. Moreover, the decline of the antinuclear movement during the late seventies and its kinship with the peace movement on nuclear issues may have produced a transfer

Table 8.2. Number of protest events of the peace movement by quarter in the four countries

	Germany	Netherlands	Switzerland	France
1/1981	10	3	1	0
2/1981	13	1	2	1
3/1981	17	13	3	1
4/1981	15	13	7	0
1/1982	3	23	3	1
2/1982	26	9	2	1
3/1982	9	11	3	1
4/1982	10	14	7	1
1/1983	6	5	11	0
2/1983	43	14	8	1
3/1983	52	5	7	4
4/1983	86	13	7	10

of the mobilization from the former to the latter through the shifting of activist and participant energies from one movement to the other, hence creating a process of diffusion within the country.

In both the Netherlands and Switzerland, the protest followed the early mobilization of the German peace movement. The almost simultaneous mass mobilization by the peace movement in the three countries was repeated in April 1982. That was the period of the so-called Eastern marches, which represented a tradition of strong mobilization by the movement in Germany and Switzerland for many years. Finally, a third subwave of protest involving all three countries occurred between September and December 1983. This represented the peak of mobilization around this issue, especially in Germany. Again, protest began in Germany and, by our account, shortly spread to the Netherlands and Switzerland.

At a minimum, the data provided above show two things. First of all, even when the origin of an international protest wave lies in the simultaneous reactions of social movements in different countries, diffusion processes may be involved, thus reinforcing mobilization in countries where strong political opportunities are present. Switzerland is a case in point. The fact that mobilization in Switzerland, which is not a member of NATO, always followed what occurred in Germany suggests that diffusion at least reinforced the protest in that country. Obviously, this has not been definitively tested, but in our view it is a more plausible account than one focusing only on the independent reaction of the Swiss peace movement to NATO's decision. The temporal sequence of protest, with Switzerland always following other countries—above all, Germany—suggests that the reaction of the Swiss peace movement was not totally independent from those of its counterparts in other countries. The external influence of mobilizations in other countries on Switzerland was not limited to the beginning of the protest wave but probably played a role later on as well. Although a dynamic internal to the Swiss situation had been triggered, the mass mobilization that took place at the end of 1983 can hardly be understood without referring to previous strong mobilizations in other West European countries such as Germany and the Netherlands. In addition, the fact that the Swiss peace movement has usually mobilized on internal issues (Bein and Epple 1984) makes diffusion more likely in the case of an international issue such as that of the cruise missiles.

The second thing the data show is that there was almost no mobilization in France. Only in June 1983 did the French peace movement mobilize in a significant way, and it seems not to have followed the general trend toward protest at the most salient moments. Why did protest against the missile issue spread to Switzerland, which is not even a member of NATO, and yet spread much less so to France? Of course, France is not a full member of NATO either. However, unlike Switzerland, it has its own nuclear weaponry. The French peace movement had an opportunity to call into question France's *force de frappe* when the issue of missiles was at the center of the political debate. This did not occur and diffusion was reduced to a weak initial surge. The relative failure of protest to spread to France can hardly be understood without referring to the country's internal situation. When the protest wave against the NATO decision began, the French peace movement had already lost its institutional support. The two largest left parties—its main potential allies— had already given up support for the movement. Additionally, the coming to power of the Socialist Party in 1981 reinforced this situation, which greatly weakened the political opportunities to mobilize on behalf of disarmament. Hence, the Committee for Nuclear Disarmament in Europe (CODENE)—a non-Communist Party organization—was able to form toward the end of 1981 because of the international protest wave, but was unable to survive the decline of the wave. The strong pronuclear consensus among French political parties contributed to a situation in which the only challenger to the French government—the peace organization CODENE—was completely isolated. As a result, the French peace movement mobilized to a much lesser degree than its Dutch and German counterparts.

In contrast, the Swiss peace movement at the beginning of the eighties mounted a rather strong mass mobilization against cruise missiles, in addition to a strong effort for relaxation of the international climate. This is all the more surprising in light of the more internal orientation of the Swiss peace movement, compared to the internationally oriented French peace movement. The difference between France and Switzerland with regard to protest against the cruise missiles can be partially explained by the previous endogenous development of this movement, the development of the new social movement sector in general, and the resulting differences in political opportunities for peace movement mobilization in the two countries. In Switzerland, mobilization against the peaceful use of nuclear energy was quite strong and led to several successes for the antinuclear movement (see chapter 9). Opportunities for mobilization were forthcoming during the second half of the seventies. Switzerland's combination of a weak state and a prevailing inclusive strategy by the political authorities offered favorable conditions for mobilization by new social movements, although in some cases their demands concerned high-profile policy domains. Most important, the chances of success for these movements were quite strong. As a result, people were sensitive to external stimuli. After the relative decline of the antinuclear movement at the end of the seventies, the peace movement was ready to take up the challenge. Its proximity to the antinuclear movement with regard to the nuclear issue facilitated such a relay. The result was that, in addition to the independent reaction by the Swiss peace movement to the international stimulus provided by NATO's decision to station the cruise missiles, diffusion processes could take place and bring about a sustained mass mobilization. Additionally, the reactivation of the peace movement around international issues helped articulate internal issues, such as the struggle against the national army. Not incidentally, the organization that was eventually to lead this challenge, in particular through the launching of a national popular initiative — the Group for a Switzerland without an Army (GSoA) — was formed in 1982, during the protest wave.

Diffusion and Political Opportunities

Let us compare the three examples described earlier as illustrating the three central arguments of this chapter. First, an international protest wave, if we exclude a random-based account, may result from two sources: a simultaneous reaction of social movements in different countries to an international theme or stimulus, or a diffusion process. The diagnosis of diffusion is problematic by itself. Yet, when no international stimulus comes to mind that could have set in motion a series of reactions by social movements in different countries, the temporal proximity among mobilizations suggests that a process of diffusion is involved. The examples of the antinuclear and urban autonomous movements point in this direction. Second, international stimuli and diffusion often combine to create international protest waves. In other words, diffusion may take place alone or within an internationally shaped protest wave. The example of the peace movement illustrates such a combination. Third, and most important, protest does not spread freely from one country to the other. Antinuclear protest took primarily a one-way ticket from France to Germany, whereas exchanges between Germany and Switzerland mutually reinforced protest in these two countries. The demands of the Dutch urban autonomous movement took hold in Switzerland and Germany, but not in France. Assuming that diffusion took place, mass mobilization by the peace movement against cruise missiles spread from Germany to the Netherlands and to Switzerland, but much less so to France. Let us elaborate on this point.

Under certain circumstances, there may be fertile ground for diffusion. Such ground is comprised of organizational, cultural, and political conditions. In our view, political conditions are particularly important and, moreover, have been neglected in literature on the topic. Therefore, we have focused on political factors—specifically on the political opportunity, structure—as conditions for diffusion. The absence of such ground would seem to have been characteristic of France, at least in our examples. Of course, the paths of diffusion we have just sketched oversimplify the actual ones, which are far more complex. However, they represent some major cross-national diffusion processes that can plausibly be assumed to have taken place during the period considered. This is true for the examples of the antinuclear and the urban autonomous movements, whereas in the case of the peace movement, diffusion is more difficult to assess.

Are all these paths the result of pure coincidence? We might tend to answer this question affirmatively if we were to look only at cases where diffusion did occur. Yet if we take into account situations where diffusion did not take place, an affirmative answer loses much of its pertinence. The fact that antinuclear protest did not spread so much to France after the events that took place in Wyhl and Kaiseraugst; the almost nonexistent reaction of the French urban autonomous movement to the events in Amsterdam, Zurich, and Berlin; the practically failed mass mobilization by the French peace movement at the beginning of the eighties—all these examples of failed diffusion (despite the fact that it is more than justified to think that contacts through direct as well as indirect channels had been established) suggest that it is internal conditions of a given country that allow protest to cross borders. Similarly, we may think of the absence of certain modes of collective action in given contexts as resulting from the fact that those contexts are not prepared to adopt such forms of action. A case of point is terrorism during the seventies. Wisler (1993) has shown that terrorism could hardly be exported from countries such as Italy and Germany to Switzerland, although the latter is geographically squeezed between the other two.

All these examples point toward an explanation of the diffusion of collective action that takes into account certain aspects of the national political context and their impact on diffusion, as well as the possibility of diffusion's failure. In a sense, to ask about the results of diffusion and the conditions of its occurrence calls for a similar kind of inquiry. Regarding these two interrogations, we may oppose two models of diffusion. The first model suggests that diffusion is a means to remobilize a movement, or generally reinforce protest in a given context, which is independent of the characteristics of that very context. According to this model, the fact that a movement adopts certain features of another movement or begins a series of actions following the example of a similar movement abroad depends exclusively on its willingness to follow the foreign example. This model may be seen as an application of classical diffusion theory to collective action. Tarrow's (1983, 1989a, 1989b) reasoning implicitly assumes this as well. Thus, diffusion is always considered as reinforcing protest and may be viewed as a way of "escaping" the constraints posed by the political opportunity structure. In our view, although it is true that diffusion often has a "stimulating" effect, this perspective runs the risk of teleology. By looking at diffusion only ex post facto, it fails to take into account situations where diffusion does not take place, and consequently it fails to consider the role of certain aspects of the political context within which adopters are going to apply the message given by transmitters.

The second model, as we have said, sees diffusion as constrained or facilitated by three kinds of conditions: organizational, cultural, and political. It thus takes into account internal variables in explaining diffusion across social movements. We think that it is much more fruitful to consider diffusion as a possible outcome of a complex interaction of internal and external factors, rather than simply as a way to reinforce protest. Since the examples we have given concern cross-national diffusion, this means that international exchanges and the national context of adopters combine to spread the

protest from one country to the other. Although we acknowledge the importance of organizational and cultural conditions for diffusion, our main argument is that certain aspects of the political context largely constrain or facilitate diffusion. This means—to use a central concept of this book—that the
political opportunity structure is partially responsible for the diffusion of protest across countries. In all the examples of cross-national diffusion that led
to a significant increase in the level of mobilization in the country hosting
the adopters, political opportunities were rather favorable for such a transfer. Opportunities were strong for antinuclear protest in Germany and in Switzerland when the French antinuclear movement gave the example to its counterparts in the two neighboring countries. The openness of the system and
of the legislative process regarding this policy domain provided fertile ground
for diffusion of protest. On the other hand, opportunities for the urban autonomous movement were weak in France at the beginning of the eighties.
Moreover, in this case the example shows how the change of the specific
political situation in Berlin was responsible for the delayed response of the
urban autonomous movement in that city. Finally, opportunities for mass mobilization by the peace movement during the same period were also weak in
France. After the Socialist Party took power, the whole new social movement
sector was in sharp decline, so the chances of success for such mobilization
were weak.

Conclusion

The main argument of this chapter is that cross-national diffusion of protest
is much less likely under conditions of weak political opportunities. Yet, before
one can sketch a model of diffusion, one has to determine which of two possible accounts of international protest waves is the more plausible. The first
account implies the presence of a transnational theme or stimulus that provokes an almost simultaneous reaction by social movements in different
countries. The second account conceives of the protest wave as the result of
a diffusion process. We have argued that, in the absence of international stimulus, a diffusion-based explanation is more plausible and that both processes
often interact to create a protest wave.

   As far as diffusion is concerned, in the first section we discussed classical
theory of diffusion and suggested some distinctions that may be useful for
studying how mobilization spreads across movements and across countries.
The basic distinctions concern the contents and the channels of diffusion.

Two major types of diffusion result, one implying the adoption of a social movement's specific features and the other consisting of the spread of protest itself. In a second step, we advanced a model of cross-national diffusion of protest that stresses three sets of conditions for diffusion: organizational, cultural, and political conditions. However, by trying to show that (national) political opportunities are crucial for cross-national diffusion of protest, we focused here on political factors. In this regard, we counterposed a model that does not take into account internal factors to a model that considers diffusion as being filtered by political opportunities. The examples we have given provide some evidence in favor of the second model. Our stress on political conditions, nevertheless, should not make us overlook the importance of the presence of political potential for action and the social contruction of similarity as facilitating factors of diffusion.

Further research should test these ideas more systematically. Here, we have focused on diffusion occurring within the same social movement. A second object of inquiry would be diffusion that takes place between different movements. The importance of such intermovement diffusion emerged from the example of the antinuclear movement. It is more than likely that specific features of protest and protest itself spread from the antinuclear movement of the seventies to the peace movement of the eighties, especially when the latter was dealing with the nuclear weapons issue. Additionally, the fact that activists and participants in new social movements largely overlap increases the likelihood that such intermovement diffusion processes take place. As McAdam and Rucht (1993) have suggested, we should distinguish between intramovement diffusion, intermovement diffusion within the same country, and cross-national diffusion, which may take place both within the same movement and between different movements. Further research should shed light on the specific dynamics involved in each type of exchange and point to how different contents of diffusion spread either within movements, across movements, or across countries.

Chapter 9

Outcomes of New Social Movements

Students of social movements have traditionally focused on factors determining or influencing their emergence and development. Yet the literature on this subject has largely neglected the consequences of social movements' action. Although a lot of work on social movements at least mentions some of their outcomes, systematic studies on the sources and causes of their success are still underrepresented.[1] Moreover, cross-national studies, which are most suited to inquiry into the conditions under which certain types of social movement outcomes occur, are almost completely absent. In general, there is a controversy in the literature between authors who stress the movement characteristics and those who underline external (political) factors as crucial for the success of social movements or other outcomes. Most studies have focused on the effects of insurgency or the use of violence by protesters. The urban riots that took place in American cities during the sixties have often been the object of empirical analyses of such effects.[2]

The lack of theoretical as well as empirical analyses of social movement outcomes is primarily the result of a number of methodological difficulties. Two of them are worth mentioning here. First of all, there is the problem of defining and measuring social movement success or other outcomes. As far as success is concerned, "subjective" and "objective" aspects raise the problem of how to assess it. Furthermore, success can be an intended as well as an unintended consequence of a movement's action. Other types of outcomes as well present definitional and measurement problems that make them difficult to study. Because of these problems, research has tended to focus on policy changes. Second, the most fundamental obstacle to research on social movement outcomes is the problem of causality, that is, the difficulty of assessing the extent to which the movement has contributed to producing a certain effect. The observed change constitutes the explicandum, but the movement's action is far from being the only explanatory factor. Moreover, social movements may be successful independent of their action—for instance, because reformist political authorities are in power.

Thus, research on social movements has dealt more with explaining their mobilization than with searching for the causes and conditions of their outcomes. In doing so, each approach has stressed a particular set of factors. Classic theories (e.g., Turner and Killian 1957; Smelser 1962) have focused on the structural strain and the effect it has on the level of frustration or deprivation in explaining collective action. This approach has identified the level of mobilization of a movement with its success, which, in turn, was considered to depend on the factors just mentioned. The first real attempt to assess the outcomes of social movements came with the resource mobilization approach. In this approach, internal variables such as the organizational infrastructure and the level of resources are at the center of the analysis. This approach has generally associated variables such as bureaucratization, professionalization, centralization, and varying strategic factors with increasing chances of success by social movements or, more precisely, by social movement organizations (e.g., Gamson 1975). Supporters of the political process approach have criticized this perspective for neglecting the political context of social movements. According to these critics, the success of social movements derives more from opportunities created by political crises or from the structural context of mobilization than from their internal organization (e.g., Goldstone 1980; Kitschelt 1986). The determinants of social movement success are thus a function of the general approach adopted to study them.

According to the political process perspective, social movements can reach some measure of success when they are able to take advantage of the weakness of their opponents, in particular the state and political authorities. In line with the general approach of this book, this perspective serves as the main source of material for this chapter, in which we shall try to link the outcomes of new social movements to certain political conditions of protest—specifically, to the political opportunity structure. We think that certain aspects of the general political context, summarized through the concept of political opportunity structure, influence the likelihood that a movement, a campaign, or an organization will produce a given outcome. Yet, as we suggested in chapter 4, to properly assess the role of the political opportunity structure on the outcomes of social movements we have to take into account two intervening factors. First, political opportunities vary according to the type of movement. Whereas, for instrumentally oriented movements, all four concrete opportunities are relevant, for identity-oriented movements those opportunities influencing the ends of action are less constraining. Moreover, each type of movement reacts differently to concrete opportunities. Second, the political opportunity structure is not constantly open or closed throughout the whole new social movement sector. On the contrary, it varies according to the policy domain the protest is addressing. Therefore, within a given political opportunity structure, we expect the outcomes of social movements to vary according to the movement type and to the policy domain. Before discussing the link between the political opportunity structure and the outcomes of new social movements in greater detail, we shall attend to the definition of the outcomes of social movements.

Defining the Outcomes of Social Movements

To begin with, we would like to make a clear distinction between the outcomes or impacts of social movements and their level of mobilization. As we have already indicated, we cannot mistake the former for the latter, unless we take for granted what Kitschelt (1986) has pointed out as being a mistake — namely, using the level of mobilization of a social movement as an indicator of its success. If this mobilization can be seen as a success — at least a partial one — by participants and activists of the movement, it can hardly be viewed as an impact on the political system or on society. The outcomes of a social movement imply that its activities produce some changes in at least one of the three following arenas: the movement itself, the political system, or the general public.

Thus, we can distinguish between *internal impacts* and *external impacts*. The former are produced within the movement itself and can be further subdivided into impacts on *identity* and impacts on *organization*. Identity impacts imply a reinforcement of the identity of participants, whether at the individual or the collective level. Organization impacts imply a change in the organizational structure of the movement. Since subcultural and countercultural movements are mostly identity-oriented, they often pursue internal goals. Hence, when the conditions are favorable, they are likely to have internal impacts. In contrast, instrumental movements mostly pursue external goals. Hence, when the conditions are favorable, they are likely to have external impacts. In this chapter, we shall analyze internal impacts when referring to subcultural and countercultural movements, and external impacts when dealing with instrumental movements.

To state the link between the political opportunity structure and the outcomes of new social movements, we have to further distinguish between different types of external impacts. In one of the first systematic attempts to analyze the success of social movements, Gamson (1975) broadly defined success as the outcome of a resolved challenge and made a fundamental distinction between two types of success. On the one hand, an organization may get a certain degree of acceptance from political authorities. On the other hand, it may obtain new advantages. Following Kitschelt (1986), we may call these two types of success *procedural impacts* and *substantive impacts,* respectively. Gamson subsequently combined them to create a typology of the possible outcomes of a challenge. The four types of outcomes in Gamson's work are full response, co-optation, preemption, and collapse. Procedural impacts refer, then, to access to the system by challengers. This may occur by establishing consultation procedures, by undertaking negotiations, through formal recognition, or through general inclusion of challengers. We can further distinguish between *ad hoc access* and *permanent access,* according to the frequency and regularity of the access.

To assess the influence of the strength of the state on the chances of success of new social movements, Kriesi (1991) made a further distinction within the category of substantive impacts. *Reactive impacts* imply the prevention of "new disadvantages," that is, challengers avoid a worsening of the situation regarding their goals. In this case, challengers are able to exert a veto against a policy or against a decision taken by political authorities. *Proactive impacts* imply the introduction of "new advantages," that is, challengers obtain substantive concessions by political authorities. In this case, they acquire policy-making power. The importance of this distinction lies in the fact that it allows us to link the outcomes of social movements to the strength of the state, which is a crucial dimension of political opportunity structure.

Kitschelt added a further type of outcome to those stressed by Gamson. In his comparative study of the antinuclear movement in four Western countries, he introduced *structural impacts*. These refer to the possibility that a movement will produce some changes in certain aspects of the political context of protest itself, that is, in the political opportunity structure. This is a crucial kind of outcome because it alters one of the most important sets of causes of a movement's action, which may in turn modify its chances of success. We may distinguish between two types of structural impacts, depending on whether a movement produces a change in the *institutional structures* or in the *alliance structures.* An example of the first type is a change in the form of political institutions; an example of the second type is a political realignment or a split in the government. In their most radical version, structural impacts take the form of a revolution, or, more precisely, of a revolutionary outcome (Tilly 1978, 1993).[3] Obviously, this has not been the case in the countries we have studied during the period covered. Structural impacts less easily modify the two other dimensions of political opportunity structure—the cleavage structures and the prevailing strategies—at least in the short term.

We would like to introduce a fourth type of external impact, which we may call *sensitizing impacts*. These refer to the possibility that a movement will provoke a sensitizing of some social actor in the political arena or in the public arena, which goes in the direction of the goals of the movement. We may make a further distinction within this type of outcome according to whether the target of change is one of these two arenas. On the one hand, a social movement may have a sensitizing impact in putting one or many of its demands on the *political agenda*. The agenda-building approach has described such processes in detail. Supporters of this perspective distinguish between the *systemic agenda* and the *institutional agenda* (Cobb and Elder 1983). The former refers to a general set of political controversies in the public space. The latter refers to a set of concrete and specific items to be treated by political authorities, and is also known as governmental or formal agenda. On the other hand, we have a sensitizing impact insofar as a social movement changes *public attitudes*. This is similar to what Klandermans (1984, 1988) calls "consensus mobilization" and can be done by expanding a goal to a larger public or by intensifying the motivations of already sensitized people. More generally, following Snow et al. (1986), we may distinguish among four types of framing that may sensitize the general public: *bridging, amplification, extension,* and *transformation.* Figure 9.1 summarizes the types of outcomes just described.

The Link between the Political Opportunity Structure and the Outcomes of Social Movements

Thus far, we have indistinctly touched upon the notions of success, impact, and outcome. We already noted the ambiguity of the term "success" with regard to the problem being investigated. The notions of impact or outcome are more neutral and more encompassing than the notion of success. They not only eliminate its subjective component but they take into account the unintended consequences of the action as well. The mobilization by social movements sometimes results in their success, sometimes leaves things

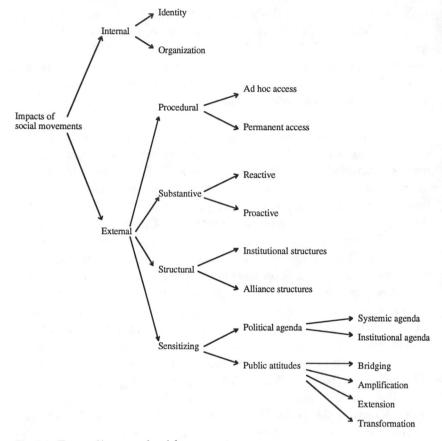

Fig. 9.1. Types of impacts of social movements

unchanged, and other times produces outcomes that the movements do not explicitly look for and that may even be counterproductive for them. Therefore, a distinction between success and impacts or outcomes is crucial to understanding the consequences of the mobilization by social movements.

Thus, an outcome of a social movement is a change of one of the types we have previously defined, whether this is a success for the movement or not. Yet we remain with a crucial unresolved problem: the link between a movement's action and the observed outcome. What allows us to say that a certain political change is the result of the action of a social movement or of a challenging group? Would it not have occurred anyway? In fact, we cannot directly determine whether a change is the result of a movement's action or of reform undertaken by the political authorities. We have to make the link between the movement's action and the observed change indirectly, by specifying the mechanisms through which the former produces the latter. Following the general argument of this book, our working hypothesis is that the outcomes of new social movements do not directly depend on the level of mobilization but are mediated by certain aspects of the political context of the protest. More precisely, they result from the interplay of the level of mobilization and the political opportunity structure. We shall first discuss the relationship between the political opportunity structure and the first two types of outcomes—procedural and substantive impacts—and shall briefly deal with the other types later on.

The structural political setting of a given country, which results from the combination of the institutional structures and the prevailing strategies, decisively influences the possibility for new social movements to have procedural and substantive impacts. Each combination is conducive to certain types of outcomes. Germany's setting of formal inclusion is most favorable for having reactive impacts. On the one hand, the relatively weak German state limits the possibilities of obtaining new advantages. In Germany, the capacity for getting things done is not very high, precisely because of the state's weakness. Hence, new social movements have to rely on reactive impacts to get some results from their action, which means to prevent a worsening of their situation. On the other hand, procedural impacts are not very likely because of the prevailing exclusive strategy that political authorities typically adopt in dealing with challengers. Hence, social movement organizations are unlikely to be integrated in advisory or decision-making procedures.

France's setting of selective exclusion is even less favorable for having procedural or substantive impacts. The strong French state has the means to implement policies. This prevents new social movements from having reactive impacts, because the government has the capacity to pursue its own policies. In contrast, the strength of the state would make proactive impacts more likely, but a prevailing exclusive strategy makes them quite difficult to produce. Government generally ignores the demands of new social movements, unless the configuration of power is more propitious to them (see chapter 3). Thus, proactive impacts by new social movements are possible when the configuration of power is favorable. Procedural impacts are severely limited in the French case, above all because of the prevailing exclusive strategy, except when the government attempts co-optation.

The Netherlands' setting of informal inclusion seems to be the most favorable for new social movements to produce outcomes of the types we are discussing. On the one hand, procedural impacts become more likely, because political authorities typically adopt a prevailing inclusive strategy when facing challengers. Indeed, this is the most inclusive political system of the four under study, which often implies important subsidies granted to some of the new social movement organizations. On the other hand, the relatively strong Dutch state, combined with a prevailing inclusive strategy, creates favorable conditions for proactive impacts, because the government is at the same time willing and able to make concessions to new social movements and to respond positively to their demands.

Finally, Switzerland's setting of integration, which is very favorable for mobilization by new social movements, is less propitious for their outcomes. The weak Swiss state prevents the movements from having proactive impacts, but leaves the door open for reactive impacts. Direct-democratic procedures—a peculiarity of the Swiss political system—represent a powerful tool in the hands of challengers for blocking public policies. Indeed, the referendum is a means of exerting a veto over certain governmental decisions. Figure 9.2 summarizes the possibilities of these types of impacts in each country as a function of the political opportunity structure.

Thus far, except in the case of France, the discussion has not taken into account the configuration of power. Yet we may generalize some points about this dimension of the political opportunity structure. The likelihood for new social movements to have procedural or substantive impacts depends on the configuration of power as well, more precisely, on the position of their allies within the political system, regardless of the structural political setting. When the Socialist Party—the most important ally of new social movements—is in the government, it can make concessions to them. Hence, in strong states we may expect demands by new social movements to have more chances to lead to change when their most powerful ally is in control of the executive branch. This was the case in France from 1981 to 1993—except for the period of cohabitation between 1986 and 1988—and in the Netherlands during the periods 1973–77 and 1981–82. In weak states, on the other hand, control of the executive branch makes no difference as far as proactive impacts are concerned, since the state has a low capacity to get things done. Moreover, reactive impacts can always be produced in weak states, exactly because of their weakness. Additionally, we may expect that the presence of a strong Socialist Party would improve the chances for new social movements to have procedural or substantive impacts, because support by the former increases the legitimacy of the latter and, thus, induce political authorities to make concessions to new social movements.

Institutional structures
(strength of the state)

	Weak	Strong
Exclusive	FORMAL INCLUSION •reactive impacts (Germany)	SELECTIVE EXCLUSION •proactive impacts if configuration of power is favorable (France)
Prevailing strategies	INTEGRATION •procedural impacts •reactive impacts (Switzerland)	INFORMAL INCLUSION •procedural impacts •proactive impacts (Netherlands)
Inclusive		

Fig. 9.2. Procedural and substantive impacts as a function of the political opportunity structure

Although we expect the political opportunity structure to constrain the outcomes of social movements in a crucial way, its influence is not the same for all types of movements. As we suggested in chapter 4, the relation of instrumental, subcultural, and countercultural movements to their political environment varies. The hypotheses we have stated thus far hold for instrumental movements only, that is, for movements for which all four concrete opportunities—chances of success, repression, facilitation, and reform/threat—are relevant. Their action is primarily a means to an external political goal. In contrast, subcultural and countercultural movements also possess internal goals linked to the reproduction of their collective identities. Therefore, the political opportunity structure is less decisive for their outcomes insofar as they pursue such internal, identity-linked, goals. In other words, since these types of movements do not only address political demands, there is a certain action space within the subculture or the counterculture on which they are grounded.

Additionally, according to the argument put forward in chapter 4, the political system is more closed for challengers when they raise issues that deal with high-profile policy domains. Conversely, it is more open when their issues concern low-profile policy domains. Similarly, we may think of low-profile policy domains as providing more chances for procedural impacts than high-profile policy domains. In other words, informal access to the system is more likely when challengers raise issues that do not threaten the political authorities decisively. Of course, the authorities could co-opt some organizations, but co-optation is likely to remain a rather rare event and to affect the most moderate movement organizations only. In contrast, the most radical organizations are rarely, if ever, the subject of integration into policy networks.

Regarding the other types of outcomes, it is more difficult to advance hypotheses. We shall only make some general remarks. We may expect some institutional features of the political system to have an influence on the possibilities of having structural impacts. In his comparative study on the antinuclear movement, Kitschelt (1986) argues that structural impacts are more likely in strong states—more precisely, in states in which political input structures are closed—because of the stronger structural pressures to which those states are subject. In our view, this is only partially true. Kitschelt's hypothesis holds for structural impacts that are large in scope, as, for instance, a fundamental institutional change. A revolutionary outcome is the most far-reaching example of such impacts. Yet, as far as smaller changes are concerned, a weak state seems to be more conducive to structural impacts.

Let us take the example of changes in political alignments. They are more likely in political systems with an open parliamentary arena. This is the case in proportional systems as the Dutch, the German, and the Swiss, whereas the French majority system makes this type of impact less likely. Greater access to the system facilitates the entrance of small parties into the parliament. Among these small parties there are allies of new social movements such as the Green parties. Yet proportional systems also have the effect of stabilizing the party structure. Therefore, an important change is unlikely to occur in such systems. In contrast, in majority systems such changes are more likely, but still not very frequent. The fact that a system is subject to strong structural pressures does not necessarily mean that an actual impact will occur. We have to make a distinction between the likelihood and the magnitude of an impact. A strong system offers little opportunity for structural impacts, but raises the necessity of producing them, precisely because of this lack of opportunities. On the other hand, in a weak system structural impacts become more likely, but, when they occur, their magnitude is lower.

We also expect political factors to be important for the appearance of sensitizing impacts. As far as impacts on the political agenda are concerned, supporters of the agenda-building approach have stressed a variety of factors such as definition of the issue, utilization of symbols, expansion of the issue to a relevant public, and patterns of entrance/access into the political system. Social movement organizations may play a crucial role in this respect, by helping their goals become issues on the political agenda. Yet some institutional features may facilitate this work. On the one hand, impacts on the political agenda are more likely in political systems that offer institutional channels to put issues on it. The possibility of using direct-democratic procedures in Switzerland immediately comes to mind. In particular, by launching a popular initiative, challengers may force political authorities to deal with a given problem and bring the population to a vote on it. On the other hand, it is more likely that an issue will be put on the political agenda when there are important allies within the administrative and the parliamentary arenas. This prevents political authorities from simply ignoring the demands of challengers and forces them to deal seriously with these demands. The Socialist Party is clearly the most important of such allies.

Finally, political opportunities are relevant for impacts on public attitudes as well. This was shown in chapter 6, where the discursive efficacy in the nuclear energy policy domain was related to previous mobilization and to the related chances of success. As we know, these factors depend to a large extent on the political opportunity structure.

The rest of this chapter is devoted to an empirical illustration of some of the arguments we have put forward. To do this, we present three examples, concerning the antinuclear movement, the gay movement, and the urban autonomous movement, which represent, respectively, instrumental, subcultural, and countercultural movements. We do not provide a systematic test of the hypotheses mentioned earlier for all types of outcomes. Instead, we furnish illustrations of how the political opportunity structure and the type of movement influence the possibilities of new social movements to produce certain outcomes. As far as external goals are concerned, we focus on procedural and substantive impacts, which are most closely linked to the political opportunity structure argument. We shall do this in the discussion of the antinuclear movement. When discussing the gay movement and the urban autonomous movement, we shall examine impacts on internal goals.

Outcomes of the Antinuclear Movement

The first example we would like to discuss concerns the energy policy domain — more precisely, the nuclear energy issue. The antinuclear movement is among the most successful new social movements, although its outcomes, as we shall see, have varied strongly from country to country. The case of nuclear energy has the advantage of offering a simple measure of its impacts. Since the main goal of the antinuclear movement is the abandonment of nuclear energy, which is produced through existing nuclear power plants, we can measure its substantive impacts by looking at the number of nuclear power plants at different times or by considering other, equivalent, indicators. Kitschelt (1986) has shown convincingly that nuclear programs have been scaled down in the presence of open political input structures, whereas weak political output structures have led to the most important construction schedule delays. Our argument is similar to Kitschelt's. According to our main argument, opposition to existing nuclear plants is more likely to succeed when the state is strong and the strategy of the political authorities inclusive, as in the Netherlands. This implies proactive impacts. In contrast, opposition to planned nuclear plants is more likely to succeed in weak states. Therefore, antinuclear opposition is also likely to succeed in Germany and Switzerland. This implies reactive impacts. Due to the prevailing exclusive strategy of the political authorities in Germany, who are less willing to negotiate with the movement than their Swiss counterparts, a strong and persistent movement is necessary there. Table 9.1 gives the development over time of the production of nuclear electricity in the four countries being studied.

This table shows, first, the different sizes of the nuclear capacity of the four countries. France and Germany have implemented a more important nuclear infrastructure than the Netherlands and Switzerland in each of the periods considered. Thus, the state of nuclear development in the single countries varied prior to the rise of the antinuclear movement or, at least, before the movement had converted all of its potential into action. Of course, nuclear capacity also depends on the size of the country, since large and populous countries need more energy supplies than smaller and less populated ones. To be sure, as the table illustrates, nuclear energy as a source of electricity increased from 1970 to 1985 in all four countries. Of course, this is

Table 9.1. Production of nuclear electricity per country (millions of kWh)

	France	Germany	Netherlands	Switzerland
1970	5,711	6,030	368	2,450
1975	18,248	21,398	3,335	7,391
1980	57,946	43,700	4,200	13,663
1985	213,100	125,902	3,713	21,281

Source: Etemad and Luciani 1991

partly due to the general growing need for energy and to the progressive lack of faith in the renewal of petroleum, especially after the energy crisis of 1973. We are more interested here, however, in the development of the production of nuclear electricity over time. We see that the pace of nuclear productive development varies across countries. France saw the greatest progression, inasmuch as the level of production in 1985 had increased to more than thirty-five times the level of 1970. German nuclear electricity underwent an important increase (about twenty-one times), whereas Dutch and Swiss production increased to a lesser extent (about ten times). According to these figures, the Dutch antinuclear movement seems to have been the most successful in opposing the progress of nuclear industry, since in that country the production of nuclear electricity actually decreased after 1980.

The number of nuclear plants in operation or under development provides a further indicator of the strength of nuclear energy in the four countries under study. Whereas in Germany and, especially, France the number of commercial nuclear plants in construction, operating, or decommissioned increased remarkably, in Switzerland and, especially, the Netherlands it remained rather stable. Thus, France—followed by Germany—is the country in which the government has been most able to implement its nuclear energy policy. In Switzerland and, especially, the Netherlands such an implementation proved more difficult. Yet these two indicators—the level of energy production and plant development—offer too simplistic a picture of the substantive impacts of the antinuclear movement. We need to link the development of nuclear energy production with the governmental plans concerning this policy domain. We can do this by returning to some data we discussed regarding the construction of a discourse about nuclear energy (see chapter 6). Table 9.2 compares the planned and the realized shares of nuclear energy in electricity production in the four countries.

This table shows that in 1974 the governments of all four countries relied strongly on nuclear energy for the supply of electricity. This is particularly true for France, which, compared to other countries, had in 1974 planned the highest share for the long run.[4] Through this table, we can easily see where

Table 9.2. Implementation of nuclear programs in the four countries
(percentages of total electricity production)

	France	Germany	Netherlands	Switzerland
% planned 1974[a]	68[b]	47	47	44
% realized 1988	70	34	5	37
% of plan realized	103	72	11	84

[a]Projected capacity for 1990
[b]Target for 1985
Source: Rüdig 1990

and to what extent the antinuclear movement has been able to oppose governmental plans for nuclear energy supply. According to the table, France is the country in which nuclear energy plans were pursued without taking into account the claims of antinuclear opposition, despite the existence of a rather strong antinuclear movement. The French government was not only able in 1988 to implement the whole nuclear capacity it had planned in 1974, but to slightly increase it. During the period under study, only one reactor, planned for Plogoff, was abandoned, in 1981. The centralization and nationalization of the electricity supply industry, the incorporation of utilities into government decision-making processes, and the centralization of the political system allowed the French government to implement its nuclear energy policy successfully against the opposition. The governments of the three other countries were all forced to renounce some of the planned nuclear capacity.

Germany and Switzerland are similar in this respect. German pronuclear forces were rather successful in struggling against antinuclear opponents, but to a much lesser extent than their French counterparts. In Germany, the antinuclear movement obtained some significant gains, although, judging from the figures in table 9.2, they were limited. This was due to the high-profile character of the nuclear energy policy domain and the related strong commitment to nuclear energy by the government. Yet the decentralization of the political system and of the electricity supply industries, the fact that, to a large extent, nuclear energy has been entrusted to the utilities, as well as the fact that nuclear energy legislation is particularly conducive to court litigation, offered many more opportunities for the movement to have substantive impacts. The most famous example is the renunciation of a project for the construction of a nuclear plant in the village of Wyhl, located near the French and the Swiss borders. Wyhl saw what has been considered to be the strongest antinuclear mobilization ever, which had not only a direct impact on that project but also an indirect one on other antinuclear challenges across the border (see chapter 8). In Gorleben, too, the movement was able to have a substantive impact by blocking the nuclear energy policy of the political authorities. The halting of construction on a fast-breeder reactor in Kalkar and the fate of a planned nuclear reprocessing plant provide further examples of successful antinuclear opposition in Germany. After local opposition to such a project had forced the authorities to displace the site several times, the eleventh site—Wackersdorf—could not host the plant, because the project was eventually abandoned. Thus, despite a general increase in the production of nuclear electricity and in the number of nuclear plants, the German antinuclear movement produced some important substantive impacts. The federal structure of the country and the fact that the nuclear energy policy domain is in the hands of the *Länder*—the member states—have facilitated such impacts. As far as this policy domain is concerned, Germany is more federalist than Switzerland, where the national government is responsible for nuclear energy. Moreover, since Germany's nuclear energy legislation leaves the door wide open to court litigation, the German antinuclear movement has frequently availed itself of the opportunity for legal challenges. The nuclear projects in Wyhl, Brokdorf, and Grohnde were tied up in the courts, although only in the case of Wyhl was construction permanently blocked.

The Swiss situation has been similar to that of Germany with regard to substantive impacts produced by the antinuclear movement—at least up until 1990, when a popular initiative sanctioned a ten-year moratorium on the construction of nuclear plants, provoking a nuclear stalemate. In Switzerland, too, the government implemented a large share of the planned nuclear capacity, but it was also forced to abandon some projects. Its direct-democratic system offers a decisive opportunity for opposing nuclear energy. Opponents of nuclear energy launched other initiatives and referenda, directed at the local or cantonal level, but they had a limited scope since nuclear energy in Switzerland depends on the national government. Yet direct-democratic procedures have played an important role in helping social movements to have substantive impacts. Since the mid-seventies, the Swiss antinuclear movement has had a crucial substantive impact. After years of opposition from antinuclear activists, massive antinuclear demonstrations, and interventions by local authorities, it succeeded in blocking construction of the planned nuclear plant in Kaiseraugst, which was eventually abandoned in 1988. The mobilization against this project had a strong resonance in the public opinion and played a fundamental symbolic role for the movement.

Nevertheless, it is in the Netherlands that the antinuclear movement produced the most important outcomes. Despite planning similar to Germany's and Switzerland's, the Dutch government was able to implement only about one-tenth of the planned nuclear capacity. To be sure, the need for nuclear energy and the nuclear commitment by the Dutch government were probably lower than in the three other countries, at least since the discovery of an important energy source: North Sea gas. This might have actually facilitated the movement, since nuclear energy was less crucial for the Netherlands in comparison to the three other countries. Yet the Dutch government had planned to strongly develop its nuclear energy policy anyway, which proves that the movement played an important role in blocking it. Moreover, the Dutch production of natural gas remained fairly stable from 1975 to 1986 and even decreased in 1987 (Hay 1990), which also indicates the reliance of the Dutch government on nuclear energy.

A further indicator provides a measure of the substantive impacts of the antinuclear movement. Since its emergence, antinuclear opposition to existing governmental policies has revealed its predominantly reactive character in pursuit of its ultimate goal: the abandonment of the nuclear option as a source of energy. This is considered to be one of its greater weaknesses (Rüdig 1990). Up to now, the movement has failed to concentrate its efforts on a possible second main goal: the promotion of a policy that takes into account alternative sources of energy. As a result, its substantive impacts, if any, have remained reactive. Yet reactive impacts may take another, less visible, form. Table 9.3 shows the average construction delays of nuclear power plants in France and Germany.

Although construction delays increased both in France and Germany from 1974 to 1984, they were particularly pronounced in Germany. Thus, in line with our expectations, reactive impacts are more likely in weak political systems, which have fragmented implementation structures and in which opportunities are forthcoming. The German legal system facilitates this type of outcome, which may be produced through successful court litigation. In contrast, a country like France, which has centralized implementation structures, can implement its nuclear energy policy more easily. Thus, the political opportunity structure seems to play a crucial role in explaining the outcomes of social movements, at least as far as substantive impacts are concerned.

As for procedural impacts, we have expected them to be more likely in countries in which the political authorities adopt a prevailing inclusive strategy. The French political system is closed not only formally, but also informally. This prevents social movements in general, and the antinuclear movement in particular, from having procedural impacts. The presence or absence of this type of outcome is difficult to show empirically. Yet many authors have pointed out the lack of procedural impacts of new social movements in France.

Table 9.3. Average construction delays of all nuclear power plants under construction or in commercial service in France and Germany (months)

	France	Germany
1974	0.7	6.1
1977	3.6	13.8
1980	7.1	30.6
1984	11.3	42.4

Source: Kitschelt 1986

Kitschelt (1986: 74) has remarked that "procedural impacts in France have been virtually non-existent." Suffice it to note that practically no organization of the antinuclear movement is integrated into consulting procedures, let alone into decision making. The government has been more than reluctant to grant concessions to the movement and has strictly followed a prevailing exclusive strategy. In Germany, the situation is not much more favorable for the antinuclear movement. As Kitschelt (ibid.: 75) has noted, "overall, the anti-nuclear movement in West Germany made no gains in procedural representation, for its mobilization failed to open any new party, legislative, corporist or (constitutionally forbidden) plebiscitarian avenues of representation."[5]

As expected, most procedural outcomes were produced in Switzerland and the Netherlands, the two countries in which political authorities follow a prevailing inclusive strategy. Such outcomes took the form, for instance, of the integration of organizations of the antinuclear movement into consulting procedures or, less frequently, established systems of interest intermediation. Nevertheless, especially in Switzerland, they remained rather limited and mostly ad hoc, largely because of the high-profile character of the nuclear energy policy domain. For instance, the Swiss government often consults the Swiss Energy Foundation (SES) on energy issues. Other large, more traditional, ecology organizations, such as the World Wildlife Fund (WWF) or the Swiss League for the Protection of Nature (SBN), are sometimes consulted. In contrast, purely antinuclear organizations are almost never consulted.

The antinuclear movement has, however, found other paths to institutional politics. We are alluding to structural impacts. Although the movement has not shaped any specific political party, its interests have been partially articulated in the parliamentary arena by Green parties, as well as by the Socialist Party and other left-wing parties. Despite fundamental differences in the electoral system and in the cleavage structures (see chapter 1), a Green party could enter parliament in three of the four countries under study. Only in France have the Greens been forced to remain an extraparliamentary party at the national level, despite their rather strong electoral support. Especially in the early stages, Green parties have been an ally of the antinuclear movement and helped it pursue its goals. Other small parties of the left—except perhaps in France—have also supported antinuclear demands to a similar extent. Yet Green parties, following a party logic, tend to broaden their spectrum of goals, and, as a result, the struggle against nuclear energy becomes only one facet of their political program. The remark by Rucht (1990a: 211), nevertheless, that "the structural impacts on the regime itself seem to be insignificant in all three countries" (the United States, France, and West Germany), is somewhat exaggerated.

Apart from the varying degree of substantive, procedural, and structural impacts, we may wonder whether the antinuclear movement succeeded in putting the nuclear energy issue onto the political agenda and changing the attitudes of the general public in the four countries. As far as the political agenda is concerned, the answer is clearly yes, but again to varying degrees. Not surprisingly, the shaping of the antinuclear issue in France proved more difficult than in the other three countries. This is partly because of the lack of movement allies in the parliamentary arena during the eighties—itself a result of the French party system's being organized along a bipolar social-economic cleavage, and of the indifference of the political authorities. When the Socialist Party took power in 1981, its support for the antinuclear movement rapidly vanished. As a consequence, the limited political opportunities offered new social movements by the French political system during the eighties explains the partial failure of the movement to keep the nuclear energy issue on the political agenda. This is because the lack of chances of success, particularly after the Socialist Party's coming to power, provoked a rapid decline of the movement (see chapter 3). In the three other countries, nuclear energy became a crucial issue in the second half of the seventies, when the movement was successful in challenging pronuclear policies. Yet, at the beginning of the eighties, when the peace movement reached its peak, the military use of nuclear technology replaced nuclear energy as an issue in the public space, especially in Germany and the Netherlands. In Switzerland, thanks to direct-democratic procedures, the nuclear energy issue could be kept on the political agenda for a longer time; the launching of several popular initiatives and referenda forced the political authorities and the public to deal with this issue.

Finally, sensitizing impacts by the antinuclear movement in the four countries under study seem not to have been forthcoming. If we go back and examine the data on attitudes of people toward nuclear energy (see chapter 6), we can see a general lack of sensitizing impacts. The cross-country comparison tells us that public support for nuclear energy is higher where the industry is stronger and vice versa. Thus, for instance, the French public supports nuclear energy more than the German public. As Rüdig (1990: 347) has noted, "public opinion adapts to the state of nuclear energy in these countries. Once a country abandons nuclear energy, public opinion develops a staunchly anti-nuclear flavor. And in these countries which have made a major commitment to nuclear energy, public support is quite high and opposition less pronounced." Nevertheless, despite some fluctuations over time, public attitudes toward nuclear energy have remained fairly stable in all four countries. This fact suggests that the influence of the antinuclear movement on public opinion is lower than many movement activists and observers tend to believe.

Outcomes of the Gay Movement[6]

The gay movement differs from the antinuclear movement in two substantive respects. First, it is a predominantly subcultural movement. As such, within-group interactions and collective identities play a crucial role for its mobilization and outcomes. Hence, we expect external factors such as the political opportunity structure to have only a limited influence on the impacts of this movement, at least as far as internal goals are concerned. The outcomes of a subcultural movement are often internal and depend on the readiness of the movement to respond to a threat or to promote an internal goal rather than on the external political conditions. Second, its demands concern low-profile policy domains. As a result, when external goals are at stake, the political system is more open than for the antinuclear movement and the political authorities do not repress it with the same vigor. Moreover, the political authorities may be willing to significantly facilitate the movement in certain situations, even with regard to certain internal goals. One example is the appearance of AIDS in the early eighties. In this section, we focus on the outcomes of the gay movement with regard to AIDS. Besides representing a turn in the gay community, the AIDS epidemic allows us to quantify some movement outcomes. The extent to which Western countries are affected by AIDS varies widely. Table 9.4 shows the presence of AIDS among gays in the four countries under study at the end of 1990.

In the four countries, AIDS is a serious threat for the gay community, although the problem has not reached the gravity it has in the United States. When we look at the absolute figures, France and Switzerland seem to face

Table 9.4. Presence of AIDS among gays in the four countries
(per million inhabitants, end 1990)

	France	Germany	Netherlands	Switzerland
Gays with AIDS	124.1	50.0	82.5	109.3
% gays among total of people with AIDS	53	70	80	45

Source: World Health Organization/National Commission for the Struggle against AIDS
(Netherlands)

a more serious problem than the two other countries. Yet, if we consider the
percentage of gays among the total number of people with AIDS, Germany
and the Netherlands are in a worse position. At any rate, differences among
these four countries are less striking than differences between them and other
European countries. Among gays, AIDS has done greater damage in the
richer northwest European countries than in the southern part of the conti-
nent. For instance, in Italy "only" 16 percent of the total number of people
hit by the disease are gay, which in absolute figures amounts to 21.5 per
million inhabitants. Similarly, in Spain there are "only" 30.8 gays with AIDS
per million inhabitants, accounting for 16 percent of the total. On the other
hand, the percentage of drug addicts hit by the disease in these south European countries is much higher than in the north European countries. What
accounts for these differences in the spread of AIDS between south and north
European countries? The differences cannot be accidental. They may be due
to the greater emancipation and the more sizable subculture of the gay movement in the northern countries prior to the emergence of the disease. These
factors may have facilitated the spread of AIDS through a larger number of
"self-identifying" gays and through a wider incidence of "dangerous" sexual
practices when the disease emerged. Of course, the spread of AIDS also depends on other factors, such as geographical mobility. Nevertheless, an assessment of the impact of the gay movement on the spread of AIDS is mean-
ingless unless we take into account the evolution of the disease over time
since methods of prevention became known.

   In this regard, Altman (1988: 311) has remarked that "the most effective
responses have been observed in those areas where the gay movement already existed as a legitimate and recognized pressure group." This is the
case of the Netherlands and, to a lesser extent, Switzerland. In contrast, "the
oddest case is France, where despite a considerable caseload and a leading
role in medical research, virtually no government action has been forthcoming from either socialist or conservative ministers, and where even the gay
movement, in decline throughout the 1980s, has failed to mobilize around

aids" (ibid.: 311–12). The strength of the gay movement is seen as a major factor leading to effective prevention of AIDS among gays. More precisely, according to this view, the prevention of AIDS depends on the prior existence of a movement, able to act politically. However, this is not completely accurate. If such an explanation seems to be true in the case of the Netherlands, it does not hold for the three other countries. Neither in France, nor in Germany, nor in Switzerland was the gay movement a strong political actor when the disease appeared. To be sure, in France the movement was quite strong at the beginning of the eighties. Yet, paradoxically enough, the strong facilitation by the French political authorities and the subsequent abundance of success of the movement led to its decline (see chapter 7). What remained was an important commercial subculture, while the gay movement as a political actor went into crisis. Thus France, as well as Germany and Switzerland, has proved more effective in preventing the spread of AIDS among gays than other European countries, particularly south European countries, even in the absence of a strong movement. Table 9.5 shows the increase in the number of gays with AIDS in the four countries from 1986 to 1990.

Since the great variations in the absolute figures across countries do not allow for a judgment based on them, we have to look at the relative difference between the two time periods to assess the progression of the disease. The results show that prevention was most successful in Switzerland, since the percentage of increase in AIDS cases was lower than in the other countries. Surprisingly, the Netherlands ranks lowest in successful prevention. Indeed, the pace of the spread of AIDS was higher there than in France, which had one of the worst prevention policies of all West European countries. Yet the Dutch gay subculture is one of the strongest—at any rate, stronger than in the other countries under study. Why, then, was prevention less effective in the Netherlands? The answer may lie in the very content of the prevention campaign. In the Netherlands, prevention brought less satisfactory results than in Switzerland because the Swiss explicitly advised the use of condoms from the beginning, whereas the Dutch message was ambiguous. A clear and straightforward message proved more effective than an ambiguous one.

Differences among the four countries under study are relatively weak, however, when compared with figures for other European countries. In general, south European countries show a higher increase in the number of cases than north European ones. For instance, Portugal, Spain, Italy, and especially Greece have been less effective than Denmark, the United Kingdom, Sweden, and Norway. Obviously, there has also been an international preven-

Table 9.5. Increase in the number of gays with AIDS in the four countries (per million inhabitants, 1986–90)

	France	Germany	Netherlands	Switzerland
Gays with AIDS end 1986	24.8	10.7	15.5	29.0
Gays with AIDS end 1990	124.1	50.0	82.5	109.3
% increase 1986–90	400	367	436	277

Source: World Health Organization/National Commission for the Struggle against AIDS (Netherlands)

tion effect, in the sense that in all countries the pace of the spread of the disease slowed between 1986 and 1990. Such a success strongly contrasts with the failure to slow the spread of the disease among drug addicts. Whereas the number of gays with AIDS increased by six times on a European average between 1986 and 1990, the number of cases among drug addicts multiplied by seventeen times. This fact suggests that the presence of an important subculture grounded on a strong collective identity and of a politicized social movement, such as exist among gays but are lacking among drug addicts, plays a crucial role in reducing the spread of the disease. More generally, the presence of three social networks may explain the efficacy of AIDS prevention efforts. First, a sizable commercial subculture (see chapter 7), as exists in France and the Netherlands, is an organizational tool for disseminating information about dangerous sexual behavior and "safer sex." Second, a strong noncommercial subculture, as exists in the Netherlands and Germany, may also facilitate such dissemination. Third, a powerful gay movement, as in the Netherlands, may also make prevention more effective. If all these networks are absent, prevention becomes more difficult, as the south European countries demonstrate. These factors have the function of organizing the gay community against the threat of AIDS. They also show the importance of the action space that subcultural movements have at their disposal and the role it has on the outcomes of this type of movement.

Yet, a comparison of the four countries under study shows that there are differences in the development of the disease even when all these conditions are present. To the extent that the gay subculture has an external political expression — that is, insofar as there is a social movement — the political opportunity structure may influence the outcomes of the movement. In the case of AIDS, what matters is the readiness of the political authorities to undertake prevention efforts. It appears that the quicker the reaction from the gay movement and the political authorities, the more effective the results of prevention. Thus, facilitation coming from a prevailing inclusive strategy on the part of the authorities may help the movement and the subculture on which it is grounded to produce internal outcomes. Switzerland represents perhaps the best example. Swiss political authorities decided as early as 1983 to intervene in the struggle against AIDS. The movement made its real first step in this direction in 1985, by forming a national organization (Swiss Aid against AIDS). Immediately, the Federal Office of Public Health became a member of the organization. It was the first time in Switzerland that a governmental institution had asked to become a member of a private association (let alone a new social movement). This move gave the organization legitimacy and financial support. It helped the gay subculture organize against the threat of AIDS. Thus, the Swiss state has played a crucial role in the struggle against AIDS. This is part of a new development concerning the prevailing inclusive strategy of the Swiss political authorities. The Swiss state has increasingly adopted a strategy of providing incentives for the self-organization of society (Bütschi and Cattacin 1993). Indeed, this strategy represents a new form of subsidiarity, which was traditionally conceived of as a way of delegating only those tasks to the state that could not be solved by civil society or the private sector. According to the new form of subsidiarity, a weak state not only tends to become the ally of private initiatives, but it creates and encourages them when they are of general interest. Thus, a new kind of relationship appears to be established between the state and certain social movements where social problems are concerned, AIDS and alcoholism being two major examples.

This brief example of the gay movement and AIDS suggests several provisional conclusions. First, the presence of an important gay subculture, grounded on a strong collective identity, has had a double effect. In the beginning, it increased the spread of the disease, because the "sexual revolution" made contacts easier; but thereafter, prevention proved more effective because of the very presence of a cohesive gay community. This is clear if we compare the countries of northern Europe with those of southern Europe. Second, such a comparison reveals the crucial role of three social networks for the gay movement in producing internal outcomes: a commercial subculture, a noncommercial subculture, and a politically oriented movement. The efficacy of AIDS prevention among gays is not necessarily linked to the presence of a strong gay movement. A strong gay subculture, whether commercialized or not, is at least as important as the movement in shaping the conditions of its outcomes. Third, a comparison of the four countries under study shows that the efficacy of prevention relies on other factors as well, which may further facilitate it or make it more difficult. The Swiss case illustrates the importance of the position of the political authorities in this context. Provided that the subculture is strong enough to constitute the basis for an external intervention, an early reaction by the authorities and their subsequent support may reinforce prevention efforts. Yet such intervention must be well focused. The example of the Netherlands shows that, even in the presence of a strong subculture and of facilitation by the authorities, the result is not as satisfactory as would have been expected had the content of the message resonated with the values shared by the gay community.

Of course, gay movement outcomes go far beyond the example of AIDS. Perhaps the most important one is the change of attitudes on the part of the general public toward gays. The gay movement has had procedural impacts as well. The nonthreatening character of its demands has facilitated such impacts. Moreover, the fact that AIDS represents a threat to the whole population and not only to gays has further facilitated the collaboration between the political authorities and the movement. The example we have chosen clearly shows how subcultural movements can produce some outcomes. Since they are relatively independent of the political opportunity structure, these movements have an action space for producing internal outcomes. In other words, compared to instrumental and countercultural movements, they are more likely to have certain impacts independent of political opportunities. This action space may be used properly or not used at all. The extent to which it is well used depends, above all, on the strength of the subcultural side of the movement. Among the countries under study, some type of subcultural network was present when AIDS emerged. This contributed to an initial spread of the disease, but went a long way toward making prevention efforts effective.

Outcomes of the Urban Autonomous Movement

We saw in chapter 4 that repression is the only concrete opportunity that has an impact on countercultural movements such as the urban autonomous movement. The movement's outcomes depend to a great extent, therefore, on the level of repression exercised by political authorities. As we know, the level of repression largely depends on the political opportunity structure, which can account for variations in the outcomes of the movement in different political contexts. Since the urban autonomous movement is typically a local movement, in which the local context is decisive for the outcomes of the movement, comparisons across countries become less relevant. Nevertheless, although the local political opportunity structure is the most relevant for this type of movement, the national political opportunity structure may also play a role; the configuration of power at the national level may indirectly influence policies at the local level, especially in centralized political systems as in France.

Although the openness of the political system to the demands of the urban autonomous movement varies from one context to another, two main characteristics of this movement make procedural and substantive impacts more difficult to produce than for the two other types of movements. First, this is a typical example of the countercultural movement, which has a confrontational relationship with the political authorities. Second, its demands often address a high-profile policy domain: the protection of private property, which makes this movement more threatening for the authorities than other movements. To be sure, demands of the urban autonomous movement also include the creation of autonomous youth centers, which is not a high-profile policy domain. Thus, we can distinguish between two main branches of the movement: the squatters' branch and the branch struggling for autonomous youth centers. This distinction seems to be almost exclusively significant in Switzerland, where two parts of the movement exist with distinct goals, although the two are linked to each other and frequently overlap.

What kind of implications do these two main characteristics of the movement have for the assessment of its outcomes? As compared to instrumental and subcultural movements, especially those addressing low-profile policy domains, the urban autonomous movement has much less access to the political system and no allies among the established political actors. As a result, it has virtually no procedural impacts. Such impacts are nevertheless sometimes forthcoming, but, since the political authorities generally address the most established and moderate wing of a social movement, this often reflects an attempt to co-opt certain organizations, to delegitimize the radical wing, and to calm down the protest. Thus, for instance, we expect state subsidies given to this movement to be much lower than those granted to other new social movements. As we saw in chapter 4, the urban autonomous movement is much less facilitated than the other movements. To be sure, some organizations have received state subsidies. One Dutch organization among those we studied bases its existence almost exclusively on state subsidies. In Switzerland, two organizations, one located in Zurich and the other in Geneva, received sizable amounts of money from their local governments once they obtained a youth center; these are the most moderate organizations, which aim at creating autonomous youth centers open to everybody. These organizations often subsequently follow the path of commercialization. The more radical wing of the movement is, however, generally repressed by the political authorities. This has dramatic consequences not only for procedural impacts but also for substantive impacts. For instance, in France squatters have no legal means to fight back or defend themselves after an occupation, and the authorities usually follow a prevailing exclusive strategy. Thus the French squatters' movement was practically disarmed when the government decided to carry out a police expulsion policy against squatters during the seventies and from 1983 on. Only between 1981 and 1983 did the political authorities show initial tolerance for the movement, which went so far as to grant subsidies. The attitude change by the left government soon strongly diminished the chances of the movement's having any procedural and substantive impacts.

The German situation differs in that the movement produced more visible outcomes, despite strong repression by the political authorities. The first occupations of vacant houses in Berlin in February 1979, led by a civic action group (*Bürgerinitiative*), produced some remarkable results. The favorable configuration of power — a left-wing government — facilitated certain movement successes, such as the granting of leases for a number of houses. The occupation of an empty factory in 1979 was also successful. Yet, after 1981 and a change in the local configuration of power, these early impacts waned. From then on, the movement found it more difficult to achieve its political demands. Its radicalization, at the end of 1986, led to new laws directed especially against the Autonomen, such as the reintroduction of the law against the verbal or written propagation of criminal acts and the extension of existing antiterrorist legislation. At the same time, the city authorities were undertaking a strategy aiming at preempting the moderate wing of the movement. Nevertheless, the repression of the more radical wing beginning in 1981 had devastating consequences. Whereas in June 1981 about 170 buildings (Aust and Rosenblatt 1981) housing between two thousand and three thousand people (Brand 1988; Mulhak 1983) were occupied in Berlin, at the end of 1984 no illegally occupied houses remained (Geronimo 1990). Thus the first mobilization by the squatters in Berlin produced some substantive impacts. But these remained limited, and we may see them as tactical concessions to the movement by the political authorities, because at the same time they exercised repression — which testifies to an attempt at preemption. Still, at the end of the protest wave, by which time the movement had practically disappeared, it could show some substantive impacts in Berlin: legalized buildings that became centers of alternative culture and political activity, improvements in housing policy, extra funds for renovation, and measures against housing speculation.

In the Netherlands, the urban autonomous movement mobilized mostly in Amsterdam. There the movement also had some success, but, in contrast to the German case, it was obtained before the peak of movement mobilization in the early eighties — that is, before the political authorities launched a serious policy of repression against it. The movement was able to continue to occupy a large number of buildings because the authorities only intervened in a small number of cases. Indeed, the city of Amsterdam bought many buildings and rented them to the occupants. In addition, some outcomes were produced at the level of the housing policy, such as a construction program for apartments for youngsters or the temporary renting of buildings under renovation. All this changed when the political opportunity structure became much less favorable to the movement in 1985. From then on, repression increased and legislative measures were taken against the movement.

The German, French, and Swiss cases provide examples of structural impacts. The presence and action of the urban autonomous movement had some consequences on the party system in all three countries. In Germany, the conflict between the movement and the political authorities in Berlin had a clear winner: the Christian Democratic Union. This party gained electoral advantage from the continuous confrontation and the chaotic policies of the authorities by winning the elections of May 1981. In France, the activities of the movement had an indirect influence on the change in the leftist government's policy after 1983. The attitude change by the Socialist government followed a campaign by its adversaries, who accused the Socialist Party of being too permissive toward the squatters. In Switzerland, structural impacts of this movement were more straightforward. In Zurich, the division within the Socialist Party, which was part of the local government at the time the mobilization by the urban autonomous movement peaked in 1981, became more explicit as a consequence of movement actions. One wing of the party was sympathetic to the movement's aims, while the other wing took a harder line. This led to a worsening of internal division and, eventually, to an open split in the party. The situation was similar to what happened in Berlin: in Zurich, the bourgeois coalition was able to take advantage of a perceived need to reestablish a social order that was being "threatened" by young "rioters"; it was the clear winner of the municipal elections in spring 1982.

The Swiss example illustrates the role of the local political opportunity structure in possibilities for the urban autonomous movement to have substantive impacts. In Switzerland, local political authorities are more independent of national ones than, say, in France. As a result, we can compare two different local situations and draw some conclusions about the role of local government in shaping protest and its outcomes. Political opportunities for the urban autonomous movement at the local level were quite different in the cities of Zurich and Geneva in the early eighties. Whereas in Zurich the movement had limited access to the political system and was subjected to strong repression, in Geneva the system was more accessible and negotiations took place very quickly. Apart from a radicalization of the movement, the hard line followed by the political authorities in Zurich made it very difficult to obtain an autonomous youth center. Because of the movement's strength, however, the authorities were forced to make some concession, which were supported by a fraction of the Socialist Party. Yet this victory was only temporary, because the center was closed soon after its opening. Moreover, the authorities did not wish to speak directly with the movement, or at best spoke with its most moderate wing and tried by every means to defeat the radical wing that was at the heart of the protest. To be sure, negotiations were also undertaken in Zurich, but they were soon broken off and continued only through established intermediaries. In Geneva, on the other hand, negotiations between the core of movement—that is, the organization that led the protest—and the political authorities took place from the beginning of the protest in 1985. The movement won its youth center early on and received subsidies thereafter. We might consider this substantive impact to be a movement success, but that is far from obvious. Surely we can consider the obtaining of a youth center to be a success for the movement in the short run, but this could result in a weakening of the movement in the long run, because resort to radical actions is delegitimized once a process of negotiation has taken place and the movement has reached its main goal. Hence, the confrontational character of the movement is diminished, which means the loss of the main feature of a countercultural movement. More generally, its whole mobilization decreases because there is no longer any need to mobilize, at least on this issue. Consequently, the movement tends to follow the path of commercialization and involution by concentrating its interests and resources on management of the youth center. Commercial activities tend to overwhelm political activities.

The differences between the situations in Zurich and in Geneva cast some doubt on the interactive model proposed by Karstedt-Henke (1980) (see chapter 5). This model suggests that the political authorities always react in the same way when facing countercultural protest: they always begin by overreacting to the rise of protest with indiscriminate repression, then adopting a double strategy of repression against the radical wing of a social movement and co-optation of its moderate wing; such a strategy triggers an interactive dynamic that eventually leads to both radicalization and the latency of mass protest. Karstedt-Henke provides evidence from the German case to support this argument. The example of the urban autonomous movement in Zurich also confirms this thesis. Nevertheless, the example of Geneva leads us to ask whether it is possible to generalize this model unconditionally. Indeed, the dynamics that developed in Geneva are not consistent with those described by Karstedt-Henke. It is possible for the political authorities to react differently than this model predicts. In other words, they have an action space when dealing with social movements. The political opportunity structure constrains this action space, but the specific strategic choices of the movement and of the authorities at a given time largely determine the way the political authorities make use of it. In any case, comparison of the Zurich and Geneva urban autonomous movements suggests that the patterns of reaction by the political authorities to protest are not necessarily those of simultaneous repression and co-optation following an initial overreaction.

In summary, we can stress three points. First, the urban autonomous movement apparently obtained rather limited success. This is particularly evident in political systems that offer few opportunities for procedural and substantive impacts. If the former were practically absent, the latter were somewhat easier to produce, except perhaps in France. Yet the outcomes of this movement go beyond the obtaining of free spaces, which we may consider to be its success. Its outcomes consist also in putting some fundamental issues onto the political agenda, such as the lodging and place of the young in society. In addition, this movement had some structural impacts, although to a limited extent. These impacts can be favorable for a further development of the movement, but they are often counterproductive. Second, the national political opportunity structure is less relevant to the outcomes of this movement, since their demands primarily concern the local political opportunity structure. As a result, political opportunities may vary within a single country, as illustrated by the example of Switzerland. Third, the most important result is that the possibilities for the urban autonomous movement to have procedural and substantive impacts depends largely on whether it has internal — that is, subcultural — goals. If the political authorities see its demands as being too confrontational and radical — hence, too threatening — repression becomes too strong. As a consequence, the movement is forced to turn to subcultural activities, often of a commercial kind, such as the smooth functioning of an autonomous youth center, in order to obtain some measure of success. Thus, procedural impacts are very rare, substantial impacts may be produced if repression is not too strong, and other types of impacts, such as internal, sensitizing, or structural impacts, may be produced even if the movement is subject to strong repression.

Conclusion

This chapter has dealt with the outcomes of new social movements. We have explicitly distinguished between success, on the one hand, and impacts or outcomes, on the other hand. The outcomes of a social movement may coincide with its success, but often they do not. We can define the outcomes of social movements along two main dimensions. First, the mobilization by social movements may lead to success or failure. Second, it may produce intended or unintended consequences. To assess the importance of the political context and, specifically, of political opportunities for the outcomes of social movements, one has to distinguish between success and failure, as well as to make a distinction between intended and unintended impacts.

The literature on social movements has long neglected the consequences of social movements on the political system and on society. The first step, in such an enterprise, consists of making a typology of impacts. The second step consists of looking for the possible mechanisms causing each type of impact and formulating a set of hypotheses accordingly. The third step would consist of testing the hypotheses empirically. Here, we have not done this systematically. Through three examples — one for each type of movement — we have simply tried to show the relevance of the political opportunity structure in facilitating or constraining the outcomes of new social movements. The case studies suggest that political opportunities are relevant for explaining not only the mobilization by new social movements and their action repertoire, but their outcomes as well.

Finally, the comparison of the three types of movements has shown that the political opportunity structure does not constrain the outcomes of each type to the same extent. Since instrumental movements are by definition almost exclusively politically oriented, they are the most influenced by political opportunities. Hence, their outcomes depend very much on the political opportunity structure and on changes at this level. In contrast, for identity-oriented movements the constraining role of the political opportunity structure is less important. Subcultural movements can produce outcomes even if the political conditions are not favorable for reaching political goals, because they have an action space that allows them to reach some internal goals. Countercultural movements hardly succeed in reaching radical political goals. Their strongly confrontational character and their lack of political allies make this very difficult. They have many more possibilities for obtaining some measure of success when they struggle for subcultural goals, that is, for goals that have an internal orientation. Yet they may produce other types of outcomes that we do not necessarily see as a success. These three examples show that the political opportunity structure is especially crucial for instrumental movements, but less critical for subcultural and countercultural movements. Yet insofar as the latter raise political demands, they also need political opportunities in order to produce some outcomes.

Conclusion

The Fruits of Transatlantic Cross-Fertilization

Most recent overviews of the social movement literature distinguish between a European and an American approach (Klandermans 1986; Klandermans and Tarrow 1988; McAdam, McCarthy, and Zald 1988; Tarrow 1990; Neidhardt and Rucht 1991; Eyerman and Jamison 1991). The main focus of the European tradition is on broad social-structural changes (such as individualization or the growth of the welfare state) that are supposed to underlie the rise and fall of different categories of social movements. Within the European debate, the concept of "new social movements" (NSMs) occupies a central place. Typically, these movements are seen as carriers of a new political paradigm and heralds of a new era labeled postindustrial, postmaterialist, postmodern, or postfordist, depending on the theoretical perspective of the respective author (Offe 1985; Roth 1985; Touraine 1980b; Melucci 1980). In the United States, on the other hand, not even the concept of "new social movements" has been able to gain currency, and little attention has been paid to the macrodevelopments that are central to the European discussion. Instead, American scholars working within the resource mobilization perspective (Oberschall 1973; McCarthy and Zald 1977; Zald 1992) have focused on how individual motivations are translated into participation through the mobilization efforts of social movement organizations.

Following Melucci (1984: 821), one might say that while the Europeans have focused on the "why" of (new) social movements, the Americans have emphasized "how" social movements mobilize. Exaggerated though this opposition may be, it does contain an important element of truth. European students of new social movements have made little effort to test their ambitious theories in concrete empirical research, and have generally seen the link between transformations of social structure and mobilization as direct and self-evident. Given this near absence of empirical testing and the sometimes strongly normative character of European theorizing, one might, somewhat maliciously, say that the European approach has in fact been more preoccupied with the "ought to" than with the "why" of new social movements. The American tradition, on the other hand, is characterized by a strong emphasis on concrete aspects of mobilization processes that lend themselves to rigorous empirical tests. While this has prevented the kind of free-floating and teleological theorizing that characterizes too much of the European literature, it has also tended to restrict the American horizon to those aspects of social movements that can most easily be observed and measured: large, professional social movement organizations rather than more diffuse activities, networks, or subcultures; individual attitudes as expressed in surveys rather than structural cleavages, ideologies, or collective identities. Thus, in the eyes of many European scholars, the American approach's greater methodological and empirical rigor has demanded a high price in theoretical scope and relevance.

Up to the mid-1980s, this schematic and polarized picture of the state of the art in social movement studies was by and large accurate.[1] Recently, however, a process of transatlantic cross-fertilization has begun to take shape. Theoretically, Europeans and Americans seem to have found a common ground around the concept of "political opportunity structure" (POS), which was first introduced by American scholars (Eisinger 1973; McAdam 1982) but was soon adapted and elaborated upon by Europeans (Brand 1985; Kitschelt 1986; Kriesi 1991). On the one hand, this political process perspective provides a link with the long-standing attention within the resource mobilization perspective for the effects of external support on the development of social movement organizations (for instance, Gamson 1975; McAdam 1982; Jenkins and Eckert 1986). For Europeans, on the other hand, the attractiveness of the POS lies in the fact that it can serve as a conceptual bridge to link broad social-structural changes to concrete mobilization processes.

Methodologically, a related convergence seems to be taking place. While European social movement studies become increasingly empirical, American scholars seem to have become more aware of the limits of their concentration on individual motivations and SMOs. The recently acquired popularity on both sides of the Atlantic of analyses of protest events, gathered from newspapers or other sources, should be seen in the light of these methodological trends. Just as the mesolevel of the political process allows for an integration of the American micro- and the European macrotheoretical perspectives, so the empirical focus on protest events can be seen as an attempt to strike a balance between the American empirical orientation and the European view of social movements as interconnected wholes that cannot be sufficiently grasped by taking individual participants or SMOs as the unit of analysis.

In the present study we have attempted to proceed along this integrationist line and to further combine the strengths of the European and American research traditions. To begin with, we have taken an intermediary position with regard to the relevance of "new social movements" as a theoretical and empirical category. On the one hand, we have followed the lead of European authors by taking seriously the idea that the distinction between "new" and "old" movements is crucial to understanding modern social movement politics in Western industrialized societies. Our findings in the first part of the book make clear that the European idea that NSMs form a distinct "social movement family" (Della Porta and Rucht 1991) is basically sound. For instance, our cross-national comparisons show that there is indeed a strong inverse relation between the strength of old and new movements, as has been suggested by Brand (1985: 322). That the new social movements form a separate family is also shown by the fact that different NSMs follow similar trajectories over time, which are quite unrelated to the trajectories followed by other categories of social movements.

On the other hand, we strongly relativize the claims of European authors as to the *paradigmatic* nature of the differences between the NSMs and other movements (see also Cohen 1985). Our results show that the action repertoires and organizational forms employed by the NSMs differ little from those employed by other movements. Moreover, many NSMs meanwhile display strong tendencies toward institutionalization and professionalization, which brings them even closer to the "old" movements. Most important, our results strongly refute the idea of many European scholars that the NSMs are relatively distant and independent from "established" politics. It has been our central contention that the development of NSMs has been strongly influenced by the political context in which they had to—though perhaps not always chose to—operate, and that they have over the course of time adapted their action repertoires, organizational structures, and ideologies to the exigencies of their political environment.

The impact of the European macrostructural perspective on our thinking is perhaps most clearly visible in chapter 1, where we argued that broad processes of social change affect the cleavage patterns that, at a very general level, delineate the "political space" available to new challengers. Although it may be difficult to determine unequivocally what is new about the NSMs, it is nonetheless clear that a high salience of old cleavages in politics presents an enormous obstacle to the entrance of new issues on the political agenda. More specifically, our findings show that, as a result of the fact that most new issues are conceptualized as "left-wing" topics, this constraining effect is particularly strong where traditional class conflicts are highly salient.

We should note, however, that the politically articulated cleavage structures that are relevant to the mobilization capacities of social movements have a certain degree of autonomy from the processes of social change stressed within the European literature on NSMs. In Brand's (1985) model, the blurring of class identities in society is supposed to be self-evidently reflected in a declining salience of class issues in politics. We have argued that one should allow for *nonsimultaneity* of cleavages in politics and in society as a result of the fact that changes in social structure do not automatically and immediately translate into changes in political cleavage structures. For instance, the societal transformations — the postwar rise in welfare, security, and education levels — emphasized by Inglehart in his theory (1977, 1990a) of the culture shift from materialist to postmaterialist value patterns have occurred in all highly industrialized societies, including the countries that are the object of research in this book. However, the extent to which these changes have contributed to the erosion of "old," materialist cleavages and the degree to which they have been articulated into a new political cleavage display strong cross-national variation. Thus, postmaterialist movements and parties have become significant actors in three of our four countries, but the nature of the French political system has thus far proved to be an insurmountable barrier to these representatives of the "new politics."

A further European element in our conceptualization of the POS is the distinction between strong and weak and exclusive and inclusive political systems, which introduces a statist element that has been neglected in American conceptualizations of the POS. This lack of attention to the state in most American social movement studies may be due to the less prominent role of the state in American society as compared to the European welfare states, as well as to the scarcity of cross-national studies, which has allowed American scholars to treat formal state structures and prevailing strategies as constants.[2] The prominent role of party politics, and particularly of the strategic position of social-democratic parties, in our discussion of alliance structures likewise has a strong European flavor. This, however, has little to do with a lack of attention for alliances and external support in American studies—which have generally focused almost exclusively on this aspect of the POS—but is a direct result of the greater weight of political parties in European politics and of the different compositions of the European and American party systems.[3]

Thus, European conceptualizations of the POS tend to have a more structural and statist character than their American counterparts. This engenders the danger of directly deriving movement characteristics from structural determinants, by which the European version of the political opportunity model could fall into the same pitfalls as the new social movements approach. Elaborating on a model proposed by Tilly (1978), we have therefore introduced a set of what we have called *concrete* opportunities: repression, facilitation, success chances, and reform/threat. The "values" of these parameters are directly influenced by the more structural level of the POS, but, unlike concepts like "state strength," they have direct motivational meaning for social movement participants and organizers. An additional advantage of these intermediary concepts is that they are easily applicable to a wide variety of political contexts. A study of social movements in authoritarian regimes or in non-Western societies would most probably require a very different conceptualization of the POS than the one we have employed here, which pays much attention to central features of Western political systems such as the electoral system, the party system, and the separation of powers. Factors such as repression or success chances, however, have a much more universal meaning. Therefore, the relevance of our hypotheses and findings with regard to the effects of concrete opportunities on mobilization should extend far beyond the cases we have studied in this book.

In chapter 4 we refined this motivational theory by developing a typology of three movement types, each of which has a typical way of reacting to concrete opportunities. Here as well we have striven to combine the strengths of American and European models. The new social movements approach maintains that new social movements are primarily oriented toward the (re)production of collective identities. The predominant American perspective, however, holds that social movements follow a logic of instrumental rationality. In our view, it is not fruitful to reduce the essence of social movement action to either of these two poles. Social movements always combine instrumental and identity logics, but the mix between the two varies among movements. In turn, the varying importance of instrumental and identity orientations, as well as the type of identity—internal or external—have important repercussions for the way in which concrete opportunities are evaluated by movement activists. In addition, the typology we propose helps to account for some of the cross-national similarities we identified in chapter 4. Instrumental movements, for instance, mobilize larger numbers of people than the more exclusive, identity-oriented movements, irrespective of the national political context. Likewise, countercultural movements are always more radical and, even if they act moderately, are confronted with higher levels of repression and receive less facilitation than subcultural and instrumental movements. The main characteristic of subcultural movements, finally, is their weakly developed external orientation, which accounts for the low number of protest events we have registered for the gay and women's movements.

Chapter 4 also makes clear that for a more detailed analysis of cross-national differences and similarities it is important to acknowledge that political opportunity structures not only vary across countries but also across movements. Making use of insights provided by the American agenda-building approach (especially Cobb and Elder 1983), we have tried to systematize these movement-specific aspects of the POS by distinguishing between high-profile and low-profile issues and policy domains. Movements operating in high-profile domains such as national defense or energy supply touch upon issues that are regarded by the authorities as core state tasks, and therefore face stronger institutional resistance, are more likely to be repressed, and usually do not receive state facilitation. The definition by authorities of policy domains as high- or low-profile turned out to be quite similar in the four countries. For example, irrespective of the political context, we found that the peace movement has relatively low membership figures due to a lack of state facilitation, both in the form of subsidies and in the form of incorporation into policy networks and consultative or advisory bodies. Similarly, in each country we found remarkable differences between the antinuclear energy movement, which addresses a high-profile issue and whose interactions with the state are relatively conflictive, and the rest of the environmental movement, whose demands are less threatening to the state, and which therefore is much more moderate and institutionalized.

The introduction of concrete opportunities, movement types, and movement-specific aspects of the POS already takes us a long way from the structural determinism to which especially European versions of the political process approach sometimes fall victim (for instance, Kitschelt 1986). This emphasis on the relative autonomy of movement development from broad political structures is carried further in chapter 5, where we analyzed the dynamics of interactions among different currents of social movements, their allies and adversaries, and state authorities. The central argument advanced in this chapter is that although changes in the POS may explain the start of protest waves, the further development of such waves once they are set in motion has its own dynamics. This autonomy from structural determination does not imply, however, that the development of protest waves is a more or less random process, determined merely by the wit, imagination, or luck of the various actors involved. On the contrary, among protest waves in different countries, a number of striking similarities with regard to the development of action repertoires, levels of repression and of facilitation, and the involvement of different types of organizations can be identified. The explanation presented for these dynamic patterns again combines insights from European and American perspectives, through an integration of Karstedt-Henke's focus on the containment strategies of state authorities and Tarrow's emphasis on the competition among SMOs. We thus arrive at a theory that interprets the development of protest waves as the outcome of the interplay between facilitation, repression, and success chances, which define a set of external constraints on the one hand, and movement activists' choices among three basic strategic options available to them—aiming at novelty, size, and militancy, respectively—on the other.

What Is to Be Done?

Despite our efforts to make the political opportunity perspective more flexible, encompassing, and dynamic, there are a number of points, some of which are touched upon in Part II of the book, that deserve more attention in future research. One challenge is constituted by the recent "interpretive turn" in theorizing on social movements both in the United States (Snow et al. 1986; Snow and Benford 1988; Morris and Mueller 1992) and in Europe (Melucci 1990), which focuses attention on the construction of grievances and identities by social movement activists and organizers. As we argued in chapter 6, the importance of this constructivist approach lies not so much in that it provides a rival explanation for the development of social movements: our analysis of antinuclear attitudes and movements revealed little autonomous explanatory power for Snow and Benford's frame-alignment model. However, by stressing construction and perception, these authors point at important mediating *mechanisms* that can shed more light on the translation of political opportunity structures into movement action. A potentially even more important, and thus far neglected, question that may be addressed through an integration of political opportunity and constructivist perspectives concerns the extent to which political opportunities are themselves subject to and shaped in discursive struggles. Empirically this implies that much more attention should be paid to the evaluation and perception of opportunities by movement activists and their opponents. Theoretically, it seems necessary to dig much deeper into the political psychology of the interplay among grievances, capabilities, and opportunities.

Here the work of Jon Elster seems particularly promising. Elster (1993) shows how the formation of political beliefs and preferences is shaped by political and social institutions; he analyzes how "desires" and "opportunities" may influence each other. The finding in chapter 6 that favorable or unfavorable opportunities for the antinuclear movement eventually also altered the public's preferences with regard to the development of nuclear energy is an example of the effect of opportunities on desires, but Elster shows that, conversely, desires may also affect the perception and evaluation of opportunities. Whereas the POS model presupposes that people "recognize" opportunities to act and are willing to use them, Elster lists several situations in which people may intentionally choose not to "profit" from the opportunities available to them.

Why would anyone want to throw away any options? In *Ulysses and the Sirens* (1984), Elster discusses situations in which people may follow Ulysses and "bind" themselves to limit the effects of predictable weakness of will: people may avoid those situations in which they might be seduced to act in conflict with their moral standards. In a discussion of the work of Tocqueville, Elster (1993) shows that not only weakness of will but also strategic considerations may motivate people to disregard opportunities. In our model, the idea of a selective use of opportunities has been taken into consideration to a certain extent, namely in the movement typology. Opportunities are differently valued by movements depending on their general strategic logic: instrumental, subcultural, and countercultural movements all intentionally limit themselves to a very specific action repertoire, as Ulysses did. Terrorist organizations, locked in a spiral of conspiracy, are the most selective, and do not "allow" themselves anymore to use legal opportunities. The example of terrorist movements makes clear that the "constraining" effect of "desires" upon the use of opportunities is itself part and consequence of the interactive processes sketched in chapter 5. Movements become more radical when, in the interaction with authorities, they encounter few opportunities; but once radicalization has proceeded beyond a certain level, they may not be able or willing anymore to perceive such opportunities as do occur. In other words, depending on the (time) perspective, one may say that opportunities shape desires or vice versa.

Apart from the intentional selective use of opportunities analyzed by Elster, it is necessary to devote more attention to nonintentional "overlooking" of opportunities. The emphasis put on organization, resources, and skills within the resource mobilization approach may teach that the possession of certain capacities to act is a condition sine qua non for the recognition of opportunities. Poor and powerless people often seem to deny the few opportunities they do get because they have accustomed themselves to the idea that those "up there" will never listen to their kind anyway. This illustrates the fact that a minimum sense of political efficacy and a belief in one's own capabilities are a condition for changing circumstances collectively if favorable political opportunities appear (McAdam [1982] labels this "cognitive liberation"). Of course, this evaluation of one's capacities is itself shaped by former experiences with authorities—but it may explain why, contrary to what would be expected on the basis of a simple POS model, people sometimes do not use the opportunities available to them. Since we have dealt in this book with movements primarily rooted in the middle classes, this problem has not come to the fore prominently in this research, but it is likely to be much more important if one studies the mobilization (or apathy) of less privileged groups.

This is just one illustration of the extreme importance of the perception and evaluation of opportunities. The "framing" of success chances may also change under the influence of experiences in other countries, inspiring people to a more positive estimation of their national political opportunities (which may not have changed in any "objective" sense). Of course, the margins of this "framing" of opportunities are limited because people are immediately and concretely confronted with the consequences of nonrealistic estimations. On the other hand, "illusory" estimations of success chances have had factual consequences in history, which might not have occurred if challengers had known the "real" power balance. "Illusion" may have an empowering effect, whereas "realism" often leads to apathy. In that sense, one may turn Marx's famous statement in *The German Ideology* on its head: different interpretations of the world are sometimes a necessary condition for changing it.

Related to this, we have to take into consideration the fact that capacities such as self-esteem and efficacy are not only rooted in political history but shaped by cultural traditions as well. Whether people of a specific "caste" will ever revolt against another caste is a question of both politics and "culture." Chapter 7 most clearly called attention to the "cultural factor." There we traced the respective influences of the cultural and political contexts upon the development of the homosexual movement. Interestingly, we found that even cultural movements, which are less explicitly politically oriented, are not necessarily less influenced by the political context. Moreover, the mechanism that desires adapt to opportunities turned out to be at work in the relation between politics and movement culture as well: subcultural traditions, norms, and codes are not free-floating, extrapolitical phenomena, but are themselves inherently political. Not only do the "instrumental" aspirations of the homosexual movement vary according to political openness, but the very nature of the subculture mirrors the political conditions as well: the "deconstruction" of sexual identities that was propagated in the early 1980s could only take place in a situation where gay men and lesbians suffered less from discrimination; the relativization of identities presupposed relative freedom. The power of politics could also be established in the relation between politics and the dominant culture: antihomosexual political campaigns often resulted in less permissive moral attitudes in society at large. To suggest a simple, one-way relation between politics and cultural norms is, however, misleading: politicians generally avoid taking too much distance from dominant opinions, since that might endanger their chances of being reelected. In that sense, politics is bounded by cultural standards as well. Since the precise relation between culture and politics calls for much more research, American political science should be less one-sidedly oriented toward instrumental movements, disregarding the specific characteristics of culturally oriented movements. The opposite holds for the European "culturalization" of the new movements, which stresses the message of these movements and neglects the fact that new social movements have become by and large part of "normal politics."

Apart from these theoretical issues, the political opportunity perspective also faces some methodological challenges. Although we have provided abundant quantitative data on the mobilization of social movements, we have relied mainly on qualitative information for the independent variables in our model. As a result, the evidentiary basis for the relationships we have suggested between the POS and movement mobilization has sometimes been less "hard" than we would have liked it to be. In addition, the lack of more precise data on aspects of the POS to some extent limits the possibilities of verification and replication of our findings by other scholars. To an important extent this may be inevitable, given the complex and multifaceted nature of political opportunity structures. On the level of *concrete* opportunities, however, the possibilities for quantification seem more favorable. In fact, crude measures of facilitation and repression have already been included in our analyses. However, we believe that much more can be done in this direction. Thus, we might use newspapers not just to trace protest events, but also to develop more precise measures of facilitation, repression, success, and reform/threat. This implies that one should not just code protest events, but many more events (statements by politicians and other relevant actors, court decisions, parliamentary discussions, etc.) related to the themes addressed by the movement or movements one is studying. Data of this kind may also help us to arrive at more reliable assessments of the success of social movements. As we argued in chapter 9, measurement problems have thus far greatly hindered research on movement success. A solution to these problems is not only important because success and success chances are among the most important determinants of the development of social movements. The questions of the extent and determinants of movement success is also important in its own right, not least because it is highly relevant for evaluating the functioning and responsiveness of democratic political systems.

The Future of National Politics and New Social Movements

All very well, some readers may think, but will national politics remain relevant in the future? Given the increasing importance of supranational and transnational political institutions like the United Nations and the European Union, the global scale of social and environmental problems, the ever denser maze of interdependencies that spans the world, and the exponential increase in the speed and density of worldwide information flows, is an approach that focuses on national political opportunities not already antiquated? And do we not see similar trends within the field of social movements, where themes, strategies, and organizational forms spread across the globe through processes of diffusion, increasing international cooperation and the rise of transnational SMOs such as Greenpeace and Amnesty International (Hegedus 1990)? In short, what is the use of an elaborate theory that explains cross-national variation in a world where such variation is likely to become increasingly negligible?

Internationalization will doubtless substantially alter the role of nation-states and the context of social movement mobilization, although recent developments—the rise of nationalism, the crisis of the European Union "of milk and money" (i.e., serving mainly farmers and big business), the failure of the international community in Bosnia—suggest that the process might not go as far or as fast as has been supposed. There are further reasons to be somewhat skeptical about the supposed effects of internationalization on the politics of social movements. In this study we have discussed several examples of internationalization of social movements: the peace movement's international campaign against cruise missiles; the antinuclear energy movement's reactions to the transnational effects of the Chernobyl disaster; and the international diffusion of tactics and themes. Despite the internationalization of social problems, political decision making, and diffusion processes to which these examples attest, the most striking finding in each of these cases was the widely varying ways in which such international events impinged on the mobilization of social movements in different national settings.[4] Therefore, it seems that, at least for the time being, internationalization makes national political opportunity structures more rather than less interesting. Precisely because of the homogenization of many other context variables, and because the internationalization of politics lags far behind the globalization of mass media, culture, and social problems, the effects of national POS show up even clearer than before.

Nevertheless, if internationalization proceeds, it is highly likely to affect the realm of politics as well, and will eventually erode the role of the nation-state (see Tilly 1993). However, this in no way means that political opportunity structures will cease to affect the development of social movements. The POS concept is not tied to the national state, but can also—and will increasingly have to—be applied at the international level. Because it seems unlikely that the national state will wither away altogether, this means that the development of social movements will be determined by the interplay of national and international—and, if we may believe those who also see a trend toward localism, perhaps also local—opportunity structures. This increasing complexity of political decision making will perhaps make political process analyses more difficult—although not fundamentally different from the analysis of federal states such as Germany or Switzerland—but certainly not less relevant.

But is there also a future for the not-so-new-anymore "new social movements"? Since the mid-1980s, the activity level of the NSMs has declined in the countries discussed in this study, and the same seems to be the case elsewhere. An exception to this trend is formed by the strong growth of a limited number of professional SMOs representing these movements. Thus, the NSMs seem not so much to have disappeared as to have become part of established interest-group politics, and thus to have followed a trajectory similar to that followed earlier in this century by the labor movement. At the same time, we see a worldwide revival of nationalist, ethnic, and religious movements, that is, a remobilization of some of the "old" cleavages.

These trends notwithstanding, we think it is too early to conclude that the "new cleavage" has been pacified once and for all. To begin with, the institutionalization of the NSMs has thus far remained confined to a limited number of countries. The French — and more generally the southern European, not to speak of countries outside Western Europe and North America — NSMs still have a lot of catching up to do with their counterparts in countries like Switzerland or the Netherlands. But even in the latter countries, the themes advanced by the NSMs provide enough fuel still for new rounds of conflict. One obvious example is the issue of the environment, which at present may seem highly consensual (after all, who is against a clean environment?) but is unlikely to remain so for long:

> The consensual phase of recent years has led to an unprecedentedly high level of environmental concern among the general public. On the other hand, concrete measures to combat the present environmental problems ... lag very much behind. The resolution of these problems will require substantial sacrifices and changes in life-styles, and it is therefore highly probable that a new phase of confrontation will emerge, either because governments do not act upon the concerns they have helped to stir, or because the policies they try to implement come to face resistance from those whose interests are threatened by such policies. (Van der Heijden, Koopmans, and Giugni 1992: 35–36)

Another possible focus for a new round of NSM protests is constituted precisely by the rise of nationalist, fundamentalist, and xenophobic movements. To an important extent, the values propagated by the NSMs are the exact opposite of those advanced by the new extreme right, and the rise of the latter is therefore likely to provoke countermobilization by the NSMs, as was already the case in the second half of the 1980s in France, and more recently in Germany, where millions of people demonstrated against violent attacks on foreigners.[5] Thus, in line with the analyses presented in chapter 5, the tendencies toward demobilization and institutionalization may well be temporary. About the conditions under which a new wave of NSM protest may occur, we can only say that the answer will continue to lie not so much in the seriousness of the issues at stake, or in the organizational strength of the NSMs, as in the opportunities presented by the political systems in which these movements operate. About the when, where, and how of such a new wave of protest, we choose, however, to remain silent; for if there is one thing recent history has taught us, it must be that the politics of social movements will continue to surprise us.

Appendix
The Newspaper Data

Why Newspapers?

Protest-event data derived from newspapers were an important source of information for this study. At least among American scholars, this form of data gathering on social movements has become increasingly popular (see, for instance, Tilly, Tilly, and Tilly 1975; Tilly 1978; McAdam 1982; Tarrow 1989a). This popularity has mainly been the result of a negative choice. Anyone studying social movements will be aware of the fact that newspapers reflect only a selective part of reality, and that even that part is always colored by the subjective interpretations of reporters and editors. Similarly, it is one of the eternal complaints of movement activists that many of their actions are either not reported at all in the press, or are covered in a negatively biased way. Therefore, newspapers can hardly be seen as superior sources of information on protest in any absolute sense; rather, it is the poverty of the alternatives that makes newspapers so attractive.

The most common alternative is, of course, to refrain from quantifying protest altogether and to rely solely on qualitative sources and methods. Such an approach is appropriate if one's interest is limited to qualitative aspects of social movements, such as the internal structure of their organizations or the motivations and ideologies of their activists. However, most qualitative studies also aim at explaining quantitative aspects of social movements, such as the development of their strength over time or the composition of their action repertoire, and thus they cannot avoid making quantitative statements. In the absence of systematic empirical data, such statements are likely to be even more selective and biased than newspaper reports. To an important extent, the quantitative assertions in qualitative studies are themselves implicitly derived from the reflection of social movement activities in the media. Because this happens in an unsystematic way, the resulting statements are in fact the product of a double process of selection and bias, in which the subjective interpretation and selection of the social scientist are added to those of the journalist. Therefore, explicit and systematic quantification, difficult as it may be, is a necessary complement to qualitative information.

Among the possible sources of quantitative data on protest development, newspapers are clearly the best choice. With the partial exception of strikes, official data on social movement activities are usually lacking, and if they exist, their criteria of selection and categorization are often vague and subject to changes over time, and at any rate are likely to be different from those of the social scientist. Further, the number of variables employed in these statistics is very limited; usually they are no more than counts of a specific action form. Finally, and perhaps most important, such listings are themselves usually derived from newspapers (see Danzger 1975).

Archives are another possible source of information. Police archives—if accessible—are one option, but for obvious reasons they are likely to be heavily biased toward violent or illegal events, and they can hardly be expected to provide an impartial reflection of even the most basic aspects of protest events. This is also true to some extent for social movement archives. In addition, these tend to be discontinuous, incomplete, unsystematic, and so disorderly as to be virtually inaccessible.

Newspapers have distinct advantages over these sources. They report a large number of news events on a regular, day-to-day basis, and because they are in competition with each other and need to maintain their credibility as reliable news sources, they—or at least those "quality" papers with an educated readership—are obliged to cover important events with some degree of accuracy (see Danzger 1975). Of course, the reliability of newspapers depends on the kind of information one wants to get from them. Here, Tuchman's (1973) distinction between "hard" and "soft" news is often cited. Newspapers can be considered relatively reliable when it comes to reporting the "hard," factual aspects of protest events, such as their timing and locality, the number of participants, the action form, the stated goal of the protesters, and the number of arrests that were made. For "softer," more subjective aspects of social movements, such as whether the participants are motivated by universalistic values or merely by self-interest, or whether they were motivated by their stated goal or were merely out for a riot, it is obvious that newspapers are as reliable or unreliable as anyone else's subjective judgment.

Of course, even some of the "hard" facts will sometimes be distorted. This is especially true for the number of participants and for whether or not a demonstration was violent. Although it is impossible to solve this problem, it should be stressed that bias as such is not always a real problem as long as we are not interested in "absolute" truth, and as long as the bias is systematic. If, for instance, a particular newspaper systematically presents only the police estimate of the number of demonstrators, we would still be able to trace changes in the level of participation over time, because even the police estimate is a reflection of the actual size of a demonstration. Similarly, a significant increase in the amount of movement violence would show up in the columns of any newspaper, no matter how sympathetic or unsympathetic to the protesters it may be: differences in sympathy among newspapers may affect the absolute level of violence reported, but they are unlikely to affect the trends. An important conclusion that can be derived from this is that for variables that are possibly subject to bias or for which different versions of an event are presented in a report (for instance, both the police and the movement estimates of the number of participants, and both sides' accounts of who initiated violence), the best solution is not to let the coder try to infer what "really" happened, but to create coding instructions that make the bias systematic.[1]

The Choice of Newspapers

The following criteria were employed in choosing the newspapers in the four countries:

1. *Continuity:* first, the newspaper had to have appeared continuously during the entire period under study, and, second, there had to be no significant changes with regard to any of the other criteria;
2. *Frequency:* because we decided to code only Monday issues, which report news events that took place during the two weekend days, newspapers that also appear on Sundays had to be excluded;
3. *Quality:* the newspaper had to be recognized as a high-quality source of information;
4. *National scope:* the newspapers chosen had to cover the entire national territory;

5. *Political color:* the four newspapers had to be roughly comparable with regard to political color, preferably neither very conservative nor extremely left-wing;
6. *Selectivity:* the newspapers' selectivity in reporting protest events had to be comparable and not too high.

On the basis of these criteria, the choice of newspapers was soon narrowed down to one or a few in each of the countries. Germany, for instance, has only five quality newspapers that serve as national sources of information. Of these, *die tageszeitung (taz)*, an alternative newspaper that pays much attention to the new social movements, had to be excluded because it has only appeared since 1979. In addition, the *taz* can be considered too partisan, and it has no real equivalent in the other countries. *Die Welt* was excluded for the opposite reason of being too conservative and too selective in reporting protest events. This left three papers to be seriously considered: the *Frankfurter Allgemeine Zeitung (FAZ)*, the *Frankfurter Rundschau (FR)*, and the *Süddeutsche Zeitung (SZ)*. A possible problem with these newspapers is that all of them have a regional as well as a national focus: the *FAZ* and the *FR* on Frankfurt and Hesse, the *SZ* on Munich and Bavaria. The same problem occurred in the case of Switzerland, where major newspapers either focus on the French-speaking or German-speaking parts of the country. More implicitly, the relevant newspapers for the Netherlands and France also have such a regional bias, on the western Netherlands and on the Paris region, respectively.[2] Since a certain amount of regional bias was inevitable, it was important to make this bias comparable among the countries. In France and the Netherlands, all newspapers taken into consideration were biased toward the cultural, political, and economic centers, so we decided to choose similarly biased newspapers in Germany and Switzerland. For Germany, this consideration led us to favor the two newspapers based in Hesse over the *SZ*. Hesse is not only situated in the center of the former West Germany, but it is also — culturally and economically as well as politically — probably the state most representative of the Federal Republic as a whole. Choosing the Bavarian *SZ* would have introduced a bias toward what is probably the most exceptional state in the Federal Republic — atypical for its pronounced conservatism and its strong traditional Catholic orientation, and, moreover, the only state governed by a regionally based party (the Christian Social Union). Of the two remaining papers, we ultimately chose the *Frankfurter Rundschau* because the *Frankfurter Allgemeine Zeitung* turned out to be much more selective in reporting protest events and is politically less close to the newspapers ultimately selected for the other three countries (*Le Monde* for France, the *Neue Zürcher Zeitung* [*NZZ*] for Switzerland, and *NRC/Handelsblad* [*NRC*] for the Netherlands).

Unfortunately, it is impossible to conduct tests to compare the selectivity and bias of newspapers in different countries, simply because their coverage is based on different facts. Although the papers finally selected seemed to be roughly comparable as regards political color—from moderately left-wing (*Le Monde*, *FR*), to the political center (*NRC*), and somewhat to the right of center (*NZZ*)—there was no way to know beforehand whether the four papers would really be comparable.

It was, however, possible to conduct a selectivity test a posteriori. As Snyder and Kelly (1977) have demonstrated, the chances of a protest event being reported in a particular newspaper depend on two factors: the newspaper's sensitivity with regard to protest events, and the intensity of protest. They distinguish three determinants of intensity: size, violence, and duration (110). As we argued in chapter 5, novelty can be added as an additional determinant. If different newspapers are equally sensitive to protest events, there should be no differences in the likelihood of events of the same intensity being reported. For such a comparison, legal and nonviolent demonstrations and public assemblies are particularly suited because their intensity varies in only one dimension. They last no longer than one day, they are characterized by the same low level of militancy and, as a particularly traditional form of protest, they are not likely to be reported because of their novelty. In other words, the intensity of demonstrations and public assemblies is simply a function of their size. If, then, the four newspapers are equally selective, demonstrations and assemblies of the same size should have the same likelihood of being covered in the four countries. Of course, we do not have data about those actions that were not reported in the newspapers, but the question can nevertheless be answered in an indirect way by looking at the frequency distribution of the number of participants of the demonstrations and assemblies that were reported.

Table A.1 presents the mean, mode, and median of the number of participants for these events in each of the four countries. For Germany, the table also shows these measures for those events that took place in Hesse. The mean is the least informative of these measures because it is very much influenced by relatively few very large demonstrations and assemblies, which are likely to be reported in any newspaper, no matter how selective it is. In

Table A.1. Characteristics of the frequency distribution of participation in demonstrations and public assemblies in France, Germany (total and Hesse), the Netherlands, and Switzerland

	Mean	Mode	Median	N
France	11,237	500	1,000	838
Germany (total)	9,483	500	1,000	1,288
Hesse	3,497	500	500	482
The Netherlands	4,845	500	500	534
Switzerland	2,073	500	500	557

Germany, for instance, the largest 1 percent of these events (150,000 participants or more) contributed 33 percent, and the largest 10 percent (15,000 or more) contributed 75 percent to the total number of participants. Precisely because the total volume of participation is so insensitive to newspaper selectivity, it is particularly suited to comparing levels of social movement activity among countries (provided, of course, that it is related to the population size of a country).

The mode (the most frequently reported size) and the median (the size of the average reported demonstration or assembly), on the other hand, are more likely to reflect newspaper selectivity. Both measures may be expected to be higher if a newspaper is more selective, because a higher intensity will be required to reach its columns. As it turns out, no differences at all are found with regard to the mode. In all four countries, demonstrations or assemblies with five hundred participants are the most frequently reported ones.[3]

With regard to the median, however, there is a difference between the two larger and the two smaller countries. In France and Germany, the average reported demonstration or assembly has one thousand participants, in Switzerland and the Netherlands five hundred. However, it is very likely that this difference is not due to differences in selectivity but is related to the countries' sizes. The intensity of a particular demonstration is likely to be lower in larger than in smaller polities: a demonstration of three hundred in Switzerland may be as politically relevant and newsworthy as a demonstration of three thousand in Germany. This argument can be checked by looking at the median for demonstrations and assemblies in Hesse. If the *Frankfurter Rundschau*'s selectivity is comparable to that of the Dutch and Swiss newspapers, the median for those events taking place in the small-size polity of Hesse should be the same as that for Dutch and Swiss events. As the table shows, this is indeed the case. Therefore, we may conclude that there are no significant differences in the four newspapers' selectivity.

Why Monday Issues?

No researcher interested in the public's opinion on a certain subject would go door-to-door and interview each citizen individually. Such a research strategy would of course produce very reliable results. However, provided that the sample is large enough, survey techniques can reach a level of reliability that is almost as high, with much less resource investment. Therefore, public opinion researchers agree that there are better ways of spending one's time, energy, and resources than by investigating the whole population. As obvious as this may seem, sampling has not yet penetrated the field of protest event analysis, which is still characterized by "the fetish of thoroughness," as Tarrow has called it (1989a: 363).[4]

Still, there is no reason why sampling could not be used equally well in the analysis of newspaper data on protest events. Our decision to sample was to an important extent forced on us by the discrepancy between our ambitions and the limited available resources. Because we wanted to study protest events produced by any conceivable movement in four countries over a period of fifteen years, nonsampled data gathering would have required enormous investments, which we were unable to make. Moreover, the range of protest events we were interested in ensured that even a sampled database would contain enough cases to allow for statistically relevant analyses.[5]

If one decides to sample, several options are possible. The most complicated method, which is closest to the methodology of surveys, is to draw a random sample of newspapers to be coded. A similar, but more practical, method is to draw a sample not of individual newspapers but of months or weeks, of which all newspapers are coded (for instance, Tilly 1978). Although such methods of random selection at first sight seem to be most appropriate, they fail to appreciate an important difference between protest events and human individuals as units of analysis. In survey research, each individual's opinion or characteristics is of equal importance, and thus a random selection method is most appropriate. Protest events, however, are not all of the same value: they have varying intensities, and their importance to politicians, to movement activists, to the media, as well as to researchers, differs widely.[6] In fact, as argued earlier, the newspaper coverage already constitutes a nonrandom selection of protest events based to a large extent on the criterion of intensity (see Snyder and Kelly 1977; McCarthy, McPhail, and Smith n.d.). Thus, when sampling protest events, the question arises as to whether one should sample randomly, or whether the selection method should take into account differences in intensity.

Examples of the latter type of sampling can be found in the literature. Tilly, for instance, used violent events as "a biased but useful tracer of collective action in general." Within this category, he sampled on intensity as well: only those violent events with at least fifty participants were included (1978: 245, 251). The results presented in this book cast some doubt upon the usefulness of violent events as an indicator for the development of protest at large. If we had focused on violent events we would probably have overestimated the level of protest in France, and underestimated social movement activity in Switzerland, simply because the share of violent events in total social movement activity differs greatly from country to country. Similarly, violence can only be used to a limited extent as a tracer of the development of social movement activity within a country because violence often increases in periods when the general level of activity declines (see chapter 5). Most important, this sampling method would not have allowed us to investigate one of the most interesting topics in protest development: shifts over time and differences among movements and countries in the action repertoire. In other words, violence as an indicator is not so much "biased but useful" as it is, for most purposes, too biased to be useful.

The main problem with choosing violence as an indicator is that it represents only one element of intensity. Theoretically, an intensity-directed sample should take into account militancy, size (possibly in combination with duration), as well as novelty. The problem, of course, is that these three elements cannot be related to each other in any meaningful way. We could, for instance, decide to include demonstrations only if their size exceeds a certain maximum, say one thousand (Tilly 1978: 247). But what is the equivalent of such a size in terms of militancy or novelty? Attempts to resolve this insoluble problem will always be arbitrary.[7]

In sum, random sampling has the advantage of methodological straightforwardness, but will also lead to the exclusion of many important protest events from the sample. Sampling on intensity has the theoretical advantage of including all important events in the sample, but is practically impossible to implement in a consistent way. Our choice to concentrate on Monday issues of newspapers constitutes a compromise between these two options.[8] A first, pragmatic reason to choose Monday newspapers is that they cover the news of two days, Saturday and Sunday. Thus, with the same investment in time and resources, Monday issues allow one to trace substantially more information than other issues. Second, the weekend is a popular time for many types of unconventional mobilization. Because most of these forms depend on the involvement of many people, important actions are often organized during the weekend, when more people have time to protest. However, it is clear that the weekend is not the most popular time for all forms of protest. The most important exception is labor strikes, which by definition take place on workdays. The weekend may also be less suited to detecting conventional actions — particularly juridical action, which almost never takes place on the weekend — which may be expected to follow to some degree the rhythm of conventional politics in general, that is, to be concentrated on weekdays. Other action forms may be expected to be neither overrepresented nor underrepresented on weekend days. This is especially the case for forms of severe violence (bombings, for instance) that depend on the involvement of very few people, and more generally for radical (confrontational and violent) actions, which are often based on a constituency of students and unemployed youth, whose availability for protest activities does not much depend on the day of the week.

A small pretest conducted for Germany for eight weeks in 1986 confirmed these expectations.[9] First, this test showed that the Monday issues included a sizable share — more than a third — of the total number of protest events reported. Second, strikes, conventional actions, and heavy violence were more frequently reported in non-Monday issues. On the basis of these results, we made two decisions.

First, we decided to exclude labor strikes from the sample, even in the few cases where they were reported in the Monday paper. Although — following the argument that a systematic bias does not preclude the detection of trends and differences — we considered a certain amount of Monday bias not to be problematic, it was clear to us that for labor strikes the representativeness of the weekend would be so low as to make the data useless for this type of mobilization. In addition, our primary interest was in the new social movements, which do not use this action form (apart from a few very exceptional cases, such as a short work stoppage organized by the German and Dutch unions within the framework of the campaign against medium-range nuclear weapons). Finally, insofar as we needed information about the level of strike activity as a context variable for NSM mobilization, we could rely on the available official data on labor strikes.

Second, we concluded that the choice of Monday issues would not ensure that all important actions were included in the sample. We could be quite certain to capture the vast majority of large-size actions, such as mass demonstrations, but we would probably miss many important actions of a more conventional or more radical nature. Therefore we decided to broaden the range of actions to be coded by including all actions that were referred to in the Monday paper, but had taken place during the preceding week or would take place in the following week. For instance, an action that had taken place on Thursday might be referred to in several ways: in an article that mentioned the release of those arrested during the action; in a report of a demonstration demanding the release of those arrested; in statements by politicians referring to the action; in a press statement by an organization claiming responsibility for the event; in a report on the closing event of an action campaign, and so on. Similarly, the Monday issue sometimes contained information referring to an event that would be taking place on one of the following days: in published announcements or advertisements by SMOs; in statements of the authorities (who, for instance, might express their fears that the action would get out of hand); in articles on preparatory actions or meetings by movement activists; in articles reporting the opening event of an action campaign, and so on. In all these cases, the coders were instructed to consult the newspaper (or newspapers) in which the event (or campaign) to which the Monday issue referred was reported to find the necessary information.[10] Although this strategy significantly increased the amount of time needed for coding (particularly for those periods in which the level of protest activity was very high), we considered this to be a worthwhile investment because it would substantially lower both the Monday bias and, more important, the chances that we would miss high-intensity events. Indeed, our sample seems to include the great majority of important events. For instance, of the fifty-seven actions (for the period 1975–88) reported in Rucht's listing of important protest events in West Germany, fifty-two, or 91 percent, are represented in our sample (1989b: 340–44).

Table A.2 gives an impression both of the number of nonweekend events included in the sample as a result of our method of tracing references and of the differences between these events and those actions that took place during the weekend. As the table shows, our sample contains a substantial number of events (20–25 percent) that did not take place during the weekend. These events were, on the average, more radical than weekend actions, which were largely of the moderate, demonstrative type.

Because nonweekend events are still strongly underrepresented in our sample, this implies that our data cannot be used to infer the "true" distribution of protest events over the different strategies (then again, as we saw earlier, this is true for all data based on newspapers). However, because this

Table A.2. Weekend and nonweekend events by action form
(Germany, 1982 and 1986, excluding conventional events)

	Weekend days	Nonweekend days
Demonstrative	72.5	52.8
Confrontational	11.8	25.8
Light violence	6.1	3.3
Heavy violence	9.6	18.0
Total	100.0%	99.9%
N =	313	89
(100%)	(77.9%)	(22.1%)

Note: We have presented figures only for two years of the West German sample because
the day of the week was unfortunately not included among the coded variables.
Therefore, the day had to be reconstructed from the date, which was too labor-intensive
to do for the whole sample. Conventional events were excluded, because for many of
these events the newspaper did not report a date. In that case, the coders were instructed
to code the date of the newspaper, following the reasoning that media statements become
events at the moment they are published. This coding strategy made it impossible to
distinguish conventional events reported in the Monday issue from events that were
reported in the Tuesday issue but were dated on Monday.

bias is systematic, it is not likely to affect trends over time and differences
among countries. The inclusion of at least a sizable number of nonweekend
events ensures that we have enough events of each different strategy to be
able to make significant statements about these trends and differences.

Definition of Protest Events

Our definition of protest events is relatively simple and encompassing. The
main part of the sample consists of politically motivated unconventional actions. Rather than developing a definition of unconventional action forms,
we decided to provide the coders with a detailed and broad list of action
forms that should, in our view, be included in this category (see the list in
the next section). Such a strategy avoids confusion about whether or not an
event should be included. Kriesi et al. (1981), for instance, have employed
the criterion that protest events should be characterized by "grassroots mobilization." Rucht and Ohlemacher (1992: 98) exclude "routinized activities." In practice, such criteria are already difficult to employ in a consistent
way for specialists in the field, let alone for coders.

The criterion of political goals is somewhat less clear-cut. Here as well,
we provided the coders with an encompassing list of possible goals, which
allowed them to decide whether or not an event should be included. In addition to their numeric codings, we asked the coders to give a short descrip-

tion of each event, which should at least include the action form and the goal. Thus, we were able to exclude those (few) events that had been coded but that did not fulfill one or both of the criteria, or to correct wrong codings for these two core variables.[11]

For five new social movements—the peace, ecology, solidarity, squatters', and homosexual movements—we also coded conventional events. Here, an additional criterion was employed, namely that conventional events directed toward the goals of one of these movements should only be coded if they were initiated by an SMO or by a group of activists of one of these movements. Thus, statements or other conventional actions of political parties (including Green parties), labor unions, government officials, and so on, were excluded, even if they were clearly in favor of the goals of one of the five movements. For two reasons, this part of our sample was less useful than the data on unconventional events. First, the limitation to only five movements made the data on conventional events useless for all analyses that were not restricted to the new social movements. Second, because we suspected the coverage of (low-intensity) conventional events to be very sensitive to a newspaper's sympathy for the NSMs, the data on conventional events were less useful for international comparison.[12]

A further question with regard to the definition of protest events concerns their delimitation. We employed the timing and the locality of events as basic criteria in this respect: if an article reported a series of actions that were separated in time (different days or clearly separated periods of one day) and/or space (different cities or clearly separated parts of one city), we coded each of them as a separate event. The only exception to this rule was when an article reported different events occurring at the same time in different cities, but without any specification of the different events apart from their locality. An example of such a report could be "Yesterday, a total of 100,000 people marched in demonstrations against nuclear weapons in Frankfurt, Munich, Bonn, and Hamburg." In such cases, we judged that the information contained in the article was insufficient to warrant coding the four demonstrations as separate events, and therefore treated them as one (dispersed) event with one hundred thousand participants.[13] The compound nature of such events was registered in a separate variable representing the number of component parts of the event. Through this variable we could still turn back our decision of coding such compound actions as one event by weighting events according to the number of their component parts. However, for a number of reasons, we stayed with our original choice. First, the number of compound events was very low (less than 3 percent of the unconventional events). Second, some of them had such a high number of component parts (hundreds, or even thousands) that dividing them into separate events would influence the aggregate distribution of events to an extent not justified by their actual importance. Third, when a less extreme form of weighting was used — using a maximum weighting factor of nine for events with nine or more component parts — it did not lead to any significant changes in the distribution of events on any important variable (strategies, goals, etc.).

Sometimes articles described different actions that were not clearly separated in time and/or space, however. Often, several forms followed each other in a chain of events. For instance, an action might start with a demonstration to a central place (a government building, for instance), where it would turn into a public assembly where speakers addressed the crowd, which then might be followed by the presentation of a petition to the authorities. Or, to give another example, a series of actions might start with a peaceful demonstration against housing speculation that later turned violent, and was then followed by a demonstration to demand release of the arrested activists.

In such cases, coders were instructed to code different actions as separate events as soon as significant changes with regard to either the goals or the supporting group of the action occurred.[14] If, in the first example, the number of participants both in the demonstration and in the public assembly was ten thousand (or if the number of participants in the demonstration slowly grew to a maximum of ten thousand when the demonstrators arrived at the assembly place), but the petition presented was signed by, say, fifty thousand, the demonstration and the assembly would be coded as one event, and the petition as a second event. If several action forms supported by the same group and with the same goal were thus summarized into one event, coders were instructed to code the most radical action form of the two — in this case, a demonstration. Similarly, the second example of a peaceful demonstration that turned violent would be seen as one event (to be coded as a violent demonstration) if the same group of protesters was involved in both episodes. If, as happened relatively often, the violent confrontation was provoked by a small group of demonstrators that split off from a larger demonstration, the peaceful and the violent demonstrations would be coded as two separate events. A subsequent demonstration to demand the release of prisoners would also be coded as a separate event, because its goal differs from that of the initiating events.

The Coding of Variables

For two reasons, the amount of information on protest that can be gathered from newspapers in a systematic and reliable way is limited. First, as mentioned earlier, newspapers can only be used as a source for relatively "hard" features of protest. Second, even with regard to these aspects, newspaper reports tend to be highly disparate in the amount of information and detail they contain: some actions are extensively covered, but many are dealt with in a few lines providing only basic information. As a result, only a limited number of core variables will be available for the majority of events. Therefore, our coding scheme focuses on the following limited number of variables:

1. *Date of the event.* Year, month, and day.
2. *Duration in days.*
3. *Locality.* This variable contained several questions: first, the *region* in which the event took place; second, the *size* of the locality (large city, medium-sized town, or rural area); third, the *name* of the locality. Codes for the latter variable were taken from a prestructured list of large cities and other important sites. The question was left open for localities that were not mentioned on the list. Coders could also use this list to decide whether a locality should be included among the large cities. To decide among the other two categories of size, coders were to rely on their own knowledge or ask the supervisor.
4. *Frame of reference.* International, national, regional, or local. Level of the political system at which the movement's demands are directed. If several political levels were addressed at the same time, coders were instructed to code the lowest of these.
5. *Goal.* To be coded from a prestructured list of some one hundred possible goals arranged into larger themes (peace, ecology, etc.). If the action was directed at more than one goal simultaneously, the most important of these was coded.
6. *Action form.* To be coded from the following prestructured list of forms, arranged into broader strategies. If more action forms were used in the same event, the most radical of these should be coded (the overarching strategies [conventional, direct-democratic, demonstrative, confrontational, violence] are arranged in ascending order of radicalness). As for the question of whether a demonstration should be coded as violent, the coders were instructed to do so only if

it was clear from the report that the demonstrators had initiated the violence. Initially peaceful demonstrations that turned violent because of violent police intervention were coded as peaceful demonstrations. If the report mentioned two different versions of who initiated violence or if the evidence was inconclusive, the coders were instructed to give the demonstrators the benefit of the doubt and code the action as a peaceful demonstration (i.e., systematization of bias).

List of Strategies and Action Forms
Conventional
Juridical. Administrative lawsuit; civil lawsuit; criminal lawsuit; other.
Political. Lobbying; participation in hearings; letters to politicians; participation in advisory bodies/consultations/negotiations; voting advice; foundation/dissolution of an SMO; other.
Media-directed. Direct information to the public (leaflets, etc.); information through the media (press conferences, etc.); tribunals, hearings (if movement-initiated); advertisements; other.

Direct-Democratic
People's initiative. Launching; presentation of signatures.
Referendum. Launching; presentation of signatures.

Demonstrative
Petition; public assembly/rally; demonstration/protest march (if legal and nonviolent); protest camp; collection of money or goods for party in political conflict (i.e., excluding help in case of natural catastrophes or food aid); recruitment of volunteers for party in political conflict; festival or celebration with political content; nonconfrontational symbolic or playful actions; other.

Confrontational
Legal. Boycott (including boycott of lectures, etc.); hunger strike, politically motivated suicide; disruption of institutional procedures (if legal); confrontational but legal symbolic or playful actions (such as burning effigies); other.
Illegal. Illegal demonstration (if nonviolent); tax boycott and other forms of illegal boycott; blockade; occupation (including squatting); publication of secret information; disruption of meetings and assemblies; illegal noncooperation (for instance, census boycott); bomb threat (if no actual bomb was placed); symbolic violence (paint "bombs," etc.); other.

Violence
Light. Limited property damage (for instance, breaking windows); theft, burglary; threats to persons; violent demonstration (if movement-initiated); other.
Heavy. Bomb or fire attacks and other severe property damage; sabotage; physical violence against persons (including political murders and kidnappings).
Note: the term "unconventional" refers to demonstrative, confrontational, or violent actions.

7. *Number of participants.* If more estimates were given in the report, the highest estimate (usually that of the organizers) was coded (i.e., systematization of bias). If no exact figures were mentioned, rough estimates were converted into figures according to the following rules: some = 5; (several) dozens = 50; (several) hundreds = 500; (several) thousands = 5,000, and so on. If neither figures nor estimates were given in the report, coders were to code "missing" unless they were able to derive an estimate from contextual information (pictures were sometimes helpful).

8. *Supporting organizations.* For this variable, fourteen yes/no questions were coded for different types of organization: no organization; regional or local SMO; regional or local peak SMO; national SMO; national peak SMO; labor union; church or affiliated organization; social-democratic party; Communist party; Green party; other left-wing party; center or right-wing parties; parties of the extreme right; other established organizations (interest groups, farmers' organizations, etc.). In addition, SMOs mentioned by name were entered on a card index. Codes for the three most important organizing SMOs were later added to the file.[15]

9. *Reactions of the authorities or the police.* Two questions were used for this category. The first was based on a prestructured list including both supportive or accommodative reactions and repressive reactions, either in the form of denunciations or police violence. This list turned out to be not very useful because most categories remained empty or very small due to insufficient information. The variable was therefore only used in a much simplified form (repressive reaction, yes or no?). Second, the number of people arrested was coded. If no exact figures were given, rough estimates were converted into figures in the same way as for the number of participants. In many reports, nothing was

said about the number of arrests. Coders were instructed to code
zero in such cases, because it can be assumed that newspapers
generally do not report nonevents (the fact that no one was arrested
would only be newsworthy if this was unexpected or exceptional
given the type of action). Coders were to code "missing" only if, on
the basis of contextual information, it seemed probable that arrests
had been made, even though the report did not mention this.

10. *Number of people wounded.* Estimates and treatment of missing
    information as for the number of people arrested. Deaths were
    counted as wounded, but were additionally entered on a separate list
    containing the name and affiliation of the persons who had died.

11. *Institutionalized event.* Yes/no question to mark actions that take
    place on a regular (weekly, yearly, etc.) basis, such as May Day
    demonstrations and Easter marches.

12. *Issue campaign of which the event is part.* Code from a list produced by
    the coders to denote an event's linkage to a broader campaign
    directed at a specific goal (i.e., more specific than those included in
    the list of goals). Examples of such campaigns include those against
    medium-range missiles or against U.S. intervention in Nicaragua.

13. *Action campaign of which the event is part.* Code from a list produced
    by the coders to denote an event's linkage to a series of events with a
    common specific goal and a common strategic framework. An
    example of an (international) action campaign is constituted by the
    series of mass demonstrations in various European capitals against
    the deployment of cruise and Pershing missiles in the fall of 1981.

14. *Number of component actions.* Number of separate actions
    summarized in the event.

Intercoder Reliability

Intercoder reliability was generally high. Tests were conducted for two pairs
of coders, and showed no significant differences in coding. Differences that
did occur were all between adjacent categories. Thus an event could be coded
as a public assembly by one coder and as a demonstration by another; as directed against the violation of human rights in the Third World by one coder
and against a specific regime by another; as having a local frame of reference by one coder and as having a regional focus by another. In many cases,
such differences were less a result of wrong coding than of the multidimen-

sional nature of the events themselves. Moreover, because for the analyses much broader categories were used (demonstrative forms, solidarity movement, regional or local frame), they did not affect the results in any significant way.

In one respect, however, there were substantial differences among the coders. Whereas *coding* events in a consistent way proved to be no problem, actually *finding* events was certainly not the easiest part of the job. Large or spectacular events were usually so prominently displayed in the paper that none of the coders missed them, but less important events were often dealt with in small, low-key articles that were easily overlooked; moreover, the articles' headlines did not always make clear that they described a protest event. Protest events might also be hidden in articles whose main subject was something else — for instance, a party statement or a church conference. Furthermore, during periods of intense social movement activity, one article sometimes contained information on a large number of events at the same time, which were not always neatly distinguished by the reporter, so that coders could easily fail to register one or two of them. As a result, none of the four coders who were compared attained a 100 percent score by registering all reported protest events.

Although differences among coders were not dramatic — in both paired comparisons, around 60 percent of the events were registered by both coders, with the better coder reaching a score of 85–90 percent and the worse coder 70–75 percent of the total — they are too large to be ignored. Fortunately, these differences were not systematically related to any of the important variables used in the analyses. For instance, small demonstrations were missed as often as low-intensity confrontational or violent actions, and peace movement actions were not better registered than, say, mobilizations of the labor movement. Therefore, all tables in which aggregate distributions over different strategies, goals, movements, localities, and so on, are presented were not affected by this form of intercoder unreliability.

However, because coders were responsible for the coding of specific periods, the interpretation of all figures in which data are presented on a yearly basis — with the exception of participation figures, which are not significantly affected by the inclusion or exclusion of small events — should take into account the fact that some of the fluctuation may in fact be due to intercoder unreliability. On the basis of the tests it could be concluded that, in a worst-case scenario, intercoder unreliability might be responsible for a margin of error of plus or minus 20 percent in the number of events registered for a certain year.[16]

Figure A.1 shows how these considerations affect the interpretation of figures that may be influenced by unreliability. The figure shows the curve of NSM mobilization in Germany, and shows in addition the lower and upper bounds of the margin of error for each year. The figure demonstrates that unreliability does not affect the interpretation of the general trend of NSM development. For instance, even if we assume that the 1970s were coded by very inattentive coders, and the 1980s by very attentive ones, it is still unmistakably clear that the level of protest in the 1980s was much higher than in the 1970s (compare the upper bounds of the margin of error for the 1970s with the lower bounds for the 1980s). However, some of the smaller differences among years may indeed be artifacts produced by differences in coder attentiveness. For instance, we cannot conclude with certainty whether the level of protest declined (as suggested by the data) or increased between 1979 and 1980, as both possibilities fall within the margin of error.

Conclusion

From this discussion a number of conclusions can be drawn that may be helpful for future newspaper-based data gathering on protest. First, given the fact that newspapers are always biased, it is futile to spend too much energy on trying to eliminate bias. Given the fact that trends and differences are usually more interesting than precise levels, one should rather try to make the bias as systematic as possible.

Second, the number of participants was often excluded in newspaper-based analyses, probably because researchers feared that such figures would be unreliable as a result of bias. This omission is unfortunate because (provided that the bias is made systematic by instructing coders always to code the highest [or lowest] estimate given in the report) participation figures are highly informative. To begin with, aggregate participation figures are relatively insensitive to differences in selectivity among newspapers, and are therefore particularly suited to comparing levels of protest among countries or regions. In addition, the frequency distribution of participation in a particular action form (such as demonstrations) can be used to compare the selectivity of newspapers that focus on different regions or countries.

Third, quantitative research on social movements has not yet sufficiently discovered the advantages of sampling. Sampling can significantly reduce the amount of time and resources needed to gather newspaper data, and can therefore contribute to a more frequent use of the method, which is desirable given the lack of data in the field. Our focus on Monday issues

Number of events per year

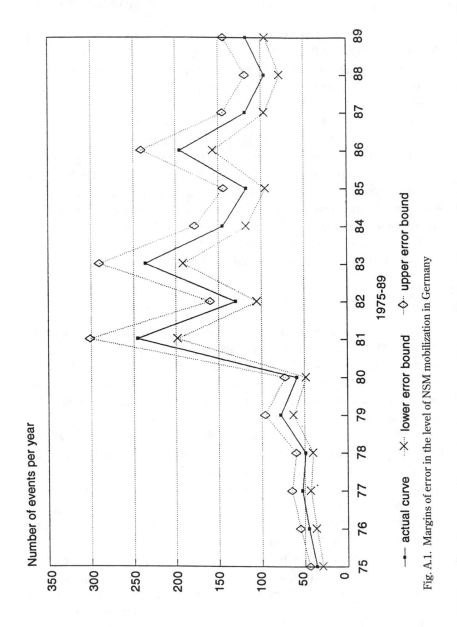

—■— actual curve   ···×··· lower error bound   ···◇··· upper error bound

Fig. A.1. Margins of error in the level of NSM mobilization in Germany

seems a particularly efficient way of sampling, because these issues contain more — and more important — protest events than other issues. In addition, our method of tracing references allows one to capture the majority of important events that did not take place during the weekend.

Finally, the discussion of intercoder reliability has demonstrated that the most important problem is not the coding of protest events, especially when one provides coders with clear instructions of how to code in case of conflicting or ambiguous information. The most important source of unreliability, which has so far been neglected in the literature, is rather the varying degree to which different coders will actually find protest events that are not displayed prominently in the newspaper columns. Estimates of this form of unreliability are necessary to allow one to determine the margin of error in time series, and to distinguish real trends from possibly spurious ones.

Notes

Introduction

This introduction was written by Hanspeter Kriesi and Marco G. Giugni and should be cited accordingly. The authors would like to thank Stefano Bartolini for his comments on an earlier version of this chapter.

1. *Le Monde,* October 25, 1983.
2. *Der Spiegel,* October 17, 1983.
3. This argument was made by one of our reviewers.
4. Those familiar with our previous work (Kriesi 1991; Kriesi et al. 1992) will notice that we have added the component of the "national cleavage structures" to the other three elements originally included in our concept of the POS. In doing so, we have followed the conceptualization proposed by Koopmans (1992a). Moreover, the previously used concept of the "configuration of power" has been more fully specified in the present model, where it is replaced by the concept of the "alliance structures."
5. A similar analysis has also been provided by Brint (1984), Lamont (1987), and Parkin (1968).
6. We are aware of the fact that Charles Tilly does not use the term "protest events." Rejecting it as being too narrow, he prefers to use the term "contentious events."

1. National Cleavage Structures

This chapter was written by Hanspeter Kriesi and Jan Willem Duyvendak and should be cited accordingly. The authors would like to thank Stefano Bartolini for his comments on an earlier version of this chapter.

1. It is important to add that Bartolini and Mair do not speak of "political cleavages," but simply of "cleavages." All cleavages are, for them, politically constituted, which is why they equate "cleavages" with "political cleavages." We prefer to make a conceptual distinction between political cleavages and their social and cultural base, that is, societal cleavages.
2. Collective identity concerns the definition of who "we" are, shared by the members of the social group in question; solidarity concerns the loyalty and commitment to the group; and consciousness refers to the extent to which a definition of the social situation shared by the members of the group implies collective action (Gamson 1992: 55).
3. More precisely, the German federalism was congruent until the fall of the Berlin Wall. With the addition of the new *Länder,* German federalism has become more incongruent and more like Swiss federalism. This would imply a reinforcement of the traditional center-periphery cleavage in this country. The period covered in this book does, however, not include the "reunification."
4. In incongruent systems, federalism can be viewed as a functional alternative to the Dutch system of pillarization (Kriesi 1990a). While preserving a segmented structure with internally highly integrated groups, it still serves to pacify their mutual relationships.

5. It is, by the way, surprising to find highly contradictory statements about the development of the impact of the traditional cleavages with respect to France in the volume just cited. Although the chapter devoted to France comes to the conclusion that the French electorate is "stalled" in terms of the traditional cleavages of religion and class (Lewis-Beck and Skalaban 1992), the editors consider France to be one of the forerunners in the historical process of the declining impact of traditional cleavages on the citizens' voting behavior. The difference is explained by the fact that they do not use the same data, but it is somewhat perplexing for the reading audience.

6. We would like to thank Stefano Bartolini for providing us with the data for the elections in the eighties, which are not covered in the book. We have recalculated the figures for the periods indicated in the text.

7. This corresponds to what Bartolini and Mair (1990) call "block volatility." It is the volatility between the block of the parties on the left and that of the parties on the right.

8. The Appendix explains in more detail how we have tried to arrive at reliable estimates for this indicator. Briefly: if several estimates of size were given in the newspaper report, we have coded the highest one. If no exact figures were mentioned, rough estimates were converted into figures according to some simple rules. We might add that direct-democratic events are excluded from this indicator, too.

9. In his study of protest and politics in Italy, Tarrow (1989a: 68f.), for instance, considers strikes as entirely conventional.

2. Institutional Structures and Prevailing Strategies

This chapter was written by Ruud Koopmans and Hanspeter Kriesi and should be cited accordingly.

1. From our point of view, Kitschelt (1986) takes a rather arbitrary decision to consider the level of centralization and of the separation of power between the executive and the judiciary as output structures, but to treat the separation of power between the legislature and the executive as an "input" structure.

2. We consider only national elections here. The French situation, for example, is quite different on the level of regional and local elections or in elections to the European parliament (see Machin 1989).

3. However, given that the Swiss system of government is not a parliamentary, but a directorial one, the government does not fall when some members of the coalition abandon it on a specific piece of legislation (see, for example, Lauvaux 1990).

4. Under the Fifth Republic, the French system of government is, of course, not a parliamentary system, but a "semipresidential" one. Especially paragraph 3 of Art. 49 is important in this context (see Duverger 1985: 408ff.).

5. Kitschelt refers to the pattern of intermediation without taking into consideration the structure of the actors being involved in this process. Moreover, he considers this pattern again exclusively as an aspect of the input structures.

6. In other words, arrangements of a "corporatist" type will be stronger and less accessible than policy networks of a "pluralist" type. See, for example, Lehmbruch (1979), who uses these terms to distinguish between various forms of policy networks or arrangements of policy making in the administrative arena.

7. The German case, incidentally, points out that neocorporatist arrangements in the administrative arena are not necessarily indicative of a generally integrative strategy. Germany is exceptional among the larger European states, since its policy networks in the ad-

ministrative arena are quite corporatist in structure and function accordingly. Hall (1986), for example, uses the term "tacit tripartism" to characterize the German case. Nevertheless, as we have argued, the strategy of German authorities with respect to challengers has remained quite repressive, for reasons not directly linked to the functioning of the administrative arena.

8. In our previous presentation of this typology (Kriesi et al. 1992: 225; Kriesi 1991: 12), we used the term "full exclusion" to characterize this situation. In adopting the term "selective exclusion" now, we are following the lead of Duyvendak (1992: 79), as well as the suggestions of one of our reviewers.

9. We are aware of the fact that facilitation by allies is very important, especially in the case of France. We shall come back to this point in chapter 3.

10. Given the fact that the presentation of signatures for referenda and initiatives usually takes place during the week, our sample, which is based on the Monday issues of major newspapers, is much less representative for these events than for other forms of mobilization like demonstrations, which tend to be concentrated on the weekends. The official figures for national-level referenda and initiatives, which we have collected in order to check this point, are much higher than those we found in our newspaper data. However, we should note that even these official figures provide only an approximation of the effective mobilization by direct-democratic procedures, since they only include initiatives and referenda at the federal level. We do not have at our disposal corresponding figures about cantonal and local events.

11. In some German *Länder*, certain limited direct-democratic opportunities exist, too.

12. Note that these data are based on our newspaper file only.

3. Alliance Structures

This chapter was written by Hanspeter Kriesi and should be cited accordingly.

1. This implication and the subsequent arguments in this paragraph were suggested to me by Ruud Koopmans.

2. Not until 1978 did the Socialists become the first force on the left in the elections to the National Assembly.

3. This argument was also suggested to me by Ruud Koopmans.

4. The results for the more exclusive category of unconventional events differ hardly at all from those presented in the text.

5. Switzerland was not considered since the composition of the federal government did not change in the period under study.

6. Following the model of the federal government, the Zurich city government is a grand coalition including all the major parties.

4. Social Movement Types and Policy Domains

This chapter was written by Jan Willem Duyvendak and Marco G. Giugni and should be cited accordingly.

1. We do not use the terms "strategic-" versus "identity-oriented" because they suggest that the identity movements cannot act in a strategic, well-planned manner with clearly circumscribed goals. The real difference is, however, the one between movements pursuing goals in the outside world, for which the action is instrumental for goal reali-

zation, and identity-oriented movements that realize their goals, at least partly, in their activities.

2. One may argue that identity also plays a role in new instrumental movements, such as the peace and ecology movements. With regard to hard-core members in particular, this indeed holds true. But it is not valid to argue that identity distinguishes new movements from old ones since identity plays a certain role in all instrumental movements, irrespective of whether they are old or new. This does not suggest a paradigmatic shift: identity has always been important for all movements.

3. There may be some doubt about the reliability of the *French* newspaper with regard to information given on repression. Even if we take into consideration the fact that powerful states do not always have to use their power in order to be effective, the data seems to show that *Le Monde* is not extremely reliable in reports on government reactions.

4. This table omits the case of Switzerland, since no change in the configuration of power occurred in this country at the national level during the period under study.

5. Alternative terms for a "policy domain" are "policy area," "policy sector," "policy field," or "policy arena." Although some differences may exist between these concepts, we use the first one and consider the others to be synonymous.

6. We have to take into consideration, however, that in France in particular traditional left-wing actors support primarily old social movements; their support to NSMs is limited to those with which historical bonds exist.

7. These seven policy domains do not, of course, include all issues relevant to the three instrumental movements concerned, let alone issues raised by NSMs in general. Here we have only considered those issues that can be brought back to a policy domain. Therefore we have excluded all mobilization for abstract or general goals of the three movements, as well as all mobilization that cannot be directly related to one of the policy domains we have distinguished.

5. The Dynamics of Protest Waves

This chapter was written by Ruud Koopmans and should be cited accordingly. It is largely based on an article that appeared in the *American Sociological Review,* "The Dynamics of Protest Waves: West Germany, 1965 to 1989" (vol. 58, no. 5 [1993]: 637–58).

1. The reader will note that I do not adopt Tarrow's term "protest *cycles,*" but instead use the term "protest *waves.*" As Weber (1987) has argued, the use of the cycle concept is only legitimate if a more or less constant periodicity (i.e., a regular distance between peaks and troughs) in the phenomenon under study can be demonstrated empirically. Since Tarrow neither asserts nor demonstrates this, it seems more appropriate to use the term "protest waves," which does not evoke associations with theories of endogenously self-reproducing oscillation (e.g., between periods of crisis and growth; between private interest and public action [Hirschman 1982]; or between conservatism and liberalism [Schlesinger 1986]).

2. The year 1984 has not been included in the first period because the level of participation in 1984 was only slighly above the average for the fifteen-year period, while the number of events in that year was very low (see figs. 3.1 and 3.2).

3. This strategy, which was particularly popular in Germany, consists of occupying the site of a future nuclear power plant, runway, or road. This strategy had the advantage that, in most cases, the protesters were not immediately evicted because the authorities lacked a legal basis to intervene. Subsequently, the occupiers often constructed makeshift "hut villages" on the site, which developed into small, self-sustaining worlds serving as

organizational centers and places where solidarity could be forged, bridges between moderates and radicals could be built, and the continuity of mobilization could be assured (Ehmke 1987: 67-76).

4. Because the numbers of violent protests and confrontational protests were low in some years, I combined data for three-year periods.

5. In the Netherlands, there is some fluctuation in the level of repression against violent protests, but this instability is related to the low absolute numbers for this strategy. For the same reason, the figure for the Netherlands does not contain a value for repression against violent protests in the period 1975-77, for which our sample includes only one violent event.

6. The figure makes clear that the relatively high level of repression in Germany that we reported in chapter 2 is a result in particular of the higher frequency of repression against legal and nonviolent, demonstrative protests.

7. The substantially lower maximum of facilitation in the Netherlands reflects our finding, reported in chapter 3, that the involvement of the traditional left in unconventional protests is higher in countries like Germany and France where the labor movement has a strong tradition of extraparliamentary action.

8. Della Porta and Tarrow (1986) explained the particularly high level of violence in the Italian protest wave in a similar manner: "To the extent that violence is a tactical differentiation within an overcrowded social movement sector, it is the size of the 'market' for social protest that determines the extent of violence that will result from it. And Italy's was surely a highly developed social movement sector" (629). A comparison of the German protest waves of the 1960s and 1980s does not confirm this. Although the protest wave of the 1980s was more "developed" in every respect than the wave of the 1960s and thus more "overcrowded," violence played a much larger role in the action repertoire of NSMs in the 1960s wave (Koopmans 1992a: 89, 100).

9. Adherents of the resource mobilization approach have challenged this position and have demonstrated the important role of organizations in the diffusion of disruptive protests, even in the cases studied by Piven and Cloward (Gamson and Schmeidler 1984; Morris 1984; Valocchi 1990).

10. Tarrow remarked that almost all violent conflicts in his sample were of this type (Tarrow 1989a: 304). In other words, violence within the Italian protest wave can only to a limited extent be seen as the result of competition for a single constituency. This violence can more aptly be described as a "war" between the extreme left and the extreme right. Of course, wars can be interpreted in terms of competition, but competition that aims to destroy competitors differs sharply from competition among parties for the support of the electorate or competition among SMOs for the support of a constituency. In the case of war, the most violent competitor is indeed likely to win. In competition for a constituency, violence is only one option and probably not the most effective choice, since competition for a constituency often hinges on winning the support of the moderate center.

11. "Unorganized" protests are not purely spontaneous outbursts of collective action by isolated individuals as suggested by "classical" models of collective behavior. In many cases, such protests originate in informal networks and subcultural and countercultural infrastructures, that is, in the social organization of a movement's constituency. The term "unorganized" means only that such protests are not the result of mobilization by formal SMOs, although they may be an unintended by-product of such efforts.

12. The analyses of strike waves in Haimson and Tilly (1989) confirm this conclusion. In their introduction to the volume, Haimson and Brian concluded: "This process of 'deinstitutionalization' [wildcat strikes] was to a degree characteristic of all the major strike

waves scrutinized in this volume" (Haimson and Brian 1989: 39). Cronin summarized the conclusion of his contribution as follows: "Strike movements built unions, but unions did not overall do a great deal to increase strike propensity" (Cronin 1989: 98).

13. Terrorist SMOs have been defined as organizations that almost exclusively use heavy forms of violence, such as the Rote Armee Fraktion in Germany or RARA in the Netherlands. Professional SMOs have been defined as movement organizations with large financial asssets and a paid professional staff. The category "other SMOs" includes all other movement organizations.

14. Within the German ecology movement, for example, the percentage of protests involving civic initiatives dropped from 78 percent in 1975–77 to 39 percent in 1987–89, while the involvement of professional SMOs increased from 8 percent to 31 percent over the same period (Koopmans 1992b: 219–20).

15. Witness, for instance, the enormous impact of the successful actions against a planned nuclear reactor in Wyhl in southwest Germany in 1975–76 (see, for instance, Rucht 1980).

16. Of course, what is novel and unconventional may vary over time and among countries. Thus, civic initiatives in West Germany initially attracted attention by their mere existence, although their action repertoire initially consisted mainly of moderate actions like petitions and small demonstrations. In West Germany, the average citizen has long been politically passive. Thus the fact that citizens who did not belong to the small radical fringe were challenging decisions of the authorities was novel enough to be of interest to the media and to concern the authorities.

6. The Political Construction of the Nuclear Energy Issue

This chapter was written by Jan Willem Duyvendak and Ruud Koopmans and should be cited accordingly. It is largely based on an article that appeared in *Social Problems*, "The Political Construction of the Nuclear Energy Issue and Its Impact on the Mobilization of Anti-Nuclear Movements in Western Europe" (vol. 42, no. 2 [1995]: 201–18).

1. This section largely draws on Koopmans 1992a: 206–11.

2. To make the Chernobyl effect detectable, the second trimester of 1986 also comprises the last five days of April, from the 26th — day one of the accident — onward.

3. The only way this finding can be made to agree with Snow and Benford's hypotheses is by assuming that, objectively, nuclear energy is not problematic at all. In that case, antinuclear attitudes should be seen as expressions of an irrational fear, which *lose* their empirical credibility the more people are actually confronted with the harmlessness and beneficial effects of nuclear power. However, as we will show further on, there is no need for this relapse into the classical imagery of social movements, as it is perfectly possible to understand cross-country differences without resorting to the assumption that about half the population of Western Europe is guided by irrational and unfounded fears.

4. This result has important implications for research on social movements. Survey researchers often use data on adherence to a movement's goals or "sympathy" for a movement as indicators of a movement's strength. As our findings indicate, such data run the risk of confusing cause and effect, and tell us more about the successful or unsuccessful history of a movement and about its present opportunities than about the actual level of mobilization of a movement.

5. Several examples of near or real disasters in the 1950s and 1960s received little, if any, attention at the time have by now become known, (e.g., major leakages from the

Windscale reprocessing plant in the United Kingdom, the contamination of a huge area in the Russian Urals, and the partial meltdown of a fast-breeder reactor in the United States; for the latter example, see Gamson 1988: 231–32).

7. Gay Subcultures between Movement and Market

This chapter was written by Jan Willem Duyvendak and should be cited accordingly.

1. Although I acknowledge that gay identities formed in the (commercial) subculture can be politicized, I prefer to start by distinguishing between movement and subcultural identities. I do so in order to enable an analysis of the conditions under which movement and subculture do, or do not, overlap. Mixing up movement and subculture in the concept of "community," as many American authors do, makes it impossible to raise the question if, and to what extent, a subculture is politicized. The start of the new gay movement with the Stonewall Riots of 1969 provides a good example of the need to make such a distinction. The homosexuals present in the Stonewall bar on the evening of June 27, 1969, did not intend to provoke any reaction by their behavior. They were not "politicized" until the attack of the police forces, after which they started the gay liberation movement (Duberman 1993).

2. In this section, I will mainly cover the male wing of the gay movement and the male subculture. To the extent that an organization focuses on interest representation (a more instrumental orientation), a mixed organization may develop — on condition that discrimination of lesbians is seen by them primarily as a form of homophobia and not of women's repression — whereas in a subculture nonmixed organizations prevail: in their desires, gay men and lesbians exclude each other. Since, as we will see, the period of instrumental interest representation in France was rather short, nonmixed pleasure-oriented organizations were predominant, in contrast with the Netherlands where the movement clearly chose a more instrumental direction. In Switzerland and Germany, SMOs were also rather instrumentally oriented, but the groups pursuing these interests often partly overlapped the subculture. Therefore, Swiss and German groups were more mixed than French gay organizations, but less so than Dutch ones.

3. An elaborated version of this history can be found in Oosterhuis and Duyvendak (1995).

4. Later, it became the International Lesbian and Gay Association (ILGA).

5. Not included are all kinds of sexual subcategories such as SM/leather, transvestites, transsexuals, pedophilia, and safe sex.

6. In political science literature, "pillarization" refers to the process by which groups of people organize their entire social and political life on the basis of their beliefs. In the Netherlands, till the 1960s the clearest example of a pillarized society, Roman Catholics and Protestants, for instance, had their own separate schools, sports clubs, cultural organizations, housing agencies, old folks' homes, welfare institutions, hospitals, political parties, and so on (Lijphart 1977, 1984).

7. In France, intellectuals possess a kind of immunity against repression. This explains why famous authors and artists could deal relatively openly with issues related to homosexuality (Proust, Gide, Jouhandeau, Cocteau, Genet, Foucault, Colette, Fernandez, Tournier, and Guibert). However, this openness does not have much bearing on the public's rather hostile attitude toward homosexuality. Researchers who stress this cultural tradition one-sidedly overlook the fact that these extraordinary people have rather exceptional points of view that are not generally shared by the broader society. Although their contribution may have been of support to the emancipation movement as a whole,

most writers did not become an active part of it. This was so because they had artistic freedom and were not directly confronted with discrimination and related problems in their work.

8. Of course, comparatively, national coordination seems to be more simple in a small country like Switzerland than in Germany. In Switzerland, however, the language cleavage made cooperation difficult; regarding pleasure-oriented, *cultural* activities in particular, German-speaking Swiss were looking at what was happening in Germany, and French-speaking Swiss at French activities.

9. What subsidies the German and Swiss gay movements receive are for AIDS work.

10. In 1985, the *Gai Pied*/Pollak survey showed that 45 percent of the readers of *Gai Pied* did not consider themselves as belonging to a *groupe social particulier.*

11. This reasoning only holds true, of course, on condition that the "permissive" respondents do not change their opinion during the course of their lives. Inglehart indeed shows with the help of longitudinal data that so-called postmaterialist attitudes are rather stable.

12. In the German situation, government policies seem less directed at equal treatment than in Switzerland. However, it is difficult to generalize since in both countries, because of their federal systems, differences come to the fore. In some parts of Germany — in Bavaria, for instance — really discriminatory policies regarding AIDS have been implemented. These differences in turn cause a rather divergent mobilization pattern within a country.

8. The Cross-National Diffusion of Protest

This chapter was written by Marco G. Giugni and should be cited accordingly. The author would like to thank Doug McAdam and Florence Passy for their comments on drafts of this chapter.

1. See, for instance, Turner and Killian (1957). For earlier works, see Tarde (1895).

2. See, for instance, McAdam (1994) and Tarrow (1983, 1989b) with respect to diffusion within protest cycles, McAdam and Rucht (1993) as to diffusion of movement ideas, Oberschall (1993) as to diffusion of a movement tactic such as the sit-in, and Pitcher, Hamblin, and Miller (1978) as to diffusion of collective violence.

3. This term is sometimes used for the region around Basel, including parts of Swiss, French, and German territory.

9. Outcomes of New Social Movements

This chapter was written by Marco G. Giugni and should be cited accordingly. The author would like to thank Florence Passy, Charles Tilly, and the other members of the proseminar on state formation and collective action (academic year 1993–94) at the New School for Social Research, New York, for their comments on drafts of this chapter.

1. Important empirical contributions have been made by Amenta, Carruthers, and Zylan (1992), Gamson (1975), Kitschelt (1986), Schumaker (1975, 1978), and Snyder and Kelly (1976). Gamson's (1975) work is particularly important, because it has raised a number of criticisms and a series of reanalyses, some of which are included in a more recent edition of the book (Gamson 1990). At the theoretical level, see, in particular, Tarrow (1983, 1989b). See Gurr (1980) for a useful review of the literature, though focusing on the

outcomes of violent conflict. A more recent—but also a more partial—review, can be found in Amenta, Carruthers, and Zylan (1992).

2. A number of studies are related to Piven and Cloward's (1971) well-known thesis about the functions of public welfare. In a more recent edition of the book, the authors discuss this controversy by reviewing several criticisms of their work (Piven and Cloward 1993).

3. Tilly has made a useful distinction between a revolutionary situation and a revolutionary outcome.

4. This is all the more true if we take into account the fact that the target for France was 1985.

5. For a comparison between France and Germany in this respect, see, among others, Nelkin and Pollak (1981).

6. This section is based for the most part on Duyvendak and Koopmans (1991b).

Conclusion

This chapter was written by Ruud Koopmans and Jan Willem Duyvendak and should be cited accordingly.

1. This is true only as long as one does not take the labels "European" and "American" too literally. Thus, for instance, many students of Latin American social movements and some political philosophers (Seidman 1992; Walzer 1992) use concepts very similar to those employed by European students of new social movements. Conversely, several European scholars work within the resource mobilization perspective (Opp and Gern 1992; van Noort 1988; see also Neidhardt and Rucht 1991: 440).

2. It should be noted, however, that American studies of revolutions have given much more attention to the state (for instance, Skocpol 1979; Tilly 1993). This perspective of "bringing the state back in" (Evans, Rueschemeyer, and Skocpol 1985) has, however, hardly penetrated the broader field of social movement studies in the United States.

3. In a similar fashion, it is hardly useful in the European context to include support from private foundations in the discussion of alliance structures, since such support is negligible in Europe.

4. This is also indicated by the widely varying strength of national branches of transnational SMOs. To give just one example: Greenpeace's membership in France numbers only a few thousand, whereas in the much less populous Netherlands it is about six hundred thousand!

5. For an analysis of the dynamics of the interaction between the NSMs and countermovements, see Koopmans and Duyvendak 1991.

Appendix: The Newspaper Data

This chapter was written by Ruud Koopmans and should be cited accordingly.

1. Once the choice to use newspapers as data sources has been made, a final question is whether to code from the newspapers themselves or to take the data from the newspaper's index (if one exists). The latter strategy has the distinct advantage of being less time-consuming, but its disadvantages are more important. First of all, by tracing protest events by certain index keywords, one runs the double risk of missing protest events that may have been classified under different headings, and of including events that do not fulfill the scientist's criteria for a protest event but are included under the keyword (see Olzak [1989:

1316]), who found that nearly half of all "candidate events" she derived from the *New York Times* index did not meet her criteria when checked with the original report). The first problem could be remedied by also looking at all keywords that are in some way related to the subject of the study, but in that case the advantage of saving time and resources is quickly lost. The second problem may be solved by using the index only as a tracer, and to code every event by going back to the original report (Olzak 1989) — which also does away with much of the original advantage of using an index, and does not solve the problem of possible protest events classified under different headings. Despite these drawbacks, using a newspaper index — provided that it is a good one — may still be a preferable choice when one is interested either in a limited range of collective action (in which case the number of possibly relevant keywords may be limited) or in a relatively infrequent type of event (in which case looking through every daily issue would not be worth the effort relative to the small number of events thus found). Because in this study we were interested in all types of unconventional protest of all social movements, using an index would not have been a workable option. Moreover, the comparative character of the project precluded the use of indexes. It was difficult enough to find roughly comparable newspapers in each of the four countries; finding newspapers in all four countries that had indexes structured in a comparable way turned out to be impossible.

2. In the Swiss and German newspapers, the bias is explicit in the sense that they are subdivided into national, regional, and local sections. A solution to the bias problem might have been to code only events reported in the national section. However, this would have led to underrepresentation for Germany and Switzerland, because the Dutch and French papers in fact also overreport on some regions but do this in a less consistent way, which makes it difficult to separate news of national, regional, and local importance. Moreover, even in Switzerland and Germany this distinction is not always so clear-cut, because events that take place in a region but that, judging by objective standards, seem to be of national importance are often reported in the local or regional sections.

3. Moreover, the relative breadth of this category of demonstrations and assemblies is comparable among the countries: it ranges from 12 percent of all events in France to 16 percent in the Netherlands.

4. Tarrow regretfully remarks: "Had we sampled events, we might have had more time and resources available to devote to studying their environment, and in this way learned more about their dynamics than by recording each event" (1989a: 363).

5. This implies that sampling is not always a viable option. If one is interested in a limited range of phenomena (a short period, one movement, etc.), sampling is both less necessary and less adequate because it will probably result in too few cases to be analyzed. Our sampled database, however, was sufficiently large, and comprises 9,022 events (of which 5,979 are NSM events). Of these, 7,010 (NSMs: 4,129) were unconventional events, on which most of the comparative analyses are based.

6. To illustrate this point, one could make a comparison with earthquakes. If we would depend on newspapers to trace earthquake incidence over time, random sampling would give very small quakes the same chance of being included as very big ones. Most likely, the researcher would in this case prefer a sampling method that includes the most important earthquakes.

7. An example of a (not very selective and therefore not so problematic) attempt to solve this problem is Tarrow's decision to code only those actions with at least twenty participants or in which violence occurs (1989a: 359).

8. If, for whatever reason (public holiday, strike, etc.), no Monday issue was available for a particular week, coders were instructed to code the first subsequent issue of the newspaper.

9. This test was conducted for the *FAZ*, which we were then still considering as the newspaper to be chosen for Germany.

10. Any protest events that were reported in other issues, but to which no reference was made in the Monday paper, were to be ignored, no matter how important they might seem to the coder.

11. In addition, the information contained in these descriptions—which might be anything the coders thought to be remarkable but could not be conveyed in the numeric codings—helped us very much to gain qualitative insight into the development of protest.

12. With the benefit of hindsight, it might have been more fruitful had we concentrated our coding of conventional events on one movement only, for which we then could have coded all conventional events in favor of or in opposition to that movement's goal, including statements and actions of established actors. This would have allowed us to study, for instance, processes of institutionalization (such as the degree to which the movement's demands have penetrated established politics) for one movement in a detailed way, and in addition could have supplied us with measures of the POS derived from the newspaper. Obviously, it would have been impossible to do this for all movements; to do so would have required coding virtually every political event reported, or virtually the whole newspaper.

13. If any distinguishing information apart from the locality was reported, an action was coded as a separate event; for instance, if the report mentioned different participation figures, different organizers, or different reactions of the authorities (arrests, etc.) for different cities.

14. Of course, the term "significant" leaves room for interpretation. With regard to the goals, different aims expressed during one (series of) actions were not seen as significantly different if they all belonged to the domain of the movement. For instance, a demonstration directed simultaneously against nuclear missiles and against a military training ground was treated as one single event (the goal to be coded depending on the newspaper's and the coder's judgment as to which of the two was most prominent). With regard to the group aspect, participation figures (exact numbers or indications such as "a small part of the protesters") or group specifications mentioned in the report were usually sufficient to determine whether two actions were supported by the same group.

15. We could have added more SMOs, but there were almost no cases in which more than three SMOs were mentioned.

16. The figure of 20 percent has been derived from comparing the best with the worst of the four coders that were tested; most intercoder differences will be smaller.

References

Adam, Barry D. 1987. *The Rise of a Gay and Lesbian Movement*. Boston: Twayne Publishers.

Altermatt, Urs. 1991. *Der Weg der Schweizer Katholiken ins Ghetto*. 2d ed. Zurich: Benziger

Altman, Dennis. 1983. *The Homosexualization of America*. Boston: Beacon Press.

———. 1988. "Legitimation through Disaster: AIDS and the Gay Movement," pp. 307–15 in *AIDS, The Burdens of History*, edited by Elizabeth Fee and Daniel M. Fox. Berkeley: University of California Press.

Amenta, Edwin, Bruce G. Carruthers, and Yvonne Zylan. 1992. "A Hero for the Aged? The Townsend Movement, the Political Mediation Model, and U.S. Old-Age Policy, 1934–1950." *American Journal of Sociology* 98: 308–39.

Archer, Dane, and Rosemary Gartner. 1976. "Violent Acts and Violent Times: A Comparative Approach to Postwar Homicide Rates." *American Sociological Review* 41: 937–62.

Atkinson, Michael M., and William D. Coleman. 1989. "Strong States and Weak States." *British Journal of Political Science* 19: 47–67.

Aust, Stefan, and Sabine Rosenbladt, eds. 1981. *Hausbesetzer. Wofür sie kämpfen, wie sie leben und wie sie leben wollen*. Hamburg: Hoffmann und Campe.

Aya, Rod. 1990. *Rethinking Revolutions and Collective Violence: Studies on Concept, Theory, and Method*. Amsterdam: Het Spinhuis.

Badie, Bertrand, and Pierre Birnbaum. 1979. *La sociologie de l'Etat*. Paris: Grasset.

Bartolini, Stefano, and Peter Mair. 1990. *Identity, Competition, and Electoral Availability: The Stabilisation of European Electorates 1885–1985*. Cambridge: Cambridge University Press.

Beck, Ulrich. 1983. "Jenseits von Klasse und Stand?" *Soziale Welt* (Sonderheft): 35–74.

———. 1986. *Risikogesellschaft: Auf dem Weg in eine andere Moderne*. Frankfurt: Suhrkamp.

Bein, Thomas, and Rudolf Epple. 1984. "Die Friedensbewegung in der Schweiz," pp. 446–83 in *Kriegsursachen*, edited by R. Steinweg. Frankfurt: Suhrkamp.

Berelson, Bernard, Paul F. Lazarsfeld, and William McPhee. 1954. *Voting: A Study of Opinion Formation in a Presidential Campaign*. Chicago: University of Chicago Press.

Best, Steven, and Douglas Kellner. 1991. *Postmodern Theory; Critical Interrogations*. London: Macmillan.

Blumer, Herbert. 1971. "Social Problems as Collective Behavior." *Social Problems* 18: 298–306.

Brand, E. 1988. *Staatsgewalt. Politische Unterdrückung und innere Sicherheit in der Bundesrepublik*. Göttingen: Verlag Die Werkstatt.

Brand, Karl-Werner. 1985. "Vergleichendes Resümee," pp. 306–34 in *Neue soziale Bewegungen in Westeuropa und den USA. Ein internationaler Vergleich*, edited by Karl-Werner Brand. Frankfurt: Campus.

———. 1987. "Kontinuität und Diskontinuität in den neuen sozialen Bewegungen," pp. 30–44 in *Neue soziale Bewegungen in der Bundesrepublik Deutschland*, edited by Roland Roth and Dieter Rucht. Frankfurt: Campus.

Brendle, U. 1992. "Deutschland," pp. 53–114 in *Umweltverbände und EG. Handlungsmöglichkeiten der Umweltverbände für die Verbesserung des Umweltbewußtseins und der Umweltpolitik in der Europäischen Gemeinschaft*, edited by C. Hey, U. Brendle, and C. Weinber. Freiburg: EURES — Institute for Regional Studies in Europe.

Brint, Steven. 1984. "'New Class' and Cumulative Trend Explanations of the Liberal Political Attitudes of Professionals." *American Journal of Sociology* 90: 30–71.

Bütschi, Daniel, and Sandro Cattacin. 1993. "L'Etat incitateur: nouvelles pratiques de la subsidiarité dans le système du bien-être suisse." *Annuaire Suisse de Science Politique* 33: 143–62.

Castles, Francis G. 1978. *The Social Democratic Image of Society.* London: Routledge and Keegan Paul.

Cavailhès, Jean, Pierre Dutey, and Gérard Bach-Ignasse. 1984. *Rapport gai. Enquête sur les modes de vie homosexuels.* Paris: Persona.

Cobb, Roger W., and Charles D. Elder. 1983. *Participation in American Politics: The Dynamics of Agenda Building.* Baltimore: Johns Hopkins University Press.

Cohen, Jean L. 1985. "Strategy and Identity: New Theoretical Paradigms and Contemporary Social Movements." *Social Research* 52: 663–716.

Coleman, James S., Elihu Katz, and Herbert Menzel. 1966. *Medical Innovation: A Diffusion Study.* New York: Bobbs-Merrill.

Copley, Anthony R. H. 1989. *Sexual Moralities in France 1780–1980: New Ideas on the Family, Divorce and Homosexuality.* New York and London: Routledge.

Cramer, Jacqueline. 1989. *De groene golf. Geschiedenis en toekomst van de milieubeweging.* Utrecht: Uitgeverij Jan van Arkel.

Crenson, Matthew A. 1971. *The Un-Politics of Air Pollution: A Study of Non-Decisionmaking in the Cities.* Baltimore: Johns Hopkins University Press.

Cronin, James E. 1989. "Strikes and Power in Britain," pp. 79–100 in *Strikes, Wars, and Revolutions in an International Perspective: Strike Waves in the Late Nineteenth and Early Twentieth Centuries,* edited by Leopold H. Haimson and Charles Tilly. Cambridge: Cambridge University Press.

Cruikshank, Margaret. 1992. *The Gay and Lesbian Liberation Movement.* New York and London: Routledge.

Dalton, Russel J. 1988. *Citizen Politics in Western Democracies: Public Opinion and Political Parties in the United States, Great Britain, West Germany and France.* Chatham, N.J.: Chatham House.

Danzger, M. Herbert. 1975. "Validating Conflict Data." *American Sociological Review* 40: 570–84.

Della Porta, Donatella, and Dieter Rucht. 1991. *Left-Libertarian Movements in Context: A Comparison of Italy and West Germany, 1965–1990.* FS III 91–102. Berlin: Wissenschaftszentrum.

Della Porta, Donatella, and Sidney Tarrow. 1986. "Unwanted Children: Political Violence and the Cycle of Protest in Italy: 1966–1973." *European Journal of Political Research* 14: 607–32.

D'Emilio, John. 1992. *Making Trouble: Essays on Gay History, Politics and the University.* New York and London: Routledge.

D'Emilio, John, and Estelle B. Freedman. 1988. *Intimate Matters: History of Sexuality in America.* New York: Harper and Row.

De Nardo, James. 1985. *Power in Numbers: The Political Strategy of Protest and Rebellion.* Princeton, N.J.: Princeton University Press.

Diani, Mario, and Hein-Anton van der Heijden 1993. "Anti-Nuclear Movements across States: Explaining Patterns of Development," pp. 355–82 in *States and Anti-Nuclear Movements,* edited by Helena Flam. Edinburgh: Edinburgh University Press.

Dodd, Stuart C. 1953. "Testing Message Diffusion in Controlled Experiments: Charting the Distance and Time Factors in the Interactance Hypothesis." *American Sociological Review* 18: 410–16.

———. 1955. "Diffusion Is Predictable: Testing Probability Models for Laws of Interaction." *American Sociological Review* 20: 392–401.

Downs, Anthony. 1972. "Up and Down with Ecology—the 'Issue Attention Cycle.'" *Public Interest* 28: 38–50.

Duberman, Martin B. 1993. *Stonewall*. New York: Penguin Books/Dutton.

Duverger, Maurice. 1985. *Le système politique français*. Paris: Presses Universitaires de France.

Duyvendak, Jan Willem. 1990. "Profiles and Trajectories of Five Social Movements." Unpublished paper, University of Amsterdam.

———. 1991. "Hoe uitdagend is de homoseksuele subcultuur?" pp. 124–34 in *Over normaal gesproken; hedendaagse homopolitiek,* edited by I. C. Meijer, J. W. Duyvendak, and M. P. van Kerkhof. Amsterdam: Schorer Imprint/Van Gennep.

———. 1992. "The Power of Politics. France: New Social Movements in an Old Polity." Ph.D. thesis, University of Amsterdam.

———. 1993. "Une 'communauté homosexuelle' en France et aux Pays-Bas? De blocs, tribus et liens." *Sociétés* 39: 75–81.

———. 1995. "The Development of the French Gay Movement 1975–89." *Journal of Homosexuality* (forthcoming).

———. ed. 1994a. *De verzuiling van de homobeweging*. Amsterdam: SUA.

———. 1994b. *Le poids du politique. Nouveaux mouvements sociaux en France*. Paris: Editions L'Harmattan.

Duyvendak, Jan Willem, Hein-Anton van der Heijden, Ruud Koopmans, and Luuk Wijmans, eds. 1992. *Tussen verbeelding en macht: 25 jaar nieuwe sociale bewegingen in Nederland*. Amsterdam: SUA.

Duyvendak, Jan Willem, and Mattias Duyves. 1993. "Gai Pied, je t'aime. Gai Pied Ten Years: A Commercial Success, a Moral Bankruptcy?" *Journal of Homosexuality* 25: 205–13.

Duyvendak, Jan Willem, and Ruud Koopmans. 1989. "Structures politiques, processus interactifs et le développement des mouvements écologiques." Paper delivered at the European Council for Political Research, Paris.

———. 1991a. "All Quiet on the Home Front? Protest against the War in the Gulf in Germany, the Netherlands, and France." Paper delivered at the conference on social problems and social policy in Visegrad, February 8–17.

———. 1991b. "Résister au sida: Destin et influence du mouvement homosexuel," pp. 195–224 in *Homosexualités et sida,* documents from the international symposium, edited by M. Pollak, R. Mendes-Leite, and J. van dem Borghe. Paris: Cahiers Gay-Kitsch-Camp.

———. 1992. "Protest in een pacificatiedemocratie. Nieuwe sociale bewegingen in het Nederlandse politieke systeem," pp. 39–58 in *Tussen verbeelding en macht: 25 jaar nieuwe sociale bewegingen in Nederland,* edited by Jan Willem Duyvendak et al. Amsterdam: SUA.

Ehmke, Wolfgang, ed. 1987. *Zwischenschritte: Die Anti-Atomkraft-Bewegung zwischen Gorleben und Wackersdorf*. Cologne: Kölner Volksblatt Verlag.

Eisinger, Peter K. 1973. "The Conditions of Protest Behavior in American Cities." *American Political Science Review* 67: 11–28.

Elster, Jon. 1984. *Ulysses and the Sirens*. Cambridge: Cambridge University Press.

———. 1989. *Nuts and Bolts for the Social Sciences*. Cambridge: Cambridge University Press.

———. 1993. *Political Psychology*. Cambridge: Cambridge University Press.

Etemad, Bouda, and Jean Luciani. 1991. *World Energy Production: 1800–1985*. Under the direction of Paul Bairoch and Jean-Claude Toutain. Geneva: Droz.

Evans, Peter B., Dietrich Rueschemeyer, and Theda Skocpol, eds. 1985. *Bringing the State Back In*. Cambridge: Cambridge University Press.

Eyerman, Ron, and Andrew Jamison. 1991. *Social Movements: A Cognitive Approach*. Cambridge: Polity Press.

Fireman, Bruce, and William A. Gamson. 1979. "Utilitarian Logic in the Resource Mobilization Perspective," pp. 8–44 in *The Dynamics of Social Movements: Resource Mobilization, Social Control, and Tactics,* edited by Mayer N. Zald and John D. McCarthy. Cambridge, Mass.: Winthrop Publishers.

Fisher, Claude S. 1978. "Urban-to-Rural Diffusion of Opinions in Contemporary America." *American Journal of Sociology* 84: 151–59.

Flanagan, Scott. 1987. "Value Change in Industrial Society." *American Political Science Review* 81: 1303–19.

Foucault, Michel. 1976. *Histoire de la sexualité,* vol. 1: *La Volonté de savoir.* Paris: Gallimard.

———. 1982. "Afterword: The Subject and Power," pp. 208–26 in *Michel Foucault: Beyond Structuralism and Hermeneutics,* edited by Hubert L. Dreyfus and Paul Rabinow. Chicago: University of Chicago Press.

Franklin, Mark N., Tom T. Mackie, Henry Valen et al., eds. 1992. *Electoral Change: Responses to Evolving Social and Attitudinal Structures in Western Countries.* Cambridge: Cambridge University Press.

Freeman, Jo. 1979. "Resource Mobilization and Strategy: A Model for Analyzing Social Movement Organization Actions," pp. 167–89 in *The Dynamics of Social Movements: Resource Mobilization, Social Control, and Tactics,* edited by Mayer N. Zald and John D. McCarthy. Cambridge, Mass.: Winthrop Publishers.

Friedman, Debra, and Doug McAdam. 1992. "Collective Identity and Activism: Networks, Choices, and the Life of a Social Movement," pp. 156–73 in *Frontiers in Social Movement Theory,* edited by Aldon D. Morris and Carol McClurg Mueller. New Haven: Yale University Press.

Fuchs, Dieter, and Dieter Rucht. 1992. *Support for New Social Movements in Five Western European Countries.* FS III 92–102, Berlin: Wissenschaftszentrum.

Gallie, Duncan. 1983. *Social Inequality and Class Radicalism in France and Britain.* Cambridge: Cambridge University Press.

Gamson, William A. 1975. *The Strategy of Social Protest.* Homewood, Ill.: Dorsey Press.

———. 1988. "Political Discourse and Collective Action," pp. 219–44 in *From Structure to Action: Social Movement Participation across Cultures,* International Social Movement Research, vol. 1, edited by Bert Klandermans, Hanspeter Kriesi, and Sidney Tarrow. Greenwich, Conn.: JAI Press.

———. 1990. *The Strategy of Social Protest.* 2d ed. Homewood, Ill.: Dorsey Press.

———. 1992. "The Social Psychology of Collective Action," pp. 53–76 in *Frontiers in Social Movement Theory,* edited by Aldon D. Morris and Carol McClurg Mueller. New Haven: Yale University Press.

Gamson, William A., and David S. Meyer. 1995. "The Framing of Political Opportunity." In *Opportunities, Mobilizing Structures and Framing: Comparative Applications of Contemporary Movement Theory,* edited by John McCarthy, Doug McAdam, and Meyer N. Zald. New York and London: Cambridge University Press.

Gamson, William A., and Emilie Schmeidler. 1984. "Organizing the Poor." *Theory and Society* 13: 567–85.

Geronimo. 1990. *Feuer und Flamme. Zur Geschichte und Gegenwart der Autonomen.* Amsterdam: ID-Archiv.

Giddens, Anthony. 1992. *The Transformation of Intimacy: Sexuality, Love and Eroticism in Modern Societies.* Oxford: Polity Press.

Giugni, Marco G. 1992. "Entre stratégie et opportunité. Les nouveaux mouvements sociaux en Suisse." Ph.D. thesis, University of Geneva.

Golden, Miriam. 1986. "Interest Representation, Party Systems and the State: Italy in Comparative Perspective." *Comparative Politics* (April): 279–301.

Goldstone, Jack A. 1980. "The Weakness of Organization: A New Look at Gamson's *The Strategy of Social Protest.*" *American Journal of Sociology* 85: 1017–42, 1426–32.

Griliches, Zvi. 1957. "Hybrid Corn: An Exploration in the Economics of Technological Change," *Econometrics* 25: 501–22.

Gurr, Ted R. 1970. *Why Men Rebel.* Princeton, N.J.: Princeton University Press.

———. 1980. "On the Outcomes of Violent Conflict," pp. 238–94 in *Handbook of Political Conflict, Theory and Research.* New York: Free Press.

Hagerstrand, Torsten. 1967. *Innovation Diffusion as a Spatial Process.* Chicago: University of Chicago Press.

Haimson, Leopold H., and Charles Tilly, eds. 1989. *Strikes, Wars, and Revolutions in an International Perspective: Strike Waves in the Late Nineteenth and Early Twentieth Centuries.* Cambridge: Cambridge University Press.

Haimson, Leopold H., and Eric Brian. 1989. "Introduction to Part II," pp. 35–46 in *Strikes, Wars, and Revolutions in an International Perspective: Strike Waves in the Late Nineteenth and Early Twentieth Centuries,* edited by Leopold H. Haimson and Charles Tilly. Cambridge: Cambridge University Press.

Hajer, Maarten. 1991. "Bias in Environmental Discourse: An Analysis of the Acid Rain Controversy in Great Britain," pp. 45–76 in *The Argumentative Turn in Policy and Planning,* edited by F. Fischer and J. Forester. Durham, N.C.: Duke University Press.

Hall, Peter. 1986. *Governing the Economy: The Politics of State Intervention in Britain and France.* Cambridge: Polity Press.

Harré, Romano, and Paul F. Secord. 1972. *The Explanation of Social Behaviour.* Oxford: Basil Blackwell.

Hawkes, N., G. Lean, D. Leigh, R. McKie, P. Pringle, and A. Wilson. 1986. *The Worst Accident in the World. Chernobyl: The End of the Nuclear Dream.* London: Pan Books/William Heinemann.

Hay, Nelson E. 1990. "The Emergence of Natural Gas," pp. 1–31 in *Natural Gas: Its Role and Potential in Economic Development,* edited by Walter Vergara, Nelson E. Hay, and Carl W. Hall. Boulder, Colo.: Westview Special Studies in Natural Resources.

Hegedus, Szusza. 1990. "Social Movements and Social Change in Self-Creative Society: New Civil Initiatives in the International Arena," pp. 263–80 in *Globalization, Knowledge and Society,* edited by M. Albrow and E. King. London: Sage.

Heijden, Henin-Anton van der. 1990. *Tussen wetenschap en politiek.* Kampen: Mondiss.

———. 1992a. "Niederlande," pp. 145–87 in *Umweltverbände und EG,* edited by C. Hey, U. Brendle, and C. Weinber. Freiburg: EURES — Institute for Regional Studies in Europe.

———. 1992b. "Van kleinschalig utopisme naar postgiroactivisme?" pp. 77–98 in *Tussen verbeelding en macht: 25 jaar nieuwe sociale bewegingen in Nederland,* edited by Jan Willem Duyvendak et al. Amsterdam: SUA.

———. 1993. "The Dutch Nuclear Energy Conflict, 1973–1989," pp. 101–28 in *State and Environmental Oppositions,* edited by Helena Flam. Edinburgh: Edinburgh University Press.

Heijden, Hein-Anton van der, Ruud Koopmans, and Marco G. Giugni. 1992. "The West European Environmental Movement," pp. 1–40 in *The Green Movement Worldwide,* edited by Matthias Finger. Research in Social Movements, Conflicts and Change, supplement 2. Greenwich, Conn.: JAI Press.

Hibbs, Douglas A., Jr. 1978. "On the Political Economy of Long-run Trends in Strike Activity." *British Journal of Political Science* 8: 153–75.

Hilgartner, Stephen, and Charles L. Bosk. 1988. "The Rise and Fall of Social Problems." *American Journal of Sociology* 94: 53–78.

Hirschman, Albert O. 1982. *Shifting Involvements: Private Interest and Public Action.* Princeton, N.J.: Princeton University Press.

Inglehart, Ronald. 1977. *The Silent Revolution: Changing Values and Political Style among Western Publics.* Princeton, N.J.: Princeton University Press.

———. 1990a. *Culture Shift in Advanced Industrial Societies.* Princeton, N.J.: Princeton University Press.

———. 1990b. "Values, Ideology, and Cognitive Mobilization in New Social Movements," pp. 43–66 in *Challenging the Political Order: New Social and Political Movements in Western Democracies,* edited by Russel J. Dalton and Manfred Küchler. Cambridge: Polity Press.

Jameson, Fredric. 1992. *Postmodernism, or the Cultural Logic of Late Capitalism.* London: Verso.

Jamison, Andrew, Ron Eyerman, and Jacqueline Cramer. 1990. *The Making of the New Environmental Consciousness: A Comparative Study of the Environmental Movements in Sweden, Denmark and the Netherlands.* Edinburgh: Edinburgh University Press.

Jansen, Steven. 1983. "Schakel, Schellinkie en Rozenstraat. Het recreatiedebat in het COC, 1970–1980," pp. 190–202 in *Homojaarboek.* Amsterdam: Van Gennep.

Jeffrey-Poulter, Stephen. 1991. *Peers, Queers and Commons: The Struggle for Gay Law Reform from 1950 to the Present.* New York and London: Routledge.

Jenkins, J. Craig. 1983. "Resource Mobilization Theory and the Study of Social Movements." *American Review of Sociology* 9: 527–53.

Jenkins, J. Craig, and Craig M. Eckert. 1986. "Channeling Black Insurgency: Elite Patronage and Professional Social Movement Organizations in the Development of the Black Movement." *American Sociological Review* 51: 812–29.

Joppke, Christian. 1991. "Social Movements during Cycles of Issue Attention: The Decline of the Anti-Nuclear Energy Movements in West Germany and the USA." *British Journal of Sociology* 42: 43–60.

Karstedt-Henke, Sabine. 1980. "Theorien zur Erklärung terroristischer Bewegungen," pp. 198–234 in *Politik der inneren Sicherheit,* edited by E. Blankenberg. Frankfurt: Suhrkamp.

Katz, Elihu. 1968. "Diffusion (Interpersonal Influence)," pp. 78–85 in *International Encyclopedia of the Social Sciences,* edited by David L. Shils. London: Macmillan and Free Press.

Katz, Elihu, and Paul F. Lazarsfeld. 1955. *Personal Influence: The Part Played by People in the Flow of Mass Communications.* New York: Free Press.

Katzenstein, Peter. 1985. *Small States in World Markets.* Ithaca, N.Y.: Cornell University Press.

———. 1987. *Policy and Politics in West Germany: The Growth of a Semisovereign State.* Philadelphia: Temple University Press.

Killian, Lewis M. 1984. "Organization, Rationality and Spontaneity in the Civil Rights Movement." *American Sociological Review* 49: 770–83.

Kitschelt, Herbert. 1986. "Political Opportunity Structures and Political Protest: Anti-Nuclear Movements in Four Democracies." *British Journal of Political Science* 16: 57–85.

————. 1990. "New Social Movements and the Decline of Party Organization," pp. 179–208 in *Challenging the Political Order: New Social and Political Movements in Western Democracies,* edited by Russel J. Dalton and Manfred Küchler. Cambridge: Polity Press.

Klandermans, Bert. 1984. "Mobilization and Participation: Social-Psychological Expansions of Resource Mobilization Theory." *American Sociological Review* 49: 583–600.

————. 1986. "New Social Movements and Resource Mobilization: The European and the American Approach." *International Journal of Mass Emergencies and Disasters.* Special issue, Comparative Perspectives and Research on Collective Behavior and Social Movements 4: 13–37.

————. 1988. "The Formation and Mobilization of Consensus," pp. 173–96 in *From Structure to Action: Social Movement Participation across Cultures,* International Social Movement Research, vol. 1, edited by Bert Klandermans, Hanspeter Kriesi, and Sidney Tarrow. Greenwich, Conn.: JAI Press.

————. 1991. "New Social Movements and Resource Mobilization: The European and the American Approach Revisited," pp. 17–44 in *Research on Social Movements: The State of the Art in Western Europe and the USA.* Frankfurt: Campus.

Klandermans, Bert, and Dirk Oegema. 1987. "Potentials, Networks, Motivations, and Barriers: Steps Towards Participation in Social Movements." *American Sociological Review* 52: 519–31.

Klandermans, Bert, and Sidney Tarrow. 1988. "Mobilization into Social Movements: Synthesizing European and American Approaches," pp. 1–38 in *From Structure to Action: Social Movement Participation across Cultures,* International Social Movement Research, vol. 1, edited by Bert Klandermans, Hanspeter Kriesi, and Sidney Tarrow. Greenwich, Conn.: JAI Press.

Koopmans, Ruud. 1989. "Die Entwicklung der Autonomen Bewegung in den Niederlanden und in der Bundesrepublik." Paper delivered at the workshop "Vergleichende Analysen sozialer Bewegungen," Wissenschaftszentrum Berlin.

————. 1992a. "Democracy from Below: New Social Movements and the Political System in West Germany." Ph.D. thesis, University of Amsterdam.

————. 1992b. "Patterns of Unruliness: The Interactive Dynamics of Protest Waves." Paper delivered at the annual meeting of the American Sociological Association, Pittsburgh, Pa., August 20–24.

————. 1992c. "Van Provo tot RARA. Golfbewegingen in het politiek protest in Nederland," pp. 59–76 in *Tussen verbeelding en macht: 25 jaar nieuwe sociale bewegingen in Nederland,* edited by Jan Willem Duyvendak et al. Amsterdam: SUA.

————. 1993. "The Dynamics of Protest Waves: West Germany, 1965 to 1989." *American Sociological Review* 58: 637–58.

Koopmans, Ruud, and Jan Willem Duyvendak. 1991. "Gegen die Herausforderer: Neue soziale Bewegungen und Gegenbewegungen in der Bundesrepublik Deutschland, den Niederlanden und Frankreich." *Forschungsjournal Neue soziale Bewegungen* 2: 17–30.

Krasner, Stephen D. 1978. "United States Commercial and Monetary Policy: Unravelling the Paradox of External Strength and Internal Weakness," pp. 51–88 in *Between Power and Plenty,* edited by Peter J. Katzenstein. Madison: University of Wisconsin Press.

Kriesi, Hanspeter. 1984. *Die Zürcher Bewegung. Bilder, Interaktionen, Zusammenhänge.* Frankfurt: Campus.

————. 1987. "Neue soziale Bewegungen: auf der Suche nach ihrem gemeinsamen Nenner." *Politische Vierteljahresschrift* 28: 315–34.

————. 1988. "The Interdependence of Structure and Action: Some Reflections on the State of the Art," pp. 349–68 in *From Structure to Action: Social Movement Participation across Cultures,* International Social Movement Research, vol. 1, edited by Bert Klandermans, Hanspeter Kriesi, and Sidney Tarrow. Greenwich, Conn.: JAI Press.

———. 1989. "New Social Movements and the New Class in the Netherlands." *American Journal of Sociology* 94: 1078–1116.

———. 1990a. "Federalism and Pillarization: The Netherlands and Switzerland Compared." *Acta Politica* 25: 433–50.

———. 1990b. "The Political Opportunity Structure of the Dutch Peace Movement." *West European Politics* 12: 295–312.

———. 1991. *The Political Opportunity Structure of New Social Movements: Its Impact on Their Mobilization.* FS III 91–103. Berlin: Wissenschaftszentrum.

———. 1993a. *Political Mobilization and Social Change: The Dutch Case in Comparative Perspective.* Aldershot: Avebury.

———. 1993b. "Politische Randbedingungen der Entwicklung neuer sozialer Bewegungen," pp. 32–46 in *Westliche Demokratien und Interessenvermittlung,* edited by Ralf Kleinfeld and Wolfgang Luthardt. Marburg: Schüren.

———. 1995. "The Organizational Structure of New Social Movements in Relation to Their Political Context." In *Opportunities, Mobilizing Structures and Framing: Comparative Applications of Contemporary Movement Theory,* edited by John McCarthy, Doug McAdam, and Meyer N. Zald. New York and London: Cambridge University Press.

———, ed. 1985. *Bewegung in der Schweizer Politik. Fallstudien zu politischen Mobilisierungsprozessen in der Schweiz.* Frankfurt: Campus.

Kriesi, Hanspeter, and Philip van Praag Jr. 1987. "Old and New Politics: The Dutch Peace Movement and the Traditional Political Organizations." *European Journal of Political Science* 15: 319–46.

Kriesi, Hanspeter, René Levy, Gilbert Ganguillet, and Heinz Zwicky, eds. 1981. *Politische Aktivierung in der Schweiz, 1945–1978.* Diessenhofen: Rüegger.

Kriesi, Hanspeter, Ruud Koopmans, Jan Willem Duyvendak, and Marco G. Giugni. 1992. "New Social Movements and Political Opportunities in Western Europe." *European Journal of Political Research* 22: 219–44.

Krohberger, K., and C. Hey. 1991. *Die Beteiligungschancen der Umweltverbände auf Europäischer Ebene.* Freiburg: EURES—Institute for Regional Studies in Europe.

Küchler, Manfred, and Russel J. Dalton. 1990. "New Social Movements and the Political Order: Inducing Change for Long-term Stability?" pp. 277–300 in *Challenging the Political Order: New Social and Political Movements in Western Democracies,* edited by Russel J. Dalton and Manfred Küchler. Cambridge: Polity Press.

Laclau, Ernesto, and Chantal Mouffe. 1985. *Hegemony and Socialist Strategy: Towards a Radical Democratic Politics.* London: Verso.

Ladner, Andreas. 1989. "Green and Alternative Parties in Switzerland," pp. 155–65 in *New Politics in Western Europe,* edited by Ferdinand Müller-Rommel. Boulder, Colo.: Westview Press.

Ladrech, Robert. 1989. "Social Movements and Party Systems: The French Socialist Party and New Social Movements." *West European Politics* 12: 262–79.

Lamont, Michèle 1987. "Cultural Capital and the Liberal Political Attitudes of Professionals: Comment on Brint." *American Journal of Sociology* 92: 1501–5.

Laumann, Edward O., and David Knoke. 1987. *The Organizational State: Social Choice in National Policy Domains.* Madison: University of Wisconsin Press.

Lauvaux, Philippe. 1990. *Les grandes démocraties contemporaines.* Paris: Presses Universitaires de France.

Laver, Michael, and Norman Schofield. 1991. *Multiparty Government: The Politics of Coalition in Europe.* Oxford: Oxford University Press.

Lazarsfeld, Paul F., Bernard Berelson, and Hazel Gaudet. 1944. *The People's Choice: How the Voter Makes up His Mind in a Presidential Campaign.* New York: Duell, Sloan and Pearce.

Lehmbruch, Gerhard. 1979. "Liberal Corporatism and Party Government," pp. 147–83 in *Trends Toward Corporatist Intermediation,* edited by Philippe C. Schmitter and Gerhard Lehmbruch. London: Sage.

———. 1991. "The Organization of Society, Administrative Strategies and Policy Networks," pp. 121–58 in *Political Choice, Institutions, Rules and the Limits of Rationality,* edited by R. M. Czada and A. Windhoff-Héritier. Frankfurt: Campus and Westview.

Lewis, Steven C., and Srenella Sferza. 1987. "Les socialistes français entre l'Etat et la Société: de la construction du parti à la conquête du pouvoir," pp. 132–51 in *L'expérience Mitterrand,* edited by Stanley Hoffmann and George Ross. Paris: Presses Universitaires de France.

Lewis-Beck, Michael, and Andrew Skalaban. 1992. "France," pp. 167–78 in *Electoral Change: Responses to Evolving Social and Attitudinal Structures in Western Countries,* edited by Mark N. Franklin et al. Cambridge: Cambridge University Press.

Lijphart, Arend. 1969. "Consociational Democracy." *World Politics* 21: 207–25.

———. 1977. *Democracy in Plural Societies: A Comparative Exploration.* New Haven and London: Yale University Press.

———. 1984. *Democracies: Patterns of Majoritarian and Consensus Government in Twenty-One Countries.* New Haven and London: Yale University Press.

Lipset, Seymour M., and Stein Rokkan. 1967. "Cleavage Structures, Party Systems, and Voter Alignments: An Introduction," pp. 1–67 in *Party Systems and Voter Alignments: Cross-National Perspectives,* edited by Seymour M. Lipset and Stein Rokkan. New York: Free Press.

Machin, Howard. 1989. "Stages and Dynamics in the Evolution of the French Party System." *West European Politics* 12: 59–81.

Mahajan, Vijay, and Robert A. Peterson. 1985. *Models for Innovation Diffusion.* Beverly Hills, Calif.: Sage Publications.

Mauss, Armand L. 1975. *Social Problems as Social Movements.* Philadelphia: J. B. Lippincott Company.

McAdam, Doug. 1982. *Political Process and the Development of Black Insurgency, 1930–1970.* Chicago: University of Chicago Press.

———. 1983. "Tactical Innovation and the Pace of Insurgency." *American Sociological Review* 48: 735–54.

———. 1988. *Freedom Summer: The idealists revisited.* New York: Oxford University Press.

———. 1990. "Political Opportunities and Framing Processes: Thoughts on Linkages." Paper for the workshop "Social Movements, Framing Processes, and Opportunity Structures," Berlin: Wissenschaftszentrum, July 5–7.

———. 1995. "'Initiator' and 'Derivative' Movements: Diffusion Processes in Protest Cycles," in *Repertoires and Cycles of Collective Action,* edited by Mark Traugott. Durham, N.C.: Duke University Press (forthcoming).

McAdam, Doug, and Dieter Rucht. 1993. "The Cross-National Diffusion of Movement Ideas." *ANNALS* 528: 56–74.

McAdam, Doug, John D. McCarthy, and Mayer N. Zald. 1988. "Social Movements," pp. 695–737 in *Handbook of Sociology,* edited by Neil J. Smelser. Beverly Hills, Calif.: Sage.

McCarthy, John D., Clark McPhail, and Jackie Smith. N.d. "Images of Protest: Dimensions of Selection Bias in Media Coverage of Washington Demonstrations, 1982, 1991." Unpublished paper.

———. 1992. "The Tip of the Iceberg: Some Dimensions of Selection Bias in Media Coverage of Demonstrations in Washington, D.C." Paper delivered at the annual meeting of the American Sociological Association, Pittsburgh, Pa., August 20–24.

McCarthy, John D., and Mayer N. Zald. 1977. "Resource Mobilization and Social Movements: A Partial Theory." *American Journal of Sociology* 82: 1212–41.

Melucci, Alberto. 1980. "The New Social Movements: A Theoretical Approach." *Social Science Information* 19: 199–226.

———. 1982. *L'invenzione del presente. Movimenti, identità, bisogni collettivi.* Bologna: Il Mulino.

———. 1984. "An End to Social Movements?" *Social Science Information* 24: 819–35.

———. 1990. *Nomads of the Present: Social Movements and Individual Needs in Contemporary Society.* Philadelphia: Temple University Press.

Michaelson, Alaina G. 1993. "The Development of a Scientific Specialty as Diffusion through Social Relations: The Case of Role Analysis." *Social Networks* 15: 217–36.

Morris, Aldon D. 1984. *The Origins of the Civil Rights Movement: Black Communities Organizing for Change.* New York: Free Press.

Morris, Aldon D., and Carol McClurg Mueller. 1992. *Frontiers in Social Movement Theory.* New Haven and London: Yale University Press.

Mossuz-Lavau, Janine. 1991. *Les lois de l'amour. Les politiques de la sexualité en France (1950–1990).* Paris: Payot.

Mulhak, Renate. 1983. "Der Instandbesetzungskonflikt in Berlin," pp. 205–52 in *Großstadt und neue soziale Bewegungen,* edited by P. Grottian and W. Nelles. Basel: Birkhäuser.

Müller-Rommel, Ferdinand. 1984. "Zum Verhältnis von neuen sozialen Bewegungen und neuen Konfliktdimensionen in den politischen Systemen Westeuropas: eine empirische Analyse." *Journal für Sozialforschung* 24: 441–54.

———. 1985. "New Social Movements and Smaller Parties: A Comparative Perspective." *West European Politics* 8: 41–54.

———. 1990. "New Political Movements and 'New Politics' Parties in Western Europe," pp. 209–31 in *Challenging the Political Order: New Social and Political Movements in Western Democracies,* edited by Russel J. Dalton and Manfred Küchler. Cambridge: Polity Press.

———, ed. 1989. *New Politics in Western Europe: The Rise and Success of Green Parties and Alternative Lists.* London: Westview Press.

Nedelmann, Brigitta. 1984. "New Political Movements and Changes in Processes of Intermediation." *Social Science Information* 23: 1029–48.

Neidhardt, Friedhelm, and Dieter Rucht. 1991. "The Analysis of Social Movements: The State of the Art and Some Perspectives for Further Research," pp. 421–64 in *Research on Social Movements: The State of the Art in Western Europe and the USA.* Frankfurt am Main: Campus/Boulder, Colo.: Westview Press.

———. 1993. "Auf dem Weg in die 'Bewegungsgesellschaft'? Über die Stabilisierbarkeit sozialer Bewegungen." *Soziale Welt* 44: 305–26.

Nelkin, Dorothy, and Michael Pollak. 1981. *The Atom Besieged: Extraparliamentary Dissent in France and Germany.* Cambridge, Mass.: MIT Press.

Noort, Wim J. van. 1988. *Bevlogen bewegingen. Een vergelijking van de anti-kernenergie-, kraak- en milieubeweging.* Amsterdam: SUA.

Oberschall, Anthony. 1973. *Social Conflict and Social Movements.* Englewood Cliffs, N.J.: Prentice-Hall.

———. 1978. "The Decline of the 1960s Social Movements," pp. 257–89 in *Research in Social Movements, Conflicts and Change*, vol. 1, edited by Louis Kriesberg. Greenwich, Conn.: JAI Press.

———. 1979. "Protracted Conflict," pp. 45–70 in *The Dynamics of Social Movements: Resource Mobilization, Social Control, and Tactics*, edited by Mayer N. Zald and John D. McCarthy. Cambridge, Mass.: Winthrop Publishers.

———. 1993. *Social Movements: Ideologies, Interests, and Identities*. New Brunswick, N.J., and London: Transaction Books.

Offe, Claus. 1985. "New Social Movements: Challenging the Boundaries of Institutional Politics." *Social Research* 52: 817–68.

———. 1990. "Reflections on the Institutional Self-Transformation of Movement Politics: A Tentative Stage Model," pp. 232–50 in *Challenging the Political Order: New Social and Political Movements in Western Democracies*, edited by Russel J. Dalton and Manfred Küchler. Cambridge: Polity Press.

Olson, Mancur. 1965. *The Logic of Collective Action: Public Goods and the Theory of Groups.* Cambridge, Mass.: Harvard University Press.

Olzak, Susan. 1989. "Labor Unrest, Immigration, and Ethnic Conflict in Urban America, 1880–1914." *American Journal of Sociology* 94: 1303–33.

Oosterhuis, Harry. 1992. *Homoseksualiteit in katholiek Nederland. Een sociale geschiedenis 1900–1970.* Amsterdam: SUA.

Oosterhuis, Harry, and Jan Willem Duyvendak. 1995. "A Gay History of Western Europe since 1945," in W. R. Dynes, *Encyclopedia of Homosexuality.*

Opp, Karl-Dieter, and Christiane Gern. 1992. "Dissident Groups, Personal Networks, and Spontaneous Cooperation: The East German Revolution in 1989." Paper delivered at the First European Conference on Social Movements, Berlin.

Oppeln, Sabine von. 1989. *Die Linke im Kernenergiekonflikt. Deutschland und Frankreich im Vergleich.* Frankfurt: Campus.

Pappi, Franz, and David Knoke. 1991. "Political Exchange in the German and American Labor Policy Domain," pp. 179–208 in *Policy Networks: Empirical Evidence and Theoretical Considerations*, edited by Bernd Marin and Renate Mayntz. Frankfurt and Boulder, Colo.: Campus Verlag/Westview Press.

Párkin, Frank. 1968. *Middle Class Radicalism.* Manchester: Manchester University Press.

Peters, M. 1992. *Achterban onder de loep. Geitewollensokkendragers, ecoyups of milieunairs.* Amsterdam: Vereniging Milieudefensie, University of Amsterdam.

Pitcher, Brian L., Robert L. Hamblin, and Jerry L. L. Miller. 1978. "The Diffusion of Collective Violence." *American Sociological Review* 43: 23–35.

Piven, Frances Fox, and Richard A. Cloward. 1971. *Regulating the Poor: The Functions of Public Welfare.* New York: Random House.

———. 1977. *Poor People's Movements: Why They Succeed, How They Fail.* New York: Vintage Books.

———. 1993. *Regulating the Poor: The Functions of Public Welfare.* Updated edition. New York: Random House.

Pizzorno, Alessandro. 1978. "Political Exchange and Collective Identity in Industrial Conflict," pp. 277–98 in *The Resurgence of Class Conflict in Western Europe since 1968*, edited by Colin Crouch and Alessandro Pizzorno. London: Macmillan.

Praag, Philip van, Jr. 1991. *Strategie en illusie. Elf jaar intern debat in de Pvda (1966–1977).* Amsterdam: Het Spinhuis.

Przeworski, Adam, and Henry Teune. 1970. *The Logic of Comparative Social Inquiry.* New York: Wiley-Interscience.

Przeworski, Adam, and John Sprague. 1986. *Paper Stones: A History of Electoral Socialism.* Chicago: University of Chicago Press.

Pulzer, Peter. 1989. "Political Ideology," pp. 78–98 in *Developments in West German Politics,* edited by Gordon Smith, William E. Paterson, and Peter H. Merkl. London: Macmillan.

Raschke, Joachim. 1985. *Soziale Bewegungen. Ein historisch-systematischer Grundriß.* Frankfurt: Campus.

Rennwald, Jean-Claude. 1992. "Le clivage centre-périphérie dans la perspective de la construction européenne." *Annuaire suisse de science politique* 32: 167–84.

———. 1994. *La transformation de la structure du pouvoir dans le canton du Jura (1970–1991). Du séparatisme à l'intégration au système politique suisse.* Courrendlin: Edition Communication jurassienne et européenne (CEJ).

Righart, Hans. 1986. *De katholieke zuil in Europa.* Amsterdam: Boom.

Rochon, Thomas R. 1988. *Mobilizing for Peace: The Antinuclear Movements in Western Europe.* Princeton, N.J.: Princeton University Press.

———. 1990. "The West European Peace Movement and the Theory of New Social Movements," pp. 105–21 in *Challenging the Political Order: New Social and Political Movements in Western Democracies,* edited by Russel J. Dalton and Manfred Küchler. Cambridge: Polity Press.

Rogers, Everett M. 1983. *Diffusion of Innovations.* New York: Free Press of Glencoe.

Rokkan, Stein. 1970. *Citizens, Elections, Parties.* Oslo: Universitetsforlaget.

Rokkan, Stein, and Derek W. Urwin. 1983. *Economy, Territory, Identity: Politics of Western European Peripheries.* London: Sage.

Rolke, Lothar. 1987. *Protestbewegungen in der Bundesrepublik.* Opladen: Westdeutscher Verlag.

Rosanvallon, Pierre. 1988. *La question syndicale.* Paris: Calman-Levy.

Roth, Roland. 1985. "Neue soziale Bewegungen in der politischen Kultur der Bundesrepublik. Eine vorläufige Skizze," pp. 20–82 in *Neue soziale Bewegungen in Westeuropa und den USA. Ein internationaler Vergleich,* edited by Karl-Werner Brand. Frankfurt am Main: Campus/Boulder, Colo.: Westview Press.

———. 1989. "Neue soziale Bewegungen als politische Institution: Anregungen für einen theoretischen Perspektivenwechsel." *Forschungsjournal Neue soziale Bewegungen* 2 (Sonderheft): 33–51.

———. 1991. "Herausforderung demokratischer Institutionen durch neue Formen politischer Mobilisierung. Zur Situation in der Bundesrepublik." *Schweizerisches Jahrbuch für Politische Wissenschaft* 31: 209–34.

———. 1992. "Bewegung als Institution. Neue soziale Bewegungen auf dem Wege zur politischen Institution." Inaugural diss., FB 15, Free University of Berlin.

Rucht, Dieter. 1980. *Von Wyhl nach Gorleben. Bürger gegen Atomprogramm und nukleare Entsorgung.* Munich: Beck.

———. 1988. "Themes, Logics, and Arenas of Social Movements: A Structural Approach," pp. 305–28 in *From Structure to Action: Social Movement Participation across Cultures,* International Social Movement Research, vol. 1, edited by Bert Klandermans, Hanspeter Kriesi, and Sidney Tarrow. Greenwich, Conn.: JAI Press.

———. 1989a. "Environmental Movement Organizations in West Germany and France," pp. 61–94 in *Organizing for Change: Social Movement Organizations in Europe and the United States,* edited by Bert Klandermans. Greenwich, Conn.: JAI Press.

———. 1989b. "Protestbewegungen," pp. 311–44 in *Die Geschichte der Bundesrepublik Deutschland,* vol. 3: *Gesellschaft,* edited by W. Benz. Frankfurt: Fischer.

———. 1990a. "Campaigns, Skirmishes and Battles: Anti-Nuclear Movements in the USA, France and West Germany." *Industrial Crisis Quarterly* 4: 193–222.

————. 1990b. "The Strategies and Action Repertoires of New Movements," pp. 156–75 in *Challenging the Political Order: New Social and Political Movements in Western Democracies,* edited by Russel J. Dalton and Manfred Küchler. Cambridge: Polity Press.

————. 1993. "Modernisierung und neue soziale Bewegungen. Theoretische und empirisch-vergleichende Analysen (USA, Frankreich, Bundesrepublik)." Unpublished manuscript.

————. 1995. "The Impact of National Contexts on Social Movement Structures: A Cross-Movement and Cross-National Comparison." In *Opportunities, Mobilizing Structures and Framing: Comparative Applications of Contemporary Movement Theory,* edited by John McCarthy, Doug McAdam, and Meyer N. Zald. New York and London: Cambridge University Press.

————, ed. 1984. *Flughafenprojekte als Politikum: Die Konflikte in Stuttgart, München und Frankfurt.* Frankfurt: Campus.

Rucht, Dieter, and Thomas Ohlemacher. 1992. "Protest Event Data: Collection, Uses and Perspectives," pp. 76–106 in *Studying Collective Action,* edited by Mario Diani and Ron Eyerman. London: Sage.

Rüdig, Wolfgang. 1988. "Peace and Ecology Movements in Western Europe." *West European Politics* 11: 26–39.

————. 1990. *Anti-Nuclear Movements: A World Survey of Opposition to Nuclear Energy.* Harlow, Essex: Longman.

Salmen, Andreas, and Albert Eckert. 1989. *20 Jahre bundesdeutsche Schwulenbewegung 1969–1989.* Cologne: BVH Materialien.

Schain, Martin A. 1980. "Corporatism and Industrial Relations in France," pp. 191–217 in *French Politics and Public Policy,* edited by Philip G. Cerny and Martin A Schain. London: Frances Pinter.

Scharpf, Fritz. 1984. "Economic and Institutional Constraints of Full Employment Strategies: Sweden, Austria and West Germany, 1973–82," pp. 257–90 in *Order and Conflict in Contemporary Capitalism: Studies in the Political Economy of West European Nations,* edited by John H. Goldthorpe. Oxford: Oxford University Press.

Schlesinger, Arthur M., Jr. 1986. *The Cycles of American History.* Boston: Houghton Mifflin.

Schmidt, Manfred G. 1987. "West Germany: The Policy of the Middle Way." *Journal of Public Policy* 7: 135–77.

Schmitt-Beck, Rüdiger 1992. "A Myth Institutionalized: Theory and Research on New Social Movements in Germany." *European Journal of Political Research* 21: 357–83.

Schmitter, Philippe C. 1982. "Reflections on Where the Theory of Neo-Corporatism Has Gone and Where the Praxis of Neo-Corporatism May Be Going," pp. 259–80 in *Patterns of Corporatist Policy-Making,* edited by Gerhard Lehmbruch and Philippe C. Schmitter. London: Sage.

Schneider, Joseph W. 1985. "Social Problems Theory: The Constructionist View." *Annual Review of Sociology* 11: 209–29.

Scholten, Ilja. 1980. "Does Consociationalism Exist?" pp. 329–54 in *Electoral Participation: A Comparative Analysis,* edited by Richard Rose. London: Sage.

Schumaker, Paul D. 1975. "Policy Responsiveness to Protest-Group Demands." *Journal of Politics* 37: 488–521.

————. 1978. "The Scope of Political Conflict and the Effectiveness of Constraints in Contemporary Urban Protest." *Sociological Quarterly* 19: 168–84.

Schwartz, M., and S. Paul. 1992. "Resource Mobilization versus the Mobilization of People: Why Consensus Movements Cannot Be Instruments of Social Change," pp. 205–23 in *Frontiers in Social Movement Theory,* edited by Aldon D. Morris and Carol McClurg Mueller. New Haven: Yale University Press.

Seidman, Steven. 1992. *Embattled Eros: Sexual Politics and Ethics in Contemporary America.* New York and London: Routledge.

———. 1993. "Identity and Politics in a 'Postmodern' Gay Culture: Some Historical and Conceptual Notes," pp. 105–42 in *Fear of a Queer Planet: Queer Politics and Social Theory,* edited by Michael Warner. Minneapolis/London: University of Minnesota Press.

Simmel, Georg. 1968. *Soziologie.* 5th ed. Berlin: Duncker und Humblodt.

Skocpol, Theda. 1979. *States and Social Revolution: A Comparative Analysis of France, Russia and China.* Cambridge: Cambridge University Press.

Smelser, Neil J. 1962. *Theory of Collective Behavior.* New York: Macmillan.

Smith, Gordon. 1986. *Democracy in Western Germany: Parties and Politics in the Federal Republic.* 3d ed. Aldershot: Gower.

———. 1989. "Core Persistence: Change and the 'People's Party.'" *West European Politics* 12: 157–68.

Snow, David A., E. Burke Rochford Jr., Steven K. Worden, and Robert D. Benford. 1986. "Frame Alignment Processes, Micromobilization, and Movement Participation." *American Sociological Review* 51: 464–81.

Snow, David A., and Robert D. Benford. 1988. "Ideology, Frame Resonance, and Participant Mobilization," pp. 197–217 in *From Structure to Action: Social Movement Participation across Cultures,* International Social Movement Research, vol. 1, edited by Bert Klandermans, Hanspeter Kriesi, and Sidney Tarrow. Greenwich, Conn.: JAI Press.

———. 1992. "Master Frames and Cycles of Protest," pp. 133–55 in *Frontiers in Social Movement Theory,* edited by Aldon D. Morris and Carol McClurg Mueller. New Haven: Yale University Press.

Snyder, David, and William R. Kelly. 1976. "Industrial Violence in Italy, 1878–1903." *American Journal of Sociology* 82: 131–62.

———. 1977. "Conflict Intensity, Media Sensitivity and the Validity of Newspaper Data." *American Sociological Review* 42: 105–23.

Spector, Malcolm, and John I. Kitsuse. 1973. "Social Problems: A Re-Formulation." *Social Problems* 21: 145–59.

Spilerman, Seymour. 1976. "Structural Characteristics and Severity of Racial Disorders." *American Sociological Review* 41: 771–92.

Steedly, Homer R., and John W. Foley. 1979. "The Success of Protest Groups: Multivariate Analyses." *Social Science Research* 8: 1–15.

Steiner, Jürg. 1974. *Amicable Agreement versus Majority Rule: Conflict Resolution in Switzerland.* Chapel Hill: University of North Carolina Press.

Strang, David, and John W. Meyer. 1993. "Institutional Conditions for Diffusion." *Theory and Society* 22: 487–511.

Tarde, Gabriel. 1895. *Les lois de l'imitation. Etude sociologique.* Paris: Alcan.

Tarrow, Sidney. 1983. *Struggling to Reform: Social Movements and Policy Change during Cycles of Protest.* Ithaca, N.Y.: Cornell University, Western Societies Program Occasional Paper 15.

———. 1988. "National Politics and Collective Action: Recent Theory and Research in Western Europe and the United States." *Annual Review of Sociology* 14: 421–40.

———. 1989a. *Democracy and Disorder: Protest and Politics in Italy 1965–1975.* Oxford: Clarendon Press.

———. 1989b. *Struggle, Politics, and Reform: Collective Action, Social Movements, and Cycles of Protest.* Ithaca, N.Y.: Cornell University, Western Societies Program Occasional Paper 21.

———. 1991. "Comparing Social Movement Participation in Western Europe and the United States: Problems, Uses, and a Proposal for Synthesis," pp. 392–420 in *Research on*

Social Movements: The State of the Art in Western Europe and the USA, edited by Dieter Rucht. Frankfurt am Main: Campus/Boulder, Colo.: Westview Press.

———. 1994. *Power in Movement: Social Movements, Collective Action and Mass Politics.* New York and London: Cambridge University Press.

———. 1995. "States and Opportunities: The Political Structuring of Social Movements." In *Opportunities, Mobilizing Structures and Framing: Comparative Applications of Contemporary Movement Theory,* edited by John McCarthy, Doug McAdam, and Meyer N. Zald. New York and London: Cambridge University Press.

Tielman, Rob A. P. 1982. *Homoseksualiteit in Nederland, studie van een emancipatiebeweging.* Meppel and Amsterdam: Boom.

Tilly, Charles. 1978. *From Mobilization to Revolution.* Reading, Mass.: Addison-Wesley.

———. 1984. "Social Movements and National Politics," pp. 297–317 in *Statemaking and Social Movements: Essays in History and Theory,* edited by Charles Bright and Susan Harding. Ann Arbor: University of Michigan Press.

———. 1986a. *Big Structures, Large Processes, Huge Comparisons.* New York: Russell Sage.

———. 1986b. *The Contentious French: Four Centuries of Popular Struggle.* Cambridge, Mass.: Belknap Press of Harvard University Press.

———. 1993. *European Revolutions, 1492–1992.* Oxford and Cambridge: Basil Blackwell.

Tilly, Charles, Louise Tilly, and Richard Tilly. 1975. *The Rebellious Century, 1830–1930.* Cambridge, Mass.: Harvard University Press.

Touraine, Alain. 1978. *La voix et le regard.* Paris: Editions du Seuil.

———. 1980a. *L'après-socialisme.* Paris: Grasset.

———. 1980b. *La prophétie anti-nucléaire.* Paris: Editions du Seuil.

Trüeb, Kuno, and Stephan Miescher. 1988. *Männergeschichten — Schwule in Basel seit 1930.* Basel: Buchverlag Basler Zeitung.

Tuchman, Gary. 1973. "Making News by Doing Work: Routinizing the Unexpected." *American Journal of Sociology* 79: 110–31.

Turner, Ralph H., and Lewis M. Killian. 1957. *Collective Behavior.* Englewood Cliffs, N.J.: Prentice-Hall.

Vadrot, Claude M. 1978. *L'écologie; l'histoire d'une subversion.* Paris: Syros.

Valocchi, Steve. 1990. "The Unemployed Workers Movement of the 1930s: A Reexamination of the Piven and Cloward Thesis." *Social Problems* 37: 191–205.

Vester, M. 1989. "Neue soziale Bewegungen und soziale Schichten," pp. 38–63 in *Alternativen zur alten Politik? Neue soziale Bewegungen in der Diskussion,* edited by U. C. Wasmuth. Darmstadt: Wissenschaftliche Buchgesellschaft.

Visser, Jelle. 1987. "In Search of Inclusive Unionism: A Comparative Analysis." Ph.D. thesis, University of Amsterdam.

Walser, Erasmus. 1991. *Unentwegt Emanzipatorisch. Vereinsgeschichte 20 Jahre homosexuelle Arbeitsgruppen Bern (CH).* Bern: Homosexuelle Arbeitsgruppen Bern.

Walsh, Edward J. 1981. "Resource Mobilization and Citizen Protest in Communities around Three Mile Island." *Social Problems* 29: 1–21.

Walzer, Michael. 1992. "The Civil Society Argument," 25–47 in *Dimensions of Radical Democracy,* edited by Chantal Mouffe. London: Verso.

Warmerdam, Hans N., and Pieter Koenders. 1987. *Cultuur en ontspanning. Het COC 1946–1966.* Utrecht: Publicatiereeks Homostudies 10.

Watts, Nicholas J. 1987. "Mobilisierungspotential und gesellschaftspolitische Bedeutung der neuen sozialen Bewegungen," pp. 47–67 in *Neue soziale Bewegungen in der Bundesrepublik Deutschland,* edited by Roland Roth und Dieter Rucht. Frankfurt: Campus.

Weber, Robert Phillip. 1987. "Cycles of the Third Kind." *European Journal of Political Research* 15: 145–53.

Weeks, Jeffrey. 1985. *Sexuality and Its Discontents: Meanings, Myths and Modern Sexualities.* London: Routledge and Kegan Paul.

Wijmans, Luuk. 1992. "De solidariteitsbeweging. Onverklaard maakt onbekend," pp. 121–40 in *Tussen verbeelding en macht: 25 jaar nieuwe sociale bewegingen in Nederland,* edited by Jan Willem Duyvendak et al. Amsterdam: SUA.

Wilson, Frank L. 1990. "Neo-Corporatism and the Rise of New Social Movements," pp. 67–83 in *Challenging the Political Order: New Social and Political Movements in Western Democracies,* edited by Russel J. Dalton and Manfred Küchler. Cambridge: Polity Press.

Wisler, Dominique. 1993. "Violence politique et mouvements sociaux. Etude sur les radicalisations sociales en Suisse durant la période 1969–1990." Ph.D. thesis, University of Geneva.

Zald, Mayer N. 1992. "Looking Backward to Look Forward: Reflections on the Past and Future of the Resource Mobilization Research Program," pp. 326–48 in *Frontiers in Social Movement Theory,* edited by Aldon D. Morris and Carol McClurg Mueller. New Haven: Yale University Press.

Zald, Mayer N., and Roberta Ash. 1966. "Social Movement Organizations: Growth, Decay, and Change." *Social Forces* 44: 327–41.

Zysman, John. 1983. *Governments, Markets, and Growth.* Ithaca, N.Y.: Cornell University Press.

Index

access: exclusive, 88; inclusive, 88
actiegroepen, 131
action: campaign, 262; facilitation of, 98, 124–25, 127, 132, 134–35, 139–40; forms of, 89, 98, 102–3; of students, 261; repression of, 86, 89, 92 98, 102, 122, 124–25, 127, 132, 134–36, 139, 141–42
action repertoire, xxi, 39–40, 42–44, 46, 49, 51–52, 86–87, 89–90, 91, 93, 108, 111–12, 119, 121, 129, 240, 244, 253, 267; blockades, 49; 136; bomb attacks, 9; confrontational, 49–50, 103, 119–20 122, 125, 129, 132–33, 136, 141, 261; demonstrative, 119–20, 122, 125, 132–33, 140, 141; disruption, 128, 129, 132, 134; kidnapping, 131; occupations, 49–50, 119, 136; petitioning, 52; political murders, 132; sit-ins, 119, 136; squatting, 119, 137; teach-ins, 119; violence, 49–52, 103, 117, 119, 120–22, 125, 127–28, 131–33, 141, 261
administration, 33
agenda, 83; building approach, 83, 97, 243; political, 134
AIDS, xix, 172–73, 178, 180, 225–30
alliances, 9; structures, xiii, xiv, 53
allies, 118, 122, 129–34, 137, 244
Alsace, 192–93
Amnesty International, 48
Amsterdam, x, 115, 173, 196, 198, 203, 233
Anderschume/Kontiki, 175
antinuclear energy movement, 100, 115, 161–62

antinuclear movement, 62, 76, 100, 107–8, 116, 146, 148–52, 155, 157, 159–63, 186, 191, 199, 202–3, 206, 210, 216–20, 222–25, 244–45; Dutch, 219, 222, 223; French, 191–93, 205, 220, 224; German, 193, 199, 220, 221, 223; mobilization, 147; success of, 147, 158; support, 147; Swiss, 193, 194, 199, 202, 221, 223
antinuclear protest, 148
antiracist movement, 63; French, 77
Arcadie, 171
archives, 254
Athens, 146
Austria, 37
autonomous movement, 49, 84, 115–16
autonomy: individual, xix; work, xix

Baden, 193
Baden-Württemberg, 192
Bad Godesberg: ix; program, 15
Bartolini, S., and P. Mair, 3, 5–6, 16, 18
Basel, 66
Basque country, 10–11, 50
Bavaria, 256
Belgium, 198
Berkeley, 181
Berlin, 114, 181, 196–98, 203, 232–33
Bern, x, 115, 194; canton of, 11, 21
Bismarck's Kulturkampf, 13
Bonn, 75
Bosnia, 249
bourgeoisie, 14
Bourges, xi

Hocquenghem, G., 171
homosexuals: in France, 62; movement, 84, 247, 264
Homosexuelle Aktion Westberlin, 171
Hyde Park, x

identities, 124, 239, 242–44, 247
identity formation, 38
ideology, 239, 253; Marxist, 55
implementation process, 41
inclusion: formal, 36–37; informal, 36–37
individualization, xviii, 238
industrial relations, 60; French, 60; American, 60
informal procedures, 26; inclusion, 36–37
Inglehart, R., 146, 169, 177, 241
innovations, 121
institutionalization, 112, 118–19, 122–24, 129, 132, 138, 140–42, 240, 250
institutional structures, xiii, 46
instrumental rationality, 242
integration, 36–37
interaction context, xv
interactive patterns, 85
intercoder reliability, 269; margin of error, 270–73
interest groups, 31
International Committee for Sexual Equality, 170
International Gay Association, 171
Irish Republican Army, 142
Italy, 34, 36, 134, 198, 226–27

Jungsozialisten (Jusos), 63–64
Jura, 11, 21, 23; canton of, 11, 21

Kaiseraugst, 152, 193–94, 203, 221; Nonviolent Action Kaiseraugst (GAK), 193–94

Kalkar, 151, 221
Karstedt-Henke, 117–19, 125, 127, 235
Kehl, 150
Kitschelt, H., xiv, 27, 161, 208–9, 216, 223
Der Kreis, 169, 171

labor: movement, 14, 19, 22, 34, 45, 52, 67, 250; unions, 112
Lafontaine, O., x
Larzac, 193

leaders, 128
leadership, 134
left's participation in government, xiv, 53; Dutch, 79; French, 78
Leninist models of organizations, 132
lesbian movement, 107, 165, 178
Lijphart, A., 35
Lille, xi
London, x
Lubbers, R., 80
Lyons, xi, 192

McAdam, D., 112, 119, 1.·¯, 164, 182, 185–89; and M. Zald, 111; and D. Rutch, 191
McCarthy, J. D., and M. Zald, 145
Madrid, x
Magnus, 175
Marckolsheim, 192–93, 195
Marseilles, xi
Marx, K., 246
mass society, xviii; theories of, xii
media, 123, 135–38, 249, 253, 259
Melucci, 88, 181, 238
militancy, 135, 244
Militant Autonomen Front, 122
militant democracy, 63
minorities, 10; religious, 11
mobilization: capacity, 108, 179–80; exclusive, 179; from above, 8; from below, 9; level of, 39–40, 43–44, 46, 52, 87–88, 108–9, 111, 179; logic of, 94
mobilization potential, 5, 10, 17; exclusively mobilized, 8; French inclusive character of, 70; inclusively mobilized, 8–9, 54; latent, 7; of traditional cleavage, 70
modernization, xviii
Le Monde, ix, x, xi; source, xxiii, 257
most similar systems design, xxii
motivational factors, 83; facilitation, 38–41, 43–44, 83, 85, 86, 98, 117, 124–27, 139, 141, 168, 173–74, 243–44, 248; reform/threat, xv, 38–40, 43–44, 83, 85, 173–74, 243, 248; repression, 38–41, 44, 51–52, 84, 86–89, 92, 98, 102, 117, 121, 124–27, 132–33, 139, 141–42, 168–69, 173–74, 177–78, 242, 244, 248; chances of success, 38–40, 43–44, 83, 85, 96, 139, 168, 173–74, 178, 242, 246, 248; subsidies: 173, 175

system: closure of, 98; formal closure, 87;
    formal openness, 87
systematization of bias, 255, 261–63, 271

tactical innovation, 118–19
die tagezeitung (taz), 256
Tallahassee, 133
Tarrow, S., xiii, xiv, xv, xxii, 53, 60, 91, 111,
    118–19, 127, 132, 187, 190, 259
terrorism, 112–13, 117, 129–31, 139, 141
Third World, 142
Three Mile Island, 147
Tilly, C., xxii, xxiii, 6, 21, 119, 211, 242, 260
Tocqueville, A., 245
Toulouse, xi
Tourraine, A., 88
Treaty of Maastricht, xvii
types of movements, 84–86, 88, 90–93,
    95–96, 109, 167, 242, 245;
    commercialization, 167; confrontational,
    90, 102; countercultural, xv, 39, 51,
    82–83, 86–95, 98, 107, 109, 131, 167, 174,
    176, 243, 245, 247; demonstrative,
    90–93; identity-oriented, 84; inclusion,
    167; instrumental; 82–83, 86–95, 98,
    101–3, 107, 109, 165, 167, 176, 243, 247;
    strategy-oriented, 84; subcultural,
    82–83, 86–95, 98, 107, 109, 167, 173–75,
    179, 243, 247

Ulm, ix
Unified Socialist Party (PSU), xi, 61
union, 119, 128–29, 264; German, 75;
    membership, 48
union system, 49; French, 15; German,
    15–16, 48, 56

United Kingdom, 37
United Nations, 248
United States, 30–31, 39, 119, 134, 224
universities, 112
urban autonomous movement: 182, 188,
    195–97, 203, 205, 217–18, 230–31, 234;
    Dutch, 197, 203; French, 203, 205;
    Geneva, 235; in Germany, 186, 196–97,
    233; in the Netherlands, 186, 196, 233; in
    Switzerland, 186, 196–97

values: emancipatory, xx; libertarian, xx;
    postmaterialist, xx
Vietnam, 58
volality: class-specific, 17–18; electoral 16;
    total, 17–18

Wackersdorf, 130, 150–51, 221
Weathermen, 112
Weber, M., xix
wehrhafte Demokratie, 34
Weimar Republic, 34
welfare state, 238
Die Welt, 256
Western Europe, 182, 196
women: movement, 84, 107, 243
working class, 14
World War II, 17, 49, 56; resistance during,
    15
World Wildlife Fund, 48, 223
Wyhl, 157, 192–94, 203, 220–21

xenophobic movements, 250

Zurich, 49, 66, 115–16, 196–98, 203, 231,
    233–34; canton of, 81

Hanspeter Kriesi is a professor of political science at the University of Geneva, Switzerland. He has taught at the faculty of political and social-cultural sciences at the University of Amsterdam and at the Institute for Sociology at the University of Zurich. He has participated in a number of studies on the motivation of social movements in Western Europe. His current research interests include right-wing extremism, the impact of information on political predispositions, and direct democracy.

Ruud Koopmans received his Ph.D. from the University of Amsterdam with a dissertation on the new social movements in Germany. Currently, he is a researcher at the Science Center Berlin. He has published several articles and books on new social movements, particularly in Germany and the Netherlands. His present research focuses on violence against foreigners in Germany and nationalist and ethnic movements in the former Soviet Union.

Jan Willem Duyvendak received his Ph.D. from the University of Amsterdam with a dissertation on the new social movements in France. He is now doing research on contemporary Dutch political history at the Amsterdam School for Social Research.

Marco Giugni holds a Ph.D. from the University of Geneva, where he wrote a dissertation on the new social movements in Switzerland. He is currently engaged in a comparative research project, financed by the Swiss national science foundation, on the impacts of social movements.